THE AMERICAN MOSAIC

POLITICAL CULTURES
Aaron Wildavsky, Series Editor

Political cultures broadly describe people who share values, beliefs, and preferences legitimating different ways of life. This series is distinguished by its openness to a variety of approaches to the study of political cultures; any defensible comparison, definition, and research method is considered. The goal of this series is to advance the study of political cultures conceived generally as rival modes of organizing political and social life.

A single set of common concerns will be addressed by all authors in the series: what values are shared, what sorts of social relations are preferred, what kinds of beliefs are involved, and what the political implications of these values, beliefs, and relations are. Beyond that, the focal points of the studies are open and may compare cultures within a country or among different countries, including or excluding the United States.

Books in the Series

The American Mosaic: The Impact of Space, Time,
and Culture on American Politics
Daniel J. Elazar

The Malevolent Leaders: Popular Discontent in America
Stephen C. Craig

Handling Frozen Fire
Rob Hoppe and Aat Peterse

Cultures of Unemployment:
A Comparative Look at Long-Term
Unemployment and Urban Poverty
Godfried Engbersen, Kees Schuyt, Jaap
Timmer, and Frans Van Waarden

Culture and Currency: Cultural Bias
in Monetary Theory and Policy
John W. Houghton

A Genealogy of Political Culture
Michael E. Brint

Cultural Theory
Michael Thompson, Richard Ellis, and Aaron Wildavsky

District Leaders: A Political Ethnography
Rachel Sady

FORTHCOMING

Politics, Policy, and Culture:
Applying Grid-Group Analysis
Dennis J. Coyle and Richard J. Ellis, editors

THE AMERICAN MOSAIC

The Impact of Space, Time, and Culture on American Politics

Daniel J. Elazar

Bar-Ilan University
and Temple University

Westview Press

BOULDER • SAN FRANCISCO • OXFORD

Political Cultures

Published in 1994 in the United States of America by Westview Press, Inc., 5500 Central Avenue, Boulder, Colorado 80301-2877, and in the United Kingdom by Westview Press, 36 Lonsdale Road, Summertown, Oxford OX2 7EW

Library of Congress Cataloging-in-Publication Data
Elazar, Daniel Judah.
The American mosaic : the impact of space, time, and culture on
   American politics / Daniel J. Elazar.
      p.   cm. — (Political cultures)
   Includes bibliographical references and index.
   ISBN 0-8133-0948-4. — ISBN 0-8133-0949-2 (pbk.)
   1. United States—Politics and government.   2. Political culture—
United States.   I. Title.   II. Series.
E183.E43   1994
306.2'0973—dc20   93-1222
                                                                              CIP

Printed and bound in the United States of America

The paper used in this publication meets the requirements
(∞) of the American National Standard for Permanence of Paper
for Printed Library Materials Z39.48-1984.

10   9   8   7   6   5   4   3   2   1

For Avi, Naomi, and Eitan

Contents

List of Tables and Illustrations   xv
Preface and Acknowledgments   xvii

1 The Three-Dimensional Location of the United States   1

The Importance of Location, 1
Culture and Civil Society, 4
Political Culture and Political Behavior, 9
Cultural Themes and Their Political-
    Culture Equivalents, 9
The Rhythm of the Generations, 15
Location and Change, 16
Frontier and Section: The Political Geography
    of the United States, 20
State and Local Parallels, 28
Summary, 35
Notes, 36

2 The Generational Rhythm of American Politics   41

Early Studies of Generational Rhythms, 41
Efforts to Delineate Political Cycles in
    American History, 43
Temporal Rhythms in the United States, 45
Human Social Rhythms, 47
Generations, Centuries, and Events, 49
Generations and Frontier Stages, 55
Generations and Economic Periods, 58
Centuries, Generations, and Federalism, 58
Generations and the Ethnoreligious
    Interrelationship, 59

The Internal Structure of the Generation:
    Challenges and Responses, 60
The Bench Marks of American Political History:
    Critical Elections and New Deals, 63
The Generational Recurrence of Critical
    Elections, 63
"New Deals": Bursts of Federal Government
    Activity, 66
Summary, 69
Notes, 69

3 **A Frontier Society**   73

The Frontier and the Generational Rhythm, 74
How to Identify a Frontier, 76
The Classic Land Frontier, 77
The Urban-Industrial Frontier and Its Impact, 81
The Opening of the Metropolitan Frontier, 84
Case Study: The Automobile and the Metropolitan
    Frontier, 90
The Rurban-Cybernetic Frontier, 95
Summary, 97
Notes, 98

4 **Frontiers and Foundings**   103

THE SEVENTEENTH CENTURY (1607–1713)   104
The First Generation (1607–1648), 104
The Second Generation (1648–1676), 108
The Third Generation (1677–1713), 115

THE EIGHTEENTH CENTURY (1714–1815)   119
The Fourth Generation (1714–1754), 119
The Fifth Generation (1754–1789), 122
The Sixth Generation (1789–1815), 127
Summary, 131
Notes, 131

5 **The Flowering of Sectionalism**   137

The Three Spheres, 138
The Eight Sections, 141
The Seventh Generation (1816–1848), 143
The Eighth Generation (1848–1876), 150
The Ninth Generation (1877–1912), 155

Summary, 160
Notes, 161

6 **Sectional, Class, and Ethnic Patterns
   in the Twentieth-Century United States**   165

The Tenth Generation (1913–1947), 167
The Eleventh Generation (1948–1976), 172
The Rise and Decline of Class Conflict, 179
New England: A "Confederation" Within
    the Union, 180
The Middle Atlantic States: America's
    "Main Street," 181
The Near West: The North's First Frontier, 182
The Upper South, 184
The Lower South, 186
The Western South, 187
The Northwest, 188
The Far West, 190
Summary, 192
Notes, 192

7 **The Peoples of the United States
   and Their Cultures**   199

Who Are the People of the United States? 199
Religion, Ethnicity, and Culture in America, 200
Generations and Ethnoreligious
    Interrelationships, 201
Cultural and Structural Assimilation, 207
Conscious and Subconscious Ethnicity, 209
Political Will and Group Consciousness, 209
Ethnic Groups and the Continuing Frontier, 212
Political Culture: A Major Force for
    Ethnic Integration, 214
The "Geology" of Settlement and the Cultural
    Streams, 215
Political Culture and American Politics, 219
Contrasting Conceptions of the Political Order, 219
Marketplace and Commonwealth: The American
    Cultural Matrix, 220
Summary, 223
Notes, 223

8 **The Political Subcultures of the**
   United States   229

The Individualistic Political Culture, 230
The Moralistic Political Culture, 232
The Traditionalistic Political Culture, 235
The "Geology" of Political Culture, 237
The Distribution and Impact of Political
   Subcultures, 239
Ethnicity, Political Culture, and Contemporary
   Migration Patterns, 247
Political Culture: Some Caveats, 252
The Implications of American Diversity, 253
Summary, 254
Notes, 255

9 **Territorial Democracy and the**
   Metropolitan Frontier   259

A System of Systems, 260
Territorial Democracy, 262
The Two Faces of Territorial Democracy, 263
The States as the Keystones in the
   Governmental Arch, 272
The States as Political Systems, 275
The States as Civil Societies, 277
The Federal System and the Political Setting, 279
Federalism and Political Culture, 280
The Political Cultures of the States, 282
The Widespread Application of Federal
   Principles, 285
The Civil Community: The Vehicle for
   Local Action in the Federal System, 287
Territorial Democracy on the Metropolitan
   Frontier, 290
Summary, 292
Notes, 292

10 **A New Generation and a New Frontier**   295

Beginning the Twelfth Generation, 295
Some Implications of the Generational
   Thesis, 306
The Impact of Space, Time, and Culture on
   American Politics: A Final Word, 306

Summary, 309
Notes, 310

About the Book and Author   313
Index   315

Tables and Illustrations

Tables

2.1	The generational rhythm of American politics	52
3.1	Distribution of U.S. population by size of place: 1790–1988	86
3.2	Growth of automobile usage in the United States: 1920–1989	92
7.1	Immigration: 1820–1989	200
7.2	Immigrants by country of birth: 1961–1989	202
7.3	Religio-ethnicity and political participation, family income, and education	210
7.4	Characteristics of comparable subcultural streams	218
8.1	Characteristics of the three political cultures	238
8.2	Political culture and quality of urban life for medium-sized SMSAs	247
9.1	State political cultures: The national configuration	284
9.2	Populations of the cultural groupings, by state, 1940–1990	286

Figures

2.1	The internal rhythm of the generation	62
4.1	Patterns and trends in the first generation	106
4.2	Patterns and trends in the second generation	110
4.3	Patterns and trends in the third generation	116
4.4	Patterns and trends in the fourth generation	120
4.5	Patterns and trends in the fifth generation	124

4.6   Patterns and trends in the sixth generation   128

5.1   Patterns and trends in the seventh generation   144
5.2   Patterns and trends in the eighth generation   151
5.3   Patterns and trends in the ninth generation   156

6.1   Patterns and trends in the tenth generation   168
6.2   Patterns and trends in the eleventh generation   174

7.1   The matrix of value concepts in American culture   221

9.1   The territorial basis of representative democracy
          in the United States   264

10.1   Patterns and trends in the twelfth generation   296

Maps

1.1   The United States in North America, 1800   21
1.2   On the eve of the Civil War   27
1.3   Migration, spheres, sections, and urbanized areas   29
1.4   Two hundred years of population shift   30
1.5   Political culture of Illinois   34

7.1   Re-enacting the ride of Paul Revere   204

8.1   The regional distribution of political cultures
          within the states   242
8.2   Center of population: 1790–1990   255

9.1   Dominant political culture, by state   283

Exhibits

1.1   Religion, culture, and political life   8

8.1   Political cultural differences and Watergate   240

Preface and Acknowledgments

This is a book about location. We usually think about location as referring to spatial location only. Geographers study and map spatial location, adding system to the structure that humans give to space. Less frequently do we think of the other two dimensions of location—time and culture. In truth, both are as integral to location as is space. It is the thesis of this book that location in time and culture have structure to no less a degree than does location in space, and that their structures can be understood to be systematic or at least sufficiently systematic to be mapped.

This book looks at the people of the United States of America both in their changing spatial-temporal-cultural location and as a paradigm for understanding the three dimensions of human location. In the following pages I will discuss the systematic structures of the three dimensions of location and how they have shaped and continue to shape the lives of the American people. In the process I will do more than a little mapping, though the intention of the book is not mapping per se.

Most people have no difficulty perceiving differences among locations in space. Especially in our rapidly changing times, many people have come to understand how location in time changes meaningfully as well. In principle, differences in cultural location are also becoming more easily perceived; however, for Americans—living as they do in a vast land, sharing a common culture in which subcultures are differentiated in relatively subtle ways—recognition of cultural location is sometimes difficult, in two ways. First, there is the problem of understanding that such differences exist; and second, even if this intellectual understanding is achieved, there is the problem of understanding what they mean in real life. Thus Americans are notoriously "American" in believing that "deep down all people are really alike," even if they speak different languages or wear "exotic" dress, meaning that they are really like other Americans. This optimistic note is touching in its hopefulness, but it has led to some drastic mistakes in American foreign policy—especially those resulting from misassessments of evil and deviousness among others.

Why should we bother with location—particularly such a complex understanding of it? From time immemorial, people have puzzled over the causes and effects of human events. The problem of establishing cause and effect is an extraordinarily difficult one, as a substantial literature attests. Less obscure is the fact that what we here refer to as location has a major impact on what happens and why. Without suggesting that understanding location is a solution to the problem of understanding cause and effect, I submit that it is a necessary ingredient in trying to achieve causal explanation. At the same time it is worth significant study in its own right. What follows should be considered as an introduction to and the guidelines for such a study.

This book is the outgrowth of more than thirty years of exploration. I initially formulated the basic questions addressed in this volume and the theses presented in answer to them in 1954–1956, while a graduate student at the University of Chicago. Since then I have undertaken several major projects to explore them. The first was a major study of the workings of the American federal system in which I joined with the late Morton Grodzins, my mentor, to investigate the practice of American federalism, past and present. This study led to the publication of *The American Partnership: Federal-State Cooperation in the Nineteenth Century United States* (1962), *American Federalism: A View from the States* (1966) (by Grodzins; I edited and completed the book after his death), *The American System: A New View of Government in the United States* (1966), and *Cooperation and Conflict: A Reader in American Federalism* (1969) (with R. Bruce Carroll, Kenneth E. Gray, E. Lester Levine, and Douglas St. Angelo).

A second major project was my study of medium-sized metropolitan areas in Illinois and other states of the Mississippi Valley in the context of American political, economic, social, and cultural development. I began this, the "Cities of the Prairie" project, in 1959, at the Institute of Government and Public Affairs of the University of Illinois. In the first book to emerge from that project I developed and applied the themes dealt with in the present book. When I inaugurated the project I promised myself that I would conduct several rounds of studies of the selected metropolitan areas over a period of one generation. The project is now in its thirty-first year and its third round of research. From it have emerged *Cities of the Prairie: The Metropolitan Frontier and American Politics* (1970), *Cities of the Prairie Revisited* (1986), *The Politics of Bellville* (1971), and *Building Cities in America* (1987).

Growing out of these two projects was what became a separate effort to explore American political culture and the three subcultures that I identified early on in my research. The principal statements of that thesis are found in *American Federalism: A View from the States* and *Cities of the Prairie*.

This project, too, has led to several books, including *The Ecology of American Political Culture* (1975).

Most recently, I and my colleagues at the Center for the Study of Federalism have inaugurated a series of books on state politics and government. In these volumes we are exploring the themes presented in this book state by state.

In an enterprise of so many years' duration, it is impossible to properly acknowledge all of the people from whose assistance I have benefited. Many of them are acknowledged in the various books that I have published on aspects of this subject in the past. Hence I will confine my thanks to those who were immediately involved in the gestation and completion of this book.

As always, I must begin by thanking my colleagues and staff at the Center for the Study of Federalism, who provided the intellectual and work environment needed to undertake the various projects associated with this effort. I would particularly like to acknowledge Benjamin Schuster and John Kincaid, both originally doctoral students of mine who have since gone on to pursue their own careers, for their studies of locational and cultural factors. Along with Dr. Kincaid, Ellis Katz, Donald Lutz, and Steven L. Schechter have been invaluable as colleagues and partners for nearly two decades. Aaron Wildavsky and Joel Lieske, two close colleagues in the elusive pursuit of political culture, were particularly helpful as this manuscript developed.

I am also especially grateful to the Earhart Foundation and its leadership, David Kennedy, Antony Sullivan, and Richard Ware, for providing the support I needed for this project. Their friendship and assistance over the years have been of immeasurable benefit.

Preparation of this manuscript involved the work of people who are vital to all my projects, including Mark Ami-El of the Jerusalem Center for Public Affairs; Jeff Morenoff and Rina Edelstein, my research assistants at the JCPA; and Pam Scher, my then-secretary there. Joseph Marbach and Marian Pulaski Wolfe at the Center for the Study of Federalism played a very important role, as always—as did Marian's predecessor, Mary Duffy.

I would also like to thank the people at Westview Press—Dean Birkenkamp, Sally Furgeson, and Jennifer Knerr—for their encouragement in this project. Special thanks go to Christine Arden, whose copyediting made this book so much better.

Daniel J. Elazar
Estes Park, Colorado

THE AMERICAN MOSAIC

CHAPTER 1

The Three-Dimensional Location of the United States

THE IMPORTANCE OF LOCATION

A popular story tells about a man who returned to his home to find an intruder hiding in his closet. Turning to the intruder in outrage, the householder bellowed, "What are you doing here?" The intruder, a meek little man, replied, "Everybody has to be somewhere." The point of this truism should be so obvious that it need hardly be stated. Recent efforts to explain human behavior, however, have too often neglected or overlooked the factor of location. Everybody does, indeed, have to be somewhere, and where one is plays a crucial role in determining who and what one is and what one does (or, in other words, how one behaves). What is true of individuals is equally true of groups, societies, peoples, and nations.

Even when we do think of location, we tend to think of it simply as a spatial matter—as a matter of being some *place.* In fact, location has three critical dimensions: spatial, temporal, and cultural. All human beings and groups are located in a particular space, in a particular time, and in a particular culture. It is necessary to understand all three facets of location in order to understand how people behave and why they behave as they do. It is not sufficient to think of the United States as being geographically located between the Atlantic and Pacific oceans, bounded by Mexico and the Gulf of Mexico on the south and Canada on the north. Rather, one must also understand that the United States is historically located in the modern epoch that opened at the beginning of the seventeenth century and culturally located within what we generally term Western civilization. As a result of the first dimension, this nation has no premodern history of political consequence, which does much to explain its difficulty in understanding the driving forces behind "Old World" societies that have had to modernize. As a result of the second, the United States has been able to focus on a cultural inheritance particularly conducive to the development of an energetic, even aggressive, competitive entrepreneurial society. All of these are crucial benchmarks not only for focusing in upon the location of any particular element in the United States but also for understanding the behavior of its people and its political system.

Biologically, humans are tied to all three locational dimensions. People, in common with all other animals, are severely bounded by time, which, like space, they can manipulate only to a certain degree. People live in particular times, and each person is allotted a particular measure of time. Living in particular times means that people begin their lives with an inheritance of times gone by and must maneuver within their own times in light of the limitations and possibilities imposed by what has gone before. A person's own life span may to some degree be extended or contracted through his or her efforts (e.g., by eating or smoking habits), and certainly a person may determine how his or her available time is used within very real limits.

In any given period, people are constrained by the limits of knowledge and the habitual practices available at that particular time. There is also a sense in which time runs out before people become aware of potential dangers, before new knowledge can be developed to meet new problems, or before individuals, political leaders, and societies can complete new projects. We do not, for example, have sufficient knowledge to make solar energy economically viable now or enough technical skill to make nuclear energy comfortably safe, especially with regard to radioactive wastes. Yet the "spirit of our time" calls for a continuing increase in the use of energy in order to maintain the style of life to which Americans have become culturally accustomed. The domestic and international political problems raised by worldwide energy needs became apparent during the 1970s. Although that immediate crisis was overcome, the larger issue remains with the American people as the world moves toward the twenty-first century.

In another vein, we often speak of the frustrations and opportunities that arise for individuals or groups who are "behind the times" or "ahead of their time." Political reformers, especially, experience the latter feeling, while regarding others as being "behind the times." Finally, in terms of day-to-day political life, the timing of action is one of the most important skills of a successful political leader.

In recent years, intensive investigations have been made into human *territoriality* (the human need to have ties to a particular place). They have demonstrated that all living beings have such a need, and that it shapes their orientations toward space. Although humans have greater opportunities to maneuver than do animals, there are limits to the degree to which they can manipulate their territorial instincts, even as they organize and reorganize space to meet their needs with varying degrees of effectiveness.

Political boundaries represent one major way in which people seek to organize space for their use. Territorial boundaries, whether national borders or household property lines, sort people out in space so as to minimize conflict and aggression and organize competition and cooperation among people. The political importance of territory is heightened by the universal tendency of like-minded individuals to differentiate themselves from others. Territory helps to provide individuals and groups with a sense of security and with a place in which they can work out their own identities and destinies. We might also keep in mind the fact that individuals occupy multiple territories—from personal space, to household, neighborhood, village or city, county, state, region, section, nation, continent, hemisphere, and perhaps even planet. Each of these "places" has specific meanings and purposes for people. In at least one respect, then, politics can be understood as the means by which humans impose their own order upon both space and time, which are otherwise differentiated only by natural processes or characteristics. That order is imposed, first and foremost, through human culture.[1]

In its simplest sense, culture may be regarded as the "way of life" of a people. The concept of culture refers to the explicit and implicit or overt and covert patterns of shared beliefs, values, and traditions about life held by a particular people. It consists of a set of rules, common symbols, and common sentiments that are learned by individuals as they grow up within the group. In this way culture tends to become "second nature," affecting behavior without self-conscious reflection. Culture separates humans from animals. Anthropologists have taught us that all people, groups, and societies are located within particular cultures whose own basis is so intertwined with the biological base of humans that it is impossible to draw any precise or even imprecise line separating the two. We are all inheritors of a culture that, to some degree, we can continue to shape but which in some respects is as much beyond the reach of our influence as the land forms upon which we live or the inexorable march of time from the beginning to the end of our lives.[2]

Political culture can best be understood in terms of the framework it sets for individual and group political behavior—in terms of the political thoughts, attitudes, assumptions, and values of individuals and groups and in the range of permissible or acceptable action that flows from them. Political culture, as such, directly determines behavior within relatively few situations or in response to relatively few particular issues.[3] Instead, its influence lies in its power to set reasonably fixed limits on political behavior and to provide subliminal direction for political action in particular political systems. These limits and direction are all the more effective because of their antiquity and subtlety, whereby those limited are often unaware of the limitations placed upon them.

CULTURE AND CIVIL SOCIETY

Some General Propositions About Culture

The study of political culture is related to the study of culture as a whole.[4] Accordingly, we shall begin our exploration with some propositions about the nature of culture as a whole. Culture refers to a way of life, combining a totality of experience. Referring to culture as a "way" of life highlights its dynamic character; every culture is located in a particular time and space. Indeed, the handling of time and space is a major concern of every culture. Significantly, culture is based on communication (a term related to *communis*, meaning "common"), which involves sharing "ways" of perception and understanding within a community.

It is equally significant that the term *culture* is related to *cultivation*, for culture is, in the final analysis, learned behavior. Culture is more than custom; it is a way of thinking, feeling, and believing that not only is learned but involves selective learning. Yet culture is so much a part of human life that it can best be understood as second nature. It is the aspect of human behavior that an individual takes for granted, believing it to be universal (if it is part of that individual's culture) or idiosyncratic (if it is part of another's). Culture, like nature, is at least partly concealed. It is almost a truism that any particular culture is most concealed from those who share in it. People must make a particular effort to understand their own culture precisely because all cultures are both explicit and implicit (in Clyde Kluckhohn's terms) or overt and covert (in Ralph Linton's).[5]

In his thought-provoking book *The Silent Language,* the anthropologist Edward Hall sees culture as having three manifestations: formal, informal, and technical.[6] According to Hall, a culture's formal manifestations are to be found in its implicit rules; the core of culture is second nature. Its informal manifestations represent learned behavior that has passed out of the awareness of those who have been acculturated into it, whereas the technical manifestations of a culture are those found at the highest levels of consciousness. Hall's formulation is particularly useful in developing an understanding of political culture, which, by its very nature, generates subconscious patterns of political behavior.

The Biological Basis of Culture

It is now generally recognized that culture has a biological basis. Culture channels biological processes and modifies biological functioning. For example, "territoriality," which has been shown to have biological roots, has culturally transmuted into such diverse manifestations as the migratory range of nomadic tribes on the Asian steppes, the thrust toward ownership of detached, single-family dwellings in the United States, and the drive for *Lebensraum* (living space) on the part of the German Reich in the twentieth century.

The development from biological demands to culture can be simply portrayed in the following manner:

biological demands————infrastructure————culture

Each culture shapes the biological demands of its members in its own particular image, establishing a "social heredity" and thereby uniting nature and culture (although there is no general agreement as to the relative strength of nature and culture in shaping behavior).

Theoretically, it is possible to isolate the "natural" components behind culture; but in their unmodified state, as much as they may reveal about humankind in general, unmodified, these natural components reveal little about particular human beings or groups. In these respects, the Greek idea of "nature," which implies an underlying pattern of behavior fixed by the cosmos for every species, is less useful for understanding man as a social being than the Hebrew idea of "way," which implies that each group as well as each species moves (or develops) within a context that combines biological and cultural aspects into a single individual package. Such phenomena as cities, architecture, myths, and ideologies create sensory screens through which humans inhabit and perceive the world. Similarly, sight, sound, and smell are biological devices that regulate cultural perceptions even as the perceptions themselves are culturally attuned in particular directions. Hence different cultures create different kinds of visual, auditory, and olfactory space for those who are within them.

Language and Culture

Although culture involves both verbal and nonverbal communication, language is the "program" through which humans register and structure external reality; hence language is a major element in the creation of different sensory worlds and the formation of thought. Political language is a major factor in the formation of political thinking, even in its most elementary forms. Political culture differences often are reflected in different political terminologies, whereas different subcultures within the same overall political culture frequently infuse the same terminologies with differences in meaning. Every political culture has its own special political terms (examples from the American culture include *open primary, public servant, nonpartisanship, good government, American way of life*), with different meanings that are not transferable to any other culture. Similarly, what are to Americans common political terms—such as *democracy, freedom, the people*, and *politics*—have different meanings in different political cultures, if they exist within them at all. Any or all of these terms will have different shades of meaning in the various subcultures within a particular political culture.

"Define your terms" is a favorite intellectual game, often played with those just noted or similar words. Sooner or later we all learn that, for some terms, every precise definition begets a different and equally precise one. This phenomenon is a reflection of the difficulties of definition even within the same culture. In fact, such terms as *democracy* and *freedom* are actually "value concepts" that are infused with meaning through the culturally defined imagery that they provoke within the minds of those who use them, though not because of any agreement as to their precise definition. Value concepts are terms whose use evokes images important in shaping the attitudes and beliefs of the participants in that culture. The meanings of these terms are connotative or suggestive; precise definitions invariably fail to convey their full meanings, no doubt because value concepts get at the heart of a culture and therefore must be as dynamic as the culture itself, whereas full definition actually denies them their fullness.[7] Among the keys to understanding a particular culture are the identification and understanding of its value concepts.

Culture, Society, and Personality

A. R. Radcliffe-Brown, another anthropologist, sees culture as having three aspects: a set of rules (both counsels and precepts); common symbols (necessary for communication), with common meanings attached to those symbols; and common sentiments. In this connection, it is important to note the distinction between culture and society (in the largest sense). "Society" may be defined as an organized group of people who interact more with one another than they do with other people, cooperating among themselves for the attainment of certain ongoing ends; "culture" may be defined as the distinctive way of life of any society produced by shared experiences filtered through culturally predetermined perspectives. Culture represents "the organized repetitive responses of a society's members" (Linton) or the force for the standardization of the behavior of individuals and the "fitting together" of society (Radcliffe-Brown).[8] In short, culture is the integrating factor in society.

Just as culture is the integrating factor in society, personality is the integrating factor for the individual. Culture is the major determinant of basic personality structure; different cultures develop different personality norms. Socialization of personality traits leads cumulatively to the development of specific psychological biases in the culture of the world.

Culture and Religion

At this point, it is important to note the extraordinary influences on culture of religion (broadly defined to include the so-called secular pseudo-religions of the modern world as well as the traditional ones) as creator and legitimizer of social and political norms, patterns, and goals.[9] Religion may well be the major catalyst of cultural change (see Exhibit 1.1). Strong historical evidence assigns this role to religions or quasi-religious movements, whether Judaism, Christianity, Islam, and Communism in the West, or Buddhism, Confucianism, and Shinto in the East. At the same time, it seems that particular cultures are influenced by religion in special ways. Why, for example, did the Calvinist and Reformed churches become dominant in societies that adopted or experimented with federal modes of political organization? Religion even plays a role in the creation and diffusion of language and linguistic patterns; consider, for example, the role of Christianity (especially Protestant Christianity, with its emphasis on reading the Bible) in the spreading of literacy and certain value concepts, first in Europe and more recently in Asia and Africa.

Culture and Subcultures

The more complex the society, the more likely it is that there are subcultures within it. Subcultures represent the interaction of nuances of differences within society. They also represent the interaction of nuances of differences within larger cultures, separable to a degree but always within the framework of the overall culture. The subtleties of subcultural variations add spice to the study of political culture.

Culture and Justice

A. R. Radcliffe-Brown has argued persuasively that all societies are built around the integrating structural principle of justice, which he presents as culturally defined.[10] Justice involves both just retribution and equivalent return. (The former entails the law of retaliation, the principle that benefits must be compensated for by benefits, and indemnification for injury.) Differences in the conception of justice are rooted in cultural differences.

In this respect, at least, Radcliffe-Brown brings modern social science back to the rediscovery of the architectonic nature of politics accepted without question by the Greeks. All societies are ultimately civil, or political, societies because they involve the development and maintenance of shared principles of justice through accepted authoritative arrangements. The shared tenets of justice in a given society are largely a function of its culture and, to a considerable degree, of its political culture.

EXHIBIT 1.1   Religion, Culture, and Political Life

All signs point to religious movements—those great surges of human self-definition based on certain perceived transcendent and enduring truths embodied within some institutional framework—as being the keys to cultural development and survival. Religious movements have been central to cultural continuity and the transmission of cultural modes to succeeding generations or foreign populations, to the transcending of old ethnic or national divisions or the creating of new ones, and to fundamental changes within particular cultures leading to the emergence of new cultures or subcultures. Culture is transformed through religious experiences ranging from the Jews' covenant at Mount Sinai to the Native Americans' ghost dance movement of the 1890s, from the Protestant Reformation to the spread of Communism as a kind of secular religion.

Religious experiences may be generated by a host of factors; but once an experience takes hold among a particular people, it becomes a force promoting fundamental change and then continuity. The potency of religion is reflected in the way that the religious impulse can be found among all peoples, all times and places. Political thinkers—whether Plato or Machiavelli, Locke or Marx—have noted religion's staying power. Many philosophers and political leaders have tried to mobilize religion for their purposes, some as a way of cementing the polity; others to change it; still others to privatize religion or to abolish it as "false consciousness." Throughout all, religion retains its compelling cultural power.

Three corollary points should also be noted. First, specific religious movements, even as they change culture, are generally most successful among groups already culturally predisposed toward their fundamental tenets. Thus, Calvinistic Protestantism found its strength among peoples with a common cultural heritage along the shores of the North Sea. Their American descendants created Yankee Puritanism. And Mormonism was founded by Yankees in upstate New York (in 1830) during a period of religious ferment and revival. The latter has had the most success in terms of proselytizing, not only among the same peoples who were originally attracted to Calvinism but also among the Scandinavians, who come from a similar cultural milieu.

Second, the impact of religion on society and politics is not limited to the influence of those who formally participate in its institutional manifestations. Rather, the approaches to life embodied in particular religions tend to infuse culture as a whole, thereby continuing to influence, however subtly, even those who have formally strayed from the fold.

Third, a decline in the force of a particular pattern of religious belief and experience within the culture it has molded invariably leads to a cultural crisis of the first magnitude. This in turn usually leads to a search for religious substitutes to overcome the crisis. The Roman empire, for instance, underwent such an experience after the first century of the Christian era, and there are strong indications that the Western world is experiencing a similar crisis today.

POLITICAL CULTURE AND POLITICAL BEHAVIOR

Political culture may be defined, for our purposes here, as the particular pattern of orientation to political action in which each political system is imbedded. It is an element in general culture that is analytically separable for some purposes. The study of political culture requires that distinctions be made regarding

1. sources of political culture, such as race, ethnicity, religion, language, and life experiences;
2. manifestations of political culture, such as political attitudes, symbols, and style; and
3. effects of political culture, such as actions, institutions, and policies.

Political culture, *qua* political culture, can be studied only through its manifestations. To study the sources is not to study the political culture itself. Gabriel A. Almond and G. Bingham Powell are quite correct when they assert: "Political culture is not a residual explanatory category. [In other words, it is not something that explains only what other factors cannot explain.] It involves a set of phenomena which can be identified and to some degree measured."[11]

The manifestations of political culture may be broken down for analytic purposes into at least two levels and two kinds of patterns. Just as there are two patterns of cultural manifestations on the individual level, there are two kinds on the community level. Patterns of individual and community belief are manifested in a variety of political symbols by which the individual or the community as a whole expresses its values, its self-understanding, its goals, and so on. Similarly, political style involves communitywide patterns of action different from the personal behavior of particular actors.[12]

Political culture is not simply the aggregate of the four component manifestations. In addition, we must consider the various patterns of interaction among the four component parts. Individual beliefs concerning the meaning of community symbols and the meaning attached to those symbols by the community as a whole are also important aspects of the political culture. Similarly, it is important to an understanding of political culture that we remember the disjunctures between community symbols and individual beliefs on the one hand and individual behavior and the community's style of politics on the other.

CULTURAL THEMES AND THEIR POLITICAL-CULTURE EQUIVALENTS

Clyde Kluckhohn has posited six themes that must find expression in every culture. As we have already seen in the case of the first (language), these themes can be adapted to suggest political-culture equivalents. By making such adaptations, we are better able to define the potential scope and content of the study of political culture. *Aesthetic expression,* Kluckhohn's second theme, embodies such elements as political styles, individual and general, and their aesthetic appeal in particular political cultures; changes in political style, temporal and regional; political symbols and symbolization; and what makes certain political styles or myths, traditional or ideological, aesthetically appealing in particular political cultures.

Standardized orientation to the deeper problems of life and death, the third theme, has its equivalent in questions of political life and death. Political life can be understood as referring to such questions as What is acceptable and desirable for attaining office or acquiring political power? Hence this theme deals with the political-culture aspects of political recruitment, political socialization (learning what political actors can and cannot do), and political projections of individuals (personal appearance, public image, and the range of acceptable campaign tactics). Political death refers to the effective ending of political career possibilities. Hence this theme is also concerned with the nature of political death, factors causing political death (age, defeat, change of residence, certain kinds of controversy), and the functional utility of political death in the maintenance of political systems or the introduction of political change.

The fourth theme, the *means to perpetuate the group and its solidarity* (including its norms), deals with the character of political institutions, the institutional channels of political communication, and the common modes of political socialization as shaped by political cultural factors. *Meeting individual demands for an orderly way of life* is the fifth theme. It is concerned with the nature of such demands (commonly held theories of government and society) within particular political-culture frameworks, the accepted "price of politics," and the accepted ways of organizing to meet those demands.

The final theme, *meeting individuals' biological/survival needs,* involves the cultural definition of those needs, the ways of organizing politically to meet those needs, and, ultimately, the definition of who is a person or citizen, which in turn determines who gets what in the way of protection of life and rights.

Every civil society expresses these cultural themes in its own way and build its own synthesis of those expressions into a cultural whole. The themes and the synthesis, like all cultural phenomena, are dynamic, changing over time in response to changing conditions, but always within a context that preserves the continuity of the culture as a whole. Whereas cultural change is normal and even accelerated in the modern era, only occasional social traumas of the most intense kind can alter the fundamental character of the culture itself. Tracing the cultural constants in a world of change is one of the tasks undertaken by those who study political culture.

In a slightly different vein, Edward Hall has suggested studying culture through what he terms *primary message systems* (PMS), separate but interrelated kinds of human activity stemming from biological bases and reflecting the cultural accretions that form the building blocks of specific cultures. Combined with the cultural themes noted earlier, they enable us to penetrate further into the study of political culture. *Interaction,* the first of the ten primary message systems, is the central core of the PMS approach because it is the basis of communication. For our purposes, it leads us to recognize the kinds and patterns of political communication as shaped by particular political cultures. *Association* leads to the consideration of the forms of political organization produced by particular cultures. *Subsistence* opens up the topic of the relation of political phenomena to economic life in particular political environments. Similarly, *bisexuality* opens up consideration of the relation of political to family life in particular political cultures. *Territoriality* suggests the need to deal with the location and spread of political subcultures in space, just as *temporality* does in time. *Temporality* also provides us with a way to examine political-culture change. *Learning* leads us to study individual socialization and cultural adaptation, whereas *play* leads to an understanding of the nature and rules of the "game of politics." *Defense* leads to the analysis of the ways and means of protecting the political-culture patterns devised in every group. Finally, *exploitation* (of materials) suggests consideration of political, culturally directed thrusts and the limits imposed on political management of the environment.

We can sum up this brief introduction to the study of political culture by outlining the significant questions that must be dealt with in a systematic analysis of the political culture of any particular political system. The first is the question of *relation to authority* (government and the political system). It includes the identification of adaptive behavior in interaction with authority, personal and group ideologies, and the central conception of the relationship of authority and self that underlie, and are reflected in, behavior and ideology. Here it is important to distinguish between perceived differentiations in kinds of authority and the differentiation in responses to same. Related to a person's culturally determined sense of relation to authority is the second question of *conception of self* in relation to authority and to civil society as a whole, both as a member of civil society (citizen) and as a political actor.

Third is the question of the culturally requisite *social and individual bases for maintaining inner equilibrium* as a political system. It is closely connected with the fourth question regarding the *major forms of political anxi-*

ety within a particular cultural set, including perceived threats to the ego structure and expected consequences of value violation. Both are linked with the fifth question regarding the *primary political dilemmas or conflicts and ways of dealing with them*. It may, indeed, be possible that whole political systems are organized in terms of one or a few primary tensions that are built into their political cultures (e.g., the tension between liberty and equality in the United States) and that they play out their history through a series of accommodations of those tensions.

The study of political culture is concerned with four additional questions as well—namely, those dealing with *modes of cognitive functioning, styles of expressive behavior, handling of major dispositions* (aggression, dependency, curiosity, and so forth), and *types of social (political) sanctions*. Finally, there is the question of the *extent of political involvement* sanctioned for various individuals and groups within particular political cultures. Here we must be concerned with both the degree and the direction of involvement.

A specific political culture may or may not coincide with a particular political system or civil society, since patterns of orientation to politics frequently overlap beyond the boundaries of specific political systems. At the same time, precisely because culture is so central to human existence and politics and so important in shaping human society, every political system must create some kind of cultural synthesis within its boundaries, at least for those who actively participate in politics. Historically, cultural conflict, in part because of its ties to religion, has been among the most divisive experiences within and between polities.

One aspect of the development of American civilization has been the emergence of an American political culture created more or less simultaneously on a sectional basis as well as throughout the country. The nation as a whole, every state, and most local communities have created, synthesized, or adapted their own variations of this common political culture in response not only to the interactions among geo-historical location, demographic streams, and patterns of general culture but also to the influence of the national political process.

The study of politics concerns itself with three dimensions: political structure, political processes, and political culture. Political structure relates to the institutions of political life, political processes are concerned with political behavior, and political culture deals with the norms of politics and governance. As such, political culture is an independent variable with a dynamic of its own.

In this book, it is my intention to present a case for the place of culture—particularly political culture—as one of the three elements or bench marks of human location. In my previous work on the subject I have largely concentrated, as have others, on political culture as a dynamic variable in shaping political behavior.

Another dimension to culture in general and political culture in particular is what I refer to here as the locational aspect. In casual conversation, we talk about people and their institutions as being embedded in particular cultures. This manner of speaking reflects a reality that requires proper exploration by social scientists. Indeed, by exploring the phenomenon of location in particular, social scientists are able to place behavioral studies in a proper context—one that avoids the problem of overgeneralization from "snapshot" research. Proper consideration of location in all of its dimensions, then, is necessary for a three-dimensional political science.

Each of the three dimensions has its own properties of permanence or lack thereof. Spatial or geographic location, taken alone, is fixed. By contrast, temporal or historic location is constantly changing. Cultural location falls somewhere in between; it appears fixed but actually changes in a gradual way. Taken separately, each of the three dimensions has its own dynamic; but a different pattern emerges when all three are taken together.

In fact, there is no such thing as location in one dimension without location in the others. Thus spatial location is fixed; geo-historical location is not. The very passage of time brings with it locational change that is geographic as well as historical. So, for example, spatially the location of the United States has remained unchanged since the founding of the republic. However, in the nineteenth century, its geo-historical location was peripheral to the great events of world affairs, one of isolation from the Old World; and in the twentieth century, that isolation disappeared as a result of technological change, giving the United States a new geo-historical location at the center of the world stage—by every new measure, a location now close to the "action" on every continent. Or consider a more localized example: From the 1760s to the early nineteenth century, Pittsburgh was considered the gateway to the West; but as the land frontier moved westward, it lost that geo-historical locational characteristic and was instead enveloped by the advancing urban-industrial frontier. By the time Abraham Lincoln visited the city in February 1861, as he was making his way east to be inaugurated president, he felt it appropriate to use Pittsburgh as a platform from which to address those who were part and parcel of the new urban-industrial age. Yet a century later, Pittsburgh was commonly referred to as being located in the Rustbelt, an economic backwater tied down by a decaying urban-industrial plant and an inability to compete in world markets. Thus, its geo-historical location has regularly changed since its founding.

In this connection, culture acts as a mediating force that responds to changes in geo-historical location or their consequences in such a way as to enable people confronted by those changes to live with them, maintaining continuity yet absorbing change.

Political culture plays a significant role in all of this. As I have noted in my earlier research, political-culture similarities often provide useful assistance in bridging general cultural gaps between groups (although in some cases the reverse is true, as when political-culture differences exacerbate cultural divisions). It is precisely because culture differs from style—in that the former reflects deeper orientations to existence whereas the latter consists of more superficial manifestations of accepted behavior—that political culture serves as a steadying force.

The distinction between political culture and political style has been blurred in recent years. For example, the new political orientations influencing American urban politics are often mistakenly referred to as political cultures. Rather, they are political styles or, perhaps, ideologies.

At the same time, expressions of political culture change as geo-historical location shifts. For example, it has been demonstrated that Minneapolis, Minnesota, has as purely a moralistic political culture as one is likely to find. Between World War I and the 1960s, accordingly, the city was dominated by rather straight-laced views with regard to what are defined in American cultural politics as moral issues (e.g., gambling, prostitution, obscenity and pornography, abortion). After the "revolution" of the 1960s, however, most of that older political style fell by the wayside. Once those "illicit" activities were redefined as expressions of personal freedom, the cultural pacesetters in Minneapolis embraced the notion that they should be protected with moralistic fervor. In particular, prostitution and displays previously considered obscene or pornographic were allowed to flourish because they were now recognized as protected speech. It was only after the massage parlors and escort services became obvious breeding grounds for crime that there again occurred a shift in attitude toward them. These shifts in style were apparent to the naked eye; not always so apparent was the degree to which they were absorbed within the same political culture in each case. In short, the overt changes were the result of a shift in the temporal location of the city.

A major difficulty in the study of political culture, then, is to distinguish between culture and style. Here, too, it should be apparent that the factor of geo-historical location can be of help. Shifts in location are likely to result initially in shifts in style, which, however, may or may not ultimately induce cultural change.

My aim in this book is to show how location in the three dimensions of space, time, and culture constitutes an important factor in shaping American political life. In the process I emphasize geo-historical location as the location of a civil society in time (history) and space (geography) together. Location establishes the raw physical and ecological conditions with which settlers must come to terms, shapes the territorial limits of the society, orders the flow of human migration, and influences the forms of political institutions that are created to make use of the land. Each location is shaped by the deposits of peoples and cultures who settle it and by the varying ways in which they use the land over time. Although one can speak of national geo-historical location, what is notable about the United States is the rich diversity of geo-historical locations resulting from the variety of geographies, peoples, cultures, and settlement periods within the nation. One's particular location also shapes the way one looks at the nation as a whole.

THE RHYTHM OF THE GENERATIONS

The rhythm of the generations is the central aspect of the time element in geo-historical location. Observation of this rhythm can provide a way of organizing the flow of history and of understanding the patterns of political events in terms of the human life cycle. Although in many societies the beginnings of the generations have been lost in the mists of time, in the United States it is possible to know their foundings and to trace the subsequent generational cycles from those points. Since the first British settlement in North America there have been twelve generations ranging in length from twenty-six to forty-three years. This is roughly the period during which most people experience the productive phase of their life cycles. Each generation shares a common heritage and a set of experiences and challenges that give it a distinct identity. At the beginning of a generation the challenges of the times are introduced as political issues. After the issues have been debated and raised to the level of nationwide concerns, the generation undertakes a period of response to the issues. This is in turn followed by a period of consolidation that sets the stage for the next generation.

The generation born after World War II, for example, has been faced with the task of maintaining a two-hundred-year-old federal democracy in a vastly new historical order marked by the rise of new nations demanding a greater share of world resources, by new ideologies demanding new national and international political arrangements, and by the proliferation of nuclear weapons capable of rendering human life extinct. These, in turn, have affected the geo-historical location of the United States. The oceans are no longer a defense barrier but, instead, act as cover for submarines armed with nuclear weapons. World War II opened the skies as perhaps the most lethal new battleground.

The richness of the American continent in terms of agriculture, energy, and minerals, which allowed the United States to become the world's most affluent civilization and to handle many problems of justice by expanding the economic pie, will take on new importance for the next several generations. Both domestic and international politics will be affected by the degree to which America's standard of living requires external sources of natural resources such as energy. New territorial disputes have broken out over offshore boundaries and the exploitation of seabed resources. American agricultural abundance, for better or worse, will play an important political role in a world marked by widespread hunger. Finally, the need to preserve the environment and conserve resources will put pressure on American cultural habits and perhaps require new political policies capable of dealing effectively with issues of social justice and international peace in a time of rising expectations and uncertain solutions.

In the following chapters we will focus on the spatial, temporal, and cultural aspects of location to see how they help shape American political behavior.[13]

LOCATION AND CHANGE

Every civil society has its own particular location in space and time. That location can be seen as resting on earlier locational "strata," which in turn continue to influence contemporary life. In that sense, every polity may be said to rest upon its own "geological" base. The geology of each polity plays a fundamental role in dictating the context in which its political and social systems must operate, the broad limits of its discretion, the structuring of its political concerns, and the continuing character of the political interaction within it. In this chapter we will review some familiar history of American settlement, but from a new perspective—looking at old materials with new eyes.

The cumulative effects of location in space and time are limiting in many ways, but the very passage of time in a civilization oriented to change, such as that of the United States, also represents the opening of new opportunities. In one sense, at least, this is a new phenomenon. The opening of the modern age in the seventeenth century, which coincided with the settlement of English-speaking North America and the foundation of American civilization, initiated not only an epoch of change but also a chain reaction that has accelerated the process of change. The result has been the virtual institutionalization of change in all modern societies, especially in the United States. As change became institutionalized, time itself lost its static character, which, in premodern times, had made its passage well-nigh imperceptible from generation to generation. Now time's passage has become an almost visible force, opening new frontiers for human development in every generation.[14]

Brought down to concrete terms, the dynamics of geo-historical location (i.e., location in space and time) change the effective positioning of every civil society and virtually every generation. No polity or community ever really "stands still." Changes in location make it necessary for local American communities to perpetually reconstitute themselves politically, much as they must reconstruct themselves economically and physically. In that sense, the American novelist Thomas Wolfe was right when he wrote, "You can't go home again." Indeed, such changes can transform previously prosperous communities into depressed ones through no apparent fault of their own, especially in the case of communities that rely heavily on a single type of economic activity that becomes outmoded by time.

The ghost town is a familiar feature in American history. By definition it is a town that lives off of a particular economic function for a few years or even a generation and then is emptied when it becomes obsolete because of economic or technological changes. In terms of geographic position, it remains in the same place; but its temporal location shifts with disastrous consequences. It does not "keep up with the times." Hence "the times pass it by" and its inhabitants move elsewhere, either for greater opportunity or simply in order to survive. We think of ghost towns as being primarily associated with the mining industry, some of which emptied because the mines played out. But changes in the price of gold, copper, and iron or the discovery of deposits more easily or cheaply mined elsewhere often played the same role.[15]

Other primary examples of ghost towns in the United States are the agricultural towns and villages that grew up in the nineteenth century to serve the surrounding farms but became outmoded by changing transportation and merchandising technologies in the twentieth century. Once the automobile came along, it was no longer necessary for there to be a town within an easy walk or horseback ride of every farm. Not only were people able to travel farther in the same amount of time to secure supplies, but rising levels of prosperity and merchandising meant that there had to be large concentrations of people to provide the new levels of consumer goods and services being sought. Times changed and whole communities died out, becoming ghost towns in their own right.

The big cities of the United States today are undergoing similarly drastic transformations, also as a result of changing times. Densely populated cities developed when there was a need for large concentrations of workers to service industrial and commercial enterprises; and transportation technology required that those workers live relatively close to work sites, or at least close to the railroad and streetcar lines that took them to work. Masses of new immigrants to the cities, just starting out their new lives, put up with conditions of population density and limited space; indeed, they had no alternative but to do so. As people prospered and the automobile made it possible to travel longer distances to work, big cities lost population to the suburbs. Then cybernetic technology made even the process of gathering together less necessary, in a growing number of areas. Each of these changes effectively changed the geo-historical location of the big cities, just as similar changes had transformed the position of mining and agricultural towns.[16]

Conversely, temporal changes of this nature also make it possible for backwater communities to transcend the limitations of past location by capitalizing on new potentialities. The mining towns of Colorado, for example, were on the cutting edge of the frontier in the late nineteenth century. Then the mines played out or became uneconomic. If they survived at all, they did so as backwaters for the first half of the twentieth century. After World War II, the new leisure-time activities of skiing and mountain recreation, coupled with new developments in telecommunications, put them again on the cutting edge of American development—at least to the degree that they could become vibrant (though still small) communities once again.[17]

The "historical geology" of social phenomena is such that there is some "beginning" or founding in every social order at the point where space and time are first linked in the life of a particular social system. The bedrock upon which subsequent strata of human activity are deposited is located at the point where particular people first begin to function in systematic relationship to one another on a particular territory. The continued effects of that first linkage and their modification by the deposits of later human activity, the upheaval of subsequent events, and the simple erosion of time provide the framework within which social systems develop and, as such, constitute the basic matter for social investigation.

Alexis de Tocqueville accurately described the importance of foundings in civil society and suggested that by studying the history of the United States of America we gain the opportunity to learn the whole story of a particular country and people:

> When a child is born, his first years pass unnoticed in the joys and activities of infancy. As he grows older and begins to become a man, then the doors of the world open and he comes into touch with his fellows. For the first time notice is taken of him, and people think they can see the germs of the virtues and vices of his maturity taking shape.
>
> That, if I am not mistaken, is a great error.
>
> Go back; look at the baby in his mother's arms; see how the outside world is first reflected in the still hazy mirror of his mind; consider the first examples that strike his attention; listen to the first words which awaken his dormant power of thought; and finally take notice of the first struggles he has to endure. Only then will you understand the origin of the prejudices, habits,

and passions which are to dominate his life. The whole man is there, if one may put it so, in the cradle.

Something analogous happens with nations. Peoples always bear some marks of their origin. Circumstances of birth and growth affect all the rest of their careers.

If we could go right back to the elements of the societies and examine the very first records of their histories, I have no doubt that we should there find the first cause of their prejudices, habits, dominating passions, and all that comes to be called the national character. We should there be able to discover the explanation of customs which now seem contrary to the prevailing mores, or laws which seem opposed to recognized principle, and of incoherent opinions still found here and there in society that hang like the broken chains still occasionally dangling from the ceiling of an old building but carrying nothing. This would explain the fate of certain peoples who seem borne by an unknown force toward a goal of which they themselves are unaware. But up till now evidence is lacking for such a study. The taste for analysis comes to nations only when they are growing old, and when at last they do turn their thoughts to their cradle, the mists of time have closed round it, ignorance and pride have woven fables round it, and behind all that the truth is hidden.

America is the only country in which we can watch the natural quiet growth of society and where it is possible to be exact about the influence of the point of departure on the future of a state.

At the time when Europeans first landed on the shores of the New World, features of national character were already clearly shaped; each nation had a distinct physiognomy; and since they had by then reached the state of civilization inducing men to study themselves, they have left us a faithful record of their opinions, mores, and laws. We know the men of the fifteenth century almost as well as our own contemporaries. So America shows in broad daylight things elsewhere hidden from our gaze by the ignorance or barbarism of the earliest times. [18]

The United States provides one the very best settings available for the study of social and political systems from the geo-historical point of view because of its character as a "new society." It is one of the few countries in which the interactions among space and time, political systems, and political processes can be traced "from the beginning" with reasonable accuracy and within a manageable time span. We possess detailed information about the development of this country from the days of the first settlers, and the entire process has taken place within a span of less than four centuries (i.e., less than twelve generations). Scholars and scientists who study social phenomena in the United States thus possess an unparalleled opportunity to develop a multidimensional analysis of a society from its very foundations, with a thoroughness that can be duplicated in few other parts of the world.

FRONTIER AND SECTION:
THE POLITICAL GEOGRAPHY OF THE UNITED STATES

The American landscape, including its lands, waters, topography, and climate, has played an important part in the working out of the American experience—specifically, by

1. creating conditions that the settlers of the land and subsequent generations have been able to exploit or have had to overcome through the conquest of successive frontiers,
2. influencing the territorial limits of the United States,
3. influencing the flow of migration across the land, and
4. influencing the shape of political institutions developed to organize the land for human use.

The first settlers came to North America with the germ of what was to become a great political idea, but they brought that idea to a particular land. The character of that land; the way its rivers flow and the pattern of its mountain ranges; the quantity of rainfall in its various sections; the intensity of heat and cold; the distribution of forest, prairie, and desert; the abundance of its raw materials, flora, and fauna; the richness of its soil—all of these factors shaped the way the settlers, their children, and those who came to join them occupied the land and organized it socially and politically into the first continental nation-state in world history.

The Federalist put it in these terms:

> It has often given me pleasure to observe, that Independent America was not composed of detached and distant territories, but that one connected, fertile, wide-spreading country was the portion of our western sons of liberty. Providence has in a particular manner blessed it with a variety of soils and productions and watered it with innumerable streams for the delight and accommodation of its inhabitants. A succession of navigable waters form a kind of chain round its borders, as if to bind it together; while the most noble rivers in the world, running at convenient distances, present them with highways for the easy communication of friendly aids and the mutual transportation and exchange of their various commodities. [19]

Look at a map of North America (Map 1.1) and think a moment about how Americans perceive their land. Most Americans look at the land from east to west, a habit instilled by studying the history of settlement of their country, which was essentially a movement from east to west. Americans who live on the West Coast, however, look at the land from west to east, which, significantly enough, parallels the way in which the western third of the country was settled after the initial arrival of the settlers from the

The United States in North America

1800

←——— BRITISH FUR TRADE TRUNKLINES AND MACKENZIE'S EXPLORATIONS

DIFFUSION OF THE HORSE AND SUBSEQUENT PLAINS INDIAN CULTURE

AREA AFRO-AMERICANS MORE THAN 33% OF TOTAL POPULATIONS

------- HYDROGRAPHIC BOUNDARIES

Petropavlovsk

Aleutians

Unalaska

RUSSIAN

Kodiak

AMERICA

New Archangel

Nootka Sound

BRITISH

Fort Chipewyan

RUPERT

BRITISH AND AMERICAN SEAFARERS

NORTH

York Factory

San Francisco Bay

Monterey

ALTA

Fort William

AMERICA

CALIFORNIA

LOUISIANA

Montreal

NEW

Santa Fe

St. Louis

UNITED

MEXICO

STATES

NEW

Loreto

TEXAS

Nacogdoches

San Antonio

BERMUDA

New Orleans

AFRO-

San Blas

FLORIDA

NORTH

SPAIN

Havana

AMERICA

Mexico

CUBA

JAMAICA

SANTO DOMINGO

CURAÇAO   BARBADOS

Map 1.1   *Source:* D. W. Meining, *The Shaping of America,* vol. 1: *Atlantic America, 1492–1800* (New Haven: Yale University Press, 1986), p. 423. Reprinted by permission of Yale University Press.

East Coast. Alaskans, a small but hardy breed, look southward to "the lower 48," just as Hawaiians look to "the mainland." And, proverbially, the New Yorker sees the United States as 80 percent the five boroughs of the Big Apple; another 10 percent the surrounding suburban counties of New York, New Jersey, and Connecticut; and the remaining 10 percent divided more or less equally among the Wild West, Florida, California, and Las Vegas.[20]

In 1835, Alexis de Tocqueville already saw the United States (which at that time did not extend west of the Rocky Mountains or southwest of the Arkansas River) as an integrated whole. As a Frenchman looking at a map, he was not constrained by the cultural preconceptions that Americans would bring with them. He could see North America falling into two roughly equal natural divisions, one encompassing the territories from which the waters flowed northward (i.e., the Hudson's Bay, Arctic Ocean, and St. Lawrence River basins, which became the nucleus of Canada), and the other, from which the waters flowed southward (principally the Mississippi, Missouri, and Ohio rivers basin, with the respective coasts attached to each). Based on this understanding, he predicted fifteen years in advance that the Americans would acquire the Pacific coast, from Puget Sound to the Gulf of California, and what were then the northernmost territories of Mexico, now Texas and the American Southwest. He believed that because those relatively empty lands were part of a natural geographic extension of the Mississippi Valley, they could not long remain in the possession of another nation.

De Tocqueville was right. The force of American expansion absorbed those vast territories before the mid-century mark through purchase, annexation, and the Mexican War. The country's response to the Mexican War itself was determined largely by geography. New Englanders, who were most detached from the geographic situation, generally took a moral stand in opposition to the war as unnecessary and unjust. But the settlers of the Mississippi Valley, north and south, with a few notable exceptions (including Abraham Lincoln), saw the war as absolutely necessary to secure their flanks. They saw the absorption of the new land as the most natural outcome in the world.[21] Standing in St. Louis, at approximately the point where the Mississippi, Missouri, and Ohio rivers meet, one is likely to get a different sense of the coherence of things than when standing in Boston.

What was (and is) it about the land that had the most potent consequences for its settlement and political organization? First of all, there was its vastness. For Europeans, especially people from the British Isles, the sheer size of the continent was impressive. In 1783, when the United States and Britain signed the peace treaty ending the Revolutionary War, the territory that came under the American flag (888,655 square miles) was already larger than the area within the twelve-member European Community two hundred years later—the British Isles plus all of Spain, Portugal, France, Germany, the Low Countries, Denmark, Italy, and Greece put together. By 1819, after the Louisiana Purchase and the acquisition of Florida, the still-infant republic was larger than all of Europe excepting European Russia and Romania. Today the United States is approximately the same size as all of Europe—from the Atlantic to the Urals, as the expression goes.

Wyoming is larger than all of Great Britain, Texas is larger than France, California is larger than both Germanys combined, Indiana is larger than Austria, and smallish West Virginia is considerably larger than Switzerland. The United States now extends over eight time zones. When it is 1 P.M. in Puerto Rico or the Virgin Islands, it is 6 A.M. in western Alaska. Only Russia has a larger expanse.

The land that would become the United States was not only vast but open—that is, accessible from without and within. Indeed, it may be more than coincidence that the United States, preeminently the "open society," benefited initially from geographic openness. Its Atlantic coast features many good deep-water and ice-free harbors, and the coastal area itself is penetrated by many navigable rivers. The central part of the country is drained by the world's mightiest river system, that of the Mississippi and its tributaries, most of which were navigable in the nineteenth century when settlers first entered the basin in large numbers. And even though the country is divided by three major mountain systems, the Appalachians, the Rockies, and the Sierra Nevadas, all three are broken by broad passes at crucial points. Ease of movement, then, has been a hallmark of American geography.

A third geographic element in the shaping of American society is the country's diversity. Because of its geographic situation, the United States embraces almost every kind of climate—from Arctic cold to subtropical and even tropical heat, from rain forests to rain-free deserts—and features almost every conceivable variety of land form and vegetation. This factor contributed to the availability and abundance of the many diverse resources needed to create a large, modern civilization; it also provided a geographic undergirding to the human diversity that continues to characterize American society.[22]

The shape of the land substantially influenced the ways in which the settlers occupied it. Until 1759, North America was divided among four great powers: France, Britain, Spain, and Russia. Geography shaped the role of each. The French entered the continent through the broad St. Lawrence Gulf and founded Quebec in 1608. Using the Great Lakes they rapidly penetrated into the interior, linking up with the Mississippi River system and acquiring the entire Mississippi Valley down to the Gulf of Mexico during the seventeenth century. Although the French established outposts wherever they raised their flag, the main attraction of the land for them was its capacity to produce furs. Consequently, their wide penetration, which in the eighteenth century sent them as far west as the Great Plains, did not lay the foundation for permanent settlement even though it gave them the major share of the continent. Thus, when the British were able to capture Quebec and Montreal, the two key centers of French Canada, the entire French empire in North America collapsed.[23]

The Spanish, who had established their empire in the central and southern parts of the Western Hemisphere in the early sixteenth century, turned northward from central Mexico and established their presence in what is now the American Southwest by the end of that century. They consolidated that presence in the seventeenth century but did little more than establish outposts at the farthest end of the empire. In one last burst of energy, at the time of the American Revolution, they also settled California, partly in an effort to forestall the expected British and Russian moves in the same direction. Barely more than a generation later, they would be displaced by the revolt of the indigenous inhabitants of greater Mexico.[24]

Russian North America, today the state of Alaska, represented the culmination of another great pioneering sweep of modern times: the eastward movement of the Russians across Siberia in the sixteenth and seventeenth centuries. After acquiring the vast Siberian lands for the czar, the intrepid Russian explorers and pioneers crossed the Bering Strait and planted settlements on the North American continent, which they would hold until 1867.[25]

The farthest Russian penetration into North America was Fort Ross, approximately 90 miles north of San Francisco, on the Pacific coast (today Fort Ross State Park). It represented the culmination of four thousand years of western movement. In the 1820s, Fort Ross was the southernmost Russian outpost in North America. For a brief moment, it reflected the expansionist ambitions of certain Russian leaders, who saw in the still politically chaotic Pacific coast of North America of the early nineteenth century a chance to extend Russian hegemony southward in the face of rival British, American, and Spanish claims. The Russian effort was brief and unsuccessful. It had no real support from Moscow and was confronted by intense opposition from rival claimants. The Russians abandoned the fort in the 1830s, withdrawing to Alaska where they were to sit for another thirty years until Secretary of State William Seward arranged to purchase that territory for the United States. Today, Fort Ross is a collection of restored log structures whose piquant history attracts visitors to a lovely section of the California coast.

In one sense, however, Fort Ross is far more significant than its brief history would seem to indicate. In effect, it was at that point that the convergence of various elements of what we generally define as Western civilization brought to a culmination four thousand years or more of expansion that ultimately embraced the whole globe.

Five thousand years before the founding of Fort Ross, the West Asian civilizations, out of which Western civilization was to spring, were reaching their height in the fertile crescent from the Nile to the Tigres and Euphrates valleys. A millennium and a half later, Israel emerged on the scene at the very western end of that region to give rise to Judaism, which became the religious foundation of Western civilization. Shortly thereafter, the Greeks, much influenced by the great civilizations of ancient West Asia, began the development of what was to become Western philosophy and science, first in Asia Minor and then in Southeastern Europe. Between the Semitic peoples of the Mediterranean coast and the Hellenic peoples of the Greek isles, what became Western civilization was spread throughout the Mediterranean Basin during the course of the millennium immediately prior to the rise of Christianity.

Two thousand years ago, Christianity was born out of the Jewish people; within its first millennium it synthesized its understanding of Jewish religious thought with the contributions of Greek civilization and spread throughout Europe. The energies of the West thus organized and released, the following millennium saw the Christianized Russians move eastward and the Christianized Spanish, French, and British peoples move westward away from their European heartlands to colonize vast new territories and implant Western civilization within them. The eastward movement of the Russians and the westward movement of the other European nations finally met after having girdled the globe in northern California at Fort Ross. Thereby completed were literally millennia of migration, settlement, and cultural transformation, the consequences of which became quite apparent in the twentieth century as the entire globe acquired at least the external elements of Western civilization.

Finally, there was British North America, territorially the smallest segment of the continent before 1759, but politically the most thoroughly settled and most fully organized. Here, geography and politics intersected. For France, Spain, and Russia, their North American possessions were outposts of empire, far removed from the centers of power in the mother country and not even of great interest to the centers of settlement in the colonial areas that had served as springboards for their advance. But this was not so in the case of the settlers who came to British North America. For them, the new continent became a vast frontier of expansion. The Atlantic coastal colonies were a natural extension of the British Isles. Moreover, instead of being settled as commercial or strategic outposts of a mother country, they were settled by people who came to stay and make their homes. For them, America—not London—was the center of the world. Moreover, they were organized politically into what were, in effect, self-governing dominions, linked with the mother country in a kind of imperial federation, not as in the case of the other possessions, mere colonies, politically dependent upon the motherland in every respect.[26]

This combination of geography and politics proved irresistible. The British, significantly assisted by the British North Americans, brought about a culmination of two generations of struggle between Britain and France by eliminating the French as a significant presence in North America. Although the Americans then proceeded to eliminate the British, they did so on a basis that so consolidated their own position that in the course of the next century, as they expanded westward, they proceeded to eliminate the French, Spanish, and Russians in turn, leaving North America north of the Rio Grande essentially an English-speaking preserve. In these actions we see one important facet of politics—the ability of people to use politics to concentrate their will and impose it upon vast territories and great peoples.

A century after the elimination of the French, the gross political boundaries of North America were essentially fixed. Even the boundaries of the subunits of much of the continent were established, with political configurations already outpacing the spread of settlement in certain areas. On the eve of the Civil War, sectionalism—the expression of social and political differences along geographic lines—was a powerful political force (see Map 1.2).

The three original sections—New England, the Middle States, and the South—had expanded westward as a result of the migration of their sons and daughters from these sections. The heirs of the Puritans had established a greater New England in upper New York State, northern Pennsylvania, the northern third of Ohio, Michigan, the northern corners of Indiana, northern and northwestern Illinois, Wisconsin, Minnesota, the northern two-thirds of Iowa, northeastern Kansas, western Oregon with outposts in western Washington, and southern California.[27] The sons and daughters from the Middle States had occupied central Ohio, Indiana, Illinois, southern Iowa, northern Missouri, southwestern Wisconsin, eastern Nebraska, and the settled parts of central California.[28] Although these two streams were often separated in their patterns of *local* settlement, in most cases they found themselves within the same states—a phenomenon that was repeated on the East Coast as New Englanders began to settle in New York City in great numbers, attracted by the commercial possibilities of that metropolis. Thus, over time, these groups had grown together to become the North, despite the internal differences that still divided them. As the North, they had established a West of their own, including the old northwest (Ohio, Indiana, Illinois, Michigan, and Wisconsin) and the still barely settled trans-Mississippi west.

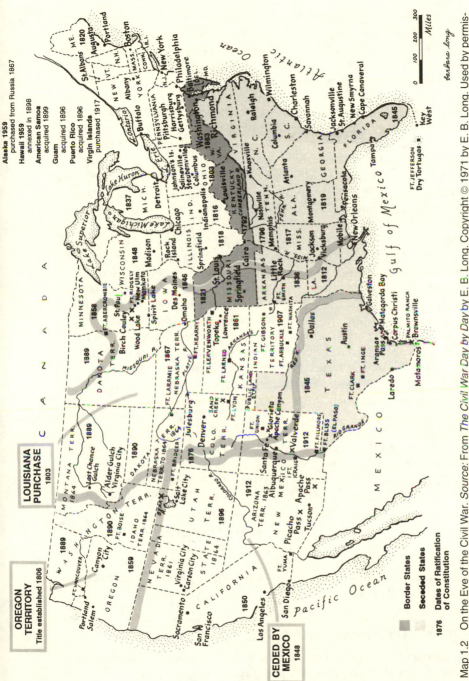
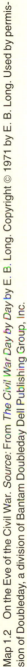

Map 1.2 On the Eve of the Civil War. *Source: From* The Civil War Day by Day *by E. B. Long. Copyright © 1971 by E. B. Long. Used by permission of Doubleday, a division of Bantam Doubleday Dell Publishing Group, Inc.*

Meanwhile, the Southerners pushing due westward had established two wests of their own—the old southwest (Kentucky, Tennessee, Alabama, and Mississippi) and the trans-Mississippi southwest. Both were tied tightly to the Old South through slavery, "the peculiar institution" that created a cohesiveness in the South, unequaled north of the Mason-Dixon line or the Ohio River.[29]

Settlements from both the North and the South had leaped over the central sections of the trans-Mississippi west, still known then as "the great American desert," to establish chains of settlements on the Pacific coast. The great area in the middle, barely penetrated by permanent settlers in 1861 (except for the Mormons in Utah and a few gold-seekers in Colorado), was to be settled essentially after the Civil War by a mixture of Northerners and Southerners quite different from that common to the pre–Civil War efforts.

More than a hundred years later, the end product of the first thrust of American settlement is still very visible (see Map 1.3). The South most clearly retains its identity as a separate section, whereas, as we shall see, the North has three components—the old northeast, the North's original west (i.e., those states settled after the adoption of the Constitution but before the Civil War), and the post–Civil War west. In the intervening century, the change in pattern of settlement reflected not simply the filling in of the vacant areas of 1861 but, rather, the transformation of the American population into an urban and then a metropolitan one, with all the essential political boundaries drawn and apparently fixed. More than a generation has passed since then. Although the nationwide pattern is generally the same, Americans have continued to move, in many cases along tried and true lines. Yet it was during these years that the migration to the Sunbelt became a flood, with so many Northeasterners and Midwesterners moving to Florida, the Gulf Coast, Texas, the southwestern desert states, California, and the Pacific Northwest. Though slowed by the economic downturn in the oil-producing states in the early 1980s, the flow from Frostbelt to Sunbelt has continued overall.

At the same time, the centrifugal movement away from central cities continued into the countryside to create belts of "rurban" development, whereby very urbanized people settled in small towns or in the rural areas around them. The series of maps in Map 1.4 graphically describes the results of this movement.

STATE AND LOCAL PARALLELS

Each state and locality has undergone a similar process of development, conditioned by its own particular geographic characteristics. Take, for example, the state of Illinois, located at the geo-historical crossroads of the

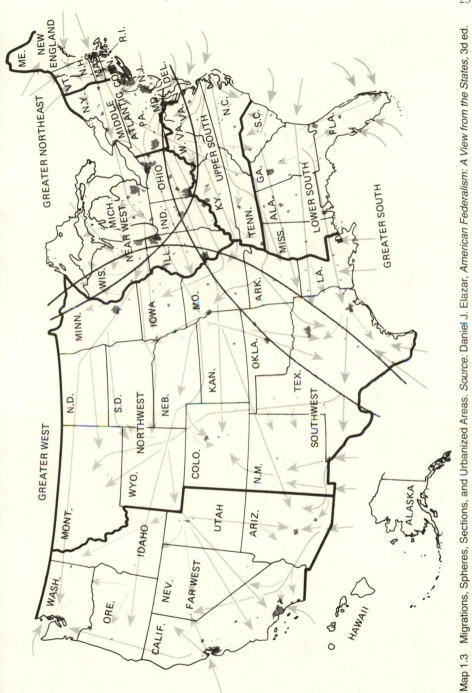

Map 1.3 Migrations, Spheres, Sections, and Urbanized Areas. *Source:* Daniel J. Elazar, *American Federalism: A View from the States,* 3d ed. (New York: Harper and Row Publishers, 1984), p. 139. Reprinted by permission of HarperCollins Publishers.

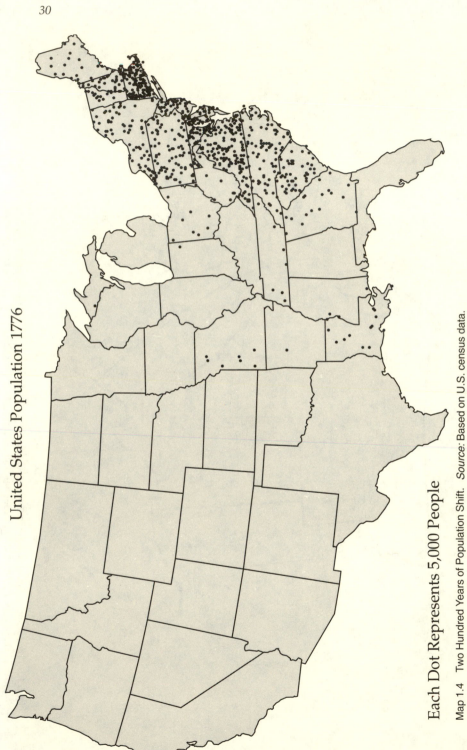

United States Population 1776

Each Dot Represents 5,000 People

Map 1.4   Two Hundred Years of Population Shift.   *Source:* Based on U.S. census data.

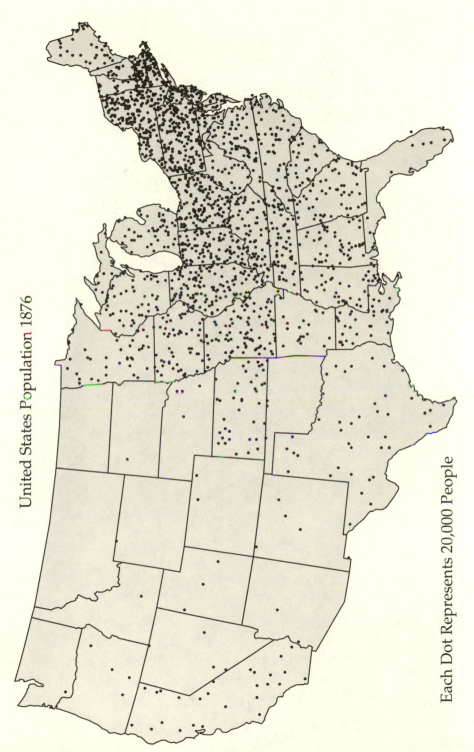

United States Population 1876

Each Dot Represents 20,000 People

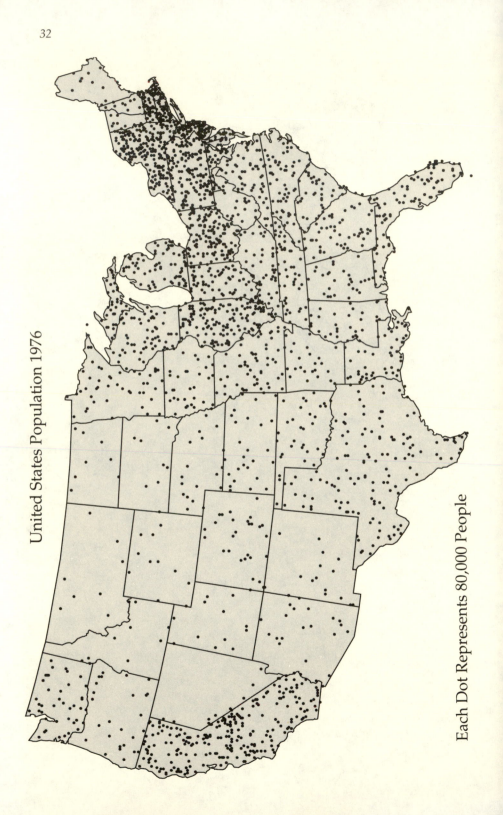

United States Population 1976

Each Dot Represents 80,000 People

United States, where North and South, East and West, and all the migratory streams meet. This state first appears in the pages of Western history, in the mid-seventeenth century, as what the French called the "Illinois country" after the Indian tribe of that name. (The tribe inhabited the land between Lake Michigan and the Mississippi River along the banks of the Illinois River.)[30]

Illinois sits astride the heart of the country's principal river system, where the Mississippi, Missouri, and Ohio rivers meet. The outlines of its future borders could be seen in the rivers themselves (though only in retrospect, since the use of any particular set of "natural" boundaries is a matter of human choice). The rivers represent one of the two distinguishing features of the flat–to–gently rolling Illinois country. The other is the line separating the wooded areas of the southern and eastern United States from the prairies that mark the beginning of the greater West.[31]

Looking at a map (Map 1.5), the keen observer will note immediately how open Illinois is—the very acme of openness in a country noted for openness. Rivers penetrate its every segment. To the northeast, the portage between the Great Lakes–St. Lawrence River system and the Mississippi River system is short and crosses a range of barely perceptible hills. No wonder it served as one of the main avenues of French exploration of the North American interior or, a century later, became the jumping-off point for the great western expeditions, beginning with that of Lewis and Clark (1803–1806). Yet in the hundred years between the time the French began their explorations and the state's conquest by Virginians during the Revolution, little had been done to settle the open Illinois country; nor had any boundaries been fixed to give Illinois meaning other than as a geographic term.

The Americans who came to settle and organize the land were the first to impose boundaries upon it. Illinois became part of the Indiana Territory. In 1809, it became a territory in its own right, taking the name of the principal Indian nation—"Illinois"—that had been located within its new borders. Finally, in 1818, Illinois became a state. In each case, the change in political status was accompanied by a redefinition of boundaries. With statehood came the most successful negotiation in Illinois' history. The territory's representative in Congress was able to secure a northern boundary for the new state that gave it an outlet on Lake Michigan, essentially the area that is metropolitan Chicago today. This boundary entitled it to fulfill its vital role as a bridge between East and West, North and South.

By 1818, the immigration to Illinois was in full swing. Politically, because of the Ohio River, Illinois is considered a Northern state (which in its earlier days meant that slavery was prohibited within its boundaries by Congress, regardless of local preference). Geographically, however,

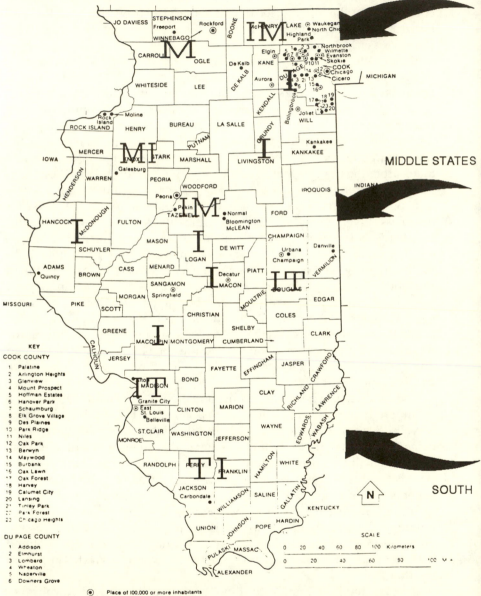

Map 1.5   Political Culture of Illinois. M: Moralistic; I: Individualistic; T: Traditionalistic.
Source: Based on author's research.

southern Illinois is due west of Virginia; hence the first waves of migration came into the new state's southern reaches and were mostly Southerners.

The rest of the state was settled between 1818 and 1861. Until the mid-1820s, Southerners were the predominant immigrants to Illinois. Then, for a decade, people from the Middle States were predominant. After 1835, the opening of lands in northern Illinois (a result of the Black Hawk War) led to an influx of New Englanders. Thus, in no more than fifty years, all three major native-population segments of the United States had entrenched themselves in the state, making its internal political life quite as complex as that of the United States as a whole, but within a much smaller territory.

The political life within Illinois' boundaries had to reflect various differences. The history of the establishment of its 102 counties encapsulates its internal political development. New counties were established to give new migrants a chance to control their own local affairs. And within those counties where New Englanders settled, townships were established (although the state constitution had to be changed to allow it, in a compromise struck between the Yankees and the Southerners in 1848). Otherwise the counties were governed as units without the benefit of such subdivision.

Nearly 150 years later, Illinois exhibits the impact of urbanization and metropolitanization within an already completely settled and politically organized civil society. The pattern of the Chicago metropolitan area reveals this impact in greater detail. Particularly evident is the way that territorial divisions have been used to achieve political goals—in this case, the goals of local self-government on a scale deemed appropriate by the decisionmakers involved.

SUMMARY

The smallest communities and the most comprehensive civil societies are alike in that they are shaped by their geo-historical location. No understanding of American politics in any arena—national, state, or local—is possible without taking this phenomenon into consideration. In the following chapters we will have occasion to explore its full meaning in detail.

Location, understood as location in space, in time, and in culture, is the critical concept to be explored in this book. It is argued here that the beginning of understanding a polity and its political system is understanding its three-dimensional location. Particular attention is paid to cultural location and its relationship to society and the individual personality, as well as to the relationship between culture and religion on the one hand and ethnicity on the other.

The changing pattern of this tridimensional location is to be found in the rhythm of the generations, a theme also introduced in this chapter. A theory of the generational rhythm is presented and outlined. With this in place we turn to look at the relationship between location and change in general, and more specifically in the United States, where the combined influence of the continuing American frontier and American sectionalism plays a special role in shaping the changing location of the United States.

The chapter concludes with an outline of these patterns at work throughout the United States and specifically in the state of Illinois, a good example of a state located at the cultural and geo-historical cross-roads of the country.

NOTES

1. See, for example, Robert Ardrey, *The Territorial Imperative* (New York: Atheneum, 1966) pp. 30–31; William Etkin, *Social Behavior from Fish to Man* (Chicago: University of Chicago Press, 1967); Stanform M. Lyman and Marvin B. Scott, "Territoriality: A Neglected Sociological Dimension," *Social Problems* 15:2 (Fall 1967): 236–249; and Jean Gottman, "The Evolution of the Concept of Territoriality," *Social Science Information* 14 (1975): 29–47.

2. See Richard Kluckhohn, ed., *Culture and Behavior* (New York: Free Press, 1962); A. L. Kroeber and Clyde Kluckhohn, *Culture: A Critical Review of Concepts and Definitions* (New York: Vintage, 1963); Edward T. Hall, *The Silent Language* (Garden City, N.Y.: Doubleday, 1959) and *The Hidden Dimension* (Garden City, N.Y.: Doubleday, 1966).

3. See, for example, Harry Eckstein, "A Culturalist Theory of Political Change," *American Political Science Review* (September 1988): 789–805.

4. This section was adapted from Daniel J. Elazar and Joseph Zikmund II, eds., *The Ecology of American Political Culture* (New York: Thomas Y. Crowell, 1975), Introduction.

5. Clyde Kluckhohn, "Cultural Behavior," *in* Gardner Lindzey, ed., *Handbook of Social Psychology* (Cambridge, Mass.: Addison, 1954); and Ralph Linton, *The Cultural Background of Personality* (New York: Appleton-Century, 1945).

6. Hall discusses the three manifestations of culture in *The Silent Language*, pp. 83–118.

7. See Max Kadushin, *Organic Thinking: A Study in Rabbinic Thought* (New York: Jewish Theological Seminary of America, 1938).

8. Ralph Linton, *The Cultural Background of Personality* (New York: Appleton Century, 1945), p. 44; A. R. Radcliffe-Brown, *The Nature of a Theoretical Natural Science of Society* (Chicago: University of Chicago, 1948).

9. For some important social science discussions of religion in America, see Gerhard Lenski, *The Religious Factor* (New York: Doubleday, 1963); Rodney Stark, *Religion and Society in Tension* (Chicago: Rand McNally, 1965); Andrew M. Greeley, *Unsecular Man* (New York: Dell, 1972); William C. McCready with Andrew M. Greeley, *The Ultimate Values of the American Population* (Beverly Hills, Calif.: Sage, 1976); Theodore Caplow et al., *All Faithful People: Change and Continuity in Middletown's Re-*

ligion (Minneapolis: University of Minnesota Press, 1983); Robert N. Bellah, *The Broken Covenant: American Civil Religion in Time of Trial* (New York: Seabury, 1975); Robert S. Billheimer, ed., *Faith and Ferment: An Interdisciplinary Study of Christian Beliefs and Practices* (Minneapolis, Minn.: Augusburg, 1983); and Davison Hunter, *American Evangelicalism* (New Brunswick, N.J.: Rutgers University Press, 1983). See also the following books by Martin E. Marty: *Modern American Religion* (Chicago: University of Chicago Press, 1986), *A Nation of Believers* (Chicago: University of Chicago Press, 1976), *The New Shape of American Religion* (New York: Harper and Row, 1959), *Pilgrims in Their Own Land: 500 Years of Religion in America* (Boston: Little, Brown, 1984), *Religion and Republic: The American Circumstance* (Boston: Beacon Press, 1987), *Religion and Social Conflict* (New York: Oxford University Press, 1964), and *Righteous Empire: The Protestant Experience in America* (New York: Dial Press, 1970).

10. See Radcliffe-Brown, *The Nature of a Theoretical Natural Science of Society.*

11. Gabriel A. Almond and G. Bingham Powell, Jr., *Comparative Politics: A Developmental Approach* (Boston: Little, Brown, 1966), p. 51.

12. For an analysis by political scientists of the national political culture in comparative settings, see Gabriel Almond and Sidney Verba, *The Civic Culture* (Princeton, N. J.: Princeton University Press, 1963). See also Daniel J. Boorstein, *The Americans: The National Experience* (New York: Random House, 1965); Seymour Martin Lipset, *The First New Nation: The United States in Historical and Comparative Perspective* (New York: Basic Books, 1963); and Louis Hartz, *The Foundings of New Societies: Studies in the History of the United States, Latin America, South Africa, and Australia* (New York: Harcourt, Brace and World, 1964).

13. See Elsworth Huntington, *Mainsprings of Civilization* (New York: Wiley, 1945), for a discussion of the influences of location and climate on social organization.

14. See Kevin Lynch, *What Time Is This Place?* (Cambridge, Mass.: MIT Press, 1972); Daniel J. Boorstein, *The Republic of Technology: Reflections on Our Future Community* (New York: Harper and Row, 1978); James J. Sheehan and Morton Sosna, *The Boundaries of Humanity: Humans, Animals, Machines* (Berkeley: University of California Press, 1991); and Peter Coveney and Roger Highfield, *The Arrow of Time* (London: W. H. Allen, 1990).

15. On the decline of mining and agricultural towns, see Lewis E. Atherton, *Main Street on the Middle Border* (Chicago: Quadrangle Books, 1966); Carle Clark Zimmerman, *Outline of American Rural Sociology* (Cambridge, Mass.: Phillips Book Store, 1946); Robert Athearn, *The Mystic West in Twentieth-Century America* (Lawrence: University Press of Kansas, 1986); and Marshall Sprague, *Money Mountain: The History of Cripple Creek Gold* (Boston: Little, Brown, 1953).

16. See Daniel J. Elazar, *Building Cities in America* (Lanham, Md.: Hamilton Press, 1987).

17. See, for example, *From Peak to Peak*, the bimonthly magazine on Front Range communities, most of which went through this cycle. The present author has also noted this phenomenon in unpublished field notes.

18. Alexis de Tocqueville, *Democracy in America*, Vol. 1 (New York: Random House, 1990), pp. 26–27.

19. Alexander Hamilton, John Jay, and James Madison, *The Federalist*, No. 2, edited by Clinton Rossiter (New York: Mentor, 1961), pp. 37–39.

20. The *New Yorker* and other publications have published classic "maps" showing these different perspectives. See also Lynch, *What Time Is This Place?;* E. Relph, *Place and Placenessness* (London: Pion, 1976); Frederick Jackson Turner, *The Significance of Sections in American History* (New York: Holt, 1932); Charles O. Paullin, *Atlas of the Historical Geography of the United States* (Washington, D.C.: Carnegie, 1932); and Ramesh D. Dikshit, "Geography and Federalism," *Annals of the Association of American Geographers* 61 (March 1971): 97–115.

21. O. B. Faulk and J. A. Stout, Jr., eds., *The Mexican War: Changing Interpretations* (Chicago: Sage Books, 1973); Nathaniel W. Stephenson, *Texas and the Mexican War.* Vol. 24, *Chronicles of America* (New Haven, Conn.: Yale University Press, 1921).

22. David M. Potter, *People of Plenty* (Chicago: University of Chicago Press, 1954).

23. See Francis Parkman, *France and England in North America,* 9 vols., several editions (Boston, 1867–1892); James P. Gibson, ed., *European Settlement and Development in North America: Essays on Geographical Change in Honor and Memory of Andrew Hill Clark* (Toronto: University of Toronto Press, 1978); Francis Parkman, *Pioneers of France in the New World* (Boston: Little, Brown, 1901); Louise P. Kellog, *Early Narratives on the Northwest* (New York: Barnes and Noble, 1959).

24. On Spain and early America, see Arthur P. Whitaker, *The Spanish American Frontier, 1783–1795* (Boston: Houghton Mifflin, 1927); French Ensor Chadwick, *The Relations of the United States and Spain* (New York: C. Scribner's Sons, 1941); and Arthur P. Whitaker, *Spain and the Defense of the West: Ally and Liability* (Westport, Conn.: Greenwood Press, 1980).

25. On Russia and early America, see Howard I. Kushner, *Conflict on the Northwest Coast: American-Russian Rivalry in the Pacific Northwest, 1790–1867* (Westport, Conn.: Greenwood Press, 1975, pp. 3–24; and Ronald J. Jensen, *The Alaska Purchase and Russian-American Relations* (Seattle: University of Washington Press, 1975), pp. 62–99.

26. On the British settlement of North America and the American colonial experience, see Parkman, *France and England in North America;* S. E. Johnson, *A History of Emigration from the United Kingdom to North America, 1763–1912* (London, 1913); Thomas Brindley, *Migration and Economic Growth: A Study of Great Britain and the American Economy* (Cambridge, England, 1954); and Rowland T. Berthoff, *British Immigrants in Industrial America 1790–1950* (Cambridge, Mass.: Harvard University Press, 1953).

27. On the Yankee migration, see Steward H. Holbrook, *The Yankee Exodus* (New York: Macmillan, 1950); Gibson, ed., *European Settlement and Development in North America;* Merle Curti, *The Making of an American Community: A Case Study of Democracy in a Frontier County* (Stanford, Calif.: Stanford University Press, 1959); Louis K. Matthews, *Expansion of New England* (New York: Russell and Pursell, 1936); Arnold M. Rose, "The Mormon Church and Utah Politics: An Abstract of a Statistical Study," *American Sociological Review* 7 (1942): 853–854; James D. Holmquist, ed., *They Chose Minnesota: A Survey of the State's Ethnic Groups* (St. Paul: Minnesota Historical Society Press, 1981), p. 56; T. J. Wertenbaker, *The Puritan Oligarchy: The Founding of American Civilization* (New York: Grosset and Dunlap, 1947); W. Lloyd Warner et al., "Yankee City" series, *The Social Life of a Modern Community* (Westport, Conn.: Greenwood Press, 1941), and *The Social Systems of American Ethnic Groups* (Westport, Conn.: Greenwood Press, 1945).

28. On the Middle States migration, see Eric F. Goldman, "The Middle States Regionalism and American Historiography: A Suggestion," in Eric F. Goldman, ed., *Historiography and Urbanization* (Baltimore: Johns Hopkins University Press, 1941); A. B. Hollingshead, *Elmtown's Youth* (New York: Wiley, 1949); John R. Seely et al., *Community Chest* (Toronto: University of Toronto Press, 1957); T. J. Wertenbaker, *The Founding of American Civilization: The Middle Colonies* (New York: C. Scribner's Sons, 1938); William Lloyd Warner, *Democracy in Jonesville* (New York: Harper, 1949); and Curti, *The Making of an American Community.*

29. On the Southern states migration, see W. J. Cash, *The Mind of the South* (New York: Alfred A. Knopf, 1960); L. C. Gray, "History of Agriculture in the Southern United States to 1860," in U.S. Department of Agriculture, *Contributions to American Economic History,* Vol. 1 (Washington, D.C.: Carnegie Institute, 1933); T. J. Wertenbaker, *The Old South: The Founding of American Civilization* (New York: Cooper Square Publishers, 1942); James W. Silver, *Mississippi: A Closed Society* (New York: Harcourt, Brace and World, 1963); and Warner, *Democracy in Jonesville.*

30. Ray Billington, "The Frontier in Illinois History," in *Journal of the Illinois Historical Society* (Spring 1950): 1–22; Theodore C. Pease, *The Story of Illinois* (Chicago: University of Chicago Press, 1947); *Illinois: A Descriptive and Historical Guide,* originally compiled and written by the Federal Writers' Project for the State of Illinois, revised in 1946 (Chicago: Munsell, 1936); Illinois Centennial Commission, *The Centennial History of Illinois,* edited by Clarence W. Alvord (Springfield: Illinois Centennial Commission, 1918); Daniel J. Elazar, *Cities of the Prairie: The Metropolitan Frontier and American Politics* (New York: Basic Books, 1970); and Paul M. Angle, *Here I Have Lived: A History of Lincoln's Springfield 1821–1865* (New Brunswick, N.J.: Rutgers University Press, 1950).

31. On Illinois' geography, see Edward L. Mullin and Ronald R. Boyce, eds., *Geography and Spatial Interaction* (Seattle: University of Washington Press, 1980); and Ronald R. Boyce and Seymour Z. Mann, *Urbanism in Illinois: Its Nature, Importance and Problems* (Carbondale, Ill.: Public Affairs Research Bureau, Southern Illinois University, 1965).

CHAPTER 2

The Generational Rhythm of American Politics

This chapter will suggest a way in which political time is actually structured in the United States. It rests on a theory of generational rhythms that I have applied to the course of American politics since the mid-1950s to forecast developments. I have also applied that model to the American polity from its beginning, in a way that usefully charts the flows of American political affairs.

EARLY STUDIES OF GENERATIONAL RHYTHMS

Students of society have noted the succession of generations since ancient times.[1] Indeed, the Bible explicitly bases its chronology on generational measures.

As the first great work to concern itself with linear time and human movement through history, the Bible marks the beginning of human understanding of the generational pattern in human affairs. It was also the first work to explain why the pattern transcends the individual lives that call it into existence. As such, it is the starting point for our understanding of the generational phenomenon, and it offers classic paradigmatic examples of the phenomenon operating in history.[2]

Time in the Bible is almost invariably measured on a generational basis, beginning with the "generations of man" (in the first recounting of human history in Genesis) and continuing through the system of Divine rewards and punishments (the latter unto the third and fourth generations and the former unto the thousandth, by the biblical account).[3] A human being is allotted two average generations (70 years) as his or her normal life span and three full generations (120 years) for exceptional virtue.[4] Indeed, biblical scholars have clearly demonstrated that the biblical expression *forty years* is an idiomatic phrase meaning "a generation."[5]

Generations in the biblical sense are also collective affairs. The "generation of the wilderness" is the best example of a collectivity of people linked primarily by their existence as adults during a common time span.[6] The concept is applied even more often to a time period or, perhaps more accurately, to a period that embraces time-plus-people. Thus the Book of Judges describes the rise of new judges in each generation to meet the challenges of that generation and to restore peace for the remainder of its allotted span.[7]

Moreover, the Bible recognizes that all societies have beginnings whose echoes are never lost. The character of the founders persists among their heirs. Israel, whose people are of central interest in the biblical narrative, is at every point reminded of its beginnings and its ancestry.

Nineteenth-century philosophers, sociologists, and historians were the first to articulate systematic theories of generational progression and its influence on human development. Auguste Comte viewed the duration of human life, particularly the thirty-year term of full activity in adulthood, as decisive in shaping the velocity of human evolution, suggesting that "the unanimous adherence to certain fundamental notions" transforms the aggregate of individuals alive at a particular time into a social cohort.[8] John Stuart Mill, influenced by Comte and convinced that "History does, when Judiciously examined, afford Empirical Laws of Society," added the idea that in every generation, the "principle phenomena" of society are different, suggesting that the differences appear at generational intervals as each "new set" of individuals comes to dominate society.[9]

These general theories led to efforts at statistical and empirical verification and elaboration, especially during the last forty years of the nineteenth century, when historians were trying to develop the scientific study of history. Antoine Augustin Cournot advanced the principle that generations are articulated through historical events and suggested the means by which continuity among generations is maintained. Giuseppe Ferrari emphasized the thirty-year interval and suggested a fourfold classification of generations as preparatory, revolutionary, reactionary, and conciliatory in repeating cycles.[10] Wilhelm Dilthey applied the concept to cultural development.[11] Leopold von Ranke and his student Ottokar Lorenz emphasized that generational periodization was one of the keys to the scientific study of history, utilizing as tools the study of genealogy and heredity.[12] Lorenz also introduced the concept of the three-generation century.[13]

After World War I, José Ortega y Gasset (in 1933 and again in 1962) made the succession of generations the basis for his philosophical theory of social life, adding, among other concepts, the distinction between contemporaries (those alive at the same time) and coevals (those who are part of the same generation).[14] His work was continued by his student, Julian

Marias. Sociologist Karl Mannheim (1952) also worked on this problem, as did such scholars as Francois Mentre (1920) and Engelbert Drerup (1933).[15] The thesis was applied to art by Wilhelm Pinder (1926) and to literature by Julius Peterson (1930) and Henri Peyre (1948).[16]

More recent efforts by political and social scientists have focused on problems of intergenerational differences and the political socialization of new generations in totalitarian regimes or with reference to parties of the extreme left or right. Sigmund Neumann (1965) was the first to apply this perspective in his study of the rise of Nazism.[17] Bauer et al. (1956) included it in their study of the Soviet system.[18] Marvin Rintala (1958, 1962, 1963) focused on right and left in Finland, whereas Maurice Zeitlin (1966) studied Cuba.[19] And S. N. Eisenstadt (1956) and Joseph Gusfield (1957) utilized the generational concept in entirely different settings, in Israel and the United States, respectively.[20]

All these studies have provided basic data for the development of a comprehensive theory of the generational rhythm of politics. Most of their authors have not attempted to formulate such a theory, and those few who *have* did not attempt to apply their theories, leaving many questions to be clarified. For example, the studies have shown that generations can be conceptualized in two parallel ways: as a discrete series of interrelated events and in terms of the people who actively inhabit a particular period of time. In fact, both phenomena represent reality, just as physicists have determined that light consists, simultaneously, of waves and particles. The linkage of the two phenomena is a prerequisite to any comprehensive theory.

None of these authors is concerned with the inner composition of a generation. Rather, they look at it as something resembling a black box that can be added with others to form even larger time periods. Indeed, some of them place more emphasis on the century, consisting of three generations. Many of the authors use the term *generation* in a common-sensical way, but without defining exactly what they mean by it. Thus empirical verification of their use of the term is impossible. Consistent with the field of interest of these scholars (whether literature, art, or music), they are interested in discussing generations as a sequence of eminent individuals rather than in putting their scheme on a more popular basis. Some (notably Mannheim) try to solve the problem of how to embrace peoples of different cultural and geographic settings under the heading of "a generation."

EFFORTS TO DELINEATE POLITICAL CYCLES IN AMERICAN HISTORY

A number of the theories of political cycles in American history advanced since Arthur M. Schlesinger wrote "The Tides of American Politics" in

1939 are related to the generational thesis presented here. Schlesinger saw American history as a series of alternating periods of conservatism and liberalism based on "the *dominant national mood* as expressed in effective governmental action (or inaction)."[21] Conservative periods reflect "concern for the rights of the few," an "emphasis on the welfare of property," and "inaction." Liberal periods reflect "concern for the wrongs of the many," an "emphasis on human welfare," and "rapid movement." Aside from Schlesinger, the authors of such theories include V. O. Key, Jr., Charles Sellers, Gerald Pomper, and Walter Dean Burnham.[22] V. O. Key's theory is based on his historical theories of party loyalty and critical elections. He traced the "more or less durable" shifts in "traditional party attachments," using the latter as "bench marks" in studying the electoral process. Key was primarily interested in the "secular realignment" of the interest coalitions that make up the party vote in the United States. Since he made no attempt to deal explicitly with historical periodization, however, his efforts are insightful but incomplete.[23]

Charles Sellers and Gerald Pomper look at political cycles in the manner established by Key with the intention of refining Key's work. Sellers looks at the party distribution of electoral votes in presidential elections and seats won in off-year elections to the House of Representatives to discover "the oscillations in actual party voting strength" as the basis for the cyclical pattern in American politics, which, like Schlesinger, he bases on the notion of an equilibrium cycle. On this basis, Sellers divides American history into six periods, each of approximately a generation in length but with minimum consistency in the overall results. He concludes that the equilibrium cycle is of little value as a predictive device since the oscillations move in irregular and unpredictable directions.

Pomper avoids some of the problems created by Sellers in his emphasis on geographic rather than personal realignment; but, because he uses the states as his primary units, he does not deal with shifts of voting behavior that do not affect his correlations of the state vote as such. Beginning with the election of 1828, he delineates three periods: the Populist (1890s–1928), the New Deal (1928–1960s), and the present.

Walter Dean Burnham links his theory of political cycles to the level of public discontent. On that basis, he identifies five periods since 1789, each of which has gone through a cycle of stability, crystallization, and discontent. "The intrusion of approximate tension-producing events" acts as a catalyst causing already growing discontent to be focused on the capture of an established political party or the creation of a new one. This, in turn, leads to voter realignment. Burnham sees a generational basis to this pattern and, in effect, suggests that such a realignment occurs in every generation.

All five political scientists use critical elections to mark the beginning or ending of particular political periods, viewing them primarily as causative factors in the generation of political cycles rather than primarily as responses to other factors, as they have been viewed here. None of these are complete theories, and all must be considered within a larger context—one that their proponents leave implicit.

Beyond these efforts at systemization, there are rough approximations of the generations or segments of generations in the commonly accepted descriptions of historical periods in the United States. In some cases, whole generations have identities; examples include the revolutionary period and the Populist era. In others, the periods of generational response have recognized names: Jacksonian Democracy, the New Deal, the Great Society. In still others, names have been given to periods of political dominance flowing from critical elections: The Jeffersonian era and the Jacksonian era are two such periods.

TEMPORAL RHYTHMS IN THE UNITED STATES

In the first few years of the 1960s, a number of political observers developed cogent and well-elaborated theories to explain why the federal government, particularly Congress, was paralyzed and could not respond to the needs of the time.[24] A few years later, however, the American people were treated to a display of federal activity (in the form of congressional legislation) paralleled only by FDR's "100 days" after March 1933. Why did these theories miss the mark so badly? What brought about the shift from the apparent truth of this thesis in the 1950s to the veritable revolution of the mid-1960s? The answers to these questions lie in a proper understanding of the temporal rhythm of political life in the United States. (*Rhythm* in the sense used here refers to the structured flow of time and events.)

The American political system, like all others, has a rhythm of its own, which, in turn, is linked with the overall rhythm of human time. By tracing those links, we can begin to lay out a discernible pattern in the progression of political events in the United States over the years and get some sense of why things happen (or do not happen).[25] The historical pattern of political events in the United States follows a generational rhythm that flows in cycles ranging from twenty-five to forty years each, approximately the biological time-span of the mature or active portion of a human life. The sequence and impact of discrete political events is substantially shaped by the rhythm of the generations, even though the events themselves may seem random.

Thomas Jefferson noted this phenomenon and built a constitutional theory around it:

> The question Whether one generation of men has a right to bind another ... is a question of such consequences as not only to merit decision, but place also among the fundamental principles of every government. ... Let us suppose a whole generation of men to be born on the same day, to attain mature age on the same day, and to die on the same day, leaving a succeeding generation in the moment of attaining their mature age, all together. Let the ripe age be supposed of 21 years, and their period of life, 34 years more, that being the average term given by the bills of mortality to persons who have already attained 21 years of age. Each successive generation would, in this way, come on and go off the stage at a fixed moment, as individuals do now.
> ...
> What is true of a generation all arriving to self-government on the same day, and dying all on the same day, is true of those on a constant course of decay and renewal, with this only difference. A generation coming in and going out entire, as in the first case, would have a right in the first year of their self dominion to contract a debt for 33. years, in the 10th. for 24. in the 20th. for 14. in the 30th. for 4. whereas generation changing daily, by daily deaths and births, have one constant term beginning at the date of their contract, and ending when a majority of those of full age at that date shall be dead. The length of that term may be estimated from the tables of mortality, corrected by the circumstances of climate, occupation &c. peculiar to the country of the contractors. Take, for instance, the table of M. de Buffon wherein he states that 23,994 deaths, and the ages at which they happened. Suppose a society in which 23,994 persons are born every year and live to the ages stated in this table. The conditions of that society will be as follows. 1st. it will consist constantly of 617,703 persons of all ages. 2dly. of those living at any one instant of time, one half will be dead in 24. years 8. months. 3dly. 10,675 will arrive every year at the age of 21. years complete. 4thly. it will constantly have 348,417 persons of all ages above 21. years. 5ly. and the half of those of 21. years and upward living at any one instant of time will be dead in 18. years 8. months, or say 19. years as the nearest integral number. Then 19. years is the term beyond which neither the representatives of a nation, nor even the whole nation itself assembled, can validly extend a debt.
> On similar ground, it may be proved, that no society can make a perpetual constitution, or even a perpetual law. ... Every constitution, then, and every law, naturally expires at the end of 34. years. If it be enforced longer, it is an act of force, and not of right.[26]

This is the elaborate scheme that Jefferson, in his search for a system that would provide the maximum degree of individual liberty, proposed to his friend and colleague, James Madison, at the outset of the French Revolution; but it represented a transient thought on his part. Once the sage of Monticello experienced the problems of constitution-making on a large scale, he did not actively try to begin anew every nineteen years. Yet in proposing his rather radical scheme, Jefferson did come to grips with an important social phenomenon, one that perceptive political leaders of every age have reckoned with in one way or another: namely, the succession of generations as the measure of location in time as well as the measure of consent.

HUMAN SOCIAL RHYTHMS

As Jefferson noted, the human biological heritage provides a natural measure of time. We often use the concept of the "generation" in a commonsensical way for just that purpose, as when we talk about the "lost generation" or the "generation gap." In fact, social time does appear to move in sufficiently precise generational units to account for the rhythm of social and political action. If we look closely and carefully, we can map the internal structure of each generation in any particular civil society and chart the relations among generations so as to formulate a coherent picture of the historical patterns of its politics.

During a period of no fewer than twenty-five and no more than forty years, averaging from thirty to thirty-five (Jefferson gives thirty-four as the average), most people will pass through the productive phase of their life cycles and then pass into retirement, turning their places over to others. Every individual begins life with childhood, a period of dependency in which one's role as an independent actor is extremely limited. Depending upon the average life expectancy in a society, he or she begins to assume an active role as a member of society sometime between the ages of 15 and 30 (Jefferson's average: 21). At this point he or she has between twenty-five and forty years of "active life" ahead, during which he or she is responsible for such economic, social, and political roles as are given to mature men and women in society. Sometime between the ages of 55 and 70, if one is still alive, most people are relieved of those responsibilities and are by convention, if not in physical terms, considered ready for retirement.

Political life reflects this generational pattern on both an individual and a collective basis. From a political standpoint, for the first fifteen to twenty years of life an individual is essentially powerless, having no right to vote and dependent upon his or her elders for political opinions. After attaining suffrage, individuals must still pass through a period of political apprenticeship before the right to vote can be translated into the chance for political leadership. Even among those who choose to be active in politics, most reach their 30s before assuming significant positions of responsibility on the larger political scene.[27] It is only then that they become serious contenders for political power and, with good fortune, are able to replace the incumbent power-holders who depart from the scene as a result of physical or political death. (The latter may be defined as the ending of one's serious political career without suffering actual physical death.) By and large the years from one's 30s into one's 60s represent the period in which one's potential influence is at its maximum. A few people begin to exercise influence earlier, and some very exceptional people remain political leaders longer; but rare indeed is the political career that exceeds forty years of meaningful influence past one's apprenticeship.

The voting behavior of the average citizen reflects a similar cycle of participation. A very high percentage of newly enfranchised young people do not bother to vote. The percentage of eligible voters who do exercise this right increases significantly for people in their 30s, remains much the same until retirement age, and then declines again. It would seem, then, that voters as well as leaders tend to "retire" after a generation's worth of activity.[28]

In addition to the generational pattern that is reflected in each individual, as Jefferson noted indirectly, a nation or civil society is, in effect, a sequential combination of generations sharing a common history and heritage. The generational pattern for any particular society, nation, or group is set at the beginning of its history by its founders. Take the United States. The historical record shows that the "founders" of the colonies, the republic, and the western states and settlements were generally "young" men, at the beginning of the productive phase of their life cycles.[29] In the process of founding new settlements or institutions, they formed leadership groups, which in the normal course of events remained in power throughout the years of their maturity. They retired when age and an entirely new generation forced them to do so and were replaced according to the very cycle that they, willy-nilly, had established.

Thus, in the first third of the seventeenth century, groups of young adults settled virgin territory at key points along the Atlantic coast and in this way initiated what was to become the generational progression of the United States. And for all intents and purposes, they did so with a free hand. Since the first generation of Americans began more or less "even," its people (particularly its leaders) passed from the scene at approximately the same time, thereby opening the door for a new generation of leaders to enter the picture and to begin the process all over again. Thus at every stage of the advancing frontier, new people would pioneer, establish their patterns, and pass from the scene at roughly the same time, thereby allowing a new generation to assume the reins.

Because such beginnings occur in history periodically, they establish a much greater regularity of generational progressions in social and political life than that found in the simple processes of human biology, which, if other things were equal, should theoretically maintain a constant "changing of the guard." In this way the biological basis for the progression of generations is modified by locational factors. Given sufficient data, we can trace the generational cycles and patterns back to the very foundations of organized society. A case in point is the United States, a society whose foundings are recorded in history.

Such changes as occur in any society are intimately tied to the progression of generations. Each new generation that assumes the reins of power is necessarily a product of different influences and has been shaped to respond to different problems. This reality heightens the impact of the change and encourages new political action to assimilate that change into the lives of the members of the new generation. In addition, the biological fact that three or at most four generations are alive at any given time creates certain linkages between generations (e.g., the influence of grandparents on grandchildren) that ensure a measure of intergenerational contacts and social continuity. Those contacts help shape every generation's perception of its past and future. In this respect, Jefferson's effort to separate generations sharply was not only socially inaccurate but also biologically impossible and politically unmanageable.

GENERATIONS, CENTURIES, AND EVENTS

Since the founding of the first European settlements along the Atlantic seaboard three and a half centuries ago, eleven generations of Americans have led the United States through a continuing series of challenges and responses, and we are now witnessing the twelfth. In due course, the centuries (each of which amounts to essentially three generation units) as well as the generations have acquired a certain distinctiveness of their own. Again, there is a common-sensical recognition of this phenomenon in the treatment of American history. The seventeenth century stands out clearly as the century of the founding of American settlement; the eighteenth stands out as the century in which an independent American nation was forged; the nineteenth stands out as the century of continental expansion; and the twentieth is the century of the United States as a world power.

Historical centuries do not cover precisely the same time periods as chronological centuries. In American history, as in modern European history, historical centuries have come to an end and new ones have begun some seven to fifteen years after the chronological dividing point. Consider the following examples:

1. The sixteenth century ended with the death of Queen Elizabeth I (1522–1603), and the seventeenth century began with the opening of the American frontier at Jamestown (1607). The decisive political

factor of the time was the emergence of conflict between the Stuarts and the Puritans.

2. The seventeenth century ended and the eighteenth century began with the Treaty of Utrecht and the conclusion of Queen Anne's War (1713), which eliminated the Netherlands as a world power and turned the Anglo-French conflict in the New World and then the American and French revolutions into primary considerations for both America and Europe.

3. The eighteenth century ended with the fall of Napoleon and the conclusion of the War of 1812 (1815), and the nineteenth century began with the "era of good feeling" and the American turn west (1816 and later).

4. The nineteenth century ended and the twentieth century began with the inauguration of Woodrow Wilson's "New Freedom" (1913), the outbreak of World War I (1914), and the final closing of America's last land frontier.

Perhaps even more saliently, the fundamental issues and alignments forming the hidden dimension that shapes political behavior show every sign of persisting over three generation periods and then dissipating in the fourth. Two examples from American history are immediately relevant. The issues and alignments revolving around the federal union and slavery that emerged during the sixth generation of American life—the first generation under the Constitution—persisted through the eighth generation (a century later), when they were resolved in the Civil War. In turn, the war created a new set of fundamental issues and alignments having to do with industrialization and the construction of a more equal society. These took form in the ninth generation, dominated American politics for a century, and then shifted in the eleventh generation to the search for pluralism, multiculturalism, and individualism. Americans are currently in the process of defining the issues and shaping the alignments that will define them.

The issues of the past century are being replaced in the twelfth generation by new issues that have surfaced in American life in the past half generation. Indeed, the crisis of the 1960s, which commentators have described as the most divisive since the Civil War, came just when it would have been predicted to come in the flow of generations—that is, when one century's set of "just" issues was losing its grip on the American people and a new set of issues of equal intensity was moving to center stage. This transition explains why the conflicts of the late 1960s and early 1970s were so intense, the sense of alienation from the American past so deep among the members of the generation then coming to maturity, and the changes in American life so vast. Since then, great healing has taken place. Although it began after Gerald Ford entered the White House, its peak was presided over and encouraged by Ronald Reagan in a decade that witnessed the renewal of American patriotism and self-confidence.

Table 2.1 graphically delineates the progression of centuries and generations since 1607. In the course of the present book, this progression will be related to major forces and factors shaping American history: (1) the stages of the continuing American frontier; (2) the principal challenges facing the American people in each generation and the central responses to those challenges; (3) the changing forms and patterns of American federalism; (4) the sequence of critical elections; (5) the dominant modes of economic organization in the country; and (6) the changing relationships among racial, ethnic, and religious groups.

One note of caution: Although this table necessarily portrays the divisions between generations and centuries in a precise fashion, the dates themselves must be viewed as approximate. Historical eras can be delineated, but they do not begin and end with such sharpness. Convenience demands that we be more precise for analytical purposes than life ever is.

The first three generations together constituted the seventeenth century, the period of initial colonization. By 1713, immigrants from the Old World—mostly from the British Isles, the Netherlands, and Germany, but already including Africans and small numbers of people from virtually every corner of Europe—had founded all but one of the original thirteen colonies. Thus they gave rise to the first generation of native Americans of European and African descent in the English colonies and started those colonies on the road toward becoming a separate nation with its own civilization.

The fourth through sixth generations encompassed the eighteenth century, which, from the first American recognition of common continental interests in 1713 to the conclusion of the "Second War for Independence" in 1815, was devoted to forging an independent American nation. These generations created the idea of American nationalism, successfully fought for the independence of the united colonies, and established the United States as a democratic federal republic. The ideas bequeathed by those three generations form the core of the political heritage of all subsequent generations of Americans.

The nineteenth century covered the seventh, eighth, and ninth generations, beginning at the point where America turned its back on European entanglements after 1815 and ending at the point where it reembraced them in World War I. These generations transformed the young republic into an industrialized continental nation with a strong national government, abolished slavery, settled the West, and created an embryonic world power ready for overseas involvements.

TABLE 2.1 The Generational Rhythm of American Politics: A Graphic Outline

Century and Generation	Dates	Challenge-Response	Critical Elections	Frontier Period	Economic Period	Intergovernmental Relations	Ethnoreligious Trends
Seventeenth	1607	Founding and establishing polities		Rural-land frontier	Colonial mercantilism	Founding and organizing colonies	Ethnic separation on religious basis
1	1648			(East Coast settled)			Establishment of churches
2	1676	Establishing local identity Building a pluralistic social base				Experiments in federal organization	
3	1713						
Eighteenth		Eliminating the French from North America					Protestant diversification and disestablishment
4	1756	Establishing national independence	1768: Stamp Act Congress	(Appalachians crossed)		Formation of Union	Increased ethnic diversity within framework of Protestantism
5	1775 1776 1781		1774: 1st Continental Congress				
	1787						

# / Period	Government	Party system	Frontier	Economic system	Federalism	Religion / Immigration
6 1789 1815	1789 Organizing a government	1796: Federalists 1800: Democratic-Republicans		Semimercantilism	Development of intergovernmental cooperation	
Nineteenth 7 1816	1816 Democratization of the American polity	1824: National Democrats 1828: Jacksonian Democrats	Urban-industrial frontier	First transition		Informal reestablishment of Protestantism Influx of Catholics and Jews
1846 8	1848 Reorganizing for an industrial society	1856: Democrats 1860: Republicans	(Continent spanned)	Free Enterprise capitalism	Era of land grants	
1876 9						
10 1913 1946	1913 First assault on problems of industrialization	1892: Democrats 1896: Republicans		Concentrated enterprise capitalism	Beginning of cash grants	Period of Eastern and Southern European migration Protestant counterattacks
Twentieth 11 1917	1917 Reformation of the industrial system	1928: Republicans 1932: Democrats	Metropolitan-technological frontier	Second transition	Grant-in-aid federalism	Discovery of pluralism

continues

TABLE 2.1 (cont.)

Century and Generation	Dates	Challenge-Response	Critical Elections	Frontier Period	Economic Period	Intergovernmental Relations	Ethnoreligious Trends
	1949	Responding to metropolitan frontier as world leader	1956: Republicans 1960: Democrats		Regulated enterprise capitalism	Concentrated cooperation	Recognition of pluralism
12	1977	Restructuring of economy and society in wake of cybernetic frontier and changed role as world leader	1980: Republicans 1984: Republicans	Rurban-cybernetic frontier	New market economy	Restoration of states' initiative	Resurgence of religious fundamentalism Political self-assertion of former excluded streams Multiculturalism Increased immigration of Asians
	1989– 1991	Generational climax: West wins Cold War New assertion of U.S. power in Gulf War					
	1993	New generation takes power					

The tenth generation—the first of the twentieth century—reformed the nation's industrial system and led the country into the arena of world politics. The eleventh generation was charged with the task of shaping America's role as a world power and of presiding over massive efforts to adjust socially and politically to the results of a technological transformation at least the equal of the industrial revolution.

As the twelfth generation began forming, it was faced with the challenge of adjusting to a world role of reduced dominance for the United States, one in which American industrial might has been diminished relative to Japan and Western Europe. Also the first generation of society transformed by the application of cybernetics, it has been faced with adjustment to this new frontier. The generational climax, however, came with the collapse of Communism and the Soviet Union, leaving the United States politically dominant though economically weakened. The results of these phenomena will constitute the basis for the agenda of the remainder of the generation.

GENERATIONS AND FRONTIER STAGES

The challenges to which each generation has had to respond are products of the country's continuing frontier experience. In American history, the continuing frontier has been the crucial if not the decisive factor in the progression of generations and centuries. As noted, Table 2.1 delineates the course of several American frontiers, their interrelationships, and their relationships to other historical and political phenomena.

Since the first settlement on these shores, American society has been a frontier society, geared to the progressive extension of human control over the natural environment and the utilization of the social and economic benefits gained from widening that control (i.e., pushing back the frontier line). The very dynamism of American society is a product of this commitment—a dynamism that is virtually self-generating since, as with a chain reaction, the conquest of one frontier has led to the opening of another. It is this frontier situation that has created the major social and economic changes that, in turn, have forced periodic adjustments in the nation's political institutions.

America's continuing frontier has manifested itself in four stages to date: the rural-land frontier, the urban-industrial frontier, the metropolitan-technological frontier, and now, the rurban-cybernetic frontier. Each stage has evolved its own form of settlement coupled with a dominant form of economic activity, which together have been decisively influential in shaping virtually all aspects of American life within that stage.

The *rural-land frontier* was the classic "frontier" described by historians that set the tone for American development. It lasted from the beginning of settlement in the seventeenth century to the end of the nineteenth century on the eve of World War I. Based on the conquest of the land (the American share of the North American continent), it was oriented toward the direct exploitation of the products of the land, even in its cities. It was characterized by the westward movement of an essentially rural population interested in settling and exploiting the land and by the development of a socioeconomic system based on agricultural and extractive pursuits in both its urban and rural components. The rural-land frontier was dominant through the middle of the ninth generation, remained an active and potent force until the end of that generation, and still exists as a factor on the fringes of the country, primarily in Alaska.

Early in the nineteenth century, the rural-land frontier gave way to the *urban-industrial frontier*, which began in the Northeast and spread westward. In the process, it transformed the nation into an industrial society that settled in cities and was dedicated to the spread of new technology as the primary source of the nation's economic and social forms. The urban-industrial frontier represented the unique impact of the industrial revolution on the United States, where it went hand in hand with the first settlement of the greater part of the country. An outgrowth of the rural-land frontier when it first emerged as a recognizable frontier in its own right, at the beginning of the seventh generation, it remained tied to the demands of that classic frontier through the next two generations, finally superseding it as the dominant frontier in the middle of the ninth generation. The urban-industrial frontier remained the dominant frontier nationally until the end of the tenth generation and continues to be important in various localities, particularly in the South and West. The dominant characteristic of this frontier was the transformation of cities from service centers or workshops for the rural areas into independent centers of opportunity, producers of new wealth, and social innovators possessing internally generated reasons for their existence and growth.

By the mid-twentieth century, the urban-industrial frontier had given way, in turn, to the *metropolitan-technological frontier.* Characterized by the radical reordering of an industrial society through rapidly changing technologies and settlement patterns, this frontier encouraged the diffusion of an urbanized population within large metropolitan regions. The radically new technologies, ranging from atomic energy and automation to synthetics and cybernetics, and the accompanying suburbanization of the population influenced further changes in the nation's social and economic forms in accord with their new demands. At the same time, metropolitan expansion offered a new kind of land base for a transformed industrial society. Like the first two frontier stages, the metropolitan-technological frontier has moved from east to west since the 1920s, taking on a clear identity of its own at the outset of the tenth generation. After World War

II, in the eleventh generation, it became clearly and exclusively the dominant frontier, setting the framework for and pace of development across the country.

The metropolitan-technological frontier reached its peak in the mid-1960s; by the mid-1970s, most of its impetus had been spent. It continues to be a force in selected areas of current metropolitanization. The late 1960s and 1970s were notable for the dominance of the backlash from that frontier. This backlash took the form of a political radicalism that confronted the frontier assumptions and policies of the 1950s, ecological challenges to frontier-generated environmental pollution, and a new school of no-growth economics that attacked the growth premises of a frontier society—all stimulated by new problems of resource management brought on by the energy crisis. Pundits were saying that, after centuries, the frontier was over.

By 1980, however, there were signs that a new frontier stage was emerging, based on the cybernetic technologies developed on the metropolitan frontier. These technologies—minicomputers, satellite-transmitted communications facilities, cable television, and new data-processing devices—fostered a settlement pattern consisting of large belts of relatively small cities, towns, and rural areas, populated by urbanites engaged in traditionally urban (i.e., not connected with rural) pursuits but living lives that mixed city and small town or rural elements. These "rurban" belts have no single metropolitan center, only a number of specialized ones for different purposes. Although this phenomenon started along the northeastern coast, as did earlier frontiers, its major expression is to be found in the Sunbelt. This *rurban-cybernetic frontier* is still in its early stages but has already brought its own challenges, initially manifested during the 1980s by the Reagan presidency and its renewed commitment to the market economy, which let loose a bevy of financial entrepreneurs who changed the face of the American economy. Globally, the end of the decade witnessed the collapse of Communism, the end of the Cold War, and the triumph of the West.

Each successive frontier stage has opened new vistas and new avenues of opportunity for the American people. At the same time, each new frontier has brought changes in economic activities, new settlement patterns, different human requirements, political changes, and its own social problems—problems that grow out of the collision of old patterns and new demands as much as they are generated by the new demands themselves. Most important for our purposes are the coincidences between the points of generational division and the shifts in the various frontier stages, as will be shown in greater detail in the following chapters. Such shifts invariably came as part of the initiating events of a new generation and, indeed, are closely related to the opening of new centuries.

GENERATIONS AND ECONOMIC PERIODS

One major consequence of the continuing frontier has been a continuing demand for public (which has generally been governmental) activity to meet frontier-generated problems, particularly economic ones. As a result of this continuing demand, the governments of the United States have always maintained a more or less active relationship to the American economy, even in the "era of laissez-faire." What has changed from era to era is the nature of the relationship and the character of the governmental response. These changes have also developed on a generational basis, with some shift in every generation since the founding of the republic. Inheriting a mercantilistic economic policy in the first generation under the Constitution (the sixth generation of American history), the American government continued a semimercantilistic policy. The next generation—the first of the nineteenth century—brought a transition from intensive government involvement in the economy to free enterprise capitalism, during which the forms remained mixed. What followed was a generation in which free enterprise flourished as never before or since. The outcome was the emergence of more successful competitors as monopoly-oriented corporations, leading to a generation of concentrated enterprise capitalism, still essentially unregulated by government.

The demands for government regulation that built up during the last generation of the nineteenth century led to the reintroduction of intensive government involvement of a different kind in the first generation of the twentieth, another transition generation. In the eleventh generation, the question was resolved in favor of active government involvement leading to a regulated enterprise system. Then, at the beginning of the twelfth, there occurred a sharp turnaround toward reinvigoration of the market economy, free enterprise, and less government intervention.

CENTURIES, GENERATIONS, AND FEDERALISM

The use of federal principles and the whole problem of union can also be traced on a generational and century basis. The very first generation of American history brought the introduction of federal principles not only through the compacts and covenants that established the colonies and the local settlements within them but also through Puritan theology. In the remaining two generations of the seventeenth century, experiments with federation were made on a local and regional basis. Then, during the eighteenth century, the idea of national federation was developed and introduced. This was an idea whose strength spread during the first generation, in increasingly concrete ways during the second, and in firmly institutionalized form during the third. The nineteenth century was a period during which the character of the federal union was tested and crystallized, building up to and then beyond the Civil War, the synthesizing event of the century. Finally, the thrust of the twentieth century from Wilson through Clinton has been to accommodate federalism and a modern technological society.

Each generation has had its own particular need to deal with questions of federalism; but in most generations, if not all, new techniques have also been devised to handle intergovernmental relations. These new techniques and the systemic adaptations they have entailed have been major elements in the concrete response to each generation's challenges.

GENERATIONS AND
THE ETHNORELIGIOUS INTERRELATIONSHIP

The relationships among racial, ethnic, and religious groups (and their various combinations) stand with the frontier and the challenge-response relationship as central factors in the shaping of American history and politics. The changes in those relationships also coincide closely with the flow of generations and centuries. British America's first generation saw an attempt to allow religious pluralism on a strictly territorial basis; that is, particular religious groups were given, or claimed, exclusive control over particular territories. At the same time, Africans were introduced as indentured servants to initiate a racial division in the country. In the second and third generations, heterodox elements were recognized in most of the colonies as elements of ethnic diversity, and sectarian differentiation spread while the Africans were reduced to slavery. Thus, by the end of the first century, a modified religious pluralism had become the norm, with locally favored churches and tolerated ones existing side by side. A racially based caste system was in the making as well.

During the three generations of the second century, ethnic and sectarian pluralism increased radically, rendering most of the original territorial arrangements obsolete and resulting in the virtual elimination of established churches in the new nation. Slavery, after increasing moderately in the South, was given a new lease on life by technological change (invention of the cotton gin).

The first generation of the nineteenth century saw the unofficial establishment of a generalized Protestant republicanism, which was almost immediately challenged by the arrival of non-Protestant immigration. The second generation was one of transition to a new post-Protestant pluralism, which remained antagonistic throughout the third generation, when the non-Protestant non-British migration was reaching its height. Slavery boomed, was abolished, and then was allowed to reappear de facto in the course of the century as the caste system was reaffirmed through the institution of segregation.

From the first, the twentieth century has been one of growing religious, ethnic, and racial pluralism in America. Barriers against full participation by those who were not White Anglo-Saxon Protestants began to fall in the tenth generation, and the elimination of those barriers was the priority problem of the eleventh. Indeed, by the late 1960s, pluralism in morals and lifestyles had begun to shape up as the great issue of the coming generation. By the middle of the twelfth generation, not only were there no more excluded groups, but those once excluded were calling for the further redefinition of American society as one based on "multiculturalism"—that is, on the granting of equal weight to all groups in the expression of American culture.

THE INTERNAL STRUCTURE OF THE GENERATION: CHALLENGES AND RESPONSES

As Table 2.1 indicates in a general way, each generation has had to face and respond to its own particular challenges. Each has also developed its own very clear and widely recognized responses.[30] The challenges and the responses provide the skeletal structure of each generation. In some cases—particularly after independence, when a nation has been able to act decisively—the responses have been very clear-cut indeed. In others, particularly during the colonial period, they were more diffuse. The third column in Table 2.1 delineates the central political challenges that have dominated the American scene and places them in their respective governmental contexts.

The emergence of such challenges is a phenomenon associated with the initial stages of each generation, during which the challenges (even though, objectively speaking, they may have originated earlier) are progressively recognized as such by the body politic. It is this growing recognition of the challenges, in conjunction with other factors such as the replacement of populations and the consequent shifts in voting behavior, that brings about the intensive response associated with mid-generation national activity. In fact, the response itself builds up in a diffused way in various public quarters, particularly in the states and localities, while the challenge is coming to public attention. Only after the appropriate responses have been tested in many quarters do they emerge as a concentrated national effort.

Aside from the fact that every generation acquires a certain discrete existence of its own, within each there is a more or less regular progression of political events revolving around the development of a particular set of challenges confronting that generation and its response to them. It is this recurring pattern of challenges and responses that gives each generation its particular character. Whereas the shape of the challenges is primarily determined by external (i.e., environmental) forces, the mode of handling those challenges is for the most part internally determined, by the members of the generation themselves.

In American history, the pattern of challenges and responses has taken two generalized forms: one pertaining to the colonial period, when each colony had its own internal politics essentially independent of its sisters; and the other since independence, when a common national constitution created a common national politics. The character of the challenges has changed from century to century. During the seventeenth century, they were essentially related to the tasks of founding a new society as manifested in the various colonies. In the eighteenth century, they were essentially related to the tasks of consolidating the supremacy, unity, and independence of British America. In the nineteenth century, they were essentially related to expanding the scope, wealth, and purposes of the American national enterprise. And in the twentieth century, they have essentially been related to the metropolitanization of American society and the assumption of an American role in world affairs.

A generalized map of the pattern of challenges and responses within each generation since independence might look something like Figure 2.1. The "border" between the old and new generations is marked by several decisive political actions, often involving constitutional change—the characteristic feature of which is the simultaneous completion of the major responses of the old generation and the opening of new directions, challenges, and opportunities for the new. The first half of the new generation is a time for recognizing the new challenges confronting it and the issues they raise, and for developing and testing proposals for political action to meet them. It is also a period of population change, as old voters and leaders pass from the scene of political activity and new ones come onto it. During that period there occur the generation's expressions of public will, which point it in the direction that the response will take, generally by raising leaders to office who have indicated that they are ready to respond to the generation's developing challenges.

The second half of the generation begins with a great spurt of governmental innovation on the national plane designed to respond to the now-recognized challenge. That effort lasts for three to five years. The remainder of the generation is then occupied with digesting the results of that spurt, modifying the new programs so that they will achieve greater success and, at the same time, integrating them into the country's overall political fabric. The end of the generation is marked by political acts that both ratify and codify its accomplishments while also serving to open up the issues of the next generation. By that time, voices calling for political

62

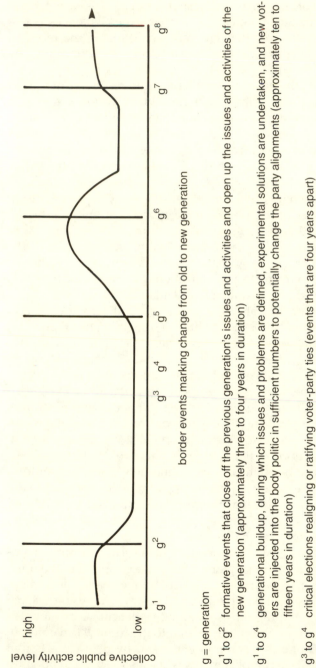

collective public activity level

border events marking change from old to new generation

g = generation

g¹ to g²   formative events that close off the previous generation's issues and activities and open up the issues and activities of the new generation (approximately three to four years in duration)

g¹ to g⁴   generational buildup, during which issues and problems are defined, experimental solutions are undertaken, and new voters are injected into the body politic in sufficient numbers to potentially change the party alignments (approximately ten to fifteen years in duration)

g³ to g⁴   critical elections realigning or ratifying voter-party ties (events that are four years apart)

g⁵ to g⁶   years of intensive political response, particularly on the national legislative front (approximately three to four years in duration)

g⁶ to g⁸   years of political stabilization and consolidation, during which the changes initiated in g⁵⁻⁶ are completed and institutionalized around a new level of public consensus (approximately ten years in duration)

g⁷ to g⁸   culminating events that bring to a close the activities of the generation, ratifying its changes and opening the door to the next generation (approximately three to four years in duration)

Figure 2.1   The Internal Rhythm of the Generation

responses to new challenges are already beginning to be recognized. This is the process diagrammed in Figure 2.1.

THE BENCH MARKS OF AMERICAN POLITICAL HISTORY: CRITICAL ELECTIONS AND NEW DEALS

In the course of mapping the topographic characteristics of a particular landscape, geologists mark off crucial points through a system of bench marks. Crucial points in the passage of time can also be seen as marked off in some way. In American political history, the crucial points of demarcation are very much in tune with the generational rhythm of events. They manifest themselves in two ways: first, as critical elections that determine who shall govern in a particular generation and, second, as "new deals," or periods of intensive federal legislative innovation, through which government initiates a systematic response to the challenges of each generation. The fourth column in Table 2.1 links both to the larger pattern.

THE GENERATIONAL RECURRENCE OF CRITICAL ELECTIONS

A major element in the movement from challenge to response is the sequence of critical elections that has preceded every major period of national response since the adoption of the Constitution. The generational thesis takes on particular clarity in light of this pattern of critical elections. A critical election is one that brings about major alterations in the party loyalties of major blocs of voters, shifting them from one political party to another. V. O. Key, who first suggested the term, defined a "critical election" as one in which "the depth and intensity of electoral involvement are high, in which more or less profound readjustments occur in the relations of power within the community, and in which new and durable electoral groups are formed."[31] These shifts and readjustments, in turn, lead to the formation of new nationwide electoral coalitions and either to a change in political ascendancy from one party to the other or, within the major party, from one major bloc to another.

Students of American electoral behavior have clearly shown that there is a tendency for one of the major parties to command the allegiance of a majority of the national electorate for a relatively long period of time.[32] Thus, for example, according to public opinion polls and election returns, between the 1930s and the 1970s a majority of the nation's voters who identified themselves with a political party considered themselves to be Democrats. As a consequence, in every national election between 1932 and 1984, the Democrats started with the advantage of having a plurality of the voters identified with them, whereas the Republican Party, as the

minority party, had to overcome the "normal" Democratic majority in order to elect presidents or even a sufficient number of senators and representatives to win control of Congress.

The results of this situation are well known. Between 1932 and 1968,
only one Republican won the presidency and the GOP controlled the
Congress for only two years (1952–1954). Dwight D. Eisenhower, a military hero with nonpartisan appeal, was twice able to overcome the "normal" Democratic majority to capture the White House for his party—because of his personal appeal, coupled (at least in 1952) with the general
feeling that it was "time for a change" after twenty years of Democratic incumbency. John F. Kennedy restored the democratic majority through a
new coalition in 1960. But these circumstances were upset by the Vietnam
War. Republican Richard M. Nixon squeaked into the presidency in 1968
in the wake of the Democrats' Vietnam problems, and he won a second
term at the expense of an extremely unpopular Democratic alternative;
but in neither case could he carry a Republican majority into either house
of Congress. Nevertheless, his victory hastened the weakening of the majority Democratic coalition and broke the Democratic lock on the presidency. It ushered in a period of split-ticket voting that kept Republicans in
the White House for all but four years (1977–1981) from 1969 to 1993, but it
also left the Democrats in full control of Congress except in 1980–1984,
when the GOP controlled the Senate.

A party becomes the majority party when it is able to put together a
nationwide coalition constituting a majority of the various permanent and
transient electoral groups. These electoral groups are based on a variety of
economic and geographic interests and on differing historical loyalties,
racial or ethnic backgrounds, religious affiliations, personal or family ties,
and responses to the specific problems of the age. The coalitions are not so
much national as nationwide. They are inspired and held together by national leaders but, in fact, are activated through the separate state parties
that form the two national confederations known as the Democratic and
Republican parties. Just as the national parties are confederations of the
state parties, so is the national coalition of electoral groups a confederation of state and sectional coalitions.

Once one of the parties is able to put together such a coalition and
thereby capture the majority of the votes, the tendency of the electorate to
remain stable in its allegiances will enable it to remain the majority party
until positive reasons develop that lead to the dissolution of the winning
combination. This dissolution, too, is virtually inevitable. Times and
moods change, new problems attract voter attention, and the opposition
party exploits the dissatisfactions that develop and sooner or later makes
the necessary inroads into the various electoral groups.

Even during its period of dominance, the majority party faces opposition and loses elections as a result of temporary shifts in public opinion. Since its coalition is never of equal strength in the fifty states, some states remain in the control of the party that is in the minority nationally. Of course, it is by no means certain that the majority party will win all the national elections during its ascendancy. Indeed, it is both possible and usual for a party to suffer losses on the national plane for a limited time without forfeiting its majority status, as long as its losses are aberrations that do not dissolve its coalition. The states that remain in the hands of the minority party serve as bases that enable it to maintain its effective existence and mend its political fences until it can develop a new majority coalition. It does so, when the time is ripe, by providing candidates for national office and sources of patronage and other political rewards for the party faithful during the years of national "famine."

As the majority coalition begins to weaken, its constituent electoral groups will become alienated from one another. Their changing needs may even bring former confederates into conflict. The members of these electoral groups may begin to find the other party more receptive to their new demands. As issues pass and problems change, whole electoral groups may decline radically in importance and new, still uncommitted groups may emerge to be wooed and won by the opposition. When the time is ripe for change, the realignment takes place. This is not the oft-discussed realignment of the liberal and conservative wings of the two parties, but a reshuffling of the parties' constituent elements, the myriad electoral groups.[33]

Whereas the beginnings of every realignment can be found in the state and congressional elections, the shift becomes a national phenomenon only through the medium of the quadrennial presidential elections, in which sufficient voter interest is aroused to firm up the embryonic realignments. Once the realignments become fixed, they are further reflected in the state and congressional elections that follow. The series of presidential and congressional elections in which the realignment takes place are the "critical elections."[34]

The very first pair of critical elections actually preceded the development of the institution of the popularly elected president. Despite the difference in modes of election, the same factors of electoral bloc representation that later came to symbolize presidential politics when the votes of the people were solicited apparently were present in the contests in the electoral college and the House of Representatives.

Key's thesis regarding the shift of political allegiance on the part of individual voters has been challenged as unprovable through the use of aggregate voting data. Doubt has also been cast on the notion that many voters do indeed shift allegiances. The generational thesis offers the key to the solution of this problem. It may very well be that the "realignment" that takes place proceeds not so much from changes in the allegiance of specific voters as from a disruption of the common pattern whereby children tend to vote as did (or do) their parents—along lines determined by issues current during their grandparents' prime. A "realignment" thus becomes the end result of an event or compact series of events so crucial that they disrupt this "normal" progression and lead a significant percentage of children to reassess their family voting patterns and alter them in light of a situation that has made the old issues lose their primary importance. As the parents die (or cease to vote), the votes of their children come to represent first the balance in the electorate and then the majority. The shift is initially felt in the period of generational buildup—precisely the period during which this "challenging of the guard" is taking place among political actives and "rank and file" alike. This is why the critical elections occur during that part of each generation and bring the generational buildup to an end. By the time the ratifying election is over, the new generation of "children" has moved from balance to majority. Column 4 of Table 2.1 links the critical elections with the overall progression of generations.

"NEW DEALS": BURSTS OF
FEDERAL GOVERNMENT ACTIVITY

The culmination of each series of critical elections is a burst of innovative federal activity—specifically, legislative activity of the kind usually referred to in connection with the New Deal of Franklin Delano Roosevelt. These periods become fixed in the public mind as the historical watersheds they are.

In the six and a half generations since the adoption of the U.S. Constitution, there have been five such concentrations of reform activity. Thomas Jefferson and Andrew Jackson are well known for their "new deals." We still speak of Jeffersonian and Jacksonian democracy. But less well known is the fact that Abraham Lincoln presided over a period of domestic reform legislation of major proportions that enabled the country to adjust to the industrial revolution in much the same way that the New Deal provided the basis for overcoming the social problems of industrialization. The Civil War upstaged that dimension of Lincoln's presidency, but the period, as such, stands out in the public mind because of that struggle. Only in the ninth generation was the moment of reform aborted. It began at the appropriate point but was cut short by a series of decisions made by an extremely unsympathetic U.S. Supreme Court. The reforms were, perforce, delayed until nearly the end of the generation, when Theodore Roosevelt was able to use the presidency to overcome some of the resistance to them. Next came Roosevelt's New Deal, which has become the model for all such periods of federal action. In the 1960s, Lyndon B. Johnson's Great Society continued the pattern—"on schedule," as it were. The next such concentration should come sometime in the 1990s, and the election of Bill Clinton to the presidency suggests that this will be the case.

The burst of legislative activity in the Great Society lasted approximately three years. Although governmental involvement continued to accelerate within the executive branch of the federal government and in the intergovernmental system for another two or three years, the election of Richard Nixon to the presidency effectively ushered in the appropriate period of generational consolidation.

The first postwar generation came to an end in the three years between 1973 and 1976, during which time the American effort in Vietnam collapsed and the United States became "gun-shy" of extensive overseas involvements as the world's policeman. Nixon became involved in the Watergate scandal and was forced to resign his presidency, thus putting an end to the growth of the "imperial presidency" and bringing about a congressional reassertion of its power. The energy crisis and some of the more critical domestic problems that arose in the last days of the Nixon administration led the governors of the American states to reassert themselves; filling the vacuum left by Washington, they thereby considerably weakenened the hierarchical understanding of American federalism whereby the states and localities had come to await marching orders from Washington before undertaking any activities.

The election of Jimmy Carter to the presidency in 1976 as an "outsider" whose task it was to clean up the Washington community marked the beginning of the second postwar generation, the twelfth in American history. The Carter administration, though scarred by many difficulties, began to define the issues of the new generation, usually in a way that was unrecognized by the public at the time. President Carter was faced with the task of restructuring America's international role in the wake of the post-Vietnam mood. He tried to shift federal government concern from social welfare to a new set of infrastructure issues revolving around energy. He tried to bring the Washington bureaucracy under control in the name of the states and localities. These were all to become principal issues during the period of generational buildup.

The election of Ronald Reagan to the presidency in 1980 brought to the White House a figure whose ability to communicate issues to the American people in a simple and direct manner intensified the tendencies introduced during the Carter years. In the eight years that followed, all those issues gained even greater focus. By the end of the Reagan administration, voices were being raised on behalf of a new wave of government activity to respond to what were referred to as the issues of the 1980s but were actually the issues of the new generation.

George Bush's presidency brought the Reagan administration's foreign policy to culmination with the collapse of the Soviet empire but let domestic affairs slide, to the detriment of the American economy and Americans' economic well-being. Hence Bush ended up an easy target for Bill Clinton, who promised active efforts for change at just the appropriate generational moment.

Politically speaking, the new programs of each generation have invariably been preceded by critical elections, through which the reconstituted electorate—which changes from generation to generation as new people reach voting age and old ones die—determines the basic pattern of party voting for the new era, either by reaffirming the majority party's hold on the public by granting it an extended mandate or by rejecting the majority party as unable to meet those demands and elevating the minority party to majority status. These critical elections, which attain their visibility in presidential contests, allow voters, blocs, and interests to realign themselves according to the new problems that face them.

Three times in American history critical elections have elevated the party previously in the minority to majority status. In the series of elections beginning in 1796 and culminating in 1800, the Jeffersonian Democratic-Republicans replaced the Federalists. In the 1856 and 1860 series, the Republicans replaced the Democrats, who had become the heirs of the Jeffersonians; and in 1928–1932, the Democrats in turn replaced the Republicans.

Between each shift the critical elections served to reinforce the majority party, which was successful in adapting itself to new times and new conditions. Thus, in 1824–1828, the Jacksonian Democrats picked up the reins from their Jeffersonian predecessors; and in 1892–1896, the Republicans were able to reconstitute their party coalition to maintain their majority position and even strengthen it. In 1956–1960, the Democrats were able to do the same thing. The old coalition put together by FDR and the New Deal, which underwent severe strains in the late 1940s and early 1950s, was reconstituted and reshaped by John F. Kennedy and Lyndon B. Johnson to give the Democrats an even stronger majority than before. This majority status made the programs of the 1960s possible but led, in turn, to a new testing period for the Democratic coalition by giving the Republicans the power to achieve deadlock.

To suggest that a generational rhythm is clearly apparent in American politics is not to say that events move in lockstep, that the rhythm of each generation is exactly the same as that of every other, or that there are no exceptions to the "normal" rules. Obviously history does not work in these ways. Hence we must note the exceptions as well as the rules and account for them if the theory is to be an accurate one. That we *can* do so is what gives the theory its power.

SUMMARY

Chapter 2 has focused in detail on the generational rhythm of American politics. Ultimately derived from the biblical understanding of time, the generational theory has, until recently, been of more interest to European social philosophers than to American social scientists. Most systematic American attention to the question has been concerned with the cycles of American politics, often confined to electoral ones and, hence, limited in their theory. Yet a systematic biostatistical basis for the generation rhythm was provided early on by Thomas Jefferson, who pointed the way to understanding that the rhythm of generations is based upon human social rhythms generally.

Political events follow the rhythm of the generations, both in terms of their internal rhythm and on an intergenerational basis. Centuries encompass three generations each and collectively exhibit a certain pattern. Table 2.1, presented in this chapter, is the basis for discussion in the following chapters as well. The contents of the several columns in this table are summarized here as an introduction to what follows.

The chapter examines the internal structure of the generation as it pertains to the generation's challenges and the responses to them. The chapter then concludes with a discussion of critical elections and "new deals" as bench marks of American political history that recur on a generational basis.

NOTES

1. Julian Marias, *Generations: A Historical Method,* translated by Harold C. Raley (Tuscaloosa: University of Alabama Press, 1970); Marvin Rintala, *The Constitution of Silence: Essays on Generational Themes* (Westport, Conn.: Greenwood Press, 1979).

2. George E. Mendenhall, *The Tenth Generation: The Origins of the Biblical Tradition* (Baltimore: Johns Hopkins University Press, 1973).

3. *Exodus,* chapter 20, verse 5.

4. *Genesis.*

5. For citations in the Bible of this idiomatic expression for "a generation," see *Judges,* chapter 3, verse 11; chapter 5, verse 31; and chapter 8, verse 28.

6. See *Joshua,* chapter 5, verse 6; and *Numbers,* chapter 32, verse 13.

7. See *Book of Judges,* chapter 3, verse 11; chapter 5, verse 31; and chapter 8, verse 28.

8. Harriet Martineau, *The Positive Philosophy of Auguste Comte,* Vol. 2 (London: G. Bell, 1896), p. 307.

9. John Stuart Mill, *A System of Logic, Ratiocinative and Inductive* (London, 1862), pp. 341–342.

10. Giuseppe Ferrari, *Coros Su Gli Scrittori Politici Italiani* (Milano: Monanni, 1929).

11. Wilhelm Dilthey, *Das Leben Schleiermachers* (1870) or *Menschen, der Gesellschaft und dem Staat*, in Gesammelte Schriften, Band 4 (1875), pp. 36–41.

12. For more information on Leopold von Ranke, see George G. Iggers and James M. Powell, eds., *Leopold von Ranke and the Shaping of the Historical Discipline* (Syracuse, NY: Syracuse University Press, 1989); Peter Gay, *Style in History* (New York: Basic Books, 1974); Theodore Hermann Van Lane, *Leopold Ranke: The Formative Years* (New York: Johnson Reprint Corp., 1970); and Felix Gilbert, *History, Politics or Culture?* (Princeton, N.J.: Princeton University Press, 1990).

13. Marias, *Generations: A Historical Method.*

14. José Ortega y Gasset, *The Modern Theme* (New York: Norton, 1933; 2nd ed. in 1962).

15. Karl Mannheim, "The Problem of Generations," in Paul Kecsdemeti, ed., *Essays on the Sociology of Knowledge* (New York: Oxford University Press, 1952); Francois Mentre, *Les Generations Sociales* (Paris: Bossard, 1920); Engelbert Drerup, *Das Generations Problem in der Griechischen und Griechisch-Roemischen Kultur* (Paderborn: F. Schoeningh, 1933).

16. Wilhelm Pinder, *Das Problem der Generation in der Kunstgeschichte Europas* (Berlin: Frankfurter Verlags-Anstalt, 1926); Julius Peterson, *Die Literarischen Generationen* (Berlin: Junker and Duenhaupt, 1930) and *Die Wesenbestimmung der Romantik* (Leipzig, 1925), Ch. 6; Henri Peyre, *Les Generations Litteraires* (Paris: Boivin, 1948).

17. Sigmund Neumann, *Permanent Revolution: Totalitarianism in the Age of International Civil War*, 2nd ed. (New York: Praeger, 1965), and "The Conflict of Generations," *Partisan Review* 39, no. 4 (1972): 564–578.

18. Raymond A. Bauer, Alex Inkeles, and Clyde Kluckhohn, *How the Soviet System Works: Cultural, Psychological, and Social Themes* (Cambridge, Mass.: Harvard University Press, 1956).

19. Rintala, *The Constitution of Silence;* Maurice Zeitlin, *American Society* (Chicago: Markham, 1970).

20. S. N. Eisenstadt, *From Generation to Generation: Age Groups and Social Structure* (Glencoe, Ill.: Free Press, 1956); Joseph Gusfield, *Protest, Reform, and Revolt* (New York: Wiley, 1970).

21. Arthur M. Schlesinger, "The Tides of American Politics," *Yale Review* 29 (December 1939): 217–230. Emphasis in original.

22. Charles G. Sellers, *A Synopsis of American History* (Chicago: Rand McNally, 1969); Walter Dean Burnham, *Critical Elections and the Mainsprings of American Politics* (New York: Norton, 1970); V. O. Key, Jr., *Public Opinion and American Democracy* (New York: Alfred A. Knopf, 1961); Gerald M. Pomper, *Elections in America* (New York: Dodd, Mead, 1968); Aletta Biersack et al., *The New Cultural History: Essays* (Berkeley: University of California Press, 1989).

23. V. O. Key, Jr., "A Theory of Critical Elections," *Journal of Politics* 17 (1955): 3–18, and "Secular Realignment and the Party System," *Journal of Politics* 21 (1959): 198–210.

24. See, for example, James MacGregor Burns, *The Deadlock of Democracy* (Engle-wood Cliffs, N.J.: Prentice-Hall, 1963). Over the years, various theories have been propounded to explain the cycles of American politics. Perhaps the best known is that of Arthur Schlesinger, Sr., *Paths to the Present* (New York: Macmillan, 1949), which proposes a cycle of swings from liberalism to conservatism approximately fifty years in duration. Unfortunately, the article itself is extremely time-bound—first, because it refers to liberalism and conservatism as the fundamental bases of American political ideas, when in fact these constructs—though relevant to the generation between World Wars I and II, when the article was written—are no longer quite as relevant today; and, second, because the cycles themselves best reflect the swings from more activist to less activist government from the Civil War to the New Deal.

25. The discussion to be advanced in the following pages was adapted from Daniel J. Elazar, "Generational Rhythm of American Politics," *American Political Quarterly* 6, no. 1 (January 1978): pp. 55–94; and from Elazar, "Generational Breaks," in Nissan Oren, ed., *When Patterns Change: Turning Points in International Politics* (Jerusalem: Magnes Press, 1984), pp. 81–110. See also Elazar, *Building Toward Civil War* (Lanham, Md.: University Press of America and Center for the Study of Federalism, 1992).

26. Letter from Thomas Jefferson to James Madison, September 6, 1789.

27. Note that the U.S. Constitution requires a person to be 25 years old to serve in the House of Representatives, 30 years old to serve in the Senate, and 35 years old to be president.

28. See Angus Campbell, Phillip E. Converse, Warren E. Miller, and Donald E. Stokes, *The American Voter* (New York: Wiley, 1960); Norman H. Nie, Sidney Verba, and Jae-on Kim, "Political Participation and the Life Cycle," *Comparative Politics* 6 (April 1974): 319–340; Mary M. Conway, *Political Participation in the United States* (Washington, D.C.: Congressional Quarterly Press, 1985); Norman H. Nie, Sidney Verba, and John R. Petrocik, *The Changing American Voter* (Cambridge, Mass.: Harvard University Press, 1976); Alex Inkeles, "The American Character," *The Center Magazine* (Santa Barbara, Calif.: Center for the Study of Democratic Institutions, November-December 1983); Morris Janowitz, *The Last Half-Century: Societal Change and Politics in America* (Chicago: University of Chicago Press, 1978); Lester W. Milbrath, *Political Participation: How and Why Do People Get Involved in Politics* (Chicago: Rand McNally, 1965); Roger W. Cobb and Charles D. Elder, *Participation in American Politics: Agenda Building* (Boston: Allyn and Bacon, 1972); James David Barber, *Politics by Humans: Collected Research on American Leadership* (Durham, N.C.: Duke University Press, 1988); and Clifton McCleskey, *Political Power and American Democracy* (Pacific Grove, Calif.: Brooks/Cole, 1989).

29. Stanley Elkins and Eric McKitrick discuss this phenomenon with special reference to the revolutionary and constitutional years in *The Founding Fathers: Young Men of the Revolution* (New York: Macmillan, 1961).

30. Arnold J. Toynbee, *A Study of History* (New York: Dell, 1965); Jurgen Habermas, *The New Conservatism: Cultural Criticism and the Historians' Debate* (Cambridge, Mass.: MIT Press, 1989).

31. Key, "A Theory of Critical Elections," pp. 3–18.

32. Campbell et al., *The American Voter*; Pomper, *Elections in America*; Phillip E.

Converse, "Of Time and Partisan Stability," *Comparative Political Studies* 2 (July 1969): 139–171.

33. On the subject of realignment, see V. O. Key, Jr. , *The Responsible Electorate* (Cambridge, Mass.: Belknap Press of Harvard University Press, 1966); James L. Sundquist, *Dynamics of the Party System: Alignment and Realignment of Political Parties in the United States* (Washington, D.C.: Brookings Institution, 1973); Burnham, *Critical Elections and the Mainsprings of American Politics* and "American Politics in the 1970s: Beyond Party?" in William Nisbet Chambers and Walter D. Burnham, eds., *The American Party System: Stages of Political Development*, 2nd ed. (New York: Oxford University Press, 1975), pp. 316–317; Samuel P. Huntington, *American Politics: The Promise of Disharmony* (Cambridge, Mass.: Belknap Press of Harvard University Press, 1981), pp. 122–129; and Anthony King, ed., *Both Ends of the Avenue: The Presidency, the Executive Branch, and Congress in the 1980s* (Washington, D.C.: American Enterprise Institute, 1983).

34. Burnham, *Critical Elections and the Mainsprings of American Politics* and *The Current Crisis in American Politics* (New York: Oxford University Press, 1982); Sundquist, *Dynamics of the Party System;* Huntington, *American Politics: The Promise of Disharmony;* David R. Mayhew, *Placing Parties in American Politics: Organization, Electoral Settings, and Government Activity in the Twentieth Century* (Princeton, N.J.: Princeton University Press, 1986); James Clotfelter, *Political Choices: A Study of Elections and Voters* (New York: Holt, Rinehart and Winston, 1980); Bruce A. Campbell, *The American Electorate: Attitudes and Action* (New York: Holt, Rinehart and Winston, 1979); Peter B. Natchez, *Images of Voting: Visions of Democracy* (New York: Basic Books, 1985).

CHAPTER 3

A Frontier Society

If students of the American character can agree upon any one thing, it is that the compulsion to move about has created a nation of restless wanderers unlike any other in the world. The people are forever on the go. They cross from place to place in a room, drive unbelievable distances to consume a meal that they could have obtained nearer home, travel interminably by car to country clubs where they transfer to electric carts from which they emerge occasionally to swat a golf ball, and seemingly spend half their lives in automobiles waiting for traffic jams to clear. They squander their vacations by hurrying to distant points and hurrying home again. They shift from country to town, from town to suburb, and from suburb to country. They abandon one home for another with such predictable frequency that bank statements and dividend checks include for convenience a change of address card. When the fever strikes, the American goes, indifferent to the risks and scornful of that attachment to place that restrains the European.

—Ray Allen Billington, *America's Frontier Heritage*

Ray Allen Billington, a leading contemporary historian of America's frontier experience, succinctly describes the American desire for mobility by touching on aspects of the nomadic culture familiar to virtually all Americans.[1] The continuing American penchant for migration is well known; its connection with the continuing American frontier is not.

Immigration to the United States was responsible for the population and settlement of the country. Emigration from settled communities to new frontiers has continued the process initiated by the first immigration through each frontier stage. The very fact of migration is a vital element in American life, affecting the shape of its civil society, the character of its communities, and the political demands of its population. It makes possible social mobility through physical movement, which breaks up fixed-status patterns and limits the development of static population groups in particular localities. And, governmentally, migration has turned public attention to national political institutions as the only ones capable of dealing with problems that it has pushed across state boundaries.

The generational rhythm of American politics is intimately connected with the continuing American frontier, which has provided the context in which Americans can express their penchant for perpetual motion, the search for new horizons. Thus, too, the continuing American frontier is intimately connected with the flow of generations. Indeed, whereas the first frontier emphasized space more than time, each subsequent frontier has shifted further toward an emphasis on time as the medium within which space is transformed. It is that shift along the space-time continuum that has made the continuing frontier possible in the American experience. This chapter explores the character and content of the American frontier through three stages and into a fourth, explaining why change in America must be seen as a frontier phenomenon and connecting the frontier movement to the rhythm of the generations.

The settlement of the United States was part of the great European frontier experience that began with Columbus, continued until the twentieth century, and transformed the society and politics of Western civilization.[2] The great frontier began with the discovery of America and spread until Europeans had colonized every uninhabited or sparsely inhabited land within their reach: the Americas, Australia and New Zealand, Southern Africa, and Siberia, to mention only the largest. The American frontier experience is unique, as is each of the others. The uniqueness of each was produced by the particular pattern of interactions among three factors: (1) the environment upon which the frontier process operated, (2) the character of the peoples who were involved in the frontier experience, and (3) the particular times in which the experience unfolded. The interactions among these three factors continue to provide the ecological basis for political life within the new societies that were created in each case.

THE FRONTIER AND THE GENERATIONAL RHYTHM

There is a close connection among the movements of the American frontier, the generational rhythm of American life, and the migratory rhythm of the American people. In many respects, the dynamics of the frontier process that played out on the American landscape over the past 350 years provide the link between the spatial and temporal dimensions of American civil society. If each generation has had to respond to challenges confronting it, the challenges themselves are products of the country's continuing frontier experience. In American history, the continuing frontier has been the crucial measure, if not the decisive factor, in the progression of generations and centuries and in the constant movement of the

American people. At the same time, it has served both as the source of natural renewal that has kept American society dynamic and open and as the stimulus for changes in the federal system.

Column 5 in Figure 2.1 adds the pattern of the several frontier stages to the generation chart begun in Chapter 2. The coincidence between the points of generational division and the shifts in the various frontier stages is nearly exact. Such shifts invariably come about as part of the initiating events of a new generation and, indeed, are closely related to the opening of new centuries.

The driving force behind American society is the continuing American frontier—the effort on the part of Americans to come to grips with untamed elements of nature and, by taming them, to reorganize their society. The continuing frontier is the source of renewal that sustains the United States as a "new society."

Each successive frontier stage has opened new vistas and new avenues of opportunity for the American people in the development of new economic activities, the creation of new settlement patterns, and the mastery of new social problems growing out of the collision of old patterns and demands. Consequently, it has generated new political concerns that revolve around the accommodation of the challenges and opportunities resulting from it.

Frederick Jackson Turner (1861–1932), the great historian of the American frontier, put it thus:

> Behind institutions, behind constitutional forms and modifications, lie the vital forces that call these organs into life and shape them to meet changing conditions. The peculiarity of American institutions is the fact that they have been compelled to adapt themselves to the changes of an expanding people—to the changes involved in crossing a continent, in winning a wilderness, and in developing at each area of this progress out of the primitive economic and political conditions of the frontier into the complexity of city life. … American development has exhibited not merely advance along a single line, but a return to primitive conditions on a continually advancing frontier line, and a new development for that area. American social development has been continually beginning over again on the frontier. This perennial rebirth, this fluidity of American life, this expansion westward with its new opportunities, its continuous touch with the simplicity of primitive society, furnish the forces dominating American character. The true point of view in the history of this great nation is not the Atlantic coast, it is the great West.
>
> He would be a rash prophet who should assert that the expansive character of American life has now entirely ceased. Movement has been its dominant fact, and, unless this training has no effect upon a people, the American energy will continually demand a wider field for its exercise. … The stubborn American environment is there with its imperious summons to accept its conditions: the inherited ways of doing things are also there; and yet, in

spite of environment, and in spite of custom, each frontier did indeed furnish a new field of opportunity, a gate of escape from the bondage of the past; and freshness, and confidence, and scorn of older society, impatience of its restraints and its ideas, and indifference to its lessons, have accompanied the frontier.[3]

HOW TO IDENTIFY A FRONTIER

Application of the frontier concept to contemporary American life is not simply a dramatic way to describe change in dynamic society. A frontier is something much more fundamental than that. It is a multidimensional wilderness (or primitive) "area," that invites human entry for purposes of "taming" it for "civilization." One major characteristic of the frontier in the American context is that it suggests the primary human confrontation is between people and nature rather than between people themselves. A frontier is the meeting of the known with the unknown.

Ten basic conditions appear to be present in every frontier situation.

1. The frontier involves extensive new organization of the uses of the land—uses so new that they are essentially unprecedented, yet so much a part of the process in question that they will be applied across the length and breadth of the continent during the course of frontier expansion.
2. Frontier activities are those devoted to the exploration of that which was previously unknown and the development of that which was previously "wild" or undeveloped.
3. The frontier generates an expanding, or growth, economy based on the application of existing technologies in new communities or new technologies in existing communities. That, it turn, requires risk taking.
4. The frontier movement, though it manifests itself as a single "whole," actually encompasses a number of different "frontiers" both geographic and functional. These exist simultaneously and successively, each with its own goals, interests, character, and pioneers; yet all are tied together by their common link to the central goals, interests, and character of the large frontier of which they are parts.
5. The opportunity to grow, change, risk, develop, and explore must be present within the framework of the frontier, thereby increasing freedom from past restraints and demanding courageous action.
6. There must be reasonably free access to the frontier sector of society for all who want it; and migration must be a major factor in gaining that access.

7. The frontier situation generates a psychological orientation toward the frontier on the part of the people engaged in conquering it, endowing them with the "frontier spirit."
8. The "feedback" from the frontier leads to the continuous generation of new opportunities on many levels of society, including new occupations to be filled by people who have the skills to do so regardless of such factors as family background, social class, or personal influence, thus contributing to the maintenance or extension of equality in the social order.
9. The frontier feedback must influence the total social structure to the point where society as a whole is significantly remade.
10. The direct manifestations of the frontier can be found in every section of the country at some time (usually in sequential order) and are visible in a substantial number of localities that either have, or are themselves, frontier zones.

These ten criteria recur in every stage of the American frontier. Because each stage is more complex than its predecessor, the manifestations of the criteria are also more complex. Moreover, the criteria obviously have different impacts at different times and are never as fully realized as the model might imply. It is not likely that everyone or even the majority in a frontier society will be involved in realizing these criteria or even be committed to their realization. In any society, the frontier sector is a relatively small one and the people occupying it are relatively few in number. But a frontier society is a perennially "emergent society," growing and changing, marked by the tone set by the frontier sector and its pioneers.

THE CLASSIC LAND FRONTIER

The original and classic frontier was, of course, the land frontier opened by the first British and Northern European settlers of America in the early seventeenth century. The land frontier—or, more properly, the rural-land frontier—was the first frontier in every state and section of the United States as Americans moved progressively westward. The rural-land frontier persisted as a major force (though not the only frontier) on the American scene until its passing at the close of World War I (1918), by which time the extended settlement of virgin land anywhere in the country had virtually ceased. As the classic American frontier, it has become the model for all subsequent frontier situations.

Characteristic of the rural-land frontier were the preoccupations of a predominantly rural America with the settlement, development, and political organization of the land itself through the establishment of a civil society based on agricultural pursuits. The cities that emerged in this period were, from the first, important institutions in American society developed to serve the rural-land frontier. Their primary function was to engage in "agribusiness," serving as commercial, social, intellectual, and political centers for agricultural regions; and, secondarily, to serve as workshops supplying the increasing number of manufactured "necessities" required by the farmer.[4] The three-hundred-year epoch of the rural-land frontier saw the formation of the basic social and political institutions, as well as the basic political culture of the United States and of its subdivisions, shaped by the frontier experience itself.

All ten frontier criteria were substantially fulfilled on the classic rural-land frontier. In the first place, there was obviously the land—a wilderness to be settled, and tamed, for a wide variety of new uses. Exploration of unknown territories and their subsequent settlement were the essence of the frontier process. The people who came to explore or tame the land were conscious of their involvement in a great task, no matter how they defined it; they had the "frontier spirit."

During the history of the rural-land frontier, excepting only temporary periods of depression and recession, the American economy was an expanding one, growing at what would be considered a phenomenal rate. The overall land frontier combined several very specific frontiers (e.g., the agricultural frontier, the mining frontier, the cattlemen's frontier, and the transportation frontier) as well as the various regional frontiers from the Atlantic seaboard to the Pacific slope. It is hardly necessary to delineate the role that various forms of risk played in the conquest of the land frontier, whether the risk of the Eastern capitalist building a railroad or the risk of a sodbuster trying to create a farm on the prairie.

Action was, of course, the basic requirement and the major emphasis of the frontier "way of life." Courage was necessary, usually in the sheer physical sense of the term. And freedom and equality were concomitants of risk, action, and courage, since the courage to take risks by acting invariably led to freedom and, on the whole, promoted social equality as well. There was a freedom to do all this out at the end of settlement, at the limits of previous human activity, where greater equality of condition was the general rule. Indeed, society's greatest rewards went to those who made use of that freedom (though obviously only to a few of them) in any number of ways.

Generally speaking, access to the frontier was unlimited, notwithstanding the limits that government imposed equally on everyone. Such access simply involved a willingness to migrate westward. Though this was not entirely true in practice, one of the major tasks of politics in the days of the land frontier was to continue making the adjustments necessary to ensure a reasonable degree of equal access.

Of course, not everyone "made it" on the rural-land frontier. There were failures, both individual and communal, as attested by the many ghost towns that still dot the American landscape (though some of these made people rich in their heyday). Just as the frontier was open to the virtuous, so also was it open to the unscrupulous who saw it as an opportunity to "make a killing," often quite literally.[5] Frontier conditions of change, movement, and loose social restraints can give rise to rapacious attitudes and violent practices toward humans and nature. Thus, among the many casualties of the frontier, the most notable and tragic were the Native Americans. In 1492, estimates have it that there were between one and two million Native Americans in what is now the United States. By 1900, they were being referred to as "the vanishing Americans" because warfare, disease, and starvation had reduced their population to about 250,000. (Since that time, their number has increased rapidly, reaching 1,789,000 identified Native Americans by 1989.) In 1984, nearly 800,000 were enrolled in their respective tribal reservations.[6]

Likewise, buffalo were slaughtered in huge numbers, trees were indiscriminately felled, and lands were worn out by improper cultivation. However, the necessarily seamy side of the frontier should not be overly dramatized, just as the virtuous side should not be romanticized. Both are part of the bundle of frontier images as well as tensions that have affected the course of American life.

Frederick Jackson Turner described the epoch of the land frontier as the period when settlement of the land was the most important factor shaping American life and democracy. He associated both the form of American civilization and its social and political functions with the peculiar set of challenges produced by the existence of the frontier. Accordingly, he viewed American institutions as adaptations to the changes experienced by a growing people whose expansion took place in an apparently open-ended arena. Contrasting the blessings of open-ended expansion with the problem of trying to expand in a clearly limited space, such as Europe, Turner concluded that democratic institutions are born and are able to take root in an open-ended frontier where the same "pie" need not be divided and redivided through internecine struggle but, rather, continues to grow so that it can potentially provide enough for all comers (see Map 1.4).[7]

Such openness, moreover, meant the absence of a need to battle an entrenched feudal class with controlling interests in existing lands, wealth, and political arrangements. The "elbow room" available on the frontier presented opportunities for individual and social advancement, wealth-getting, and political experimentation. The establishment of new communities and new enterprises tended to involve larger numbers of ordinary people in the decisionmaking and management aspects of politics and economics, thereby reinforcing grass-roots political action as well as individual self-reliance and self-confidence.[8] The rural-land frontier also gave distinctive groups of people such as the Mormons opportunities to establish new and more secure communities fashioned in accord with their own beliefs and ways of life.

Furthermore, the images of the frontier held by Americans—partly factual and partly fanciful—had a substantial psychological impact on American feelings of progress, mobility, optimism, and freedom. The grand images of the frontier and the eternal lure of a "second chance" had become so compelling that the closing of the rural-land frontier was, for a time, greeted with dismay and not a little fear that the dynamism of America would also run down. As Franklin D. Roosevelt remarked during a speech in 1932: "Our last frontier has long since been reached and there is practically no more free land. ... There is no safety valve in the form of a western prairie to which those thrown out of work by the eastern machines can go for a new start." Many believed that the Great Depression was a natural consequence of the closing of the rural-land frontier that, in turn, has generated another.

Even though many of Turner's specific hypotheses about the influence of the frontier on American life have since been revised to take into account new evidence provided by more detailed research (including his own and that of his students), the main thrust of his conceptualizing remains a valid and useful tool for understanding American life.[9] What Turner apparently did not foresee was that the rural-land frontier initiated a chain reaction that, even in his time, had led to the opening of a new frontier as the old one was fading; the new one, in turn, has since generated still another frontier that, in turn, has generated another. Turner's frontier was but one manifestation of a greater frontier that transcends the three-hundred-year settlement of the lands of North America.

The phenomena that made the land frontier a distinctive human experience have recurred in essentially similar, if progressively more complex, forms within the American experience, leading to the opening of new frontiers. The striking and patterned reappearance of certain elements originally associated with the classic land frontier at every stage of American development, including the present one, strongly suggests that the continuing frontier is a major force promoting and directing American social development, economic change, and the political responses to both.

The rural-land frontier profoundly affected the development of American society, both in the frontier zone and in the hinterland, by keeping American society in flux, rendering certain categories of privilege obsolete, providing the means whereby American society could continue to grow and change, and offering the promise of progress and a "second chance." In short, the land frontier stimulated the creation of new opportunities for people to begin "on their own" and to succeed on their own merit. Perhaps its greatest success in this regard is the manner in which it gave rise to the urban-industrial frontier out of its own accomplishments, setting off a chain reaction that enabled one frontier to breed another.

THE URBAN-INDUSTRIAL FRONTIER AND ITS IMPACT

The second American frontier was the urban-industrial frontier, which opened along the Atlantic coast after the War of 1812 and predominated in the greater Northeast after 1830, as the rural-land frontier moved westward. The urban-industrial frontier would spread across the continent by the end of the century, directly manifesting itself in the still-dominant greater Northeastern industrial heartland stretching from southern New Hampshire to beyond Lake Michigan. The essential characteristics of the urban-industrial frontier were to be most intensely expressed in this Northeastern-Midwestern belt. From the early to mid-twentieth century, the same characteristics were to find modified expression in specific cities and subregions of the greater South and greater West.[10]

The primary characteristic of the urban-industrial frontier was the development of the industrial city as the major form of organized land use. New cities were established and old ones expanded, not merely as service centers for rural areas but as independent centers of manufacturing, opportunity, capital and wealth accumulation, and social innovation. This new industrial frontier stimulated the development of intensive urban concentrations in the latter two-thirds of the nineteenth century and first third of the twentieth, as it transformed the United States into an industrialized nation.

The urban frontier began the urbanization of American society before it became recognizable as a major frontier manifestation in its own right. Migration to urban areas has been on the increase at least since the eighteenth century. Since 1790, the year of the first U.S. census, the rate of rural and urban growth has been the same in only one decade, between 1810 and 1820, before the emergence of the urban frontier as a force to be reckoned with. After 1820, the rate of urban growth accelerated whereas the rate of rural growth began to decline. When the urban frontier came into its own, the city became the center of American life, even though city dwellers still represented only a small minority of the total population. Virtually every city was taken in hand by its "boosters," who fervently desired to enlarge its size and position as a metropolitan center, to make it a bigger and supposedly grander metropolis than any other city ever, and, in the process, to glamorize urban living.[11]

By 1850, the urban frontier had become the dominant frontier in the East and the city had become the vanguard of the land frontier in the West. In general, the period between 1816 and 1876 was the "heroic age" for the foundation, incorporation, and growth of what are now the nation's largest cities, just as it was the heroic age for the conquest of the last land frontier. Indeed, the two phenomena went hand in hand. This overlapping of frontiers occurred at a time when the shape of the United States was being crystallized. It is significant that the bulk of the nation's population growth in the past two generations has taken place in the metropolitan areas surrounding the cities established in that era.

During this period, when the distinctive American urban pattern took root, the largest cities in the United States were (with one or two exceptions) no bigger in population than the middle-sized cities of today. These cities grew really large only after 1890, by which time the land frontier had become secondary to the urban frontier and the latter had become the primary source of individual opportunity and social development. In the years between the Civil War and the turn of the century, the combined influence of the two frontiers stimulated a process of "natural selection" that transformed some of those cities such as New York, Chicago, and San Francisco into national and world centers while limiting others equally as old to lesser frontiers.

As with the land frontier, the opening and progress of the urban frontier led to great changes in American life, in a manner that substantially met the ten conditions of the frontier thesis. It involved extensive new organization in the uses of the land through the development of industrial cities with concentrated urban populations as the dominant form of social and economic organization in American life. The assault upon nature, once a relatively simple matter of turning wilderness into productive (usually agricultural) land, was transformed into a continuous innovative effort to exploit natural phenomena (steam, electricity) or extract and reform raw materials (coal, iron) in some unprecedented way. In place of the land explorer, the scientific innovator, so well typified by Thomas Edison (1847–1931), became the source of new discoveries and the trailblazer into the unknown, whereas the industrial entrepreneur and the factory worker replaced the commercial entrepreneur and the agriculturalist as pioneers in the development of the discoveries of the inventor-explorer.

This process had its price, of course. Some of the successful entrepreneurs were justifiably referred to as "robber barons." Relatively small groups of individuals, by accumulating vast fortunes, could have a disproportionate effect on economic and political affairs. Meanwhile, cities teemed with poor immigrants who crowded into squalid tenements and sweatshops and worked long hours at low wages. Before the Civil War, for example, the New York City house occupied by George Washington during his first years as president was reduced to a crowded tenement. The urban-industrial frontier also saw the rise of urban political bosses—men like George Washington Plunkitt of New York who "seen" their "opportunities" and "took 'em." The notorious Republican Gas Ring of Philadelphia earned that city the title of "City of Brotherly Loot." Labor-management violence replaced Native American–settler violence on the urban-industrial frontier. And class, ethnic, and racial conflicts became serious factors in American politics.

This period also witnessed the emergence of the organizational society in the United States as people sought to create new bonds of association. Replacing older, organic bonds of family and community, these new bonds served a more mobile and complex society. This fact was reflected in the organization of labor unions, political parties, professional associations, large and small corporations, free public school systems and libraries, self-help organizations and philanthropic foundations, conservationist and other "do-gooder" associations, and civic as well as ethnic clubs, not to mention Protestant churches, Catholic parishes, and Jewish synagogues. It was also reflected in the emergence of a civil service system accompanied by growing government bureaucracies. This organizational activity was primarily a consequence of the strife and flux of the urban-industrial frontier. Organizational strength was needed during this period in order to take advantage of the urban-industrial revolution. But organization was also necessary to defend oneself against the exploitative tendencies of this revolution or to reform its more rapacious aspects.

Despite frequent corruption and periodic depressions, the nation's economy continued to expand at an even more rapid rate, past the "takeoff" period described by W. W. Rostow and through the period of rapid industrialization with its corresponding increase in national wealth.[12] A new technology, fostered in great part by the demands of the land frontier, emerged to become a major force in the promotion of urbanization, industrialization, and economic growth, creating new secondary frontiers of its own. Cities grew up to produce not only ever more sophisticated agricultural implements but also the machine tools needed to make the former. The railroad, itself a revolutionary instrument in transportation technology, generated further revolutions in the patterns of settlement on both frontiers. These, in turn, led to the emergence of new specialized functional frontiers (textiles, steel, food processing) or reorientations of old ones (transportation, mining, merchandising), plus new geographic ones.

The urban frontier provided new opportunities for making fortunes, for getting away from home, for taking financial and personal risks, and for bringing about achievements based on the willingness to act. There also existed the same kind of freedom to engage in these enterprises previously associated with the land frontier, both for the entrepreneur interested in the development of a new product and a new market and for the "man in the street" interested in new forms of earning a livelihood. The same "boom or bust" spirit, sense of boosterism, and feeling of pioneering found among the pioneers of the land frontier could be found among the developers of the industrial cities on the urban frontier. The popular literature of the day reflects this phenomenon quite clearly.[13]

As on the classic land frontier, talent remained more important than either family background or inherited money, so access to the challenges and benefits of the urban frontier remained reasonably free. This access was extended broadly as new occupations developed at a rapid rate, with openings for people on all social levels. These new occupations, coupled with the professionalization of old ones, served to break down developing inequalities in the agricultural sector. What people needed to do was migrate to the city, whether from the American countryside or from the Old World. As in the case of the land frontier, where the promise of the frontier did not appear to be materializing as a matter of course, seekers of the promise took political action to rectify matters. Despite the tendencies of the new industrialism to promote large fortunes (which almost invariably were made by entrepreneurs from humble backgrounds), the forces of the urban frontier still promoted a rough equality of conditions for the majority—by destroying many of the established inequalities of the past.

The coming of urbanization transformed the social structure of American life, moving first the most energetic and ultimately the majority of the nation's population into the cities, where they had to modify aspects of their agrarian outlook in an effort to meet the problems of high-density living in a complex, highly organized society. Urbanization also changed the nation's demographic base by adding a polyglot population of Catholics and Jews from all over Europe to an overwhelmingly Protestant Anglo-Saxon base. In its turn, industrialization, with its introduction of recurring technological obsolescence, introduced a level of continuing change unheard of in any earlier society.

THE OPENING OF THE
METROPOLITAN FRONTIER

The history of the urban frontier in the United States appears to envelop two contradictory trends. On the one hand, the urban frontier brought about the urbanization of American society. On the other hand, even as the rate of urbanization began to accelerate, a counter, almost anti-urban, trend began to develop as well. This trend would not become dominant until four generations later, in the 1920s, when the physical setting of American society had become thoroughly urbanized.

Americans moved to the cities with seeming reluctance. Only in 1890, when the urban frontier was entering its highest stage of development, did the number of urban places in the United States exceed 1,000 and the urban population exceed one-third of the total population (Table 3.1). Not until after 1900 was one-quarter of the nation's total population living in cities of more than 50,000.

The urban population did not exceed the rural population until 1920, when the urban frontier was already passing the peak of its influence. That same year, the total population in cities of 100,000 and more came to exceed the total population in all smaller urban places. The age of the big city had seemingly arrived. However, no sooner did the big city become the apparent embodiment of the American style of life than it began to be replaced by a less citified style. As Table 3.1 indicates, the upward trend in the growth of big cities ended during the Great Depression, giving way to the development of medium-sized and smaller cities within large and medium-sized metropolitan areas as a new embodiment of American urban life and a major aspect of the third American frontier.

By 1950, the trend toward big-city living had been reversed and the number of people living in cities of more than 100,000 had declined to fewer than the number of people living in smaller urban places. By 1990, only 25 percent of the total population in the United States lived in urban places of more than 100,000 people, the lowest figure since 1910 and less than the percentage living in rural areas. The percentage of population living in cities of more than 1 million, which peaked in 1930, declined sharply since then and had fallen below the 1920 level by 1970. By 1980, the new trend was even sharper, with the percentage dropping below that of 1900.

All this occurred despite the increasing metropolitanization of the nation's population. By 1970, 6 percent of the nation's total population lived in the 243 Census Bureau–defined Standard Metropolitan Statistical Areas (SMSAs). Although these SMSAs occupied only about 11 percent of the nation's land area, their population had increased by 23.5 percent between 1960 and 1970, in contrast to the overall national growth of 13.3 percent. By 1980, fully 74.8 percent of all Americans lived in SMSAs, which now covered 16 percent of the total U.S. land area; and by 1990, this number had grown to 77.5 percent.[14]

The positive yet reluctant response of most Americans to urbanize reflects a basic desire on their part to have their cake and eat it too. They want to have the economic and social advantages of urbanization, which they value for essentially hedonistic reasons, while preserving the erstwhile "rural" amenities of life, both physical and social, which they value for essentially moral and aesthetic reasons.[15]

TABLE 3.1 Distribution of U.S. Population by Size of Place: 1790–1988

Year	% Urban	No. Urban Places	More than 1 million No.	% of Pop.	500,000–1 million No.	% of Pop.	250,000–500,000 No.	% of Pop.	100,000–250,000 No.	% of Pop.	50,000–100,000 No.	% of Pop.	10,000–50,000[a] No.	% of Pop.	Less than 10,000 No.	% of Pop.	% Rural
1790	5.1	24	—	—	—	—	—	—	—	—	—	—	5	5.1[a]	19	—	94.9
1800	6.1	33	—	—	—	—	—	—	—	—	1	1.1	5	5.0	27	—	93.9
1810	7.3	46	—	—	—	—	—	—	—	—	2	—	9	—	35	—	92.7
1820	7.2	61	—	—	—	—	—	—	1	1.3	2	1.3	10	4.6	48	—	92.8
1830	8.8	90	—	—	—	—	—	—	1	—	3	—	19	—	67	—	91.2
1840	10.8	131	—	—	1	1.8	1	—	2	1.2	2	1.1	32	6.7	94	—	89.2
1850	15.3	236	—	—	1	—	1	—	4	—	3	—	52	—	174	—	84.7
1860	19.8	392	—	—	2	4.4	1	0.8	6	3.2	7	1.4	77	10.0	299	—	80.2
1870	25.7	663	—	—	2	—	5	—	7	—	11	—	143	—	495	—	74.3
1880	28.2	939	1	2.4	3	3.8	4	2.6	12	3.6	15	1.9	188	13.9	716	—	71.8
1890	35.1	1,348	3	5.8	1	—	7	—	17	—	30	—	296	—	994	—	64.9
1900	39.7	1,737	3	8.5	3	2.2	9	3.8	23	4.3	40	3.6	362	7.3	1,297	—	60.3
1910	45.7	2,262	3	9.2	5	3.3	11	4.3	31	5.3	59	4.5	586	10.4	1,665	8.7	54.3
1920	51.2	2,722	3	9.6	9	5.9	13	4.3	43	6.2	76	5.0	608	11.5	1,970	8.8	48.8
1930	56.2	3,165	5	12.3	8	4.7	24	6.5	56	6.1	98	5.3	791	12.6	2,183	8.6	43.8
1940	56.5	3,464	5	12.1	9	4.9	23	5.9	55	5.9	107	5.6	878	13.2	2,387	8.7	43.5
1950	64.0[b]	4,743[b]	5	11.5	13	6.1	23	5.5	65[b]	6.3[b]	126[b]	5.9[b]	1,030[b]	13.7[b]	3,479[b]	10.1[b]	36.0
1960	69.9[b]	6,041[b]	5	9.8	16	6.2	30	6.0	81[b]	6.5[b]	201[b]	7.7[b]	1,566[b]	18.1[b]	4,142[b]	10.1[b]	30.1
1970	73.5	7,062	6	9.2	20	6.4	30	5.1	100	7.0	240	8.2	1,905	19.3	4,761	10.8	26.5
1980	73.7	8,765	6	7.7	16	4.8	34	5.4	117	7.5	290	8.7	2,440	22.5	5,862	17.1	26.3
1988	77.0	9,252	7	8.0	17	5.0	37	5.0	125	8.0	300	8.0	1,898	16.0	6,868	12.0	23.0

[a]Percentages of population include all cities of less than 50,000 through 1900.
[b]Current Urban Definition. Not included in this table is the population of unincorporated parts of urbanized areas, which equaled 4.9 percent of the total in 1950 and 5.5 percent in 1960.

Sources: U.S. Department of Commerce, Historical Statistics of the United States (Washington, D.C.: Bureau of the Census); and Statistical Abstract of the United States (Washington, D.C.: U.S. Department of Commerce, various years).

The expansion of cities continued as long as city life was able to offer most of the amenities of "rural" living, as well as the economic, social, and cultural advantages of urban life, to those who were in a position to determine their city's growth. Throughout the nineteenth century, many newly settled suburbs and smaller cities were annexed to already large cities because their residents, or those holding power locally, felt reasonably confident that loss of their suburbs' independent political status would not mean an end to their suburban style of life. Not only did large cities continue to grow larger but small cities still aspired to become great metropolitan centers. City leaders were infected with the idea that "bigger is better" and that large organizations were more efficient and businesslike.

As the full impact of big-city life in its less attractive aspects—crowding, apartment living, tenement slums, governmental remoteness, and lack of such natural amenities as clean air, grass, and trees—had not become sufficiently apparent to the majority of the residents in their cities, the idea of indefinite city growth evoked no negative response. Thus, in 1854, Philadelphia grew from 2 to 129 square miles as the result of a gigantic consolidation of city and county, which absorbed the formerly independent suburbs of Northern Liberties, Spring Garden, Kensington, Southwark, and Moyamensing. In 1898, the population of New York City increased by some 2 million; and its land area jumped from 40 to 300 square miles when Manhattan (the original New York City) was joined with Brooklyn (then the fourth largest city in the United States), Staten Island, much of Queens, and a portion of Westchester County (which became known as the Bronx) to form a single city of five boroughs—essentially the New York City of today.

The truth of the matter was that, before 1890, big cities in the United States had not yet become big enough to evoke negative reactions, except in a few isolated cases along the Eastern seaboard. This is not to deny that many industrial cities had extensive tenement sections before 1890; but even in them, the majority of the socially and politically articulate population could still live in private or semiprivate homes along tree-lined streets. Tenement living remained the preserve of newly arrived immigrants who as yet had little or no voice in civic affairs and little means to escape the circumstances to which they were effectively confined.

There came a point in the development of most of the larger cities, however, when even the politically articulate city-dwellers found it difficult to maintain their semi-urban style of life. Even enlargement of the city limits came to mean enlargement of the city's problems without any reasonable recompense. At the same time, several other factors coalesced to encourage metropolitanization in place of simple urbanization.

As maintenance of even the simpler rural-style amenities began to cost more money within the large cities, the wealthier city-dwellers began to seek new residences outside the city limits. The cities themselves began to run up against increased difficulties in their attempts to annex new areas, coming up against already-existing cities that, although they were undergoing suburbanization both socially and economically, desired to retain their political independence in order to better maintain their distinctive character. It had become apparent that annexation to the great cities was tantamount to absorption into a citified environment, with little or no possibility to control the extent of citification. Hence neither old residents nor new settlers fleeing the big city were willing to be brought into its embrace. Annexation, which had been relatively easy under the law in most cases, was made more difficult as the small cities on the fringes of the giants went to the legislatures with their demands for self-preservation. In fact, as these fringe-area cities began to attract settlers from the central city, they frequently annexed vacant land themselves, often in small and even medium-sized cities within the larger metropolitan regions that were in the process of formation.

Simultaneously, improved transportation technology made it possible for more people to move out of the great cities into surrounding areas, while retaining jobs within the cities they had left. This movement, begun in the days of the railroads and streetcars, intensified with the development of the automobile and the construction of roads suitable for heavy motor traffic. At the same time, the previously deprived groups living in the substandard areas of the large cities had become prosperous enough to seek alternatives to their relatively poor living conditions, while their offspring acquired the American taste for a semi-urban environment. Following the "old tenement trail"[16] to the suburbs, they began to move out to a new metropolitan frontier where it became possible to live in the same style that earlier prestigious groups had endowed with considerable status. Moreover, as the movement to the metropolis accelerated in the country as a whole, many rural residents moved directly into the suburban fringes of the major cities, preferring them over city living from the first.

"Permanent" metropolitanization (as distinct from the "temporary" suburbanization of earlier years) began in the East in the last third of the nineteenth century in response to the urban frontier and spread to the larger cities in the middle and far West by the turn of the century, just as the urban frontier had begun in the heyday of the land frontier as a response to the needs of the land frontier and had spread in the same manner. However, it was not until the close of World War II that the metropolitan frontier came into its own: The pressures to leave the great cities, which had been building up through the depression and war years, finally burst their bounds. Thus, between 1960 and 1970, the population of central cities in metropolitan areas grew by 6.4 percent whereas their suburban areas grew at the rate of 26.8 percent.

The great migration to the suburbs was simply one aspect of the new metropolitan frontier. The urban-industrial frontier lost its primacy during the Great Depression. With the completion of the nation's basic urbanization and industrialization, the complex of opportunities needed for frontier-style development temporarily disappeared. Urbanizing and industrializing trends had persisted until then in regions on the peripheries of the urban-industrial frontier, just as pioneering on the land frontier continued in isolated areas. However, the opportunity to foster the continuous reconstruction of the social order associated with the frontier was no longer available through simple urbanization and industrialization.

So, after a brief hiatus brought about by the Great Depression and World War II, the third great manifestation of the American frontier began to unfold. Its reappearance as the metropolitan-technological frontier of science, suburbia, and synthetics led to the emergence of new versions of old frontier situations. As in the case of the land and urban frontiers, the metropolitan frontier initially manifested itself as a local phenomenon that spread within and across the sections in a generally east-west direction, ultimately becoming a nationwide phenomenon. Movement on this new frontier, however, has not been tied to national geography alone. Although this movement is headed across the continent, almost every one of the nation's urban centers responded to the new frontier locally by developing a metropolitan frontier of its own.

Thus frontier areas of new growth emerged around the fringes of the great majority of the nation's urban centers. But within those urban centers, areas of decline have developed because of an inability to respond positively to the new frontier's demands. They have come to resemble the "backwash" regions left in the wake of the earlier frontiers, with all the problems of areas returning to "wilderness."

On the metropolitan frontier, land once again became a crucial factor. The "metropolitan fringe"—the area of expanding urbanization and the nonurban area into which it expands—was the locus of frontier expansion. Within the metropolitan area, it even became possible to delineate a frontier line (where settlement falls below a density of 500 people per square mile) that marks the limit of metropolitanization and to watch that line move as settlement expands. The metropolitan frontier organized the use of land in a new way: Densities that would be considered rural in much of the Old World combined with urban social and economic organization to create quasi- (or sub-) urban, metropolitan complexes encompassing cities of all sizes, towns, villages, and rural dwellings.[17]

By the standards of the urban frontier era (which all too often are still applied in discussions of contemporary metropolitanization), the land uses of the metropolitan frontier are considered "urban sprawl." But in view of the goals of deconcentration implicit in the development of these variegated metropolitan land use patterns, this so-called sprawl is what makes urban living tolerable to many (if not most) Americans. By 1987, even with the spreading of metropolitan forms of land use, 16.2 percent of the land area of the United States was included within Standard Metropolitan Statistical Areas and only about 4 percent of the land outside the federal public domain (which represents approximately one-third of the total U.S. land area) was viewed as actually urbanized, or 3 percent of the total,[18] leaving what is, in effect, a near-limitless area for future expansion of metropolitan settlement in this country, a key manifestation of its frontier character. Although land is no longer "free" or unoccupied and there is no longer the once-prevalent feeling that it is limitless, the facts regarding the availability of new land for metropolitanization do not differ substantially from similar facts regarding the land frontier.

The physical world of the metropolitan frontier appears to be highly tamed; but, in a sense, humanity has never before confronted the "wilds" of nature to the extent that it does today, with its ability to explore the oceans and outer space, its increased mastery of the physical, chemical, and biological structure of the universe, and its new technology. Of course, these wilds (or the wilderness they add up to), whether they be of this earth, below it, or beyond it, must be approached through the techniques of science rather than through the simple exertion of brute physical force (not that science did not supplement brute force on the land frontier or that physical power is no longer needed). This shift to the primacy of intellectual effort, with all its consequences for society as a whole, is itself one of the most profound impacts of the contemporary frontier.

The metropolitan land boom and the growth of "brain" industries are but two manifestations of the twenty-year economic boom that began with the opening of the new frontier and, though occasionally slowed by recessions, has continued as the feedbacks of the frontier (ranging from the demands of space exploration to the needs of newborn babies) have exerted increasing influence on the economy. Moreover, the results of scientific exploration on the new frontier have stimulated the pioneering of many new technologies. Their importance is such that technological change has become the equivalent of land and industrialization as the motive force of the metropolitan frontier.

CASE STUDY: THE AUTOMOBILE
AND THE METROPOLITAN FRONTIER

As in the case of earlier frontiers, changes in transportation and communication technology were crucial to the opening of the metropolitan-technological frontier. On this new frontier, the key to the expansion of settlement was the automobile, whose development is illustrative of the frontier impact of science and technology. From certain theoretical principles of physics, "discovered" by the first scientific explorers a century or more ago, the inventor-pioneers of the urban-industrial frontier were able to create the internal combustion engine and, ultimately, the automobile. The new vehicle and the technology it represented rapidly revolutionized society, creating myriad new industries— automobile manufacturing, the oil industry, an expanded military industry, and many others—and providing a wide range of opportunities for those willing and able to take advantage of them. By 1963, at the height of the metropolitan frontier, more than 7 million jobs were directly dependent on the automobile. None of these jobs had existed two generations earlier.

American society became automobile oriented, leading in turn to a revolution in its physical organization, its social structure, and its moral sense (see Table 3.2). The automobile, like the railroad before it, made possible the opening of new geographic frontiers. Whereas pre-automobile communities could develop only along rail lines, new ones were able to develop wherever roads could be built. This fact was of particular importance around the nation's cities. Suburbs, previously few in number and largely the preserves of the rich because they had to be located along railroad lines, now became accessible to the vast majority of the people, offering them better housing, lands and open space, and a greater feeling of community. This outcome, in turn, radically changed the uses of land in potentially suburban areas, the social structure of urban populations, and the political organization of metropolitan regions.

The automobile also extended freedom of travel to people who were unable to travel before, transforming isolated villagers into participants in wider regional communities. It changed the pattern of rural settlement no less than that of urban areas, turning villages into ghost towns and towns into small cities. Meanwhile, farm equipment using the internal combustion engine increased the size of economic farms manyfold.

The impact of the automotive frontier had some important (and often unforeseen) by-products as well. The new automotive society enriched numerous automobile manufacturers and dealers as well as manufacturers and dealers in subsidiary products, creating a whole new class of millionaires with interests and values reflecting the culture that made them. Thomas H. McDonald, for thirty-four years head of the federal Bureau of Public Roads, put the matter succinctly: "The roads themselves helped us create a new wealth, in business and industry and land values. ... So it was not our wealth that made our highways possible."[19] It transformed the socioeconomic structure of entire states, creating, among other things, modern Michigan, contemporary Texas, and twentieth-century California (the very acme of the new frontier). The automotive frontier also contributed to the new "five-dollar day," making it possible for African-Ameri-

TABLE 3.2   Growth of Automobile Usage in the United States: 1920–1989

	1920	1940	1950	1960	1970	1980	1989
Auto registrations (in thousands)	8,136	27,465	40,339	61,682	89,280	121,600	144,400
Percentage of families with 1 auto	NA	NA	52%	62%	54%	34%[a]	
Percentage of families with 2+ autos	NA	NA	7%	15%	28%	53.7%[a]	
Avg. auto speed	NA	NA	48.7	53.8	60.6	NA	NA
Auto fuel consumption (in millions of gallons)	NA	16,759	25,037	41,996	66,728	71,900	71,700
Total traffic deaths	12,500	34,501	34,763	38,137	54,633	53,200	46,900
Traffic deaths per 100,000	NA	261	23.0	21.2	26.8	22.6	18.4

[a]Percentage in 1987.

Sources: U.S. Department of Commerce, *Historical Statistics of the United States* (Washington, D.C.: Bureau of the Census, 1975), pp. 716–720; and *Statistical Abstract of the United States* (Washington, D.C.: U.S. Department of Commerce, 1990).

cans as well as others to earn a living wage for the first time in their history and promoting their migration northward. In this and other ways, it readily broadened the opportunities of a people previously restricted in every way and contributed mightily to stimulating the present drive for African-American equality.

Not the least of the automobile's effects were the changes it induced in family life, giving children greater freedom from parental control than at any other time in history. These changes, in turn, forced a variety of adjustments in traditional American social institutions. In the political realm, they profoundly influenced the structure and scope of local, state, and national government, raising new problems of police patrol and changing the span of political control and pressure.

The automobile also produced new environmental, economic, and social problems for America. Auto emissions raised levels of air pollution, especially in highly congested cities (although, ironically, the automobile was at first greeted by urbanites as a relief from the pollution and odor created by hundreds of tons of horse manure along with dead horses lying about city streets). New legislation, such as the various clean air acts, and new technologies have been required in an effort to reduce auto pollution. Moreover, although street, highway, and parking spaces occupy no more than about 2 percent of the land area of the United States, auto critics have charged that highways are devouring the land. The increased number of automobiles and their travel speeds have also produced a new source of death, along with charges that automobiles are "unsafe at any speed." During the early 1970s, the automobile consumed about 30 percent of all the oil used in the United States (another 10 percent was used by trucks) and was thus linked to the "energy crisis."

More serious social problems arose with the construction of inner-city freeways, which, in many cases, destroyed pleasant neighborhoods and displaced people, especially the poor, whose homes stood in the way of automotive "progress." By facilitating the movement of people and jobs to the suburbs, freeways also contributed to the erosion of tax bases in some big cities and to the increase in the proportions of poor and unemployed persons living within the big cities. In turn, urban renewal programs designed to attract suburbanites back to city centers displaced still more low-income people as their homes gave way to office buildings, shopping areas, and upper-income housing developments. On a national scale, the interstate highway system, coupled with air travel and refrigeration, facilitated the migration of people and jobs from the Frostbelt to the Sunbelt cities—a migration that became especially evident during the 1970s.

Nevertheless, despite the problems generated or facilitated by the automobile, neither social criticism nor any mass transit scheme has yet been able to lure Americans from their cars. In their eyes, the benefits still outweigh the costs, and many of these costs can be appreciably reduced without significant reductions in automobile usage.[20]

Like its predecessors, the metropolitan frontier was also a composite of many specialized geographic and functional frontiers. The automotive and suburban frontiers have already been mentioned. The recreation and consumer frontiers, as well as those of the Eastern megalopolis or southern California, constitute still others. Each of these specialized frontiers offered many opportunities for exploration, growth, and development; all required the taking of risks and the active pursuit of frontier-style goals while offering great material and moral rewards. The builders of subdivisions, the creators of franchised "chains," the researchers in laboratories, and perhaps even the promoters of psychedelic art and psychic renewal all potentially shared this aspect of the frontier experience insofar as their courageous application of effort brought them the rewards that proceed from exploring or pioneering.

The very complexity of the metropolitan frontier and variety of specialized frontiers within it heightened the freedom of access to the frontier zone in one way or another. In particular, the existence of a standard body of scientific and technical knowledge—formally (if not actually) available to all on the basis of ability alone, and the mastery of which offered access to the frontier—is simply a more complex variation on the kind of equality of access that prevailed in the days of the land frontier. Then the "standard body of techniques" grew out of physical prowess rather than intellectual ability, but it served the same general purpose. Of course, the use of intelligence as a prime means of access to the frontier has not been confined to the realms of science and technology. Migration, also a factor in

promoting access, involves movement not only from central cities to suburbs but from suburb to suburb and metropolitan area to metropolitan
area as well.

If the publications and pronouncements of the press and mass media
and the orientation of recent political campaigns were at all indicative of
public attitudes, popular awareness of the frontier-like opportunities present in American society during the metropolitan frontier had reached a
very high level and public response to the challenges of that frontier was
no less impressive than in earlier periods in American history. All in all,
the repeated mass-media references to "new frontiers" were not simply a
matter of rhetoric. This frontier psychology existed despite the strong tendency in American society to view the problems of each era as unique—an
outlook that, in itself, reflects the thinking of people engaged on a frontier.

Frontier-based economic change brought even greater social fluidity.
Rapid technological change stimulated the creation of new industries,
producing new occupations on all levels of society that demanded talents
not transmitted by heredity and that consequently had to remain open to
those who qualified regardless of their social backgrounds. It has been re-
liably estimated that some 80 percent of the jobs that exist in the United
States today were not in existence two generations ago, when the urban-
industrial frontier was at its peak. Moreover, a shift has occurred in the
character of American occupational structure from production to service,
comparable to the shift from agriculture to industry caused by the advance of the urban frontier.[21]

At the same time, the social "feedback" from the advancing frontier
continued to have strong pro-democratic effects on American social structure and civil society, promoting both freedom and equality through its
continued fostering of social mobility and its expanding conception of the
rights of all to participate equally in social and political life. The civil
rights movement, the war on poverty, and the emergence of radically new
forms of individual freedom and self-expression—all occurred in response to the frontier-related developments in postwar American society.

The greatest social contribution of the metropolitan frontier was the impetus it gave to the breakdown of major social and economic differences
among population groups. As a result, the older institutions of the republic and its subdivisions, which had more or less excluded nonwhite, non-
Protestant, and non–Northern European people, had to readjust to include the rest of the country's population in the system of politics and
power, public and private, through which decisions are made.

That readjustment included desegregation of African-Americans and
the election of the first Roman Catholic president, new access to the corporate world for Jews, and the revival of ethnicity for the children of Southern and Eastern European immigrants. All these changes were secured in

a manner consonant with the American mystique and the basic institutions and traditions through which that mystique is expressed. As the very name of the new frontier indicates, most of these adaptations had to be made in the local arena. Indeed, the best expression of the sociopolitical consequences of the new frontier can be seen in the transformation of urban America into metropolitan America. The key to the adaptation lies in that very transformation as the postwar extension of the continuing American frontier.[22]

THE RURBAN-CYBERNETIC FRONTIER

In 1976, the post–World War II generation came to an end. Nothing symbolized this better than the election of Jimmy Carter, the first American president to have come of age since World War II, a man who ran on a platform that suggested that the issues of the post–World War II generation were no longer central to American life. As the new generation began, the third stage of the American frontier no longer seemed compelling. At the same time, despite the "limits of growth" rhetoric, there was every sign that a fourth stage was beginning—a rurban- or citybelt-cybernetic frontier generated by the metropolitan-technological frontier, just as the latter had been generated by its predecessor.

The rurban-cybernetic frontier first emerged in the Northeast, as did its predecessors, as the Atlantic coast metropolitan regions merged into one another to form what Jean Gottman called "a 600-mile-long megalopolis"—a matrix of urban and suburban settlements in which the older central cities came to share importance if not prominence with smaller places.[23] It was a sign of the times that the computer was conceived at MIT in Cambridge, first built at the University of Illinois in Champaign-Urbana, and developed at IBM in White Plains—three medium-sized communities. Two of these cities located in the megalopolis (Cambridge and White Plains) have become special centers in their own right, and the other two (Champaign and Urbana) form a freestanding small metropolitan area. Here we see a reflection of the two primary characteristics of the new frontier: The new locus of settlement is in medium-sized and small cities, and in the university centers of the megalopolis.

The spreading use of computer technology in everything from direct-dialing of telephone calls throughout the world to microwave ovens is the most direct manifestation of the cybernetic tools that make such citybelts possible. In 1979, the newspapers in the Northeast published the first reports of the revival of the small cities of the first industrial revolution, particularly in New England, as the new frontier engulfed them. A decade later, such places were booming—in New England, in the southern Piedmont, in the Colorado Rockies, and along the West Coast.[24] At the same time, population growth shifted into rural areas countrywide.[25] Both phenomena are as much a product of direct-dialing as of the longing of older Americans for small-town or country living. Both reflect the urbanization of the American way of life no matter what lifestyle is practiced, or where.

In 1983, the U.S. Office of Management and Budget (OMB) recognized this phenomenon by changing its definition of Standard Metropolitan Statistical Area (SMSA) to Metropolitan Statistical Area (MSA).[26] Like its predecessor, an MSA is defined as including at least one city with 50,000 or more people. The difference is the addition of a Census Bureau–defined urbanized area of at least 50,000 inhabitants and a total MSA population of at least 100,000. New standards provide that an MSA can be based upon "central counties"—that is, areas in which there is no clear-cut central city (a reflection of the new rurban settlement patterns). Although a larger city in each MSA is designated as a "central city," there are often situations such as that of the Benton Harbor metropolitan area in Michigan, which has a total population of 75,000; of that number, only 12, 000 live in Benton Harbor, a depressed older city that is actually the area's backwater but has been designated the "central city" in deference to old habits.

While the Northeast, like its predecessors, was first to follow this pattern of settlement, the new frontier is finding its true form in the South and West, where citybelt matrices are not being built on the collapse of earlier forms but, rather, are developing as an original form. The present Sunbelt frontier—spread out along the Gulf coast, the Southwestern desert, and the fringes of the California mountains—is classically megalopolitan, given its citybelt characteristics. It has cybernetic properties as well, given its aerospace-related industries and its Sunbelt living made possible by air conditioning and the new telecommunications.

It is still too early to delineate with surety all the imperatives, or even propensities, of the rurban-cybernetic frontier; but some are already visible. Perhaps first and foremost is the new sectionalism, the reemergence of an older basis of American politics in new form. The urban-industrial frontier brought in its wake a politics of class, reflected at its height in the New Deal and the political realignment of which it was a part. This politics of class attacked the division of urban America into "two cities"—the "Protestant" and privileged versus the "ethnic" and denied. It persisted through the metropolitan frontier years in no small measure because, even after affluence and influence came to Protestants and ethnic groups alike, it was reinforced by the transformed politics of race. As African-Americans moved from the Southern backwaters (remaining from the old rural-land frontier) to the world of the metropolitan frontier, their problems took on an economic dimension previously submerged by the legally enforced caste system.

The politics of class divided the country into liberals and conservatives, a division that has become very blurred in recent years. The blurring of what were once relatively clear-cut differences is a reflection of the emergence of the new frontier, its new problems and politics revolving once again around "have" and "have not" sections whose economic interests are often diametrically opposed. Significantly, the emergence of this renewed sectionalism is tied to the end of the economic dominance of the Northeast. The Sunbelt-Frostbelt division is only one aspect of this new sectionalism; presidential contests have revealed how sharp are East-West divisions as well. The reallocation of House seats in the wake of the 1990 census further sharpened these divisions as they are translated into new power balances in Congress and the Electoral College. These sectional divisions are reflected in lifestyle differences as well.[27]

The issues associated with whatever current idiom denominates "lifestyle" for the moment have contributed to a great weakening of the political party system and single-issue politics. Although these particular manifestations may be less long-lived than the conventional wisdom suggests, it is very likely that a continued concern with lifestyle issues will be a major propensity of the rurban-cybernetic frontier and that at least some resolution of the conflicts associated with those issues will become a major imperative. This "lifestyle" problem is intensified inasmuch as the citybelt dimension, with its emphasis on smaller communities, will encourage recrudescence of the kind of territorial democracy that potentially allows different lifestyles to flourish in different places without clashing. Meanwhile, the cybernetic dimension, with its propensity to foster a global village that is tied together by telecommunications, will work in the opposite direction.

SUMMARY

The United States is a "new society" founded by immigrants from old societies who came to this once relatively open territory to establish new lives and communities. In the New World, the settlers underwent a frontier experience that has continued to shape American political life. Each of the four successive stages of the American frontier has generated sets of political, social, and economic challenges as well as problems and opportunities. (1) The rural-land frontier saw the initial opening, settling, and cultivating of the continent. (2) The urban-industrial frontier witnessed a rapid growth in the number and size of cities and of great centers of industry and capital. (3) The metropolitan-technological frontier has seen a second industrial revolution, accompanied by a reverse in the trend toward big-city living; that is, suburbs and free-standing towns in the small and medium-sized range have experienced the greatest growth during the third frontier. And (4) the rurban-cybernetic frontier, now in its early stages, rests on a global revolution in communications and information technology that, in turn, is further dispersing urban life. This frontier has also involved the exploration of new space, such as the undersea and outer space, as well as the development of wholly new and exotic technologies.

The global village is the key to the latest frontier stage, which, even as it follows the tried and true paths of spatial diffusion of earlier frontiers, has a global—indeed, even extraterrestrial—reach. In the final analysis, the frontier is the driving force for the reshaping of time and space in the United States. In the forthcoming chapters we shall see how it is also the driving force for the transformation of American culture and politics.

NOTES

1. Ray Allen Billington, *America's Frontier Heritage* (New York: Holt, Rinehart and Winston, 1966).

2. See Walter Prescott Webb, *The Great Frontier* (Boston: Houghton Mifflin, 1952).

3. Frederick Jackson Turner, *The Significance of the Frontier in American History* (New York: Holt, Rinehart and Winston, 1920), pp. 1–3.

4. See Carl Bridenbaugh, *Cities in the Wilderness: Urban Life in America, 1625–1742* (New York: Capricorn, 1964) and *Cities in Revolt: Urban Life in America, 1743–1776* (New York: Capricorn, 1964); and Richard C. Wade, *The Urban Frontier* (Chicago: University of Chicago Press, 1973).

5. See Richard Slotkin, *Regeneration Through Violence: The Mythology of the American Frontier, 1600–1860* (Middletown, Conn.: Wesleyan University Press, 1973).

6. This information was provided by the U.S. Census Bureau and the Bureau of Indian Affairs at the U.S. Department of the Interior. However, since thousands of Native Americans have intermarried with other Americans and assimilated into the larger society over the years, it is impossible to give a completely accurate figure for their number. How does one define a Native American? A full-descent Native American? One of partial descent? See also C. Matthew Snipp, *American Indians: The First of This Land* (New York: Russell Sage Foundation, 1989).

7. See Turner, *The Significance of the Frontier.* And for a sampling of the literature on Turner's theories, see the bibliography in Ray Allen Billington, *Westward Expansion* (New York: Macmillan, 1967).

8. See Stanley Elkins and Eric McKitrick, "A Meaning for Turner's Frontier," *Political Science Quarterly* 69 (September 1954): 321–353 and (December 1954): 565–602. See also the Amherst pamphlet series, *The Turner Thesis Concerning the Frontier in American History* (Amherst, 1949).

9. The Turner thesis was widely accepted by American historians after 1893 and soon became the regnant explanatory theory in American studies. By the 1930s, however, it was being challenged by a new generation of historians who pointed out what they took to be empirical flaws in Turner's evidence and criticized the essentially romantic nature of Turner's presentation (see, for example, Henry Nash

Smith, *Virgin Land* [New York: Vintage, 1957]). By and large, Turner's students met those challenges and, even though they conceded specific points, were able to defend the thesis itself.

In the 1950s, historians suggested counter-theories that encompassed the frontier thesis but broadened it in different directions (e.g., David Potter, *People of Plenty* [Chicago: University of Chicago Press, 1954]). These counter-theories continue to enjoy a certain popularity. Then, beginning in the mid-1970s and continuing into the early 1990s, yet another generation of historians challenged both the idea of the winning of the West and the notion of European settlement in the Americas as progress, applying the anti-colonialist political ideas developed in regard to the Third World in the postwar generation or the new environmentalist sensibility. The myth of the West itself is challenged from this perspective. Among the contemporary revisionists are Patricia Nelson Limerick, who, according to Larry McMurtry, claims "that America's westward expansion was a mosaic of failure, financial and personal, but also, in the largest sense, moral"; and Kirkpatrick Sale, who, in *The Conquest of Paradise* (New York: Alfred A. Knopf, 1990), attacks Columbus as a committer of genocide. For an overview of these challenges and a reply to them, see McMurtry, "The Winning of the West in Retrospect," *New Republic* (1990). Also responding to these revisionists are William H. Goetzmann in *New Lands, New Men: America in the Second Great Age of Discovery* (New York: Viking, 1986) and *The West of the Imagination* (New York: Norton, 1986); and Robert Athearn, *The Mythic West in Twentieth-Century America* (Lawrence: University Press of Kansas, 1986).

As McMurtry puts it, the major problem with "historical revisionism about the west is its post-ness." None of the information presented by the revisionists is new. True students of the frontier experience, not to mention those involved in it directly, were well aware of the difficult and tragic elements of the frontier; but today that information has an audience willing to draw negative conclusions about the whole enterprise, something it did not have in the past.

In this writer's opinion, the revisionists are also morally wrong. The settlement of the West did change the Western environment and its ecology; but the settled West is at least as pleasant a place as the harsh landscape and climate of the primordial West, and it is equally useful to people as well. Unless we are species self-haters, we can be rather thankful for that pleasantness.

The theory presented in this book may be described as neo-Turnerian. It encompasses all the criticisms, empirical and normative, and still argues that while everything has its price, the frontier challenge is itself the engine of liberty and equality.

10. See Constance McLaughlin Green, *The Rise of Urban America* (New York: Harper and Row, 1965); Charles N. Slaab and A. Theodore Brown, *A History of Urban America* (New York: Macmillan, 1967); Howard P. Chudacoff, *The Evolution of American Urban Society* (Englewood Cliffs, N.J.: Prentice-Hall, 1975); and Arthur M. Schlesinger, *The Rise of the City, 1878–1898* (New York: Macmillan, 1933) and *Prisoners of Progress: American Industrial Cities, 1850–1920* (New York: Macmillan, 1976).

11. For a discussion of urban "boosters," see Daniel J. Boorstein, *The Americans: The National Experience* (New York: Vintage, 1965), pp. 113–168. See also Anselm L. Strauss, *Images of the American City* (Glencoe, Ill.: Free Press, 1962) ; and Christopher Tunnard and Henry H. Reed, *American Skyline* (Boston: Houghton Mifflin, 1955).

12. W. W. Rostow, *The Stages of Economic Growth: A Non-Communist Manifesto* (Cambridge, Mass.: Cambridge University Press, 1960); Brigitte Berger, *The Culture of Entrepreneurship* (San Francisco: ICS Press, 1991).

13. See R. Richard Wohl, "The 'Rags to Riches' Story: An Episode of Secular Idealism," in Reinhard Bendix and Seymour Martin Lipset, eds., *Class, Status and Power,* 2nd ed. (New York: Free Press, 1966), pp. 501–506.

14. The U.S. Census Bureau reports five types of urban concentrations: (1) *Urban* is defined as any incorporated or unincorporated place having 2,500 or more people. (2) An *urbanized area* is defined as a central city and all contiguous territory having population densities of 2,000 per square mile or more. (3) According to the Office of Management and Budget, which established the definition of MSAs, the general concept of a Metropolitan Statistical Area is one of "a large population nucleus, together with adjacent communities which have a high degree of economic and social integration with that nucleus" (*Statistical Abstract of the United States* [U.S. Department of Commerce, 1988]). The current standards, which were adopted in 1980 for what were then called Standard Metropolitan Statistical Areas (as noted, the OMB changed the name from SMSA to MSA in 1983), provide that each MSA must include at least "(a) One city with 50,000 or more inhabitants, or (b) A Census Bureau–defined urbanized area of at least 50,000 inhabitants *and* a total MSA population of at least 100,000 (75,000 in New England)." The MSA must also include as "central counties" the county in which the central city is located and any adjacent counties that have at least 50 percent of their population in the urbanized area. Other "outlying counties" to be included in the MSA must meet specifications regarding requirements for commuting to the central counties as well as standards concerning metropolitan character. Although the SMSA (now MSA) concept was not developed until 1940, if we were to project these criteria backward, we would have found 44 MSAs in 1910, 169 MSAs in 1950, 265 in 1974, and 281 as of 1987. (4) By 1980 standards, metropolitan complexes of 1 million or more people contain separate component areas if specified criteria are met. "Such areas are designated primary metropolitan statistical areas (PMSA's); and any area containing PMSA's is designated a consolidated metropolitan statistical area (CSMA)" (*Statistical Abstract of the United States 1988*). As of 1980 there were 21 CSMAs, most of which were previously known as Standard Consolidated Areas. These areas contain contiguous MSAs that are somewhat interdependent, such as New York–Northeastern New Jersey and Chicago–Northwestern Indiana. (5) Although the term *city* is sometimes used to describe any urban concentration of people, in the United States a city (like a state or the nation itself) is also defined politically. It is a municipal corporation, a body politic created by the state for purposes of local government. Thus, in any metropolitan area there are many cities, each with a separate local government of its own.

15. Daniel J. Elazar, *Building Cities in America* (Lanham, Md.: Hamilton Press, 1987) and "Are We a Nation of Cities?" *The Public Interest,* no. 4 (Summer 1966): 42–58.

16. See Samuel Lubell, *The Future of American Politics* (Garden City, N.Y.: Doubleday Anchor, 1956), p. 65; and Kenneth J. Jackson, *Crabgrass Frontier* (New York and Oxford: Oxford University Press, 1985).

17. See Scott Donaldson, *The Suburban Myth* (New York: Columbia University Press, 1969); Robert Wood, *Suburbia* (Boston: Houghton Mifflin, 1959); John J. Harrigan, *Political Change in the Metropolis*, 3rd ed. (Boston: Little, Brown, 1985); and Jean Gottman, *Megalopolis* (Cambridge, Mass.: MIT Press, 1961).

18. U.S. Department of Agriculture, Resources Inventory Division, *1982 National Resources Inventory* (Washington, D.C.: Government Printing Office, 1984); and Joel Garreau, *Edge Cities: Life on the New Frontier* (New York: Doubleday, 1991).

19. *The Impact of Freeways in Washington State: A Report* (Washington, D.C.: Bureau of Records, 1956).

20. On automobiles and their political/social impact, see Robert E. Passwell, *Problems of the Careless* (New York: Praeger, 1978); David L. Lewis and Lawrence Goldstein, eds., *The Automobile and American Culture* (Ann Arbor: University of Michigan Press, 1983); Garth Mangum, ed., *The Manpower Revolution* (Garden City, N.Y.: Doubleday, 1965); and Daniel J. Elazar, *Cities of the Prairies* (New York: Basic Books, 1970), pp. 41–42.

21. See Mangum, *The Manpower Revolution;* and Kenneth E. Boulding, *The Meaning of the 20th Century* (New York: Harper and Row, 1964).

22. For further discussion of these frontier themes, see Elazar, *Cities of the Prairie.*

23. See Gottman, *Megalopolis.*

24. Just a generation earlier the OMB had changed the definition from Standard Metropolitan Area (SMA) to Standard Metropolitan Statistical Area (SMSA). The history of these definitions is itself a reflection of the metropolitan frontier. The Standard Metropolitan Area was established as a category by the Bureau of the Budget, in 1949, just as the metropolitan frontier was becoming dominant. The term was changed to SMSA in 1959 while that frontier was in its heyday. The criteria for the establishment and definition of SMSAs were modified in 1958, 1971, and 1975—each time, in the direction of deemphasizing the central city and with the recognition that metropolitanization was increasingly becoming a form of noncentralized low-density urbanization. Another modification was made in January 1980, and the term itself was changed in 1983 to Metropolitan Statistical Area. Further revisions of MSA definitions were made in 1984, 1986, and 1987. They were principally designed to add newly qualified MSAs or central cities, always in the direction of less population and less density for each.

25. On the small town, see John Herbers, *The New Heartland* (New York: Times Books, 1986).

26. On the shift of population growth to rural areas, see Herbers, *The New Heartland.* See also "Final Court Will Shift Seats to Far West, Southeast," *Congressional Quarterly* 48, no. 35 (1981): 2793–2794; "Census Data Shows Sharp Rural Losses," *New York Times* (August 30, 1990); and "West Coast, Sun Belt States Show Big Gain in Census," *Wall Street Journal* (August 30, 1990) .

27. Applying the theory presented here, I was able to forecast many of these trends, in "Megalopolis and the New Sectionalism," *The Public Interest* 11 (Spring 1968): 62–85.

CHAPTER 4

Frontiers and Foundings

The theory of the continuing frontier is what is known as a dynamic theory—one that not only takes account of movement and change but also is based on movement and change as permanent realities. It is a theory that emphasizes action and interaction. In American history one of the major interactions was that between frontiers and foundings. As de Tocqueville noted, the manner of founding contributes much to shaping the patterns of later development.[1]

Part of the process of founding involves determination of the generational rhythm of the particular civil society, the way in which it is likely to respond to challenges, and the basic tensions around which it is constructed. I refer here to those great questions that must be reconciled in the process of founding but whose reconciliation is never entirely complete. Indeed, such great questions, which reinforce each other and remain in tension with one another, need to be reconciled anew in each generation.

For example, American civil society was founded on the dual bases of liberty and equality. On the one hand, the two reinforce each other; each makes the other possible. On the other hand, at a certain point they also stand in tension with each other, when the liberty for all individuals to make of themselves what they wish flies in the face of equality and, conversely, when the press for equality limits individual liberty. The tension between the two has been reconciled anew in every generation of American history. If frontiers bring new challenges to a civil society, its foundings strongly influence the character of the responses.

In this chapter we will review the founding of the United States from the first new settlement at Jamestown in 1607 through the War of 1812, often known as the second war of independence, which completed the separation of the United States from its European challengers and completed the founding work of the revolutionary and constitutional periods. We will do so by applying the generational model presented in Chapter 3.

THE SEVENTEENTH CENTURY (1607–1713)

The five generations before 1789 were responsible for the founding of the thirteen original colonies and five other states-to-be, the establishment of civil societies in all of them, the establishment of an American civilization, the forging of a national identity, and the winning of American independence. During the first three generations, the English established their presence in North America and began the process of becoming Americans. At first, the colonies proceeded to develop more or less separately. The fact that their development followed along the same generational patterns, even to the point of adjusting to a common time-span, reflects the universal character of the generational flow. By the beginning of the third generation, a common generational pattern of events was beginning to emerge, although substantial local variations were still evident. The transfer of the generational pattern from England to America and the movement from locally discrete to increasingly continental patterns are the subjects of this chapter.

THE FIRST GENERATION (1607–1648)

The first generation of American history was marked by the founding of Virginia, New York, and Massachusetts, the three "mother" colonies of the original three sections of the United States, the colonies that created the country's three basic cultural patterns. Although Virginia, founded considerably before the others in 1607, reached its years of political response at a time when the other colonies were still in the first stages of founding, by the end of the generation the alignment of events was becoming clear for all three, as shown in Figure 4.1.

Major Political Patterns and Events

Virginia's pattern was indeed the most orthodox, inasmuch as the majority of its founders were young men and women at the beginning of their mature years.[2] From 1607 through 1609, they underwent the trials of the founding and then settled into a nine-year period of generational buildup in the area between the James and York rivers. Here they became entrenched in the land and developed demands for self-government and economic growth. These demands were met during the years of political response from 1619 through 1624, beginning with the establishment of representative institutions and culminating in Virginia's becoming a colony. For the next twenty years, the colony consolidated itself and developed its institutions. Then, in the years immediately following the Indian War of 1644, it completed its generational cycle and turned toward the interior.

New York, or New Netherlands, followed a pattern nearly as straight-forward.[3] Beginning with a fort and trading post in 1613, the colony developed in a desultory fashion during eleven years of generational buildup. It took a giant step forward in 1624 with the purchase of Manhattan Island, the appointment of the first resident governor of stature, and the intensification of colonization activities. The period of political response came to an end in 1629 with the introduction of the patroon system as a means of fostering permanent rural settlement. The colony then entered an eighteen-year period of settlement and consolidation along the Hudson River from Staten Island to Albany, culminating in the appointment of Peter Stuyvesant as governor in 1647 and the introduction of an expansionist policy.

Massachusetts had something of a dual founding.[4] The Plymouth colony established in 1620 followed the usual pattern of settlement but its influence was limited, and it remained for the Massachusetts Bay colony of 1629 to found Massachusetts. The latter colony was founded at mid-generation by men in mid-career. The founding was itself a decisive political response to the struggles of the Puritans in England and, hence, did not follow the orthodox generational pattern. Its leaders had generally been leaders of the Puritan movement in the old country who had come to despair of real success there and decided to build a new "city upon a hill" in the New World.

Because the colony itself was a decisive political response, it embarked immediately on a series of activities appropriate to that period within the generational cycle, establishing institutions and even daughter colonies (Connecticut, Rhode Island, and New Hampshire) that reflected different versions of the new society the Puritans hoped to build. The decade from the founding in 1629 to the adoption of the Fundamental Orders of Connecticut in 1639 was one of decisive political response.[5] It was followed by nine years of stabilization and consolidation, culminating in the New England colonies' response to the English Civil War. This, in turn, led to a number of constitutional actions to ratify and institutionalize the gains of the Puritans' first generation in the New World, ultimately bringing their pattern into harmony with the overall generational movement.

Government and the Economy

The relationship between government and the economy was essentially the same in all three colonies.[6] The notion of separation between the governing authorities and the economy did not exist in the contemporary sense. All three colonies were established under the aegis of trading companies, which were government monopolies; these, in turn, were responsible for governing the settlers. At first, it was assumed that the colonists would not pursue individual goals but would work collectively for their

106

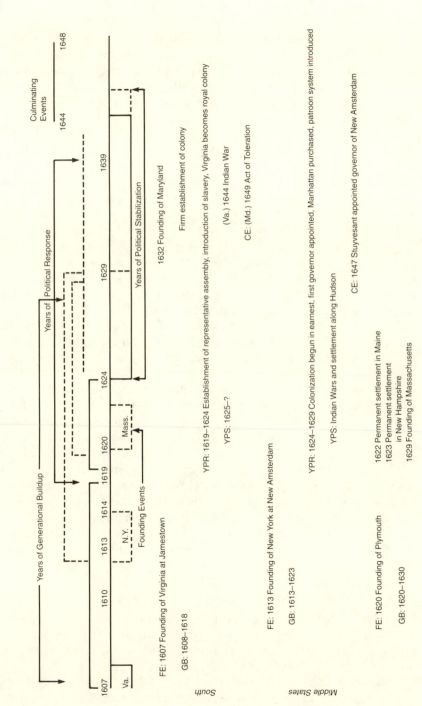

Years of Generational Buildup

Years of Political Response

Culminating Events

1607 1610 1613 1614 1619 1620 1624 1629 1639 1644 1648

Va.

N.Y.

Mass.

Founding Events

Years of Political Stabilization

South

FE: 1607 Founding of Virginia at Jamestown

GB: 1608–1618

YPR: 1619–1624 Establishment of representative assembly, introduction of slavery, Virginia becomes royal colony

YPS: 1625–?

(Va.) 1644 Indian War

1632 Founding of Maryland

Firm establishment of colony

CE: (Md.) 1649 Act of Toleration

Middle States

FE: 1613 Founding of New York at New Amsterdam

GB: 1613–1623

YPR: 1624–1629 Colonization begun in earnest, first governor appointed, Manhattan purchased, patroon system introduced

YPS: Indian Wars and settlement along Hudson

CE: 1647 Stuyvesant appointed governor of New Amsterdam

FE: 1620 Founding of Plymouth

GB: 1620–1630

1622 Permanent settlement in Maine
1623 Permanent settlement in New Hampshire
1629 Founding of Massachusetts

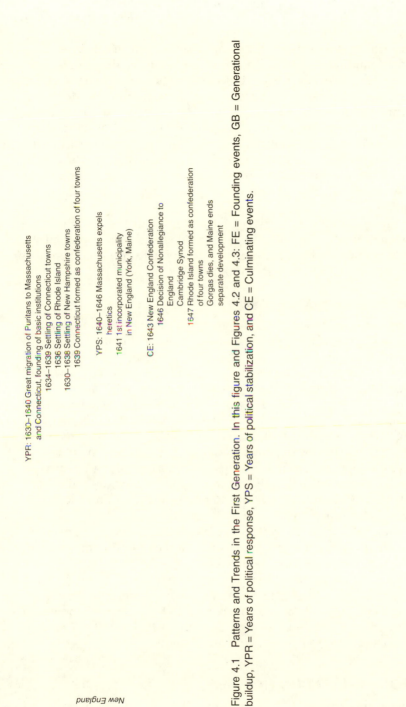

New England

YPR: 1630–1640 Great migration of Puritans to Massachusetts
and Connecticut, founding of basic institutions
1634–1639 Settling of Connecticut towns
1636 Settling of Rhode Island
1630–1638 Settling of New Hampshire towns
1639 Connecticut formed as confederation of four towns

YPS: 1640–1646 Massachusetts expels
heretics
1641 1st incorporated municipality
in New England (York, Maine)

CE: 1643 New England Confederation
1646 Decision of Nonallegiance to
England
Cambridge Synod
1647 Rhode Island formed as confederation
of four towns
Gorgas dies, and Maine ends
separate development

Figure 4.1   Patterns and Trends in the First Generation. In this figure and Figures 4.2 and 4.3: FE = Founding events, GB = Generational buildup, YPR = Years of political response, YPS = Years of political stabilization, and CE = Culminating events.

respective companies. This collective approach failed in all three cases during the founding period and was replaced during the generational buildup by progressively greater individualization of economic effort, though still under the relatively rigid control of the authorities. Moreover, a significant aspect of the years of political response was the struggle between the colonists and the mother company for the right of self-government. This right was substantially won in Virginia and Massachusetts during the first generation (Rhode Island and Connecticut, as offshoots of Massachusetts not beholden to a trading company, simply claimed it as their own). New York did not win that right until the British conquest a generation later.

When the governing powers were transferred to the colonists, the power of control over the economy was divided such that the domestic economy was controlled locally whereas the imperial authorities assumed control over foreign and intra-imperial trade.

Principal Ethnoreligious Manifestations

Ethnoreligious homogeneity was the goal of all three colonial establishments in the first generation, and in all three it was maintained with great difficulty from the beginning.[7] All three had established churches and found it necessary to combat dissenters. Virginia was Anglican, New York was Dutch Reformed, and Massachusetts was Puritan (what later came to be known as Congregational). Nonconformists were expelled from the colonies whenever possible. At the very least, they were forced or encouraged to go out into the wilderness to establish their own settlements in which theirs would be the reigning orthodoxy. This was territorial democracy of the old kind, in which territories stood for something but anyone could go out and establish his own territorial community. Catholic Maryland, heterodox Connecticut, tolerant Rhode Island, and Protestant pluralist New Hampshire were all cases in point.[8]

In this first generation the settlers in the various colonies were of either English or Dutch stock. Only scattered individuals from other ethnic or national groups could be found, and they generally assimilated or left. The introduction of African-Americans was the beginning of significant ethnoracial pluralism in North America.[9] Native Americans, however, were looked upon not only as separate nations but as potentially powerful antagonists, since throughout the first generations their numbers were no less than those of the settlers, if not greater.[10]

THE SECOND GENERATION (1648–1676)

Just as the events of the first generation revolved around foundings and were concluded by constitutional actions designed to institutionalize the progress made, the second generation was concerned with nativizing the colonies and transferring control over their domestic institutions from the Old World to the New (see Figure 4.2). The impetus to do so stemmed in part from the simple fact that a native-born generation had begun to reach maturity, in part because the English Civil War had eliminated or reduced the mother country's role in colonial affairs for the first half of the generation, and in part because the restoration of the throne in England was followed by the consolidation of English authority along the Atlantic coast between Canada and Florida.

Major Political Patterns and Events

Given the equivocal position of Maryland as a border colony of Catholics exposed to Puritan and Cavalier influences even in the seventeenth century, the South continued to consist essentially of Virginia.[11] Virginians began to filter into what was to become North Carolina in the 1650s, at the beginning of the generation, and they were there in sufficient numbers to mount a rebellion against the Navigation Acts (Culpepper's Rebellion) that coincided with Bacon's Rebellion to close that generation. But it was not until the next generation that North Carolina required identity as an entity in its own right.

Virginia itself became virtually independent in the wake of the Civil War. Its leadership, consisting primarily of freeholders and merchants, refused to acknowledge the authority of the Commonwealth and the colony became a dominion, managing its own affairs until the Restoration in mid-generation (1660). Overall, this generation was dominated by the relations between autocratic Governor William Berkeley, whose two terms (1641–1652, 1660–1677) virtually encompassed it, and the new native generation of Virginians who ultimately secured his removal in their struggle for self-rule.

The major political responses of the generation in Virginia revolved around the restoration of English authority through Berkeley and the Navigation Acts (which crippled the local economy) and the institutionalization of slavery, which, through a series of acts in the 1660s, was made the permanent and irrevocable condition of all African-Americans in the dominion. The generation culminated in Bacon's Rebellion, the first major American challenge of British authority. Provoked by the impact of the Navigation Acts, Berkeley's autocratic rule, and Indian Wars encouraged by the governor to prevent the expansion of the settlement, this response marked a fitting completion to the task of the generation—namely, the defining of separate American (or, more properly, Virginian) interests in contradistinction to English ones.

New Netherlands–New York continued to be the sum of the Middle States in the second generation, just as Virginia continued to be the sum of

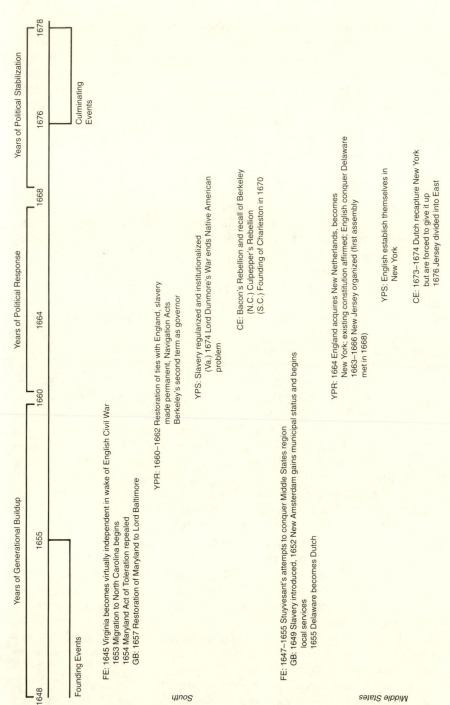

Years of Generational Buildup | Years of Political Response | Years of Political Stabilization

1648 — 1655 — 1660 — 1664 — 1668 — 1676 — 1678

Founding Events

Culminating Events

South

FE: 1645 Virginia becomes virtually independent in wake of English Civil War
1653 Migration to North Carolina begins
1654 Maryland Act of Toleration repealed
GB: 1657 Restoration of Maryland to Lord Baltimore

YPR: 1660–1662 Restoration of ties with England, slavery made permanent, Navigation Acts
Berkeley's second term as governor

YPS: Slavery regularized and institutionalized
(Va.) 1674 Lord Dunmore's War ends Native American problem

CE: Bacon's Rebellion and recall of Berkeley
(N.C.) Culpepper's Rebellion
(S.C.) Founding of Charleston in 1670

Middle States

FE: 1647–1655 Stuyvesant's attempts to conquer Middle States region
GB: 1649 Slavery introduced, 1652 New Amsterdam gains municipal status and begins local services
1655 Delaware becomes Dutch

YPR: 1664 England acquires New Netherlands, becomes New York; existing constitution affirmed; English conquer Delaware
1663–1666 New Jersey organized (first assembly met in 1668)

YPS: English establish themselves in New York

CE: 1673–1674 Dutch recapture New York but are forced to give it up
1676 Jersey divided into East

New England

and West Jersey
1675 1st American-based business corporation chartered
1673 English legal system introduced in Delaware

FE: 1651–1653 United Colonies of New England; 1652 Massachusetts annexes Maine, mint established in Boston

GB: 1652–1661 Massachusetts attempts to enforce religious orthodoxy and fails

YPR: 1662 Half-way Covenant, end of open persecution of heretics
1661 Quakers organize in Rhode Island
1662 Connecticut secures charter from Crown recognizing its independence
1665 New England Commission established, New Haven joins Connecticut

YPS:

CE: 1675–1678 King Phillip's War
1673 Massachusetts elects 1st native governor
1677 Massachusetts legalizes its acquisition of Maine

Figure 4.2   Patterns and Trends in the Second Generation

the South. In fact, the first part of the generation (which effectively commenced when Peter Stuyvesant became governor and infused new energy into the colony) was devoted to Dutch efforts to use New Netherlands as a base from which to literally conquer the entire region. Between 1647 and 1655, the Dutch established their hegemony from Delaware to upper New York State, threatening even southern New England. As a result, the entire generation was taken up with the struggle between the Dutch and the English for regional control (1647–1674). In 1664, the tide turned against the Dutch, who lost New Amsterdam and the Hudson Valley as well as the peripheral areas of their domain. New Amsterdam was briefly reconquered in 1673 but returned to English control in 1674, permanently ending the Dutch threat to conclude a generation of conflict.

Internally, the period of generational buildup saw New Amsterdam acquire municipal status and introduce the first rudimentary municipal services. Meanwhile, the political response revolved around the English conquest and confirmation of the established constitutional arrangements. The major change brought about by the English was to legitimize the ethnic and religious pluralism of the colony—particularly that of New York City, which had already begun to develop under the reluctant Dutch. New York became a colony devoted to business and open to virtually all who were interested in pursuing the goals of commerce. Fittingly enough, the generation closed with the chartering of the first entirely American business corporation in 1675.

The peripheral regions of Stuyvesant's greater New Netherlands were given their own identity by the English in a second generation. New Jersey, a kind of no-man's-land for the first half of the generation, was anglicized between 1663 and 1666.[12] Representative government was introduced in 1668; and then, to conclude the generation, the territory was divided into East and West Jersey in 1676. Delaware, conquered in 1664, remained in political limbo until 1673, when the English legal system was introduced there and life was normalized within the context of an English colony.[13]

New England was the only region that had spawned several colonies during the founding generation. Of the six states of contemporary New England, only Vermont was without any settlement in 1640. Ideological differences within the overall framework of Puritan theology and the use of the federal principles that formed the organizational basis of all Puritan settlements both functioned to encourage a proliferation of towns and the federation of like-minded towns into colonies. In fact, by the end of the first generation, several of the independent towns and colonies had begun to experiment with regional or intercolonial confederation.[14]

The period of intracolonial constitutional activity that marked the closing of the first generation also marked the opening of the second. This activity was followed by a period of generational buildup that saw the introduction of further federal experiments on the regional plane. These, in turn, led not only to the United Colonies of New England, which functioned on and off during the generation, but also to further efforts to shape the internal structure of the individual colonies themselves. Massachusetts clarified its hegemony over New Hampshire (which would not become an independent colony until the next generation) and annexed Maine in 1652. (The latter act was legalized in 1677 at the very end of the generation, when the colony formally bought the rights of the heirs of Sir Ferdinand Gorges, the founder of Maine's settlement.)[15] This process continued during the years of political response, when Connecticut obtained a royal charter affirming its autonomy and added New Haven to round out its territory.

The New England colonies were highly sympathetic toward the Puritan victors in the English Civil War. At the same time, they welcomed the opportunity provided by the Commonwealth to assert their political equality with England and consequently became virtually independent between 1646 and 1660, at best with the acquiescence of the new power in England. It was during these years that the authorities in Massachusetts, beset by the arrival or emergence of various kinds of Puritan sectarians (particularly Baptists and Quakers), made their strongest efforts to enforce religious orthodoxy within the colony. Their failure was clinched when Charles II reestablished himself in the mother country, actively asserted his authority over the colonies, and decreed the end of persecution of heretics.

The struggle over orthodoxy during the period of generational buildup was a reflection of the great challenge of the second generation in New England. As the "saints" who pioneered the holy Commonwealth during the first generation died or removed themselves from the active life of the community, their children grew up with a less intense religious commitment or, at least, with different religious ideas. Strictly speaking, this made them ineligible for admission into the covenant that could make them citizens. They were thus relegated, with the real heretics, to the peripheries of Puritan society.

Once the Puritan leadership discovered that it could not suppress heresy or stimulate the same level of religious inspiration among the sons as among the fathers, they had to find a new way to bring people of goodwill into the community as citizens. This was the task of the period of generational buildup. It was accomplished in 1662 by the introduction of the Half-way Covenant, the great political response of the second generation that provided citizenship in the political community for those otherwise qualified who were unable to become full-fledged Puritan "saints."[16]

In the years of political stability that persisted from the mid-1660s to the outbreak of King Philip's War in 1676, the New England colonies expanded their settlements, accommodated their religious differences, developed their confederacy, and attempted to work out viable relations with royalist—and hence hostile—England. Those years came to an end with the outbreak of the King Philip's War, which introduced a new generation and a new set of problems on all fronts.

Government and the Economy

The principal characteristic of the second generation was the growth of commerce as a factor in the colonial economies and increased influence of the commercial classes in political matters. Even agriculture began to take on a commercial cast, with increased production for export as well as for subsistence. In Virginia, commercial agriculture—particularly tobacco culture—led to plantations that would have a permanent impact in the next generation. In New York, agriculture was hardly a factor, as commerce remained central to the colony's existence. And in New England, the growth of freehold agriculture and growing commercial interests went hand in hand.

Government regulation of internal and external economic activities remained pronounced. Government monopolies as well as price controls continued to be common. In short, mercantilism under the aegis of the mother country was further institutionalized.

Principal Ethnoreligious Manifestations

The difficulties of maintaining orthodoxy were compounded in the second generation by the continued influx of nonconformists, sectarians, and peoples of varying ethnic and religious backgrounds throughout the colonies. Not only Protestants of every shade but also Catholics came. And at least two colonies had small Jewish communities by the end of the generation. Grudging accommodation was the order of the day, a situation further complicated by the interest of the English Crown in promoting relative toleration for commercial reasons.[17]

Immigrants of English stock still predominated, but Dutch, Swedes, and Scots began to appear and African-Americans continued to be imported. The second generation witnessed an increase in conflict as the settlers became more confidently aggressive and the Native Americans began to see that there was no place for their way of life in the new societies that were emerging. The culminating events of that generation were major Indian Wars from north to south in which the colonists won decisive victories that ended any serious threats to the future of their colonies.

THE THIRD GENERATION (1677–1713)

Major Political Patterns and Events

The third generation, which closed out the seventeenth century, was marked by the emergence of new colonies in all three sections, thus virtually completing the English settlement of the Eastern seaboard.[18] At the end of the second generation, it was only in New England that the settlers had broken out of scattered coastal bridgeheads; but by the end of the third generation, all the other colonies, except Georgia—which had not yet been founded—had settled inland from the coast. Moreover, whereas only New England had cross-colony interests at the outset of the third generation, by mid-generation such interests had been extended to embrace New York and New Jersey as well; and by the end of the generation, Queen Anne's War was well-nigh universal in its impact to become the first "continental" issue to confront the colonies. (See Figure 4.3.)

Several other phenomena new to the third generation had continental implications. The Huguenot migration after 1685 had an impact on all three sections.[19] The "Glorious Revolution" of 1688 had continental repercussions and, indeed, triggered the generation's years of political response. In the North, Governor Edmund Andros was deposed and local self-government was restored. In the South, the aftermath of the deposing of the Stuarts led to constitutional changes in Virginia, Maryland, and the Carolinas. King William's War, which began in 1689 and continued until 1697, was the first of the French and Indian Wars, which involved the entire continent to a greater or lesser degree.

Last, but hardly least, efforts were made throughout the entire generation to impose Anglicanism as the established church from Maine to South Carolina. Wherever these efforts came up against other established patterns of church-state relations, they were soundly rejected—sometimes only after serious conflict and, in the case of North Carolina, open rebellion. At the same time, the Anglican Church was successful in establishing toeholds in colonies where it had previously been excluded. The struggle over Anglican establishment in New England hastened the end of Puritan dominance in that section.

Slavery as a permanent condition and a significant institution was firmly established during the third generation. The Southern colonies, excepting only North Carolina, settled the issue of the permanent bondage of African-Americans, slavery spread in the Middle Colonies, and New England entered the slave trade.[20] In the meantime, non-English immigration (Welsh, Scots, Huguenots, and Germans) expanded in all sections of the country in the last half of the generation.

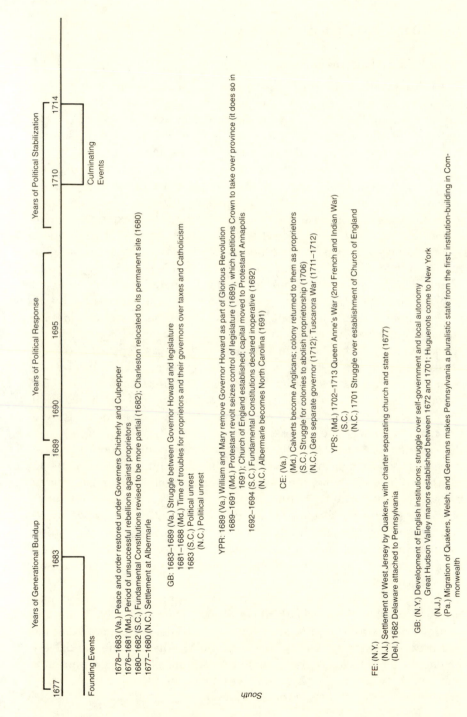

Middle States

YPR: (N.Y.) 1689 Leister's Rebellion fails but secures representative government for New York City; professional municipal services introduced in New York City
(N.J.) 1688 Jerseys temporarily joined to New England
(Pa.) 1701 Charter of Privileges, Pennsylvania's final constitution
(Del.)

YPS: (N.Y.)
(N.J.) 1702 New Jersey reunited under governor of New York
(Pa.) Presbyterians and Baptists add to Pennsylvania pluralism
(Del.)

CE: (N.Y.)
(N.J.)
(Pa.) 1718 Founding era ends with termination of Pennsylvania
(Del.)

New England

FE: 1675–1676 King Philip's War
1680 New Hampshire made separate colony by royal order

GB: 1680–1689 Struggle between local authorities and Governor Andros over local political and religious autonomy

YPR: 1691 Union of Plymouth and Massachusetts; toleration extended to all except "Papists"
1692–1697 Salem witch trials and aftermath
1696 New England enters slave trade
1699 Massachusetts governor also appointed governor of New Hampshire

YPS: Completion of classic Puritan theological movement;
fight between centralizers and noncentralizers in the church; beginning
of spread of Anglicanism

CE: 1701–1713 Queen Anne's War
1709 Beginning of significant migration of
non-English-speaking people to New England

Figure 4.3 Patterns and Trends in the Third Generation

The third generation marked the beginning of the French and Indian Wars. These global conflicts had special implications for North America and were to persist intermittently for two generations. King William's War lasted from 1689 to 1697, through the years of political response; and Queen Anne's War picked up the years of political stabilization from 1701 to 1713. The Treaty of Utrecht, which concluded the latter conflict, also brought the seventeenth century to an end in both Europe and America.[21]

Government and the Economy

The completion of English occupation of the Atlantic seaboard tightened the imperial control over colonial trade in the mercantilist manner. In the South, plantation owners increased their political power at the expense of merchants and freeholders—a reflection of shifts in the internal economies of the Southern colonies. Commerce continued to be the central consideration in the Middle Colonies and became increasingly important in New England as well.

Principal Ethnoreligious Manifestations

This was the last generation of Puritan political dominance in New England. It was marked by strong official efforts to foster Anglicanism, struggles within the Puritan fold between those who favored presbyterian organization and unreconstructed congregationalists, and the witch trials. Both Puritan theology and Puritan "blue laws" flowered in the struggle against non-Puritan elements. All of these factors reflected a generation of religious crisis during which traditional faith and the powers of the leaders of the faithful were undermined.

In the Middle Colonies, religious pluralism was established once and for all. It was even made the formal cornerstone of Pennsylvania, Delaware, and the Jerseys, but was no less true of New York as well. Indeed, religion was banished from world affairs in those colonies and made a private matter, while political economics became thoroughly secularized in spirit as well as practice.

In the South, old orthodoxies persisted more easily because they were less demanding. The beginnings of Huguenot and Scotch-Irish settlement in the southern and western areas of those colonies led to the introduction of Calvinism on a very limited scale, though in territories relatively distant from the established centers of Anglicanism.

Relations with Native Americans in the third generation became entangled with international politics as the great Indian nations aligned themselves with the English and the French in the struggle for control of North America that was to dominate two generations. The Native Americans who were allied with the French became very aggressive under stimulus from the allies, transforming a conflict that had involved periodic wars with relatively peaceful intervals into a virtually continuous scenario of raid and counter-raid that greatly heightened hostilities between the two peoples.

THE EIGHTEENTH CENTURY (1714–1815)

The three generations that constitute the eighteenth century—the fourth, fifth, and sixth in American history—had as their central task the founding of the American nation. At the beginning of the century, the Americans-to-be were still psychologically as well as politically divided by colonial boundaries. Only one man, an anonymous Virginian, is known to have publicly suggested federation of British North America, and his book remained in obscurity.[22] Although the colonists had already begun to share common problems and experiences, they were generally unaware that they did so. By the end of the century, the young American republic was clearly established under its own federal constitution, had expanded its territory two-thirds of the way across the continent, had waged two wars with Britain to gain and maintain its independence, and was being viewed by the wiser heads of Europe as a world power in the making.

THE FOURTH GENERATION (1714–1754)

Major Political Patterns and Events

The Treaty of Utrecht represented a great gain for Great Britain, ratifying as it did the improved geopolitical status of Britain that had resulted from a generation of conflict; but it left the boundaries among the French, Spanish, and British possessions undefined and thereby sowed the seeds for future conflict on the basis of local issues. Among the formative events was the Yamasee War between the South Carolina and Florida Indians, which opened the door for the settlement of Georgia during the years of generational response.[23] This was just one of a series of localized Indian Wars that took place on the peripheries of colonial settlement throughout the generation (see Figure 4.4).

In general, however, this first generation of the eighteenth century was devoted to the quiet advance of the colonists. It was during this generation that settlement advanced from the coastal areas inland as far as the mountains, such that, by the end of the generation, the first crossings of the Appalachians were inaugurating a whole new era of westward expansion.[24] Population increased fourfold in this generation, from less than 360,000 to nearly a million and a half. Cities developed that rivaled those

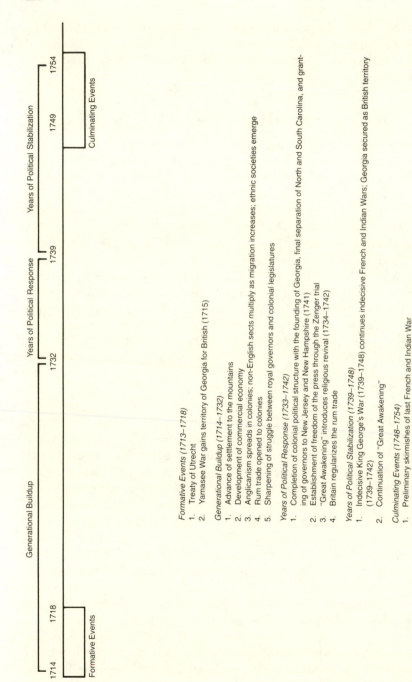

Generational Buildup

Years of Political Response   Years of Political Stabilization

| 1714 | 1718 | | 1732 | 1739 | | 1749 | 1754 |

Formative Events

Culminating Events

Formative Events (1713–1718)
1. Treaty of Utrecht
2. Yamasee War gains territory of Georgia for British (1715)

Generational Buildup (1714–1732)
1. Advance of settlement to the mountains
2. Development of commercial economy
3. Anglicanism spreads in colonies; non-English sects multiply as migration increases; ethnic societies emerge
4. Rum trade opened to colonies
5. Sharpening of struggle between royal governors and colonial legislatures

Years of Political Response (1733–1742)
1. Completion of colonial political structure with the founding of Georgia, final separation of North and South Carolina, and granting of governors to New Jersey and New Hampshire (1741)
2. Establishment of freedom of the press through the Zenger trial
3. "Great Awakening" introduces religious revival (1734–1742)
4. Britain regularizes the rum trade

Years of Political Stabilization (1739–1748)
1. Indecisive King George's War (1739–1748) continues indecisive French and Indian Wars; Georgia secured as British territory
   (1739–1742)
2. Continuation of "Great Awakening"

Culminating Events (1748–1754)
1. Preliminary skirmishes of last French and Indian War
2. Albany "Plan of Union"
3. Beginning of exploration and settlement of the trans-Allegheny west

Figure 4.4   Patterns and Trends in the Fourth Generation

in England in both size and sophistication, and an urban culture was established. America became an important factor in international trade, primarily as an exporter of agricultural products.[25]

The period of generational buildup was given over to these developments. Philadelphia flowered as the country's major city in what may well be called the "Age of Franklin," pioneering modern urban living in a host of ways. Boston ceased to be a town in all but name and form of government. New York expanded its position as the commercial entrepot *par excellence*. Baltimore was founded to handle the milling and export of flour from the new hinterlands between the Potomac and the Susquehanna. Richmond emerged as the first city of Virginia. Charleston developed a distinctive urban culture as the queen city of the deep South.

During the years of generational response, the Scotch-Irish and the Germans settled the Piedmont frontier and the great valleys that led southward from Pennsylvania to the Carolinas. At the same time, the Yankees began their last wave of town-building in southern New England and sent fingers of settlement into all sections of northern New England. Georgia was founded and fought a war with Spanish Florida to ensure the English colonists' survival. The Scots in particular represented a new element. Consisting mostly of people who had resisted the union of parliaments that eliminated Scotland's autonomous governmental structure (in 1707, one of the culminating events of the century in Britain), they were implacably hostile to English rule anywhere.

At the same time, the English were attempting to consolidate their rule in the colonies, converting proprietary colonies into royal ones, strengthening the hands of the royal governors, and generally trying to introduce more aristocratic elements into the colonial governments. The colonial legislatures fought back, strengthening themselves in the process, and the colonial courts began to write colonial ideas of liberty into the law over the opposition of the governors, as in the Zenger case.[26]

After nearly three decades of peaceful consolidation, the generation was brought to an end by nine years of intermittent warfare (King George's War) that further consolidated the borders of British America and set the stage for the final assault on French Canada. For the first time, the Americans themselves bore the brunt of the fighting outside their boundaries and proved themselves successful in the North and South wherever they were led by their own commanders.

At the generation's end, young George Washington was setting off for the Ohio River frontier and Benjamin Franklin was proposing his Plan of Union at the first general congress of colonial representatives convened in Albany. Although neither effort was successful, both marked turning points in the developing American nation.

Government and the Economy

The British relaxed their mercantilist policies in the fourth generation to allow the Americans a wider ambit for trading, though under close imperial regulation. The rum trade was opened to the colonies, and the American traders extended themselves in many directions in the north and south Atlantic. In general, the growing productive capacity of American agriculture, the expansion of the new commercial cities in the colonies, and the introduction of more sophisticated machinery for processing local natural resources made British America a more important and increasingly more equal trading partner.[27]

A wealthy American merchant class began to develop, with all the accoutrements one might expect of such a class in the eighteenth century—from "respectable" religion (Anglicanism) to fancy dress balls. At least in some quarters, the new colonial merchants began to develop rivalries with their British counterparts and expressed dissatisfaction with the limitations of imperial mercantilist policies, even relaxed ones.

Principal Ethnoreligious Manifestations

The great population increase of this generation was the result of heavy migrations from Scotland, Ulster, Ireland proper, and the Germanys. Although 60 percent of the population remained of English stock, the fact that 40 percent was non-English by the end of the generation was of great significance for America's future—not the least reason being that many of those who came were not merely uninterested in English rule but actively opposed to it. Most of the new immigrants settled on the frontier, but a significant number rose to prominence in the cities as well, by exploiting the commercial adjunct of the land frontier.[28]

Religiously speaking, the great event of the generation was the "Great Awakening," the first intersectional (if not countrywide) revival that dominated the years of political response.[29] Although the character and impact of the "Great Awakening" are matters of some dispute, it is generally acknowledged to have brought America another step down the road away from the law-centered Puritanism of the seventeenth century and toward the more individualistic and antinomian Protestantism that was to become quintessentially American.

THE FIFTH GENERATION (1754–1789)

Major Political Patterns and Events

The fifth generation was responsible for the founding of the United States.[30] The formative events and generational buildup of that generation revolved around the last of the French and Indian Wars and the elimination of the French as a North American power (see Figure 4.5). The war itself began on the frontier in 1754, though officially not until 1756. Between those two years, the colonists were once again made painfully aware that the burden of frontier defense against Native Americans would be theirs unless and until British imperial interests were more involved. Not only were they unable to depend upon the mother country to protect their interests on the frontier, but there were conflicts of interest between them. The colonists also learned how vulnerable the British could be through their experience with Braddock, while at the same time discovering the special military capabilities they had derived from their frontier experiences. Finally, for the first time, the colonists and the imperial power were formally asked to consider a plan of national federation: namely, Benjamin Franklin's Albany Plan of Union, proposed in 1754 on the eve of the war as a defense measure.[31]

By 1713, the French had been eliminated and the disposition of the continent east of the Mississippi became a matter of contention between the Americans and the British imperial authorities. The issue was heightened when, during the culminating events of the previous generation, the Americans broke the Appalachian barrier: Settlers began to move west of the mountains as soon as the war was over, only to find their way blocked by the British, who decided to keep the West wild for the fur trade. Thus the question of Western settlement became a key point of confrontation during the generational buildup.

The aftermath of the last French and Indian War also brought with it a controversy over who was to pay for the conflict and a struggle over colonial taxation that became the proximate cause of the break with England. The series of parliamentary tax measures added almost yearly increments to the tension between the colonists and the mother country, beginning with the Sugar and Currency Acts of 1764 (the latter struck at the established power of the colonies to issue paper money); continuing with the Stamp Act of 1765, the Townshend Acts of 1767, and the tea tax of 1770; and culminating in the Tea Act of 1773.

The main thrust of the generational buildup, in the direction of American independence, combined the multiplication of controversies with Britain, the spreading sense of American nationalism, and the emergence of an intercolonial political structure to mobilize the public and to represent its common interests. The two major prerevolutionary nationwide "expressions of public will" were the Stamp Act Congress in 1765 and the first Continental Congress of 1774, both of which genuinely anticipated the role played by critical presidential elections after independence. The Stamp Act Congress was essentially loyalist in its composition, but it gave the independence party a chance to organize on an intercolonial basis. By

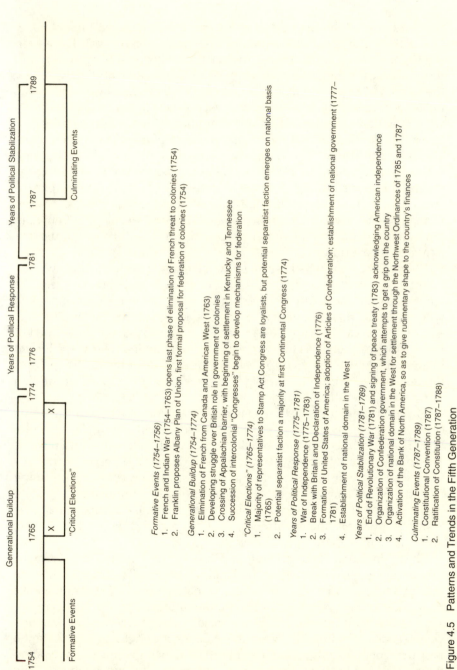

Figure 4.5 Patterns and Trends in the Fifth Generation

Formative Events

Generational Buildup

"Critical Elections"

Years of Political Response

Years of Political Stabilization

Culminating Events

1754   1765   1774   1776   1781   1787   1789

Formative Events (1754–1756)
1. French and Indian War (1754–1763) opens last phase of elimination of French threat to colonies (1754)
2. Franklin proposes Albany Plan of Union, first formal proposal for federation of colonies (1754)

Generational Buildup (1754–1774)
1. Elimination of French from Canada and American West (1763)
2. Developing struggle over British role in government of colonies
3. Crossing of Appalachian barrier, with beginning of settlement in Kentucky and Tennessee
4. Succession of intercolonial "Congresses" begin to develop mechanisms for federation

"Critical Elections" (1765–1774)
1. Majority of representatives to Stamp Act Congress are loyalists, but potential separatist faction emerges on national basis (1765)
2. Potential separatist faction a majority at first Continental Congress (1774)

Years of Political Response (1775–1781)
1. War of Independence (1775–1783)
2. Break with Britain and Declaration of Independence (1776)
3. Formation of United States of America; adoption of Articles of Confederation; establishment of national government (1777–1781)
4. Establishment of national domain in the West

Years of Political Stabilization (1781–1789)
1. End of Revolutionary War (1781) and signing of peace treaty (1783) acknowledging American independence
2. Organization of Confederation government, which attempts to get a grip on the country
3. Organization of national domain in the West for settlement through the Northwest Ordinances of 1785 and 1787
4. Activation of the Bank of North America, so as to give rudimentary shape to the country's finances

Culminating Events (1787–1789)
1. Constitutional Convention (1787)
2. Ratification of Constitution (1787–1788)

the first Continental Congress, even though it, too, took a generally loyalist stance, those who would vote for independence two years later were already dominant.

The second Continental Congress initiated the years of political response (1775–1781), of which the central events were the War and Declaration of Independence and the adoption of the Articles of Confederation, the constitution that formalized the existence of the United States as a "perpetual union." The decisive actions taken during that period need hardly be mentioned. The Continental Congress created an independent nation, gave it a constitution and a government, established an army and navy, created a monetary and banking system (the first bank in North America), gave it the accoutrements of statehood, and ensured that the Western lands would be a common national resource, all the while waging a war of independence. In a very real sense, this first intensive period of national political response to the challenges of the generation was paradigmatic of those that were to follow.

After the years of political response came those from 1781 to 1789, which, despite their reputation as years of upheaval, were actually characterized by political stabilization as the country got on its feet and began to organize itself as an independent nation. The newly ratified Articles of Confederation were made operative and legislation effectuating the actions of the Continental Congress was enacted, particularly in regard to the Western lands (under the terms of the Northwest Ordinance of 1785 and 1787). A favorable peace treaty with Great Britain "wrapped up" the War of Independence, and the last of the unreconstructed loyalists left the country with considerable local encouragement.[32]

The culminating events of the generation were fully in line with the post-1781 trends. The constitutional convention of 1787 did not create a new union but, rather, in its own words, established a "more perfect" one, ending the generation that struggled for independence and opening the doors to the future for the new nation under a more durable form of government.[33]

Government and the Economy

The political revolution of the fifth generation was accompanied by an economic revolution. The colonialist economic policies of the British were serious factors in provoking the independence movement, and greater opportunity for international trade was a major American war aim. As soon as conditions permitted, Americans began developing their international trading capabilities. Internally, many of the most powerful economic figures in the country remained loyalists and, as a consequence, lost their positions and even their wealth. What followed was a redistribution of power—both political and economic—as a result of the war. The degree to which this was so varied from state to state: The fewest changes occurred in the South, where much of the planter class sided with the revolutionaries. And the greatest changes occurred in the Middle States, where many of the great merchants were Tories through and through and were attacked as such. Finally, the triumph of the Americans raised questions regarding intercolonial commerce that led directly to the constitutional convention and the creation of what may anachronistically be called the American "common market."[34]

Principal Ethnoreligious Manifestations

Revolutionary changes in the patterns of church-state relations accompanied the independence struggle. Most states disestablished their churches during the course of the generation, establishing governments that, although they had pledged to support "religion and morality," were forbidden to support particular denominations. Equal rights of citizenship were extended to non-Protestants and non-Christians throughout most of the new republic.[35]

The war itself reflected the impact of the growing ethnic diversity that was a particular feature of the eighteenth century. Scots, for example, played an important role in the conflict, displaying their strong anti-English feelings. Quakers and the German sectarians, on the other hand, were generally loyalists because of their general anti-war posture, if not their prosperity under British rule. The war itself attracted military figures from various parts of Europe to give the revolutionary army a certain cosmopolitan veneer that would likely be transformed into a part of the American tradition whereby every ethnic group to settle in the country could find its special Revolutionary War hero.

The revolution was also a partial revolution for African-Americans. Slavery was abolished in the North under the impetus of the drive for equality and liberty and might have disappeared even in the South had it not been for the invention of the cotton gin and the opening of the Western lands. This partial victory was written into the Constitution, providing a date for stopping the importation of slaves, as part of the achievement of the revolutionary generation.[36]

Most of the Native Americans sided with the British during the revolution, recognizing that the Americans were now their implacable foes. The British, in turn, used the Native Americans for raiding on the frontier, much like the French had done a generation earlier. As a result, many Americans adopted an implacably hostile attitude toward all Indians—an attitude that was rapidly incorporated into the national policy of the young republic.

THE SIXTH GENERATION (1789–1815)

The major concern of this first generation under the Constitution was the establishment of the political institutions and character of the new federal republic. This concern was accompanied by more or less successful efforts to expand the nation's borders and ensure its independence from both Great Britain and European wars in general. By the end of the generation, the outlines of such institutions as the presidency, Congress, and judiciary were coming clear; the nature of the federal-state relationship was well on its way to definition; party politics had successfully taken root; and the continental expansion of the United States was more or less assured.

Major Political Events and Patterns

The sixth generation began with the adoption of the Constitution in 1789 and its initial implementation by President Washington and the First Congress during the next three years.[37] These were founding events that not only gave that generation its direction but shaped the subsequent framework of political life in the republic (see Figure 4.6).

By the time of the writing of the Constitution, it was already apparent that the older generation of revolutionary leaders was giving way to younger individuals—either to the subalterns of the Continental army or to men who had risen to prominence during the revolution itself. Indeed, now a few of the great revolutionary leaders—such men as Patrick Henry, George Mason, and Samuel Adams—opposed ratification of the Constitution and, for that reason or some other, retired from the political scene after its adoption. This process accelerated during the 1790s such that by 1800 only Jefferson, alone among the great revolutionary leaders, remained politically active—and he had not emerged as a figure until 1776, when, as a 32-year-old, he wrote the Declaration of Independence.[38]

During that period of generational buildup (1789–1800), the coalitions that had originally formed around the struggle over ratification of the Constitution became institutionalized as the Federalist and Democratic-Republican parties. The party struggle they initiated led to the first set of critical elections in 1796 and 1800. The first of these, in turn, cemented the Jeffersonian coalition, even though the Federalists won. And the second shifted majority-party status from the Federalists to the Republicans.[39]

The Jeffersonian political response to the problems of the sixth generation came between 1801 and 1808, a period that encompassed the ratifying election of 1804, which Jefferson won by an overwhelming majority. The response was less one of specific programs than one befitting a still-young republic; it entailed the establishment of ground rules for the transfer of national power from one party to another, the firming up of the conditions

| 1787 | 1789 | 1790 | 1792 | 1796 | 1800 | 1801 | 1807 | 1812 | 1816 |

Generational Buildup | Years of Political Response | Years of Political Stabilization

Formative Events | Critical Elections | Culminating Events

Formative Events (1787–1792)
1. Writing and ratification of the Constitution (1787–1788)
2. Adoption of the Bill of Rights (1789–1791)
3. First Congress lays down basic operational pattern of federal government and federal system (1789–1792)

Generational Buildup (1789–1800)
1. Struggle between Hamilton and Jefferson leads to creation of Federalist and Democratic-Republican parties
2. Impact of French Revolution leads to division of country into those for and those against the revolution, to undeclared war with France, and to the ending of Franco-American alliance
3. First struggles between nationalists and proponents of states' rights (national bank, revolutionary debt assumption, alien and sedition acts, Virginia and Kentucky resolutions, 11th Amendment)
4. Westward expansion includes final federal assumption of states' Western lands, admission of first new states, establishment of regular army to open way for settlers

Critical Elections (1796–1800)
1. Federalists win with Adams, but Jeffersonian coalition linking Southern farmers and Northern city dwellers is completed (1796)
2. Jeffersonian coalition decisively defeats Federalists to become majority party (1800)

Years of Political Response (1801–1808)
1. Establishment of principle and practice of peaceful transfer of power from party to party, and clarification of presidential election procedures (12th Amendment)
2. Establishment of judicial independence and review powers (Marbury vs. Madison, failure to impeach Judge Chase)
3. Westward expansion (Louisiana Purchase, Lewis and Clark and Pike explorations, admission of Ohio as first public land state)
4. Federal involvement in internal improvements (national roads, Internal Improvement Fund, Gallatin Report on Internal Improvements, first federal joint-stock companies)

Years of Political Stabilization (1808–1815)
1. Public and governmental attention diverted to the international arena in light of Napoleonic wars, ending forward thrust of Jeffersonians
2. Tabling of Gallatin Report
3. Demise of first national bank

Culminating Events (1812–1816)
1. War of 1812 (second war for independence) shifts territorial expansionism away from Canada and ends direct American involvement in European politics
2. Wartime experiences (suspension of specie payments, militia problems, New England opposition to war) lead to greater support among Jeffersonians for expanded federal role in domestic affairs
3. Hartford Convention marks beginning of political decline of New England

Figure 4.6   Patterns and Trends in the Sixth Generation

of westward expansion, and the inauguration of the internal improvement movement. [40]

America's growing need to adjust to the changes in the international balance of power as a result of the Napoleonic wars led not only to a turning away from domestic issues but also to a period of political stabilization that lasted until the end of the generation (1808–1815). The tabling of Gallatin's Report on Internal Improvements (itself a hint of things to come in the next generation) marked the end of the forward thrust of the Republicans. From then on, foreign affairs dominated the scene, culminating in the inconclusive War of 1812.

The war and its impact on the nation constituted the generation's culminating events. The need for national fiscal controls and better internal communications opened the door to an expansion of the federal role in domestic affairs in the next generation, and the failure of the Hartford Convention heralded a shift of political power southward and westward, away from New England.

Government and the Economy

During this, the formative generation of the American Republic, all governments pursued an activist policy designed to regulate private enterprise in general while assisting in the expansion of specific enterprises either by granting monopolies or by joining with private parties in joint enterprises. All arenas of government were actively concerned with improving the "economies" they served.[41]

Government-chartered monopolies were common in all fields requiring large-scale organizations, with banking in particular serving a governmental or quasi-governmental function. Where direct government participation was involved, joint-stock companies, created through the combination of government and private investments, were established to undertake specific projects. A moderate protective tariff was applied to maintain government economic and foreign trade policies. Price regulation and market controls were common in the local arena. And although systematic use of the public domain for development purposes was still in the future, specific government land grants for specific projects were common as well.

Principal Ethnoreligious Manifestations

The first generation under the Constitution witnessed the virtual completion of the movements to separate the American churches from their English organizational ties and to disestablish the state churches, which had emerged in the revolutionary generation. By the generation's end, church and state were formally separated in all but four states. (Informal supports continued to exist, however—particularly in the local arena). Disestablishment was largely a result of the triumph of Unitarian and deistic ideas among the intellectual, social, and political leadership in the country and the spread of Methodism (and, to a lesser extent, Baptism) among the common people. Thomas Paine published his deistic-atheistic ideas at the beginning of the generation, and Jefferson gave expression to his humanistic deism at its high point. In New England during the early 1800s, the Unitarians seceded from the orthodox churches in a great schism.[42]

This final breakdown of the orthodoxies of the seventeenth and eighteenth centuries made it well-nigh impossible for formal religious establishment to be maintained in the states where it had previously existed. Consequently, the pattern that already prevailed in the pluralistic states, particularly New York and Pennsylvania, was introduced in the others as well. That pattern involved the localization of a socioreligious subcommunity (or perhaps more than one if it happened that such subcommunities were generally compatible) that would dominate a particular locality and informally maintain its way of life as the norm there. This led to a kind of territorialistic pluralism that not only gave a special vitality to territorial democracy but also established a framework for the assimilation of the immigrants from Europe who would begin to come in great numbers after the Napoleonic wars.

While the foregoing was transpiring on the ethnoreligious front, the racial situation was undergoing a striking change as well. At the very beginning of the sixth generation, slavery was abolished in the Northern states but became profitable once again in the South. Whitney's cotton gin revived a declining interest in slave labor below the Mason-Dixon line, again ending an eighteenth-century trend while at the same time setting up the North-South division on the issue that was to form the central political concern of the nineteenth century. The eighteenth-century spirit was to have one last nationwide victory during the generation. As part of the "tidying up" of its affairs, Congress in 1808 enacted legislation ending the slave trade as provided in the constitutional compromise of twenty years earlier.

The sixth generation also marked a shift in American attitudes toward Native Americans. At the beginning of the generation, the tribes were still viewed as nations—essentially, as the equals of the United States in political relations if not in civilization generally, and capable of allying themselves with the republic's enemies. By the generation's end, however, they had been transformed in the public mind into primitive nuisances whose impact was localized rather than threatening to the republic.[43]

SUMMARY

This chapter discusses the American founding and the first two centuries of the original American land frontier. It begins with the foundings of the thirteen original colonies and continues through the founding of the United States to the end of the War of 1812 (the so-called second war of American independence) and up to the beginning of the American turn inward and the massive westward movement of the nineteenth century. These foundings and the generational rhythms they generated, separately in the seventeenth century but increasingly as one American rhythm in the eighteenth, were based on the development of a common set of challenges and responses shared by the emerging United States of America. The foundings and frontiers are discussed in terms of the themes outlined in Chapter 2, taking into account the internal rhythm of each generation, foundings, climactic and culminating events, and the impact of these events on American society, economy, culture, federalism, and religion—all within the context of their political implications, manifestations, and ramifications.

NOTES

1. See Alexis de Tocqueville, *Democracy in America*, 2 vols. (New York: Schocken Books, 1961). See also Oscar Handlin and Lilian Handlin, *Liberty and Power* (New York: Harper and Row, 1986).

2. On the history of Virginia, see Richard R. Beeman, "Robert Manford and the Political Culture of Frontier Virginia," *Journal of American Studies* 12, no. 3 (August 1978): 169–183; Matthew P. Andrews, *Virginia, the Old Dominion* (Richmond, Va.: Dietz Press, 1949); Wesley M. Gewehr, *The Great Awakening in Virginia, 1740–1790* (Gloucester, Mass.: P. Smith, 1965); Thomas J. Wertenbaker, *The Planters of Colonial Virginia* (New York: Russell and Russell, 1959); Marshall W. Fishwick, *Virginia: A New Look at the Old Dominion* (New York: Harper and Row, 1959); Charles S. Syndor, *American Revolutionaries in the Making: Political Practices in Washington's Virginia* (New York: Collier Books, 1962); and David Hackett Fischer, *America, A Cultural History.* Vol. 1, *Albion's Seed* (New York: Oxford University Press, 1989).

3. Thomas J. Condon, *New York Beginnings: The Commercial Origins of New Netherland* (New York: New York University Press, 1968); David M. Ellis, James A. Frost, Harold C. Syrett, and Harry J. Carman, *A History of New York State* (Ithaca, N.Y.: Cornell University Press, 1967); Seymour Freegood, *The Gateway States* (New York: Time-Life Library of America, 1967); *New York: A Guide to the Empire State*, Writers' Project Administration of the WPA, American Guide Series (New York: Oxford University Press, 1940); Warren Moscow, *Politics in the Empire State* (New York: Alfred A. Knopf, 1948); Fischer, *America, A Cultural History*, Vol. 1, *Albion's Seed*.

4. Perry Miller, *Orthodoxy in Massachusetts, 1620–1650* (New York: Harper, 1933); Ronald M. Peters, *The Massachusetts Constitution of 1780: A Social Compact* (Amherst: University of Massachusetts Press, 1978) and *Conservatism in a Progressive Era: Mas-*

sachusetts Politics, 1900–1912 (Cambridge, Mass.: Harvard University Press, 1964); Murray B. Levine and George Blackwood, *Political Strategy in Massachusetts: The Complete Politician* (New York: Bobbs-Merrill, 1962).

5. On the history of Connecticut, see Neal R. Peirce, *The New England States* (New York: W. W. Norton, 1976); *Connecticut in Focus* (Hamden, Conn.: League of Women Voters of Connecticut Education Fund 1974); *Connecticut: A Guide to Its Roads, Lore, and People*, Writers' Project Administration of the WPA, American Guide Series (Boston, Mass.: Houghton Mifflin, 1938); and John Gunther, *Inside the U.S.A.* (New York: Harper, 1947).

6. On government and the economy in seventeenth-century America, see Louis B. Wrights, *The Atlantic Frontier: Colonial American Civilization* (New York: Alfred A. Knopf, 1947); Harry N. Scheiber et al., *American Economic History* (New York: Harper and Row, 1976); Howard R. Smith, *Economic History of the United States* (New York: Ronald Press, 1955); and Harold Underwood Faulkner, *American Economic History*, 8th ed. (New York: Harper, 1960).

7. On religious and ethnic groups in seventeenth-century America, see Edwin Scott Gaustad, *Historical Atlas of Religion in America* (New York: Harper, 1962); Daniel J. Boorstein, *The Americans: The Colonial Experience* (New York: Random House, 1958); W. W. Sweet, ed., *Religion on the American Frontier, 1783–1850*, 3 vols. (New York, 1931–1939); and Robert E. Shalhope, *The Roots of Democracy: American Thought and Culture, 1760–1800* (Boston: Twayne Publishers, 1990).

8. See Ralph Nading Hill, *Yankee Kingdom: Vermont and New Hampshire* (New York: Harper, 1960); and Peirce, *The New England States.*

9. On the introduction of African-Americans into Virginia, see James C. Ballagh, *A History of Slavery in Virginia* (New York: Johnson Reprint Corp., 1968); Robert McColley, *Slavery and Jeffersonian Virginia* (Urbana: University of Illinois Press, 1964); and Edmund S. Morgan, *American Slavery, American Freedom: The Ordeal of Colonial Virginia* (New York: W. W. Norton, 1975).

10. On Native Americans at the time of the first settlement, see Clark Wissler, *The American Indian* (New York: P. Smith, 1950); Alden T. Vaughn, *New England Frontier: Puritans and Indians 1620–1675* (Boston: Little, Brown, 1965); Francis Paul Prusha, *Great Father: The United States Government and the American Indians* (Lincoln: University of Nebraska Press, 1984); and L. Lyman Tyler, *A History of Indian Policy* (Washington, D.C.: U.S. Department of Interior, Bureau of Indian Affairs, Government Printing Office, 1973).

11. See George Callcott, *Maryland and America 1940–1980* (Baltimore: Johns Hopkins University Press, 1985); Newton D. Mereness, *Maryland as a Proprietary Province* (New York, 1901); Bernard C. Steiner, *Beginnings of Maryland* (Baltimore, 1903); and Matthew P. Andrews, *The Founding of Maryland* (Baltimore, 1933).

12. See John T. Cunningham, *New Jersey: America's Main Road* (Garden City, N.Y.: Doubleday, 1976); and Barbara Salmore and Stephen Salmore, *Politics and Government in New Jersey* (Lincoln: University of Nebraska Press, 1993).

13. Paul Dolor, *The Government and Administration of Delaware* (New York: Thomas Y. Crowell, 1956); Cy Libernon, James M. Rosbrow, and Harvey B. Rubenstein, *The Delaware Citizen: The Guide to Active Citizenship in the First State* (New York: Tapinger, 1967).

14. On the history of New England and the New England Confederation, see Duane Lockard, *New England State Politics* (Chicago: Princeton University Press, 1959); and Harry H. Ward, *The United Colonies of New England 1643–90* (New York: Vintage Press, 1961).

15. See Dorris A. Isaacson, ed., *Maine: A Guide "Downeast,"* 2nd ed. (Rockland, Me.: Courier-Gazette, 1970); Bernice Abbot and Chenoweth Hall, *A Portrait of Maine* (New York: Macmillan, 1968); Louise D. Rich, *State O'Maine* (New York: Harper and Row, 1964); and Peirce, *The New England States.*

16. See the following titles by Edmund S. Morgan: *The Puritan Dilemma: The Story of John Winthrop* (Boston: Little, Brown, 1958), *Puritan Political Ideas 1588–1794* (Indianapolis: Bobbs-Merrill, 1965), and *Visible Saints: The History of a Puritan Idea* (New York: Great Seal Books; Ithaca: Cornell University Press, 1961). See also John Fiske, *The Beginning of New England as the Puritan Theocracy and Its Relations to Civil and Religious Liberty* (Boston: Houghton Mifflin, 1889); Douglas Campbell, *The Puritan Holland, England and America,* 2 vols. (New York: Harper, 1892); and Vaughn, *New England Frontier.*

17. See the following titles by Edwin S. Gaustad: *American Religious History* (Washington, D.C.: American Historical Association, 1966), *Dissent in American Religion* (Chicago: University of Chicago Press, 1973), *A Documentary History of Religion in America* (Grand Rapids, Mich.: W. B. Eermans, 1983), *The Great Awakening in New England* (Gloucester, Mass.: P. Smith, 1965), *Historical Atlas of Religion in America* (New York: Harper and Row, 1968), and *A Religious History of America* (New York: Harper and Row, 1966). See also Richard Neibuhr, *The Social Sources of Denominationalism* (New York: Living Age Books, 1929) and *The Kingdom of God in America* (New York: Harper Torchbooks, 1937).

18. Ernest McPherson Lander, Jr., *A History of South Carolina 1865–1960* (Chapel Hill: University of North Carolina Press, 1960); Eric B. Herzik and Sally B. Teater, *North Carolina Focus* (Raleigh: North Carolina Center for Public Policy Research, 1981); Robert S. Rakin, *The Government and Administration of North Carolina* (New York: Thomas Y. Crowell, 1955).

19. Lucian J. Fosdick, *The French Blood in America* (New York: Flemming H. Revell, 1906); G. H. Doge, *The Political Theory of the Huguenots of Dispersion* (New York: Octagon Books, 1947); Arthur H. Hirsch, *The Huguenots of Colonial South Carolina* (Durham, N.C., 1928).

20. Philip D. Curtin, *The Atlantic Slave Trade: A Census* (Madison: University of Wisconsin Press, 1969); Stanley Elkins, *Slavery: A Problem in American Institutional and Intellectual Life,* 2nd ed. (Chicago: University of Chicago Press, 1968); Thomas R. Frazier, ed., *Afro-American History* (New York: Harcourt, Brace and World, 1970); Laura Foner, ed., *Slavery in the New World: A Reader in Comparative History* (Englewood Cliffs, N.J.: Prentice-Hall, 1969); Charles D. Rice, *The Rise and Fall of Black Slavery* (Baton Rouge: Louisiana State University Press, 1975); Irwin Unger and David Reimers, *The Slavery Experience in the United States* (New York: Holt, Rinehart and Winston, 1970); John R. Spears, *The American Slave Trade: An Account of Its Origin, Growth and Suppression* (New York: Ballantine Books, 1960); Paul Finkelman, *An Imperfect Union: Slavery, Federalism and Comity* (Chapel Hill: University of North Carolina Press, 1981); William Henry Smith, *A Political History of Slavery,* 2 vols. (New

York: G. P. Putnam's Sons, 1903); Charles P. Henry, *Culture and African-American Politics* (Bloomington: Indiana University Press, 1990).

21. On the French and Indian Wars, see Paul M. Angle, *A New Continent and a New Nation*. Vol. 1, *American Reader* (Greenwich, Conn.: Fawcett Publications, 1960), ch. 3; and Ellsworth Huntington, *The Red Man's Continent: A Chronicle of Aborigine America* (New Haven, Conn.: Yale University Press, 1920).

22. In 1701, a pamphlet proposing a plan for the federation of the colonies was issued in Virginia. The pamphlet was published anonymously and did not generate any substantial reaction.

23. Norman V. Bartley, *The Creation of Modern Georgia* (Athens: University of Georgia Press, 1983); Cullen B. Gosnell and C. David Anderson, *The Government and Administration of Georgia* (New York: Thomas Y. Crowell, 1958); Ulrich B. Phillips, *Georgia and State Rights* (Yellow Springs, Ohio: Antioch Press, 1968).

24. Bayrd Still, ed., *The West: Contemporary Records of America's Expansion Across the Continent 1607–1890* (New York: Capricorn Books, 1961); Robert W. Richmond and Robert W. Mardock, eds., *A Nation Moving West: Readings in the History of the American Frontier* (Lincoln: University of Nebraska Press, 1966); Dan E. Clark, *The West in American History* (New York: Thomas Y. Crowell, 1973).

25. Carl Bridenbaugh, *Cities in Revolt: Urban Life in America, 1743–1776* (London: Oxford University Press, 1971) and *Cities in the Wilderness: The First Century of Urban Life in America, 1625–1742* (London: Oxford University Press, 1971).

26. S. E. Johnson, *A History of Emigration from the United Kingdom to North America, 1763–1912* (London, 1913); Thomas Brinley, *Migration and Economic Growth: A Study of Great Britain and the American Economy* (Cambridge, England: Cambridge University Press, 1954).

27. On the economic history of British North America, see Brinley, *Migration and Economic Growth;* Curtis P. Nettels, "British Mercantilism and the Economic Development of the Thirteen Colonies," *Journal of Economic History* 12 (Spring 1952): 56–85; and Dorothy R. Adler, *British Investment in American Railways, 1834–1898* (Charlottesville: University Press of Virginia, 1970).

28. On the Scotch and the Scotch-Irish, see John H. Finley, *The Coming of the Scot* (New York: Charles Scribner's Sons, 1940); Charles A. Hanna, *The Scotch Irish: Or the Scot in North Britain, North Ireland and North America*, 2 vols. (New York: G. P. Putnam, 1902); and James G. Leyburn, *The Scotch-Irish: A Social History* (Chapel Hill: University of North Carolina Press, 1962).

29. David S. Lovejoy, ed., *Religious Enthusiasm and the Great Awakening* (Englewood Cliffs, N.J.: Prentice-Hall, 1969); Wesley M. Gewehr, *The Great Awakening in Virginia, 1740–1790* (Gloucester, Mass.: P. Smith, 1965); Gaustad, *The Great Awakening in New England*.

30. See John Fiske, *The American Revolution*, 2 vols. (Boston: Houghton Mifflin, 1901); Angle, *A New Continent and a New Nation;* John Richard Alden, *The American Revolution 1775–1783* (New York: Harper, 1954).

31. Richard B. Morris, *The Encyclopedia of American History* (New York: Harper and Row, 1965); J. T. Adams, ed., *Dictionary of American History* (New York: Scribner, 1976); E. B. O'Callaghan, *Documentary History of the State of New York* (Albany: Wee, Parsons and Co., 1849–1851).

32. On the "critical period" from 1781 to 1787, see Andrew McLaughlin, *The Confederation and the Constitution 1783–1789* (New York: Collier Books, 1962); and Merrill Jenson, ed., *The Articles of Confederation* (Madison: University of Wisconsin Press, 1962).

33. Charles S. Hyneman and Donald S. Lutz, eds., *American Political Writing During the Founding Era 1760–1805* (Indianapolis: Liberty Press, 1983); Donald S. Lutz, *The Origins of American Constitutionalism* (Baton Rouge: Louisiana State University Press, 1988); Andrew McLaughlin, *The Foundations of American Constitutionalism*, introduction by Henry Steele Commager (1932; reprinted in Gloucester, Mass., by P. Smith, 1972); Forrest McDonald, *E Pluribus Unum: The Function of the American Republic 1771–1790* (Indianapolis: Liberty Press, 1979).

34. Scheiber et al., *American Economic History;* Howard R. Smith, *Economic History of the United States* (New York: Ronald Press, 1955); Faulkner, *American Economic History;* Wrights, *The Atlantic Frontier.*

35. Franklin Hamlin Littell, *The Free Church: The Significance of the Left Wing of the Reformation for Modern American Protestantism* (Boston: Starr King Press, 1959).

36. Curtin, *The Atlantic Slave Trade: A Census;* Foner, *Slavery in the New World: A Reader in Comparative History;* Rice, *The Rise and Fall of Black Slavery;* Unger and Reimers, *The Slavery Experience in the United States.*

37. Charles S. Hyneman and George W. Carey, *A Second Federalist: Congress Creates a Government* (New York: Appleton-Century-Crofts, 1967); Leonard D. White, *The Federalists: A Study in Administrative History* (New York: Greenwood, 1978).

38. On generational changing of the guard, see S. N. Eisenstadt, *From Generation to Generation: Age Groups and Social Structures* (Glencoe, Ill.: Free Press, 1956); Ronald Inglehart, "Generational Change in Europe," in Mattei Dougan and Richard Rose, eds., *European Politics: A Reader* (Boston: Little, Brown, 1971); Gerald M. Pomper, "Classification of Presidential Elections," *Journal of Politics* 29 (August 1967): 535–566; and *Deadalus* 107, nos. 3–4 (1978), an issue dedicated to the concept of generation.

39. Herbert Agar, *Price of Union* (Boston: Houghton Mifflin, 1966); Manning Dauer, *The Adams Federalists* (Baltimore: Johns Hopkins University Press, 1968).

40. Henry Adams, *A History of the United States During the Administration of Jefferson and Madison* (London: Collins, 1948); Leonard D. White, *The Jeffersonians: A Study in Administrative History, 1801–1829* (New York: Macmillan, 1951); Daniel J. Elazar, *The American Partnership: Intergovernmental Co-operation in the Nineteenth Century United States* (Chicago: University of Chicago Press, 1962).

41. This section can be supplemented by reference to Scheiber et al., *American Economic History;* Smith, *Economic History of the United States;* Faulkner, *American Economic History;* Curtis Nettles, "Radicals and Empire Builders: The Diplomacy of Revolution and Independence," in William Appleman Williams, ed., *The Shaping of American Diplomacy* (Chicago: Rand McNally, 1956); and Bray Hammond, *Banks and Politics in America: From the Revolution to the Civil War* (Princeton, N.J.: Princeton University Press, 1957).

42. On the separation of church and state, see William Muehl, *Mixing Religion and Politics* (New York: Association Press, 1958); Richard E. Morgan, *The Politics of Religious Conflict: Church and State in America* (New York: Pegasus, 1968); Martin E. Marty, *Church-State Separation in America: The Tradition Nobody Knows* (Washington,

D.C.: People for the American Way, 1982); Gerhard Lenski, *The Religious Factor: A Sociological Study of Religion's Impact on Politics, Economics and Family Life* (Garden City, N.Y.: Anchor Books, 1963); Franklin Hamlin Littell, *From Church to Pluralism: A Protestant Interpretation of Religion in American History* (Garden City, N.Y.: Anchor Books, 1962); John F. Wilson, *The Church and State in American History* (Boston: D. C. Heath, 1965); Earl Raab, *Religious Conflict in America* (Garden City, N.Y.: Anchor, 1964); and Thomas G. Sanders, *Protestant Concepts of Church and State* (Garden City, N.Y.: Anchor, 1965).

43. Clark Wissler, *The American Indian* (New York: P. Smith, 1950); S. Lyman Tyler, *A History of Indian Policy* (Washington, D.C.: U.S. Government Printing Office, 1973); Thorstein Sellin, ed., "American Indians and American Life," *The Annals of the American Academy of Political and Social Science* (May 1957); Francis Paul Prucha, *Great Father: The United States Government and American Indians* (Lincoln: University of Nebraska Press, 1984); Russell L. Barsh and James Y. Henderson, *The Road: Indian Tribes and Political Liberty* (Berkeley: University of California Press, 1980).

CHAPTER 5

The Flowering of Sectionalism

In the nineteenth century, most of the nation's successful progressive movements—Jacksonian democracy, abolitionism, and populism, for example—had their origins in problems that, although obviously not generated by "raw geography," were sufficiently related to the geographic patterns of American settlement to be expressed in sectional terms and, in fact, were frequently best expressed through intersectional conflict.[1]

The reorganization of space by diverse settler groups coupled with the political boundaries that have been erected around and within geographic areas have given rise to sectionalism—the expression of social, economic, and especially political differences on a geographic basis.[2] In each section are common sets of enduring concerns and interrelationships that often foster sectional unity in response to national issues.[3] The sections have been defined as New England, the Middle Atlantic, the Upper South, the Lower South, the Near West, the Northwest, the Southwest, and the Far West. Each in itself is a product of its geo-historical location within the United States.

The War of 1812 functioned in a negative way as the founding event of the nineteenth century. Its unpopularity and indecisive outcome ended American willingness to participate in European wars for a full century, and its failure in Canada turned American expansionism clearly westward.[4] What emerged was a century of devotion to domestic concerns: completion of the acquisition, settlement, and political organization of that part of the continent destined to be American; a coming to terms with the slavery issue and its concomitant question of the nature of the federal union; entry into the conquest of the urban-industrial frontier; and a rounding out of the country's population base. All but one of these were century-long tasks whose beginning and ending between the War of 1812 and World War I are clearly visible in retrospect.

THE THREE SPHERES

Three great historical, cultural, and economic spheres form the underlying basis for American sectionalism: the great Northeast, the greater South, and the greater West (see Map 1.3).[5] The great northeastern megalopolis centered in Boston, New York, and Washington serves as the metropolis of the greater Northeast, which includes all or the major parts of three sections: New England, the Middle East, and the Near West (or Old Northwest). It embraces the old urban-industrial heartland and contains more than 40 percent of the country's population in hardly more than 10 percent of the total land area. It is the sphere where most of the patterns of American civilization originated and where the largest share of the nation's power is concentrated—even today, after the emergence of California, Texas, and Florida. The sphere's second concentration of urban areas begins in the western foothills of the Appalachians on a line from Buffalo to Pittsburgh and extends westward via the cities of Ohio, Indiana, and southern Michigan to the Chicago area, which is already a borderland. Today, this is the heart of the Rustbelt. Most of the greater Northeast is located within the eastern time zone. Its western limits coincide with those of the natural eastern woodland, past which begin the great prairies.

The greater Northeast as a whole is the area of greatest population density in the United States. Almost half of the nation's thirty-nine metropolitan areas of 1 million or more inhabitants are located within it, as are four of the eight cities of more than 1 million and nearly half of those over 500,000. Dominated by these great cities and their suburbs, with their densities of thousands of people per square mile, this sphere is also characterized by a very high open-country density, because urban-style settlement in rural areas has been relatively easy. Although the concentration of population stimulated by the metropolitan frontier has created substantial areas of open space (i.e., excluding urban places of 20,000 or more) reminiscent of land frontier days in the Appalachians and northern New England, overall the sphere is marked by a contiguous belt of settlement to its western limits with an open-country density that already exceeded 45 inhabitants per square mile in 1960.

The greater Northeast also contains the dominant manufacturing regions in the United States. Although the manufacturing belt continues beyond the limits of this sphere, it contains the most contiguous bloc of manufacturing counties along approximately the same line. This concentration of industry has enriched the greater Northeast to the point that its three sections account for more than half of the nation's personal income, a figure that has remained remarkably stable since at least 1929.

The greater Northeast was preeminently shaped by the urban-industrial frontier, which superseded the area's commercial and agricultural economy as a major developmental force early in the nineteenth century. Contemporary metropolitanization and urbanization in this sphere are rooted in the social and economic patterns established during the urban-frontier stage, ranging from the transplantation of inner-city ethnic communities into the suburbs to the necessary adaptations of an industrialization plan designed for the coal and iron age.

The politics of the greater Northeast also remains an extension of the politics of the urban-industrial frontier.[6] Although most of the people in this sphere live outside of the big cities, its politics remains big-city oriented to a substantial degree. This is the politics of competing ethnic and racial groups, living together cheek by jowl under "pressure cooker" conditions. The votes may be in the suburbs and the exurbs, but the visible political conflicts are in the big cities, which remain the first places of residence not only for new European, Hispanic, and Asian immigrants to the United States but also for African-Americans originally from the rural South. Secondarily, the politics of the greater Northeast is the politics of the political, economic, and cultural "establishment." It is a highly partisan politics, dominated by organized political parties and characterized by the sharpest ideological differences to be found in the country. It is in the greater Northeast that one can still find real programmatic differences between Democrats and Republicans—differences that were renewed during the Reagan years with the rise of the New Conservatism.

The greater South, in many ways the most easily distinguishable of the spheres, advanced westward from the Eastern seaboard to include all or major parts of the former slave states plus certain peripheral areas to their north originally settled by Southerners. It embraces three sections: the Upper South, the Lower South, and the Western South (again, see Map 1.3). Until the 1960s, this sphere was clearly distinguishable by the mandatory segregation of African-Americans within its territory. It is still held together by a perceived common concern (whether positive or negative) with "the Southern way of life" now increasingly shared by both races.

Every one of the common statistical measures readily identifies the greater South. Agriculturally, it is marked by the prevalence of cotton and tobacco farming, supplemented by widespread timber farming and cattle feeding and sustained by an annual rainfall of more than 45 inches in all the states contained wholly or partly within the sphere. And, religiously, it is unique, with a marked predominance of Southern Baptists from the Atlantic to west Texas.

Much larger than the Northeast and considerably more varied in terms of the spread of urbanization and economic activity, this sphere is characterized by metropolitan-hinterland patterns that have been more sectional than sphere-wide. Moreover, the South's historic economic dependence on the Northeast kept it from developing independent metropolitan centers of its own until the recent rise of Atlanta, Miami, Houston, and Dallas. At the same time, the relatively even spread of population in its rural areas—which support isolated homesteads and settlements even more easily than rural areas in the Northeast—gives the sphere a distinctive population and settlement pattern that has reduced the pressure for development of large cities. Although the contemporary South contains many metropolitan areas, only five of them—one in Georgia, two in Texas, and two in Florida—rank among the nation's twenty-five largest. Most are multiply centered around relatively small cities.

The contemporary South is still substantially shaped by the land frontier, as it originally manifested itself in that sphere. The plantation agrarianism of antebellum days gave way to an industrial version of the plantation system when the urban frontier moved southward. During the metropolitan-technological frontier stage, the urban frontier pattern of medium-sized and small city industrialization gave way to development in the medium-sized and small metropolitan areas (often with twice the population) that grew up around the older cities, though without being absorbed by them. Today, the South is exhibiting rapid growth in its rural areas, where rurban living has reached its most developed form.[7]

Although the desire to avoid citification is found nationwide, it is most intense in the greater South, where most urbanites have come directly from the farm during either this generation or the last. Many of these people retain possession of their farms, earning enough to pay their taxes by growing trees for lumber companies and, in this manner, maintaining tangible agrarian attachments. Many more work in the metropolitan areas but continue to live on their farms, often commuting long distances daily to avoid living in the city, even when the city is as rural as these Southern communities tend to be. Both groups help maintain the homogeneous lifestyle that unites urban and rural Southerners.

Despite the great metropolitan growth, Southern politics still owes much to older forms of settlement: small towns, crossroads courthouses, county cliques, and politicians with personal followings. All politics in the United States is local and personal—but Southern politics is even more so.[8]

The greater West includes all of two sections, the Far West and Northwest, along with perhaps the northwestern periphery of the Near West. In essence, these free-soil territories (i.e., those in which slavery was prohibited from the first) emerged from the land frontier stage of their development after 1850. It was here—in the free states west of the Mississippi River, along with parts of Illinois, Wisconsin, and Michigan—that the national democratic ideals of the nineteenth century were given concrete expression. In the process, the greater West came to be endowed with a unique character of its own.

Primarily the products of Jacksonian democracy and its influences, in this radically new physical environment of the greater West, these national democratic ideals were combined with an entirely new technology. The combination stimulated an economic system in which *laissez-faire* ideas predominated, even though it was strongly influenced by corporate organization and governmental intervention from the beginning. The same combination gave rise to a populist approach to politics that was characteristic of the Jacksonian and post-Jacksonian eras—an approach intrinsically different from the traditional or elitist approaches that characterized the other spheres. The greater West also gave rise to as unstructured a social system as the modern world has ever seen, one that allowed and even expected greater and rapid mobility both vertically and laterally within it. The sphere as a whole was populated by means of an implicit if unwitting system of recruitment that placed a premium on people with a psychology of individual initiative in economic pursuits and of social conformity in most others.

The greater West remains the most "old-stock" American of the spheres (and the most Hispanic and Native American), the most republican in its politics, and the source of most presidential candidates since the 1920s. It includes areas of greatest population growth as well as areas of greatest population decline within its sphere, as a reflection of its rapid transition from the land frontier to the metropolitan frontier within a single generation. Moreover, its politics are the most volatile and the most independent in the country.[9]

THE EIGHT SECTIONS

The three great spheres are further divided into eight sections. Most attempts to discuss politics in regional or sectional terms are based on the regional scheme devised by the U.S. Bureau of the Census. This scheme has value, but it is not necessarily the best for political analysis. For one thing, it ignores the regional patterns set by the three political subcultures. For another, it ignores the larger pattern of settlement in the country that is based on the linear thrusts of the frontier, usually westward. Proposed here is a different sectional scheme.

Although the existence of the federal system forces most sectional problems into the framework provided by the existence of the states, whereby they are shaped into matters of state concern through political action, most of the physiographic, socioeconomic, and cultural features distinguishing one section from another do not follow state lines precisely. The natural endowments of soil and water that determine where the Cornbelt or the Wheatbelt is best located, the less natural but still undirected spread of political cultures, and the actively directed search for hinterlands, pushed by every chamber of commerce—all of these factors cut across state boundaries. A case in point concerns the history of the drawing of the federal reserve district boundaries in 1912 and 1913, still among the most accurate regional schemes in use today. The nation's leading cities competed for designation as federal reserve district head-quarters, and those that won them had districts drawn to reflect their spheres of influence, regardless of state lines.

A perennial problem of the states, hardly less important than that of direct federal-state relations, is how to bend sectional and regional de-mands to fit their own needs for self-maintenance as political systems. When those demands are reinforced by the interests of the nation's great cities, that task is made even more difficult. And since the concern with regional development is now growing, this difficulty is being magnified. One way in which the states are able to overcome this problem is through the use of the formal political institutions they control. Such formal insti-tutions are the major features distinguishing one section from others that do follow state lines. The states themselves are formal institutions per-forming that role. So are their respective systems of local government. The states are protected such that no regional problems can be handled governmentally without making use of those formal institutions. Thus the representatives of the states use the formal institutional structure to influence federal action to handle problems in such a way as to allow the states a role.

Most sections have continuing intrasectional conflicts of long duration within the context of their overall sectional unity. These persist in re-sponse to national concerns. For example, the intrasectional conflict among the states of the Far West over water resources, though a peren-nial issue, does not detract from their long-term community of interest in water issues, commerce, education, and control over the public lands within the section. Even more important for our purposes is the fact that certain common sectional bonds give the states of each section a special relationship to national politics. This is particularly true in connection with those specific political issues that are of sectional importance, such as the race issue in the South, the problems of the megalopolis in the Northeast, and the problems of agriculture and agribusiness in the Northwest.[10]

Political culture, geography, and history come together in the United States through sectionalism—the more or less permanent division of the United States into geo-historical regions with distinctive political subcul-tures. The American sectionalism that we know today was developed in the nineteenth century as a product of territorial expansion and the set-tling of the land frontier from coast to coast. (See Figure 5.1.)

THE SEVENTH GENERATION (1816–1848)

Major Political Patterns and Events

The seventh generation began with an "era of good feeling" and a turning away from Europe, toward the west. The Federalist Party had ceased to function in the national arena, and for a brief period the United States was essentially a one-party country on the national plane (though, in fact, that party was hardly operative except for presidential elections). The first task of the new generation was to lay the foundations for what were to become the three goals of nineteenth-century America: the conquest of the continent, the industrialization of the country, and the consolidation of the Union.

The first Monroe administration moved toward these goals with the unsolicited aid of John Marshall's Supreme Court. The Gallatin Report was revived and, although the president did not succeed in having the Constitution amended to explicitly allow federal activity in the field of internal improvements, John C. Calhoun, his secretary of war, found ways to extend federal aid nonetheless. In the process, the army was converted into an instrument of "civic action" committed to opening the West through engineering as well as Indian fighting.[11]

At the same time, William Crawford, Monroe's secretary of the treasury, superintended the reestablishment of a national bank with central banking functions, which he designed to involve the state central banks in a common nationwide system.[12] Monroe himself devised a way to provide the states with extra funds for their internal needs by authorizing federal reimbursements of dubious state claims for the War of 1812, provided that the money would be used for education or internal improvements. Finally, between 1817 and 1823, John Quincy Adams, Monroe's secretary of state, constructed America's policy of reciprocal noninvolvement with Europe, beginning with a treaty stabilizing U.S.-Canadian relations and culminating in the Monroe Doctrine.

Whereas the administration was acting to provide the wherewithal for the new departures, the Supreme Court was handing down a series of landmark decisions that established federal supremacy in the economic realm. Two crucial decisions were handed down in 1819. In the *Dartmouth College Case*, the Court established the federal right to protect the sanctity of contracts, even those in opposition to state policy, thus opening the door to modern corporate capitalism. And in *McCulloch* v. *Maryland*, the Court established the federal right to exercise its powers anywhere in the country, again even those in opposition to state policy, thus giving rise to the subsequent expansion of federal domestic activities throughout the country.[13]

Generational Buildup | Years of Political Response | Years of Political Stabilization

1816   1820   1824   1828   1829   1837   1845   1848

Formative Events   Critical Elections   Culminating Events

Formative Events (1816–1820)

1. Monroe initiates active federal role in internal improvements to implement Gallatin Report; Calhoun converts army into instrument of westward expansion
2. Second Bank of the United States established as central fiscal agent under Crawford's direction
3. Missouri Compromise begins new phase in slavery issue
4. *Dartmouth College Case* (1819) and *McCulloch* v. *Maryland* (1819) establish basis of federal supremacy in economic sphere

Generational Buildup (1816–1828)

1. Elimination of Federalist Party as national contender, and division of Democratic-Republicans into Democrats (Jacksonians) and National Republicans (Whigs) after brief period of one-party rule
2. Monroe and J. Q. Adams crystallize new American policy of withdrawal from European affairs (Monroe Doctrine)
3. Henry Clay's "American System" crystallizes the development aspirations of the American people
4. U.S. Supreme Court's decisions form basis for industrial revolution under competitive capitalism

Critical Elections (1824–1828)

1824: Under one-party system, factional candidates emerge: victory of J. Q. Adams in House brings together Jacksonians into new party organization that seizes mantle of Jeffersonians

1828: Jackson's victory generally restores Jeffersonian coalition and Democratic majority status while forcing non-Jeffersonians to create their own party

Years of Political Response (1829–1837)

1. Jackson eliminates most special relationships between the federal government and private business (closing of Second U.S. Bank) to link free-enterprise capitalism with democracy
2. Institution of popular government along lines maintained by Americans today (popular voting for presidency, electoral college loses its discretionary powers, president becomes "tribune of the people," elimination of most barriers to universal suffrage for male citizens)
3. Principle of reform as means of improving society institutionalized on all planes of government
4. Struggle over tariff and nullification
5. Internal improvement boom, particularly in states

Years of Political Stabilization (1837–1848)

1. Panic of 1837 and subsequent depression end years of intensive government activity
2. Consolidation of gains of 1830s in legislative "package" combining national tariff, public land, and internal improvement policies into a single interrelated bundle

3.   Federal fiscal adjustments in wake of abandonment of central banking function
4.   Main strength of Abolitionist movement shifts from South to North

Culminating Events (1845–1848)
1.   Completion of continental expansion (Texas annexed, Oregon divided, Mexican War results in Mexican territorial cessions)
2.   Mexican War puts slavery issue in forefront of public concerns; Wilmot Proviso, spread of free-soil movement
3.   Drive for government-assisted internal improvements institutionalized (Rivers and Harbors Congress initiated in 1847)

Figure 5.1   Patterns and Trends in the Seventh Generation

The final formative event for this generation was the Missouri Compromise. It is significant that the slavery issue generated the first serious North-South clash at the very beginning of the first generation of the nineteenth century. The resultant compromise settled the conflict for the moment, but it also served notice that the issue had been joined.

The climax of the "era of good feeling" came with Monroe's nearly unanimous reelection in 1820. From then on, the generational buildup consisted of movement toward new conflicts and their resolution. The first great conflict led to the division of the Democratic-Republicans into two parties, a realignment that took place over the course of two critical presidential elections in 1824 and 1828. By the first of these, Andrew Jackson had emerged as the likely leader of one emerging party coalition but had not yet consolidated his position among its factions and their leaders. He lost the election; but in doing so, he achieved the larger political goal that enabled him to win in 1828. The party that coalesced around him was essentially a continuation of the old Jeffersonian coalition—one that held fast to the interests and principles of the Jeffersonians, but with suitable modifications to fit the new times.

The anti-Jacksonians also began to coalesce as a political party for the election of 1828. Aside from being anti-Jackson, they also represented the various interests who were attracted by Henry Clay's "American System," an elaborate scheme of government-sponsored internal improvements and subsidies for industry designed to continue the essentially Hamiltonian tradition of active government intervention on behalf of economic development. Initially identifying themselves with the states-rights orientation of the Jacksonians, they later adopted the name Whigs.[14]

Jackson's election inaugurated this generations's years of political response when the issues raised during the first half of the generation came to a head. On the federal plane, Jackson came down decisively against the remnant of mercantilism in his attack on the special privileges of the old gentry; his intent was to eliminate most remaining governmental barriers to free-enterprise capitalism, an issue of great importance throughout the 1820s.[15]

Equally significant, Jackson presided over and substantially assisted the institution of new forms of popular government such as the transformation of the president's role into that of "tribune of the people," the institution of popular voting for the president, the transformation of the electoral college into an essentially ministerial body, and the elimination of suffrage restrictions in the states that were acting as barriers to universal suffrage for white male citizens. All of the foregoing had been issues in the elections of 1824 and 1828; they were also issues in Jackson's great 1832 victory, which ratified the new Jacksonian majority.

The struggle over the tariff was the great issue of federalism that dominated the period from the mid-1820s on. It culminated in the Nullification controversy—South Carolina's attempt to nullify the tariff, claiming that states could nullify federal laws unconstitutionally detrimental to their interests—which Jackson resolved by taking a strong Unionist stance. In doing so, he established the limits of mainstream Democratic states-rights principles and saved the Union for another generation.[16]

The states also shared in the intensive activity of the years of political response. On the one hand, they were the major actors in the internal improvement boom that occurred after many false starts in the 1820s—the states promoted, subsidized, and even constructed roads, canals, and railroads. On the other, it was in the states that the principle of "reform" as a regularized means of improving society was institutionalized, particularly in the fields of education and social welfare. This principle—a uniquely Anglo-American idea—was born in the United States at the beginning of the sixth generation and revolved around the idea of private organizations seeking the public good. A generation later, organized reform efforts began to have their impact in the governmental realm. During the 1830s, the reformers secured the incorporation of the idea of reform into the governmental sector as a political principle of cardinal importance on the American scene.[17]

The Panic of 1837 and the subsequent depression, coupled with the end of Jackson's tenure in the White House, brought the years of political activism to an end. Between 1837 and 1846, the gains made in the early 1830s were consolidated through several legislative "packages": the surplus revenue distribution of 1837; the tariff; the preemption and internal Improvement Acts of 1841; and, finally, the abortive distribution of 1846. All were interrelated in both intention and effect. In an effort to deal with the fiscal problems created by the de-federalization of the second U.S. Bank, a number of experiments were tried after 1837; but they failed to do the job. Finally, sectional sentiment favoring the Southern way of life drove the center of the abolitionist movement northward at the same time that radical reformers in New England were embracing the anti-slavery cause as the quintessential reform.

The generation's culminating events took place between 1845 and 1848, four of the most momentous years in American history. In one fell swoop (or so it seemed), the United States expanded its boundaries to the Pacific, nearly completing its contiguous territorial expansion, and, in this way, set the stage for the showdown over slavery in the next generation. Bernard de Voto has termed 1846 the "year of decision."[18] Indeed, it was part of a crucial generational watershed that was sumultaneously both culminating and initiating in nature.

Government and the Economy

The seventh generation was one of transition from the old mercantilist economic system of the colonial period to a new, capitalist system that was tied to the whole complex of American expansion in the nineteenth century.[19] Mercantilist policies gave way to policies designed to encourage free private enterprise, under the impact of new economic ideas from Europe (Adam Smith and company) and the new economic democracy of the American frontier. Governments on all planes progressively withdrew from direct participation in economic enterprise and took on a new role as subsidizers of private enterprise. The previous pattern of government grants of special monopoly rights to particular private parties was replaced by one in which the states enacted general incorporation acts that gave all private parties relatively equal access to government charters. Direct government activity and subsidization were shifted to the arena of internal improvements (the construction of roads, canals, and railroads) so as to create the infrastructure for private economic development.

This generation witnessed the beginnings of the modern corporation, which emerged, first, in fur trading, banking, and railroading. Its greatest economic achievement was the initiation of the industrial revolution in the United States; and its most significant contribution to the country's political economy was the harmonization of capitalism and democracy, which has enabled private enterprise to flourish in the United States ever since, despite its various political and economic permutations.

The decline of government-chartered monopolies followed on the heels of the development of general incorporation legislation. Beginning in the Northeast at the very outset of the generation and moving westward by its end, banking became a free private enterprise whereby intensive competition among banks replaced the monopolistic practices of the previous generation. The generation also witnessed the stabilization and decline of joint-stock companies and their replacement by the beginnings of the modern general-purpose private corporation.

Although governments retained the theoretical right to regulate private enterprise closely and intensively, in practice the amount of regulation declined drastically in all areas. Price regulation and market controls remaining from the previous generation were generally eliminated. The tariff was reoriented to be selectively protective in order to subsidize or support specific enterprises, particularly those heavy industries that represented the coming of the industrial revolution to America.

Government internal improvement programs were expanded on all planes. This was the canal-building era. The states undertook projects directly while the federal government and the localities contributed to their subsidization. Federal subsidies began to take the form of special land grants, but, by the end of the generation, such special grants were being replaced by a general land grant program developed systematically to achieve specific national goals.[20]

The first labor unions were established in this era, built around craft skills. Although the workers were not particularly successful in gaining the right to strike, they were able to win a greater political role in American society when property barriers to the suffrage were eliminated.[21]

On another plane altogether, it was during this generation that the rise of professionalism occurred on a wide variety of fronts. Even as the Jacksonian ideology glorified the amateur (particularly the political amateur), politics in the more important states, those located in the new mainstream of American life, was becoming professionalized. Science, too, was taking its first steps toward professionalization, as demonstrated by the founding of the American Association for the Advancement of Science in 1846. Even such traditional "professions" as medicine were beginning to develop true professional standards, as evidenced by the establishment of the American Medical Association in 1847.[22]

Principal Ethnoreligious Manifestations

The period after 1815 clearly marked the end of the eighteenth century in matters of socioreligious, ethnic, and racial concern. It was during this transition generation that the Southern pro-slavery ideology was given more precise form; social pressure demanding total conformity to this ideology developed throughout the section.[23] At the same time, the abolition of slavery was becoming a matter of religious obligation among reformers in the North.[24] Territorialistic pluralism became increasingly rooted in the North and West, and non-British immigrants staked out their own "territories." An informal "reestablishment" of Protestantism in a nonsectarian way also began, with Protestants of all denominations assuming the dominant role vis-à-vis the beginnings of an influx of Catholics from Ireland and Germany. This was the generation that institutionalized revivalism on the frontier.[25]

On the Native American front, the expulsion of the five civilized tribes from the Southeastern states under the direction of President Jackson and in express violation of a U.S. Supreme Court ruling marked the end of earlier efforts to "westernize" the Native Americans within the framework of their own tribal societies. From then on they were defined as "savages," to be dealt with more or less as the white people seeking their lands pleased.

THE EIGHTH GENERATION (1848–1876)

Major Political Patterns and Events

The culminating political events of the seventh generation were also the formative events of the eighth. The Mexican War–related territorial expansion and the revival of the question of the spread of slavery that flowed from it set the stage for the new generation and dictated its primary concerns. Those concerns were further reinforced by the sharp rise in the impact of the industrial revolution on American society through the opening of the urban-industrial frontier.[26] (See Figure. 5.2.)

The new industrial cities began to set the pace in American society, and the first great products of the industrial revolution, the railroad, the telegraph, and the agricultural implement industry became the new bases for the settlement of the West. The Chicago Rivers and Harbors Congress of 1847, which adjourned and immediately reconvened as a railroad and homestead congress, marked the transition in the interests of the industrializing states of the North. The two meetings effectively set the agenda of political responses to the new frontier for the generation. The new frontier was further fueled by the discovery of gold in California in 1848, the first of a generation-long series of gold and silver strikes that opened major mining frontiers in Colorado, Nevada, Montana, South Dakota, Idaho, and Arizona before the generation ended.

Meanwhile, the anti-slavery struggle took a new turn, away from the rather abstract drive to convince existing states to end the "peculiar institution" and toward the very concrete question of the disposition of new territories whose social fabric was still to be determined. This struggle, with day-to-day developments taking place from Kansas to California, led to the polarization of North and South. This polarization was assisted by the Supreme Court's decision in the Dred Scott case, which, as Abraham Lincoln pointed out at the time, so widened the arena of conflict that the issue could no longer be postponed but had to be resolved in that generation.[27]

The third element in the generational buildup was the change that took place in the party system. The Whig party fell apart over the slavery issue, no longer able to use its common stand on behalf of an activist federal government to cover up the widely divergent positions of Northern and Southern Whigs on the question. The Northern Whigs became the nucleus of the Republican Party, which was founded as a response to the free-soil movement. The new party not only united the anti-slavery free soilers and sympathetic ex-Whigs and Democrats but also created an alliance among the anti-slavery forces, farmers seeking free land in the west, and the leading pioneers on the urban-industrial frontier. This three-faceted coalition

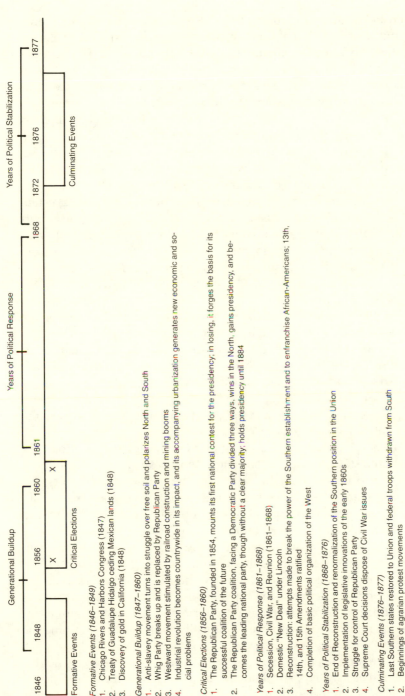

Generational Buildup | Years of Political Response | Years of Political Stabilization

1846 1848 1856 1860 1861 1868 1872 1876 1877

Formative Events | Critical Elections | Culminating Events

Formative Events (1846–1849)
1. Chicago Rivers and Harbors Congress (1847)
2. Treaty of Guadalupe Hidalgo ceding Mexican lands (1848)
3. Discovery of gold in California (1848)

Generational Buildup (1847–1860)
1. Anti-slavery movement turns into struggle over free soil and polarizes North and South
2. Whig Party breaks up and is replaced by Republican Party
3. Westward movement stimulated by railroad construction and mining booms
4. Industrial revolution becomes countrywide in its impact, and its accompanying urbanization generates new economic and social problems

Critical Elections (1856–1860)
1. The Republican Party, founded in 1854, mounts its first national contest for the presidency; in losing, it forges the basis for its successful coalition of the future
2. The Republican Party coalition, facing a Democratic Party divided three ways, wins in the North, gains presidency, and becomes the leading national party, though without a clear majority; holds presidency until 1884

Years of Political Response (1861–1868)
1. Secession, Civil War, and Reunion (1861–1868)
2. Domestic "New Deal" under Lincoln
3. Reconstruction: attempts made to break the power of the Southern establishment and to enfranchise African-Americans; 13th, 14th, and 15th Amendments ratified
4. Completion of basic political organization of the West

Years of Political Stabilization (1868–1876)
1. End of Reconstruction and renormalization of the Southern position in the Union
2. Implementation of legislative innovations of the early 1860s
3. Struggle for control of Republican Party
4. Supreme Court decisions dispose of Civil War issues

Culminating Events (1876–1877)
1. Last Southern states restored to Union and federal troops withdrawn from South
2. Beginnings of agrarian protest movements
3. Disputed election of 1876
4. Last Native American tribes capable of resisting white settlement are broken
5. Slaves abandoned to their former masters by a North weary of the "colored question"

Figure 5.2   Patterns and Trends in the Eighth Generation

came into being in anticipation of the 1856 presidential elections and, though still a sectional coalition, won the 1860 contest to replace the Democratic Party as the dominant one on the national scene. The Republican triumph not only ended two generations of Democratic Party dominance and inaugurated two generations of Republican dominance in its place; it also set the political stage for the years of political response.[28]

These years brought more than civil war and the immediate resolution of the slavery issue. They brought a response to the urban-industrial frontier in all three areas represented by the interests that constituted the Republican coalition. Parallel to the war was a domestic "New Deal" presided over by the Lincoln administration that, among other things, (1) created a new national banking system and a national currency; (2) established a policy of providing free land for homesteaders and land grants for agricultural and mechanical colleges and transcontinental railroads; (3) encouraged industrial development through programs ranging from protective tariffs to a government-sponsored program to recruit immigrants for factory work to the institution of major improvements in the postal service to aid business.

Between 1861 and 1865, a whole rash of such programs were enacted, as Congress responded to the challenges before it in the usual once-a-generation pattern. Moreover, the rest of the Western lands were organized as states or territories so as to fill in the basic outlines of the country's political map. Added to the above were the war itself, war-related amendments to the Constitution, Reconstruction, and the tidying up of the domestic reform legislation in Congress and the courts, all of which extended the period of political response to 1868.[29]

After 1868, the generation moved into its period of stabilization. The extreme manifestations of Reconstruction came to an end.[30] The Southern states were restored to their full rights in the Union, one by one. The courts and Congress began to develop interpretations of the three constitutional amendments that normalized relationships between North and South, and the legislative innovations of the early 1860s were implemented nationwide. The Supreme Court also wrote *finis* to wartime constitutional controversies during this period. Finally, the triumph of the new industrial capitalism that inaugurated the gilded age led to a conflict within the dominant Republican Party between the erstwhile abolitionists who were turning to new problems of reform and the spokesmen for industry who preferred the status quo politically, with the latter gaining the upper hand.[31]

The culminating events of the generation came in 1876–1877. The disputed election of 1876 led to the famous "deal" that gave the presidency to the Republicans and the South to the Democrats, thus restoring home rule to the last of the occupied states of the ex-Confederacy and abandoning the ex-slaves to their former masters.

While some federal troops were leaving the South, others were breaking down the last of the Native American resistance in the West capable of retarding white settlement. The latter effort took place during the intensive campaigns that followed the Battle of Little Big Horn (1876). Finally, in 1877, the U.S. Supreme Court sustained the efforts of the states to meet the first round of farmers' demands against the new industrial giants by sustaining Illinois' granger laws, thereby taking the teeth out of the farm protest movement for half a generation.

Government and the Economy

The opening of the urban-industrial frontier countrywide in the eighth generation began the transformation of the United States into a fully industrialized society. With free-enterprise capitalism dominant, only the barest vestiges of mercantilism remained. Government activities were confined to a supportive role designed to make it possible for small private enterprise to develop and flourish.

Most private enterprise was still small or middle-sized, with ownership, control, and management all vested in the same persons who maintained face-to-face contact with their employees. The exceptions were the Western railroads and, after the Civil War, the industries that the war had expanded. These large enterprises were just beginning to become powerful; by the end of the generation, however, the future was clearly in their hands. In sum, this was the era of the small entrepreneur, during which the free-enterprise myth and its ideology were developed. It was also the era that opened the door to large-scale corporate capitalism.[32]

The organizational hallmark of this generation was the spread of the corporate form of business organization. Many corporations were established under the still-new general incorporation laws, but most were still family owned. Banking was less regulated by government than ever before or since. Indeed, government regulation on all planes was at a minimum (though not nonexistent). The spread of free-enterprise ideologies and opportunities contributed to the decline of early labor unionism. Even the tariff was lowered and used primarily for revenue rather than to subsidize or encourage local industry.

Government-sponsored internal improvements concentrated on the construction of railroads and the improvement of rivers and harbors. As the number of public land states came to outnumber their non–public land sisters, general land grant programs reached their greatest extent. By the middle of the generation, federal land grants had been extended even to non–public land states through the Land Grant College Act (1862).

Principal Ethnoreligious Manifestations

During this generation, the pace of immigration stepped up. The number of Irish, German, and other Central European immigrants increased (the latter especially after the revolutions of 1848), and Scandinavians began to come to the United States in great numbers. Since it was during this period that cities began to develop in earnest, many of the new immigrants found their way to the new urban settlements, thereby creating a more complex territorialistic pluralism than was earlier the case. Many cities took on the characteristics of one or two ethnic communities (Milwaukee became "German"; Minneapolis became "Swedish"; half of Boston became "Irish"), and the very largest acquired polyglot populations. The various communities settled in sufficient numbers to generate important ethnic enclaves of their own within city limits.[33]

The rising tide of immigration further stimulated the informal hegemony of Protestantism. The first great anti-Catholic political movement emerged in this generation and, although it was not long in existence, Catholicism began to be an unwritten barrier to political office outside of districts with heavy Catholic voting majorities. The public schools that emerged as the dominant elementary educational institution in the eighth generation became the custodians of Protestant values and behavior patterns, prompting the Catholics to develop their own parochial schools.[34]

On the racial front, it was this generation that saw the struggle over slavery come to a head. The slaves themselves, reduced during the period of generational buildup to nonpersons as a result of the Dred Scott decision (1858), were emancipated a few years later as a result of the political response to the generation's challenge, raised to full citizenship by congressional fiat, and, in one of the generation's culminating events, abandoned to their former masters (or worse) by a North weary of the "colored question."

It was also during this generation that America's Hispanic and Chinese communities were founded. The Hispanic were "inherited" as a result of the Mexican War, whereas the Chinese were brought into the country as cheap labor for the construction of the Pacific slope railroads.

Meanwhile, the Native Americans were making their last effective stand in the mountain-and-plains West, beginning in Minnesota in 1862, continuing on the Pacific coast in the late 1860s and early 1870s, and ending with the defeat of the Sioux-Cheyenne alliance in the months following Custer's defeat in 1876. After 1878, only the Apache in the Southwest continued to offer meaningful resistance to American expansion—and even their resistance was confined to raids by one or two bands for eight more years.[35]

THE NINTH GENERATION (1877–1912)

Major Political Patterns and Events

The generational buildup ended when the U.S. Census Bureau was able to report (albeit prematurely) that the frontier line no longer existed; in other words, settlement was too scattered across the West to say that there was a line beyond which the land was unsettled (1890). Although the land frontier persisted for the remainder of the generation, with massive homesteading, new mining booms, and continuing railroad construction until the eve of World War I (the frontier line even reappeared briefly in the 1900 census), the basic job was done by then. Seven states were admitted to the Union between 1889 and 1896 (as part of the generational response), leaving only three territories in the continental United States, all of which were admitted as states by 1912. The Indian Wars dribbled to an end in the 1890s, though the last war scare came as late as 1916. The mining booms of the 1870s and 1880s climaxed in the 1890s with Cripple Creek and the Klondike, and continued sporadically until World War I. (See Fig. 5.3.)

Corporate capitalism remained basically unregulated during the period of generational buildup, although its excesses generated demands for its regulation from all sides. In the mines and factories, the wave of strikes that began in the mid-1870s reached a climax with the Pullman strike of 1892 and the violent Western miners' strikes of that decade; these were followed by a wave of repression in the last decade of that generation. At the same time, the farmers revived their protest movements, which also were directed against unrestricted corporate capitalism. The Agrarian revolt built up during the 1880s and burst forth in a major national third party in the 1890s, after which it, too, was aborted.[36]

The critical elections of 1892 and 1896 reflected these trends. In 1892, the Republican Party, whose majority status was in any case not secure, was rocked by the formation of the Populist Party, which drew heavily from its ranks. The Democrats won the presidency and for the third straight election gained a plurality in the popular vote. Then the Populists and the Democrats entered into an alignment, and William Jennings Bryan became their nominee. His image as an extremist served to swing great numbers of wavering Republicans back into the Republican camp. Moreover, the shift away from Bryanism came at a time when the economy was recovering from the depression of 1893, giving the Republicans the added boost of a return to "good times" under McKinley's leadership. The election of 1900 ratified the Republicans' new majority status by giving McKinley a decisive victory over Bryan. They retained the presidency for two more consecutive elections, lost it through a party split in 1912 and

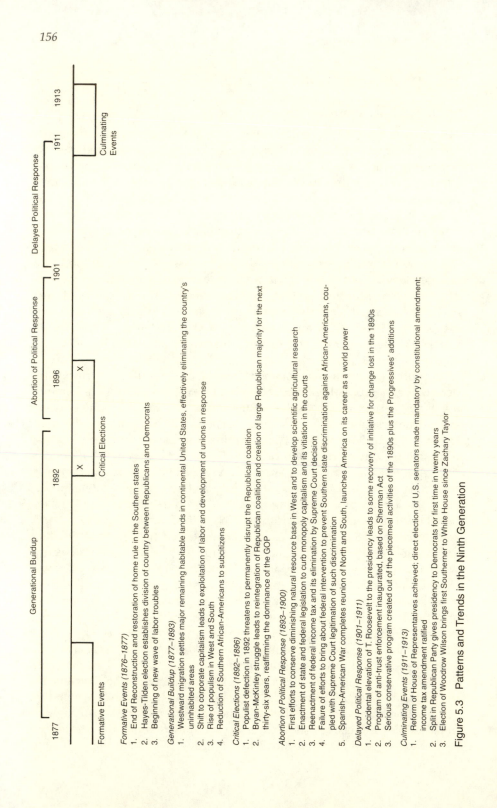

Generational Buildup | Abortion of Political Response | Delayed Political Response

1877　　　1892　　　1896　　　1901　　　1911　1913

Critical Elections　　　　　　　　　　Culminating Events

Formative Events

Formative Events (1876–1877)
1. End of Reconstruction and restoration of home rule in the Southern states
2. Hayes-Tilden election establishes division of country between Republicans and Democrats
3. Beginning of new wave of labor troubles

Generational Buildup (1877–1893)
1. Westward migration settles major remaining habitable lands in continental United States, effectively eliminating the country's uninhabited areas
2. Shift to corporate capitalism leads to exploitation of labor and development of unions in response
3. Rise of populism in West and South
4. Reduction of Southern African-Americans to subcitizens

Critical Elections (1892–1896)
1. Populist defection in 1892 threatens to permanently disrupt the Republican coalition
2. Bryan-McKinley struggle leads to reintegration of Republican coalition and creation of large Republican majority for the next thirty-six years, reaffirming the dominance of the GOP

Abortion of Political Response (1893–1900)
1. First efforts to conserve diminishing natural resource base in West and to develop scientific agricultural research
2. Enactment of state and federal legislation to curb monopoly capitalism and its vitiation in the courts
3. Reenactment of federal income tax and its elimination by Supreme Court decision
4. Failure of efforts to bring about federal intervention to prevent Southern state discrimination against African-Americans, coupled with Supreme Court legitimation of such discrimination
5. Spanish-American War completes reunion of North and South, launches America on its career as a world power

Delayed Political Response (1901–1911)
1. Accidental elevation of T. Roosevelt to the presidency leads to some recovery of initiative for change lost in the 1890s
2. Program of anti-trust enforcement inaugurated, based on Sherman Act
3. Serious conservative program created out of the piecemeal activities of the 1890s plus the Progressives' additions

Culminating Events (1911–1913)
1. Reform of House of Representatives achieved; direct election of U.S. senators made mandatory by constitutional amendment; income tax amendment ratified
2. Split in Republican Party gives presidency to Democrats for first time in twenty years
3. Election of Woodrow Wilson brings first Southerner to White House since Zachary Taylor

Figure 5.3　Patterns and Trends in the Ninth Generation

by 10,000 votes in 1916, and then decisively regained it for the next three elections.

The ninth generation, although it contained all the ingredients of a discrete generation, diverged from the normal generational pattern in several ways. In the first place, it was slightly longer than most generations, nearly reaching the forty-year maximum. Furthermore, its critical elections came after a relatively long period of generational buildup. The most important difference, however, lay in the fact that its generational political response was first aborted and then, ten years later, partially fulfilled.

The abortion of the generation's political response came not because Congress and the state legislatures refused to act but because the federal courts, led by the U.S. Supreme Court, intervened to nullify their actions. During the years of the generational buildup, the nation's legislatures made all the usual moves toward developing the basis for an intensive political response. Congress began experimenting with monetary grants-in-aid to the states in an effort to replace the land grant system, whose utility was diminishing because of the nearly exhausted supply of uncommitted marketable lands. Measures to conserve the use of the nation's natural resources and to regulate the new interstate corporations were also enacted. At the same time, the more progressive states were introducing extensive reform programs of their own to overcome the dislocations of the urban-industrial frontier. By the mid-1890s, Congress was ready for serious work, having reintroduced an income tax to finance positive new programs. It even considered action against the Southern states' efforts to deprive African-Americans of their civil rights.

Precisely at that time the U.S. Supreme Court intervened to write *laissez-faire* into the Constitution. The federal income tax was ruled unconstitutional in 1895, the Sherman Anti-trust Act had its teeth pulled in 1894, and racial segregation was upheld in 1896. The Court also struck at state regulatory legislation, substantially curtailing the states' powers to act to protect their citizens. These developments effectively aborted any massive government effort to respond to the challenges of the generation.[37] The coming of the Spanish-American War in 1898 further diverted the energies and attention of the public and the political leadership. By 1899, the reformers found themselves battling against imperialism overseas instead of for domestic reform.

The accidental elevation of Theodore Roosevelt to the presidency in 1901 reopened the possibilities for a generational response. Over the next few years, the beginnings made in the 1890s were resumed. As then, the primary efforts were in the fields of conservation and business regulation, with the vigorous new president leading the attack in both areas. In addition, Theodore Roosevelt began to develop new channels of cooperation with the states to achieve his goals.

The generation's culminating events were perhaps even more significant than those of the Roosevelt administration. They consisted of strong and successful efforts to eliminate the bottlenecks that had prevented a governmental response in the 1890s. The complexion of the Supreme Court had been changed even earlier in the decade, and progressive legislation was generally sustained after 1904. Then, in quick succession, the organization of the House of Representatives was changed to reduce the powers of the speaker, and a constitutional amendment providing for direct election of U.S. senators was submitted to the states and ratified, as was another making the levying of a federal income tax explicitly constitutional. These changes had their roots in the progressives' frustrations of the 1890s and bore fruit in the next generation.

Government and the Economy

In the ninth generation, the generation that ended the nineteenth century and the three centuries of the rural-land frontier, the American industrial revolution was completed and concentrated enterprise capitalism became the order of the day. The dominance of individual private enterprise gave way to corporate concentration and combination as large-scale capitalistic institutions with increasingly complex bureaucratic structures developed. Economic power ceased to be widely dispersed and became concentrated in the hands of those who controlled the new corporate structure. This was the age of the great entrepreneurs, individuals still big enough to build and control great enterprises, singly or in small groups; but, as the generation progressed, such individuals came to own less and less of the enterprises they controlled and had to entrust more of the management of those enterprises to subordinates.[38]

During this generation, the new enterprises became interstate in their operations and, in the process, became sufficiently powerful to challenge government on all planes. At the same time, *laissez-faire* became the dominant American policy, giving the new enterprises the latitude necessary to expand. Closely tied to "social Darwinism," *laissez-faire* was virtually written into the Constitution by the courts.

Perhaps the hallmark of the ninth generation was the progressive and inexorable closing of the land frontier. Though no longer the country's dominant frontier, it was still the great frontier, and, as Frederick Jackson Turner noted,[39] its end marked the end of a certain stage in American history. In effect, when that generation reached its high point, the land frontier was played out as a direct force on the American scene.

At the same time, the urban-industrial frontier reached the peak of its expansion and by the end of the generation had become crystallized in a certain mold. The structure of American business was transformed under the leadership of the great entrepreneurs, taking on a corporate character as the model provided by the railroad corporation was adapted for the great manufacturing and commercial enterprises that grew up in the land. Banking was developed into an interlocking nationwide system under a minimal measure of federal and state supervision in the wake of the new national banking act.

After 1877, the tariff became the great public issue of the times, with the Republicans supporting high tariffs as a political benefit to subsidize already strong industries. Until Wilson's presidency in 1913, the tariff went steadily upward.

The new corporate capitalism completely depersonalized the relations between owners and workers, leading to increased exploitation of the latter. It was during this generation that unionization began to develop, albeit with great difficulty, as a serious response to the new industrial system. Two kinds of union movements emerged after 1877: the American Federation of Labor (AFL) craft unions, which managed to gain a foothold in American society, and the very militant socialist and syndicalist unions, which did not.[40]

Government in the ninth generation began to undertake certain kinds of direct action to serve the general welfare, primarily through attempts to regulate certain business enterprises or the use of certain natural resources. Although the political demand for such regulation continued to grow throughout the generation, it was barely satisfied and, then, usually circumvented. This circumstance, in turn, promoted greater conflict between those disadvantaged by the changed economic system and the reformers, on the one hand, and the beneficiaries of the new system, on the other. Finally, the exhaustion of the supply of readily marketable public land led to the beginnings of systematic federal monetary grants-in-aid to develop new programs, particularly in the area of agriculture.[41]

Principal Ethnoreligious Manifestations

The ninth generation was preeminently the generation of mass immigration, particularly from Southern and Eastern Europe. Of the tens of millions who came to the United States, most entered the factories and mines that dominated the urban-industrial frontier. Ethnic neighborhoods became the basis of city life, and the country was effectively divided into "two cities"; an "upper" one of established Protestants who enjoyed the rights and benefits of America at its best, and a "lower" one of Catholic, Jewish, and Protestant immigrants whose rights and benefits were *de facto* limited by their position in society.[42]

This was the generation of the Protestant last stand, the last successful attempt to maintain the ways of the old America in the face of the multiple changes brought by industrialization, urbanization, and immigration. Elements of this last stand could be found in the Populist revolt, the prohibition movement, and the spread of anti-Catholic and anti-Semitic ideas and actions. The ninth generation was, by all accounts, the most overtly prejudiced in American history.[43]

If religious and ethnic prejudices led to discrimination, the virulent spread of racial prejudice led to much worse. This, after all, was the generation in which racism in the entire Western world reached its peak, justified intellectually by social Darwinism and practically by the thrust of colonialism. The compromise of 1877 abandoned the African-American population in the South to the Southern whites. What followed from 1877 to 1913 occurred in perfect generational pattern. African-Americans were disenfranchised between 1877 and the early 1890s, deprived of their civil rights from the late 1880s through the early 1900s (*Plessy* v. *Ferguson* was decided in 1895), and deprived of life itself wherever they resisted, particularly in the last decade of the generation.[44]

The segregation of Latinos, Chinese, and Japanese also intensified in the ninth generation. Generally *de facto*, their segregation was made legally and formally binding in some states (particularly California) during this period. Moreover, exclusion treaties designed to prevent the further immigration of Asians were a common feature of the generation.

So, too, was the segregation of Native Americans written into law. The Native Americans were legally deprived of the last vestiges of nationhood in the 1870s. After that, they became wards of the federal government, such that the Protestant leadership could press actively for their total Protestantization and the forcible abandonment of their old ways. This was the generation that came closest to destroying the Native Americans as peoples. Again, events followed a well-nigh perfect generational pattern. After the destruction of the last pockets of Native American resistance between 1877 and 1891 came attempts to convert the Native Americans into farmers and to remove their children from their parents' influence by sending them to distant boarding schools. These efforts reached their peak after 1890, culminating in the destruction of the last "national rights" of the Native Americans in Oklahoma in 1906 so that their territory could be added to the new state.[45]

SUMMARY

Chapter 5 has dealt with the flowering of sectionalism, its climax in the Civil War, and its culmination in the closing of the nineteenth century at the time of World War I. The chapter has encompassed three generations: the seventh, eighth, and ninth in American history. Following the pattern of themes presented in Table 2.1, the chapter looks at these themes in light of the completion of the continental expansion of the United States, the westward settlement movement, the growing controversy over slavery, the Civil War and Reconstruction, and the beginning and flowering of the urban-industrial frontier.

The frontier and sectionalism are the central themes of this chapter. The nineteenth century marked the first opportunity for the continuing frontier to enter a second stage. The pattern of sectionalism formed in the eighteenth and early nineteenth centuries around slavery brought the nation to the verge of disruption. Although the deadly danger of sectionalism was overcome, the sectional patterns that developed in the nineteenth century around economic patterns of settlement would continue to define the United States and American politics in the twentieth century as well.

NOTES

1. See the following titles by Frederick Jackson Turner: *Frontier and Section: Selected Essays* (Englewood Cliffs, N.J.: Prentice-Hall, 1961), *The Frontier in American History* (Tucson: University of Arizona Press, 1986), and *America's Great Frontiers and Sections* (Lincoln: University of Nebraska Press, 1965).

2. For a recent presentation of this subject, see Richard Bensel, *Sectionalism and American Political Development* (Madison: Wis.: University of Wisconsin Press, 1984). See also Clyde Kluckhohn, "Cultural Behavior," in Gardner Lindzey, ed., *Handbook of Social Psychology* (Cambridge, Mass: Addison, 1954); and Ralph Linton, *The Cultural Background of Personality* (New York: Appleton-Century, 1945).

3. For an assessment of sectionalism and regionalism, see Merrill Jensen, ed., *Regionalism in America* (Madison: University of Wisconsin Press, 1951). See also Howard W. Odum and Harry E. Moore, *American Regionalism* (New York: Holt, 1938); Harvey S. Perloff, Edgar S. Dunn, Eric E. Lamphard, and Richard F. Muth, *Regions, Resources, and Economic Growth* (Baltimore: Johns Hopkins University Press, 1960); John Friedmann and William Alonso, ed., *Regional Development and Planning* (Cambridge: MIT Press, 1964); and Martha Derthick, *Between State and Nation: Regional Organizations of the United States* (Washington, D.C.: Brookings Institution, 1974).

4. Ray Allen Billington, *The Far Western Frontier, 1830–1860* (New York: Harper and Row, 1962); Frederick Merck, *The Monroe Doctrine and American Expansionism 1843–1849* (New York: Alfred A. Knopf, 1966).

5. Along the borders of the three spheres (generally speaking, between and along the points of intersection of the semicircles of the map) lie three transition zones—the Ohio Valley, the western South, and the western Great Lakes—that share the characteristics of two or more spheres and have particularly diverse and complex patterns of culture and politics. The most complex of these three zones, the western Great Lakes, is the cultural and historical center of the United States.

6. For some discussions of state politics from a regional perspective, see Duane Lockard, *New England State Politics* (Princeton, N.J.: Princeton University Press, 1959); John H. Fenton, *Midwest Politics* (New York: Holt, 1966); and Neal R. Peirce, *The Megastates of America* (New York: Norton, 1972).

7. See John Herbers, *The New Heartland* (New York: Times Books, 1986).

8. See V. O. Key, Jr., *Southern Politics* (New York: Alfred A. Knopf, 1949); John H. Fenton, *Politics in the Border States* (New Orleans: Hauser, 1957); Neal R. Peirce, *The Deep South States of America* (New York: Norton, 1974); and Clifton McCleskey, *Political Power and American Democracy* (Pacific Grove, Calif.: Brooks/Cole, 1989).

9. See Thomas C. Donnelly, *Rocky Mountain Politics* (Albuquerque: University of New Mexico Press, 1940); Frank H. Jones, *Western Politics* (Salt Lake City: University of Utah Press, 1961); and Neal R. Peirce, *The Mountain States of America* (New York: Norton, 1972).

10. See David B. Walker, "New England and the Federal System," *Publius* 2, no. 2 (Fall 1972): 9–50.

11. Daniel J. Elazar, *The American Partnership* (Chicago: University of Chicago Press, 1962), pp. 57–58.

12. Bray Hammond, *Banks and Politics: From the Revolution to the Civil War* (Princeton, N.J.: Princeton University Press, 1957).

13. See Stanley I. Kutler, *The Supreme Court and the Constitution: Readings in American Constitutional History,* 3rd ed. (New York: W. W. Norton, 1984); Stanley Katz and Stanley I. Butler, *The Promise of American Progress and Prospects* (Baltimore: Johns Hopkins University Press, 1982); Paul L. Murphy, *Constitution in Crisis Times: 1918–1969* (New York: Harper and Row, 1971). See also the following titles by Edward S. Corwin: *American Constitutional History* (New York: Harper and Row, 1964); *The Constitution and What It Means Today,* 14th ed. (Princeton, N.J.: Princeton University Press, 1978); *Constitutional Revolution* (Claremont, Calif.: Pamona College, 1941); *Corwin on the Constitution,* 3 vols., edited with introduction and epilogue by Richard Loss (Ithaca, N.Y.: Cornell University Press, 1981–1988); *The Twilight of the Supreme Court: A History of Our Constitutional Theory* (New Haven, Conn.: Yale University Press, 1934); *Understanding the Constitution,* 4th ed., co-authored by J. W. Pettason (New York: Holt, Rinehart and Winston, 1967); and *The Constitution of the United States of America, Analysis and Interpretation: Annotations of Case Studies Decided by the Supreme Court of the United States to June 29, 1972* (Washington, D.C.: Government Printing Office, 1973).

14. Herbert Agar, *The Price of Union* (Boston: Houghton Mifflin, 1966); Herbert Agar and Henry Adams, *A History of the United States During the Administration of Jefferson and Madison* (London: Collins, 1948).

15. Marvin Meyers, *The Jacksonian Persuasion* (Stanford, Calif.: Stanford University Press, 1957); Joseph L. Blau, *Social Theories of Jacksonian Democracy* (New York: Hafner, 1947); Andrew Hacker, *The Study of Politics: The Western Tradition of American Origins* (New York: McGraw-Hill, 1973).

16. On the nullification controversy, see Harold C. Syrett, *Andrew Jackson* (Indianapolis: Bobbs-Merrill Co., 1953); John M. Anderson, ed., *Calhoun: Basic Documents* (State College, Pa.: Bald Eagle Press, 1952); and Glyndon G. Van Deusen, *The Jacksonian Era 1828–1848,* from the "New American Nation" series (New York: Harper and Row, 1959).

17. On the reform efforts of 1816–1848, see Leonard D. White, *The Jacksonians: A Study of Administrative History, 1826–1861* (New York: Macmillan, 1954).

18. Bernard de Voto, *The Year of Decision: 1846* (Boston: Little, Brown, 1943).

19. This section can be supplemented by reference to Harry N. Scheiber et al., *American Economic History* (New York: Harper and Row, 1970); Howard R. Smith,

Economic History of the United States (New York: Ronald Press, 1955); Harold Underwood Faulkner, *American Economic History*, 8th ed. (New York: Harper, 1960); Seymour E. Harris, ed., *American Economic History* (New York: McGraw-Hill, 1961).

20. On internal improvements, see Elazar, *The American Partnership*, ch. 2. See also Louis Hartz, *Economic Policy and Democratic Thought: Pennsylvania 1776–1860* (Chicago: Quadrangle Books, 1968).

21. On labor unions after 1816, see Bernard Mandel, *Labor: Free and Slave: Workingmen and the Anti-Slavery Movement in the United States* (New York: Associated Authors, 1955).

22. On early professions, see Daniel J. Elazar, *Building Toward Civil War* (Lanham, Md.: University Press of America and Center for the Study of Federalism, 1992).

23. On the South and slavery, see Henry Smith, *A Political History of Slavery*, 2 vols. (New York: G. P. Putnam's Sons, 1903); and Lloyd E. Abrosius, ed., *A Crisis of Republicanism: American Politics in the Civil War Era* (Lincoln: University of Nebraska Press, 1990).

24. On the North and abolitionism, see Stanley P. Hirschson, *Farewell to the Bloody Shirt: Northern Republicans and the Southern Negro 1877–1893* (Bloomington: Indiana University Press, 1962).

25. Franklin Hamlin Littel, *From Church to Pluralism: A Protestant Interpretation of Religion in American History* (Garden City, N.Y.: Anchor Books, 1962).

26. Ellis Paxson Oberholtzer, *A History of the United States Since the Civil War*, vol. 5 (New York: Macmillan, 1937); Allen Nevins, *The War for the Union* (New York: C. Scribner, 1960); James M. McPherson, *Battle Cry of Freedom: The Civil War Era* (New York: Oxford University Press, 1988).

27. Smith, *A Political History of Slavery.*

28. Hirschson, *Farewell to the Bloody Shirt*; J. Morgan Kousser, *The Shaping of Southern Politics* (New Haven, Conn.: Yale University Press, 1975); Lawrence Grossman, *The Democratic Party and the Negro: Northern and National Politics, 1868–1892* (Urbana: University of Illinois Press, 1976); Vincent P. DeSantis, *Republicans Face the Southern Question* (Baltimore: Johns Hopkins University Press, 1959).

29. On Lincoln's "New Deal," see Allen Nevins, *The Emergence of Lincoln* (New York: Scribner, 1950) and *The War for the Union* (New York: Scribner, 1960).

30. C. Vann Woodward, *The Burden of Southern History* (Baton Rouge: Louisiana State University Press, 1960).

31. John A. Crittenden, *Parties and Elections in the United States* (Englewood Cliffs, N.J.: Prentice-Hall, 1982); Oscar Handlin and Lilian Handlin, *Liberty in Expansion* (New York: Harper and Row, 1989).

32. C. Vann Woodward, *Origins of the New South: 1877–1913* (Baton Rouge: Louisiana State University Press, 1951); William A. Dunning, *Reconstruction, Political and Economic 1865–1877* (New York: Harper Torchbooks, 1935); Kenneth M. Stamp, *The Era of Reconstruction 1865–1877* (New York: Alfred A. Knopf, 1966); Robert P. Sharkey, *Money, Class, and Party: An Economic Study of Civil War and Reconstruction* (Baltimore: Johns Hopkins University Press, 1959); Harold M. Hyman, ed., *New Frontiers of the American Reconstruction* (Chicago: University of Chicago, 1961); E. Merton Coulter, *The South During Reconstruction 1865–1877*, Vol. 8, *A History of the South* (Baton Rouge: Louisiana State University Press, 1917); George Clemenceau, *American Reconstruction 1865–1867* (New York: Harper 1963).

33. Marcus Hanson, *The Great Atlantic Migration* (New York: Harvard University Press, 1961); Oscar Handlin, *The Uprooted* (New York: Grosset and Dunlap, 1951); Maldwyn Allen Jones, *American Immigration* (Chicago: University of Chicago Press, 1960).

34. Littel, *From Church to Pluralism;* Oliver Jensen, ed., *The Ninetees* (New York: American Heritage Publishing Co., 1967).

35. Woodward, *Origins of the New South: 1877–1913;* Ellis Paxson Oberholtzer, *A History of the United States Since the Civil War,* vol. 5 (New York: Macmillan, 1937).

36. On populism and labor protest, see Robert F. Durden, *The Climax of Populism* (Lexington: University of Kentucky Press, 1966); Matthew Josephson, *The Politicos, 1805–1896* (New York: Harcourt, Brace and World, 1938); Gerald Gaither, *Blacks and the Populist Revolt: Ballots and Bigotry in the "New South"* (University: University of Alabama Press, 1975); Jeffrey J. Crow, Paul D. Escott, and Charles L. Flynn, Jr., eds., *Race, Class and Politics in Southern History: Essays in Honor of Robert F. Durden* (Baton Rouge: Louisiana State University, 1989); Theodore R. Mitchell, *Political Education in the Southern Farmer's Alliance, 1887–1900* (Madison: University of Wisconsin Press, 1977); and John Donald Hicks, *The Populist Revolt: A History of the Farmer's Alliance and the People's Party* (Lincoln: University of Nebraska Press, 1961).

37. Stanley I. Kutler, ed., *The Supreme Court and the Constitution: Readings in American Constitutional History,* 3rd ed. (New York: W. W. Norton, 1984).

38. See Matthew Josephson, *The Robber Barrons* (New York: Harcourt, Brace and World, 1934).

39. Turner, *Frontier and Section, The Frontier in American History,* and *America's Great Frontiers and Sections.*

40. On labor-movement radicalism, see Josephson, *The Politicos;* Sarif Roboff, *Boston's Labor Movement: An Oral History of Work and Union Organizing* (Boston: The Boston 200 Corporation, 1977); and Eric L. Hirsch, *Urban Revolt: Ethnic Politics in the Nineteenth-Century Labor Movement* (Berkeley: University of California Press, 1990).

41. See Elazar, *The American Partnership.*

42. See Handlin, *The Uprooted;* Oscar Handlin, ed., *Immigration as a Factor in American History* (Englewood Cliffs, N.J.: Prentice-Hall, 1954); and Caroline Golab, *Immigrant Destinations* (Philadelphia: Temple University Press, 1977).

43. On religious prejudice, see John Higham, *Strangers in the Land: Patterns of American Nativism, 1860–1925* (New Brunswick, N.J.: Rutgers University Press, 1988).

44. John Whitson Call, *The Highest Stage of White Supremacy: The Origins of Segregation in South Africa and the American South* (New York: Cambridge University Press, 1982); James A. Kushner, *Apartheid in America: An Historical and Legal Analysis of Contemporary Racial Segregation in the United States* (Gaithersburg, Md.: Associated Faculty Press, 1980).

45. Colonel W. S. Nye, *Carbine and Lance: The Story of Old Fort Sill* (Norman: University of Oklahoma Press, 1943); Angie Debo, *Oklahoma: Footloose and Fancy-Free* (Norman: University of Oklahoma Press, 1949); Angie Debo, *And Still the Waters Run* (Norman: University of Oklahoma Press, 1940); Angie Debo, *Rise and Fall of the Choctaw Republic,* 2d ed. (Norman: University of Oklahoma Press, 1961); Grant Foreman, *Five Civilized Tribes* (Norman: University of Oklahoma Press, 1934); Grace S. Woodward, *The Cherokees* (Norman: University of Oklahoma Press, 1963).

CHAPTER 6

Sectional, Class, and Ethnic Patterns in the Twentieth-Century United States

At the beginning of the twentieth century, the United States underwent another change in its geo-historical as well as cultural location. Just as the end of the rural-land frontier turned the nation's focus to its urban areas, so, too, did a new urban culture begin to replace the older rural one. In the 1920s, this new urban culture was summed up by F. Scott Fitzgerald as involving "fast music, fast cars, and fast women."

The older rural culture—that of family farms and small towns servicing those farms, of traditional religious values, of face-to-face community and local self-government, with a minimum of outside involvement in which the more complex and open life of the big city was the exception rather than the rule—was replaced by new big-city standards. A loss of religious faith and practice resulted from the popularization of "science"—Darwinism popularized as the notion of humankind having evolved from the apes, anthropology popularized as cultural relativism, and Freudianism popularized as the idea that humans cannot be morally responsible for their actions because they are simply bundles of impulses whose configuration is the result of unconscious traumas. The rest of the century would reflect the results of this transformation and its extension into new areas in various ways.

The century began with a conflict between old values and new, embodied most visibly in the struggle over the prohibition of alcoholic beverages and the enactment of Sunday "blue laws." Norms that the retreating fundamentalist Protestants could not retain from voluntary adherence in earlier attempts, they tried to impose by legislation. Not surprisingly, their experiment failed, although it took the first half of the first generation of the twentieth century to establish that truth and act in response to it. Meanwhile, the reaction to Prohibition spawned the jazz age of the 1920s and the entrenchment of organized crime in the United States. In fact, oranized crime was given a great opportunity to provide a widely used service: the supplying of illicit liquor. For many of those who could afford them, the excesses of this age led to a new hedonism, a pleasure-seeking that all too often remained the shallow pursuit of new thrills, aided and abetted by a new style of music that broke down old social barriers and re-straints and by the rise of commercially owned and operated mass com-munications that, in the competition for audiences, pursued the lowest common denominator (at least the lowest common denominator allow-able by the law) to gain larger ones. The forward movement of this new hedonistic individualism was substantially slowed and in certain respects even halted as a result of the Great Depression, which dominated the sec-ond half of the generation. People had to devote their full energies to the task of surviving economically; and when World War II brought back prosperity, the war effort was the focus of their attention and resources.

The second generation of the twentieth century witnessed yet another change in geo-historical location as the big cities, whose populations had peaked in 1920, gave way to metropolitan areas and suburban living, a brief rekindling of family values, general prosperity, and television. It was the very success of these elements that led to the revolutions against them, in the 1960s—beginning with the civil rights revolution, whereby those nonwhites who had been left out of the peaceful, prosperous 1950s prop-erly and successfully asserted their demands to be included, and continu-ing with young, middle-class, white college students mounting a revolu-tion in values that transformed the American way of life. By the end of that generation, the revolution had penetrated every stratum of American society. What emerged was a far more radical individualism than before: a sexual revolution, a revolution in gender roles, and the introduction of a therapeutic society in which self-improvement and self-gratification be-came central norms.

The eve of the twentieth century found the American people without open land to the west for the taking, for the first time in their three hun-dred years of history; but what they did have was a mighty industrial plant whose expansion seemed limitless. Their country was tentatively and ambivalently stepping out onto the larger world stage as an instant star, but the American people were not at all certain that they even wanted to be in the theater. By the end of the century's first generation, they would discover that the choice was not theirs to make and that the in-dustrial system was not self-governing. Later, another generation would learn that it was possible to develop new frontiers in a wider universe and that, like it or not, the burdens of world leadership led down the path de-scribed by the isolationist Progressives, who wished to preserve Ameri-ca's character as the last best hope of mankind.[1]

As Americans approached the middle of the last generation of the twentieth century, many believed that its promises had fallen victim to the dynamics of history. For the first time, many became aware of the problematics of American history as well as of its greatness, all of which had been played out on the stage of generational progression.

THE TENTH GENERATION (1913–1947)

Major Political Patterns and Events

The formative events of the tenth generation were exceptional, primarily because so much of the response in the previous generation had been aborted. Thus, not only did some of the culminating events of the ninth generation serve as the formative events for the tenth, but the domestic activities of the Wilson administration also served to form the political responses of the new generation and, indeed, shaped those of the new century as a whole.[2] (See Figure 6.1.)

The final legitimization of the federal income tax—coming as it did at the end of the federal land grant programs and on the heels of the elimination of the tariff as a significant source of federal revenues—restored federal supremacy in the area of revenue-raising and, indeed, equipped Washington for the great expenditures of the twentieth century that lay ahead. The establishment of the federal reserve system gave the national government a means of exercising some fiscal control over American society for the first time since the demise of the second National Bank in the 1830s. The "New Freedom" programs, particularly the agricultural extension, highway, and vocational education grant programs, served as the foundation stones for subsequent developments in the twentieth century. These developments included the transformation of agricultural production that caused most farmers to move to the cities, the creation of a new transportation system based on the automobile, and the use of education as a primary vehicle for social mobility. Finally, World War I decisively catapulted America onto the world stage as a major power, thereby ending the possibility of isolation if not isolation itself.

The generational buildup that occurred between 1919 and 1932 brought the first steps in the reformation of a society no longer shaped by either the rural-land frontier with its settlement of the West or the urban-industrial frontier with its mass immigration. Politically, it was a period of consolidation of the gains made under Wilson, growing agitation for political action to reform under the country's socioeconomic system, and increasing experimentation in the states with reform programs. At the same time, the country made one last vigorous attempt to isolate itself from world affairs. The period climaxed in the Great Depression, which acted as a cata-

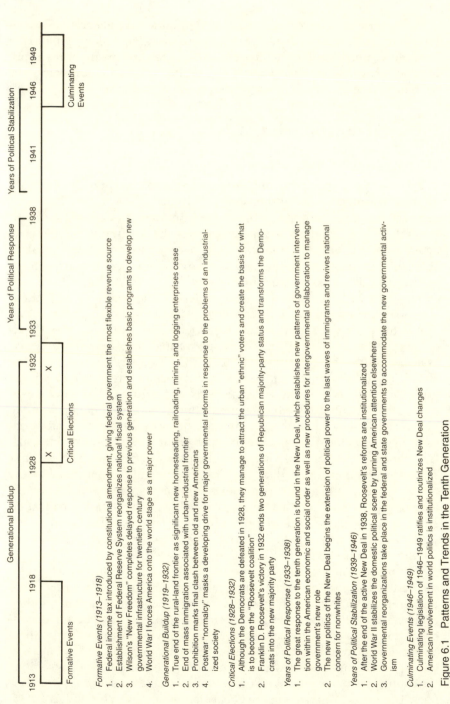

Figure 6.1   Patterns and Trends in the Tenth Generation

Formative Events (1913–1918)

1. Federal income tax introduced by constitutional amendment, giving federal government the most flexible revenue source
2. Establishment of Federal Reserve System reorganizes national fiscal system
3. Wilson's "New Freedom" completes delayed response to previous generation and establishes basic programs to develop new governmental infrastructure for twentieth century
4. World War I forces America onto the world stage as a major power

Generational Buildup (1919–1932)

1. True end of the rural-land frontier as significant new homesteading, railroading, mining, and logging enterprises cease
2. End of mass immigration associated with urban-industrial frontier
3. Prohibition marks final clash between old and new Americans
4. Postwar "normalcy" masks a developing drive for major governmental reforms in response to the problems of an industrial- ized society

Critical Elections (1928–1932)

1. Although the Democrats are defeated in 1928, they manage to attract the urban "ethnic" voters and create the basis for what is to become the "Roosevelt coalition"
2. Franklin D. Roosevelt's victory in 1932 ends two generations of Republican majority-party status and transforms the Demo- crats into the new majority party

Years of Political Response (1933–1938)

1. The great response to the tenth generation is found in the New Deal, which establishes new patterns of government interven- tion within the American economic and social order as well as new procedures for intergovernmental collaboration to manage government's new role
2. The new politics of the New Deal begins the extension of political power to the last waves of immigrants and revives national concern for nonwhites

Years of Political Stabilization (1939–1946)

1. After the end of the active New Deal in 1938, Roosevelt's reforms are institutionalized
2. World War II stabilizes the domestic political scene by turning American attention elsewhere
3. Governmental reorganizations take place in the federal and state governments to accommodate the new governmental activ- ism

Culminating Events (1946–1949)

1. Culminating legislation of 1946–1949 ratifies and routinizes New Deal changes
2. American involvement in world politics is institutionalized

lyst for all the trends and tendencies of the buildup and opened the door for the generational response.[3]

The critical elections of 1928 and 1932 bracketed the onset of the Great Depression. In the first, the Republican victory marked the formation of what was to become the winning Democratic coalition of the near future—a coalition that reflected the alliance of immigrants, dispossessed minorities, liberals, and reformers that was braced for an assault on the older "establishment." By 1932, that coalition, aided by the deepening depression, catapulted Franklin Delano Roosevelt into office. FDR judiciously cemented its components together into a national majority, ending two generations of Republican dominance. His efforts were decisively ratified in the landslide election of 1936.[4]

The political response of the tenth generation was so clearly visible in the New Deal that it need not be described in detail here.[5] When the dust had cleared, all governments—and the federal government in particular—had assumed a new role as leaders and managers of much of America's public life. In doing so, they not only changed the relationship between public and private activity in the United States but also opened the door to the integration of those people previously excluded from full participation in American life.

Despite the objective needs of a still-depressed economy, as well as the popularity and forcefulness of FDR, the New Deal came to an effective end in 1938 after a duration no longer than any of the other periods of generational political response. This spurt of activity came and went in the same way as its predecessors had done (despite its drastic character), to be followed by nearly a decade of political stabilization during which the New Deal reforms were consolidated, their administration was institutionalized, and their principles were accepted by an even wider public. The coming of World War II turned people's attention away from domestic affairs and further sharpened their New Deal–fostered tendency to turn their attention to Washington, thus adding another element to the consolidation of New Deal gains.

The culminating events of the tenth generation came after the end of the war, between 1946 and 1949.[6] They also opened the eleventh generation. Four sets of events are identifiable. First there was a spate of legislation ratifying the New Deal changes: the Full Employment Act of 1946, which ratified and affirmed the new relationship between the federal government and the economy; the Administrative Procedures Act, which crystallized the restructuring of the federal administration to allow management of the expanded federal establishment; and the Legislative Reorganization Act, which restructured the congressional committee system in light of Congress's expanded role as overseer of the new bureaucracy. Then there was the formalization of American intervention in world affairs, of which the intervention in Greece and Turkey, the Marshall Plan, and the NATO alliance were the most prominent landmarks.

Both of the foregoing sets of events took place in the shadow of the opening of the metropolitan-technological frontier, the third stage in America's continuing frontier process. Suburbanization and the replacement of the country's original industrial base with one based on more sophisticated technologies were the order of the day. These developments, in turn, generated an initial legislative response intended to better open the trail to the new frontier, about which more is noted below.

Government and the Economy

By the end of the ninth generation, the age of the great entrepreneurs had passed.[7] The tenth generation ushered in a second transition era, a generation of changes in the country's economic system parallel only to those of the seventh generation a century earlier. Corporate capitalism reached new heights of complexity and bureaucratization, while economic control passed into the hands of those able to control the capital necessary for corporate expansion. In short, financial capitalism replaced entrepreneurial capitalism, and ownership, management, and control became increasingly separated.

Agitation for increased government intervention to provide some public control over the new economic giants was finally translated into significant action in the wake of the economic crisis of the 1930s. Government regulation became widespread, effective, and accepted, and its constitutionality was ratified by the courts. Beyond simple regulation, direct government action was expanded in a wide variety of areas, leading to a great increase in the size and scope of government on all planes. One result of this increase was the emergence of a consciously cooperative federalism. The *laissez-faire*-oriented economy created in the nineteenth century was replaced by a mixed economy in which government's role as an active participant in and regulator of the economy was recognized and more or less accepted. Government regulatory programs injected the idea of the public interest into the processes of economic decisionmaking. The Federal Reserve System was introduced at the very beginning of the generation to stabilize the national fiscal system. Government regulation of the banks increased, especially after 1933, and other fiscal institutions were brought under governmental supervision. And the protection tariff was transformed from a device designed to protect the industries created by the urban-industrial frontier into a device intended to promote freer trade in anticipation of the new frontier just emerging.

As part of the transition, government support led to the development of big industrial unions as a countervailing force to the power of the big corporations.[8] Political conflict between labor and business replaced the old sectional conflicts of an agrarian age, particularly after the development of the industrial unions with federal support. This conflict was supplemented by an urban-rural conflict of some proportions. Even though the farmers finally won the government assistance they had been seeking since the 1870s, they ceased to be the decisive force in American life that they had been; but they did not retire from the scene without a fight.[9]

Principal Ethnoreligious Manifestations

One of the major actions contributing to the generational buildup of the tenth generation was the virtual closing of immigration to the United States. This action, coming at the end of the urban-industrial frontier and, indeed, related to it, helped create the conditions for the New Deal whereby an increasingly Americanized group of immigrants and their children began to function in the political arena to gain their share of America's inheritance. Ethnic politics became the basis of the Democratic Party coalition that was to sweep into power in the 1930s. By the end of the generation, the "ethnics" were in the saddle politically, both in Washington and in those cities and states where they were concentrated.[10]

Meanwhile, Prohibition—the old-time Protestants' "last crusade"—ran aground. It not only failed to place a fundamentalist stamp upon the country but also alienated many of the Protestants' own children.[11] The Ku Klux Klan of the 1920s, a more venal manifestation of the same phenomenon, was another echo of the past. The new spirit of individual liberation from social restraints that became the embodiment of the "roaring 20s" was the real portent of the future, providing a buildup not only for the generation but, it appears, for the century as well. The Great Depression and World War II temporarily turned people's attention away from the concerns of the 1920s, but by the generation's end, everything was poised for a continuation of the trends initiated during those years.

The situation of the nonwhites stabilized at the beginning of the generation, took a turn for the better at its midpoint, and was poised on the threshold of great advances by 1946.[12] The beginning of the generation saw the African-Americans at their lowest point since the Civil War. The Wilson administration's great blindspot, they were accorded no help from Washington during those years. Moreover, the wartime migrations northward led to bloody race riots in a number of northern cities. Nevertheless, the war did begin a serious diffusion of the African-American population to Northern and Western cities. The 1920s saw a continuation of lynchings meant to keep African-Americans "in their place"; but they also saw a number of significant Supreme Court decisions that began the long process of restoring their right to vote.

Further improvements came in the 1930s. Although African-Americans were not always treated equally under New Deal programs, they were included among the beneficiaries of these programs—in itself a great step forward. Moreover, the federal courts began to intervene on behalf of the civil rights of African-Americans during the 1930s, following the famous "Scottsboro" case.

The impact of World War II led in two directions. On the one hand, it broadened the horizons of many African-Americans—specifically, those in the service and those who moved to Northern and Western cities to work in the war industries. On the other, it brought the American "establishment" face to face with the problem of African-American rights. The combination of the trumpeting of the ideals underlying the American war effort, the decline of racism as an acceptable ideology on the world scene, and the growing integration of African-American soldiers in the army served to bring the civil rights issue to the fore. The generation ended with President Truman's 1946 order ending segregation in the armed services, along with the first public struggle for civil rights legislation since the 1890s.

Orientals also passed through a difficult generation, but it ended with substantial gains for them. The reaction to the forced evacuation of Japanese people from the West Coast at the beginning of World War II led to the breaking down of most of the barriers excluding them after the war. And the picture painted in the United States of China's role as an ally did much the same for Chinese-Americans.

The beginning of the tenth generation found the Native-Americans thoroughly broken and under the most severe form of colonial rule. The New Deal brought with it the Indian Restoration Act of 1934, which restored to those tribes who wanted it formal, if limited, rights of self-government and an institutional structure that could be used in the attempt to effectuate those rights. Although the end results were less favorable than anticipated, by the late 1940s all the identified tribes had organized political institutions under the act.[13]

THE ELEVENTH GENERATION (1948–1976)

Major Political Patterns and Events

The spread of the metropolitan-technological frontier and its rise to dominance in the late 1940s led to the enactment of legislation and the inauguration of programs designed to help open that new frontier to all Americans. It was during the formative years of the eleventh generation that the interstate highway and urban renewal programs were inaugurated by the federal government and state and local governments began the great expansion of their activities to build schools and roads and otherwise develop the infrastructure for the conquest of the new frontier. (See Figure 6.2.)

The generational buildup that followed these formative events dwelt primarily on the development of that infrastructure domestically while the Cold War was being fought overseas. The Korean War and its aftermath (including the period of McCarthyism in the United States) dominated the attention of the federal government and the American public. Yet throughout the 1950s, new federal aid programs were being inaugurated at the behest of state and local interests to experimentally meet the developmental demands of the metropolitan frontier. Meanwhile, other programs designed to meet the problems generated by that frontier were being suggested, debated, and shaped (but not enacted), both within and outside of Congress. Moreover, the states and localities were shouldering the great burden of providing an infrastructure of public services needed for the advance onto the metropolitan frontier.[14]

The two critical elections of 1956 and 1960 were part of that generational buildup. In the first, Dwight D. Eisenhower, the war hero whose personal popularity had enabled him to take the presidency from the Democrats after twenty years of incumbency, won a strong victory that appeared to have upset the Democratic coalition forged a generation earlier. The Republican Party, however, was unable to capitalize on Eisenhower's popularity. In 1960, the popular young Democratic nominee, John F. Kennedy, restored the Democratic coalition with the added dimension of opening the presidency to non-Protestants (a natural outgrowth of the coalition's own development in light of the social trends in the eleventh generation). In doing so, he enabled the Democratic Party to retain its majority status for a second generation, just as Jackson had done in the critical election of 1828 or, in the case of the Republicans, McKinley in 1896.

The critical elections also affirmed the full urbanization of American politics and the effective end of the old urban-rural conflict on the national plane. Kennedy's success was ratified in the Democrats' landslide victory of 1964, when the Republicans presented a candidate who not only rejected the Kennedy-Johnson response to the problems of the eleventh generation but seemingly sought to repeal the New Deal as well.

The first half of the eleventh generation brought another change in American voting patterns. As the country approached the centennial of the Civil War, the political alignments fostered by that great event began to collapse. The new generation of voters was the first to no longer have grandparents who were products of the war era or Reconstruction. Their attitudes toward the political demands of their families that were hallowed by the conflict were far less immediate than new issues that seemed to them far more pressing. The break came among Northern Republicans

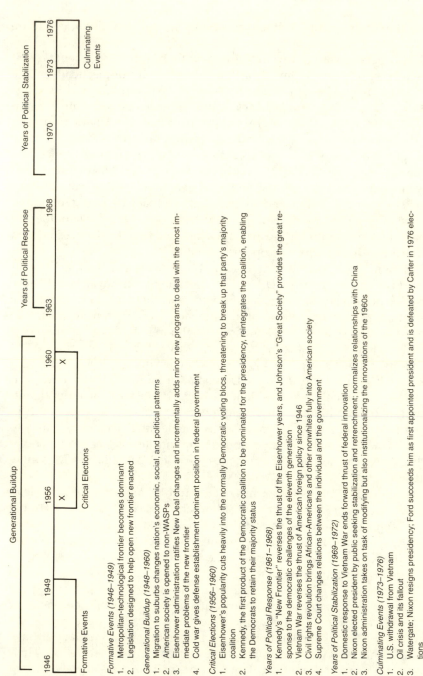

Formative Events

Formative Events (1946–1949)
1. Metropolitan-technological frontier becomes dominant
2. Legislation designed to help open new frontier enacted

Generational Buildup (1948–1960)
1. Migration to suburbs changes nation's economic, social, and political patterns
2. American society is opened to non-WASPs
3. Eisenhower administration ratifies New Deal changes and incrementally adds minor new programs to deal with the most immediate problems of the new frontier
4. Cold war gives defense establishment dominant position in federal government

Critical Elections (1956–1960)
1. Eisenhower's popularity cuts heavily into the normally Democratic voting blocs, threatening to break up that party's majority coalition
2. Kennedy, the first product of the Democratic coalition to be nominated for the presidency, reintegrates the coalition, enabling the Democrats to retain their majority status

Years of Political Response (1961–1968)
1. Kennedy's "New Frontier" reverses the thrust of the Eisenhower years, and Johnson's "Great Society" provides the great response to the democratic challenges of the eleventh generation
2. Vietnam War reverses the thrust of American foreign policy since 1946
3. Civil rights revolution brings African-Americans and other nonwhites fully into American society
4. Supreme Court changes relations between the individual and the government

Years of Political Stabilization (1969–1972)
1. Domestic response to Vietnam War ends forward thrust of federal innovation
2. Nixon elected president by public seeking stabilization and retrenchment; normalizes relationships with China
3. Nixon administration takes on task of modifying but also institutionalizing the innovations of the 1960s

Culminating Events (1973–1976)
1. U.S. withdrawal from Vietnam
2. Oil crisis and its fallout
3. Watergate; Nixon resigns presidency; Ford succeeds him as first appointed president and is defeated by Carter in 1976 elections

Figure 6.2   Patterns and Trends in the Eleventh Generation

first, no doubt because wartime memories were less compelling in the North. The well-nigh solid Republican ranks of the northernmost tier of states and those of the plains, already weakened by the forces of Populism, Progressivism, and the New Deal, crumbled in the late 1940s and 1950s as reinvigorated Democratic parties gained majority status within them.

The solid South, where the old ties were based not only on memories far more searing but also on the immediate issue of race, did not give way until the late 1950s and 1960s after it became apparent that the national Democratic Party would not defend the interests of segregationists. By that time, voting Republican no longer seemed sacrilegious to the new generation of Southern white voters, whose memories of the Civil War and Reconstruction were not reinforced by personal encounters with participants or witnesses. By the end of the 1960s, the newly reenfranchised African-Americans represented a growing proportion of Democratic voters south of the Mason-Dixon line.

Kennedy's assumption of the presidency in 1961 inaugurated the period of intensive political response to the problems of the eleventh generation, although that response did not reach its peak on the domestic front until 1964–1965. Kennedy's own efforts were most successful in the area of foreign affairs, where he shifted the emphasis of the Cold War in new directions in response to perceived changes in the Communist bloc. It fell to Lyndon B. Johnson to preside over the burst of domestic reform activities that represented the generational response. He did so through his "Great Society" program in a flurry of activity unexcelled in any other generation, during which time he secured enactment of most of the programs proposed and discussed by reformers in the 1950s.[15] At the same time, the civil rights revolution reached a climax in Congress, in the state legislatures, in the streets, and in the courts.[16] The U.S. Supreme Court took the lead in sustaining not only the rights of African-Americans but also those of criminals (or suspects) and, beyond that, in restricting the power of government to interfere with individuals' activities across a whole range of concerns previously held to be within the legitimate province of the states in their responsibility to regulate morals.[17]

The period of generational response came to an end out of its own momentum. The nation tired of the pace of innovation and the measures rushed through under pressure from the White House (Johnson apparently sensed that he had only a short time during which he could hope to gain enactment of his program, and made the best of it); now these measures needed to be "cleaned up," implemented, and consolidated. Moreover, the Vietnam War turned American attention in other directions.

The war also reversed the thrust of U.S. foreign policy since 1946, causing Americans to seek ways to pull back from the extreme interventionist position that the U.S. government had adopted by the early 1960s.[18] In doing so, the war contributed to the inauguration of the eleventh generation's period of political stabilization. As part of the quest for stabilization, the voters turned to the opposition party for a president who promised consolidation rather than new ventures.

The Nixon administration immediately took on the task of consolidating the innovations of the previous administration but, in trying to do so, was confronted by still-disaffected groups who were already looking ahead to new changes. The administration did gain more than a few successes in foreign policy that consolidated the generation. Foremost among these was the reestablishing of American relations with mainland China. On the domestic side, Nixon's New Federalism basically consolidated the strengthened federal role in the intergovernmental system developed during the generation. At the same time, the program preached decentralization.

Then the Nixon administration came apart over the Watergate scandal. During 1974, with the United States facing an energy crisis, a truckers' strike, and the collapse of South Vietnam, Washington was paralyzed and the governors of the several states had to step in to provide an appropriate American response. The president ultimately resigned, to escape impeachment. Gerald Ford, the only appointed president in American history, took over—as a caretaker president, in effect—to finish out the generation. The election of Jimmy Carter in 1976 wrote *finis* to the generation and opened the twelfth generation in American history.[19]

Government and the Economy

The economic theme of the eleventh generation may be summed up in the phrase "regulated capitalism."[20] With the opening of the metropolitan-technological frontier, the positive role of government in the economy, affirmed at the end of the previous generation, became even more fully accepted and eventually was even transmuted into the notion of government responsibility for the nation's social and economic health. This notion was casually acknowledged by the political leaders of both parties as well as by the general public—this despite a growing fringe of protest groups that demanded a "restoration" of the relationship between government and the economic system that is supposed to have existed in the nineteenth century according to the generally accepted myth of *laissez-faire*. Another fringe emerged somewhat later, disillusioned with government's ability to shoulder such formidable tasks. Furthermore, a new emphasis on partnership between governments and private economic decisionmakers took form to replace the old notion of government regulation as an unqualified interference.

Labor unions grew so strong that they became identified in the public mind as "big labor," a countervailing force in the economy that could be as threatening to the public as "big business." The federal government began to regulate them as well. At the same time, technological change began to cut into their membership and social base. Corporations became more fully manager-controlled as they accumulated enough wealth to generate their own capital for expansion without going to external money markets. The separation between ownership and management was further increased. Moreover, the pace of technological change accelerated to the point where it became an independent variable in the economic equation.

The eleventh generation witnessed a continued expansion of direct government action, government size, expenditure, and debt. Federal fiscal policies have become crucial inflationary or deflationary influences on the economy. Government regulation continued to expand or was increasingly refined. And the federal-state-local partnership was expanded into new fields including urban redevelopment and metropolitan planning.

As the generation continued, there was a general internationalization of the economy. American business became increasingly involved in overseas ventures, leading to the establishment of foreign subsidiaries in all corners of the globe. One result of this increased involvement was the growing concern of the business community with foreign policy, not only in matters of domestic concern. As the labor-business conflicts of the previous era lost their relevance, a new sectionalism began to emerge, rooted in the different responses to the new frontier in the various sections of the country. Sectional interests came through in ways far different from, but no less meaningful than, those of the old sectionalism.

Principal Ethnoreligious Manifestations

The eleventh generation brought with it a great effort to fully integrate all Americans as citizens, involving nothing less than the elimination of the division between the "upper" and "lower" cities produced by the urban-industrial frontier.[21] The first big step in this direction was the acceptance of Catholicism and Judaism as "American" religions on a par with Protestantism, an accomplished fact by the mid-1950s. Then came the opening of all political offices to non-Protestants, achieved in the 1960s.[22]

Last to come was the integration of the races. The struggle for African-American rights shifted into high gear after the school desegregation decision in 1954. It became an African-American-led struggle in the late 1950s and won its greatest political victories in the mid-1960s as part of the generational response. With the African-American victories in hand, the Latinos and Native Americans began to seek greater recognition of their rights. As the eleventh generation moved into its last years, the struggle was enlarged to involve the most excluded of the "excluded Americans."

All of these developments led to changes in the role of religion in American life and in the character of ethnic politics. During the first half of the generation, identification with one of the three major religions became the *sine qua non* of Americanism, at least among the vast majority of Americans who shared middle-class values—the Americans who "counted." Religious institutions also increasingly became the repositories of ethnic identification insofar as they continued to survive among particular groups. The 1940s and 1950s saw the transformation of explicitly ethnic churches into more Americanized ones that retained their ethnic base in less visible ways. At the same time, ethnic politics seemed to be diminishing during the first half of the eleventh generation as its conventional patterns faded in the face of suburbanization and the integration of the "two cities." Where ethnicity was strong, the "ethnics" were in the saddle politically; and where ethnicity was irrelevant, their children were successfully assimilated.

Then, in mid-generation, the acceptance extended to all religions began to include even those people of no religion. Ethnic identification underwent something of a revival in response to the "black power" movement. The erstwhile religious revival of the 1950s came to an end and organized religion even began to decline slightly as a force on the American scene, giving way at crucial points to ethnicity as the bearer of tolerated differences in American society.

The most visible aspect of the merging of the "two cities" was, of course, the African-Americans' struggle for civil rights and more. To date, this struggle, too, has followed the conventional pattern of generational flow—beginning as a matter of conventional pressure politics with a moralistic tinge, primarily in the states after World War II; becoming nationalized with the intervention of the U.S. Supreme Court in 1954; being transformed into an African-American-led struggle in the late 1950s; and reaching its climax with the marches, federal civil rights legislation, and riots of the 1960s. These events were followed by the rise of the aforementioned "black power" movement and the election of African-Americans to local political office, both of which turned the struggle into an entirely new phase.

In the middle of the generation, the African-Americans' struggle aroused the increasing militancy of other nonwhite groups such as Latinos, Native Americans, and some Orientals. The granting of statehood to Hawaii in 1960 set the stage for acceptance of such nonwhites as full citizens. By the mid-1960s, substantial federal, state, and private efforts were under way to encourage these groups to improve their economic and political lot. Moreover, this struggle, like that of the African-Americans, became a popular cause in many nonminority circles.

THE RISE AND DECLINE OF CLASS CONFLICT

By the 1930s, class and ethnic differences appeared to be far more important in American politics than sectional ones. The closing of the land frontier and the exacerbated struggle between labor and industry—which was linked closely not only with the struggle of the "ethnics" who were trying to find an equal place for themselves in American society but also with the diminution of the farmers' role as a powerful interest in American politics—shifted conflict away from the sections and into the cities, and emphasized its class dimensions. Since this was also a time when many American historians were turning to Marxian or Weberian theories, it became fashionable to reinterpret American history in terms of class conflict.[23] Soon the argument was not that class had come to replace section, but that class had always been more important. As it turned out, the class conflict was an aberration of one or at most two generations in American history. Sectionalism was to return by the next generation.

The coming of the Great Depression further obscured issues by transferring public attention to nationwide class conflicts. But World War II and the immediate postwar boom more or less successfully reduced the impact of these differences, too. Prosperity and suburbanization, by lifting the earning level of most American families into the middling range and by providing a standard minimum level of material comfort (and even a standardized form of material living) for perhaps four-fifths of the population, has considerably reduced the kind of class consciousness and class antagonisms that threatened American society in the 1930s.[24] Coupled with these factors, the normal passage of the generations has also reduced many of the overt differences between ethnic groups throughout the country, bringing the great majority of the inhabitants of this land into active participation in an overall national culture. Integration of the African-American, Latino, and Asian populations and accommodation with the Native Americans—as troubled and violent as these tasks have been—are really the last steps in this process.

With predominantly middle-class ways and a standard of living once again the shared property of the bulk of the nation, as in the years prior to the Civil War and Industrial Revolution, the old cleavages reemerged in new forms. Perhaps there was no *a priori* reason to expect that sectional differences would come to the fore again, particularly in this self-styled age of the shrunken world. Yet, paradoxically, this very shrinking of distance has given the newly emerging sectionalism sources of strength other than those that draw their vitality from mere provincialism.

Here we will examine six dimensions of sectional identity: (1) the frontier experience and its economic consequences, (2) culture and society, (3) the character of pluralism within the section, (4) educational policy, (5) relations between the section and the federal government, and (6) the character of politics within the section.

NEW ENGLAND:
A "CONFEDERATION" WITHIN THE UNION

The oldest and most coherent of the sections is New England. Its six states consciously seek to cooperate with one another in numerous ways, joining together to deal with common problems of transportation, communications, education, economic development, and law enforcement in recognition of the bonds of both history and necessity. Their cooperative efforts have been sufficiently institutionalized to create what is essentially a six-state "community" much like the European Community. Now virtually a confederation within the American federal union, it possesses a distinctiveness recognized by other Americans and, indeed, by the world.[25]

New England has always been in on the beginning of each new frontier stage.[26] Massachusetts contained the first English settlement after Jamestown. The urban-industrial frontier started in New England at the beginning of the nineteenth century; and the metropolitan-technological frontier, at the beginning of the twentieth. The particular structure of settlement in New England, based on the town system, has lent itself to the development of citybelts and rurban settlement. Today every single New England state exhibits its own manifestations of that phenomenon.

New England society is proverbially one in which "good fences make good neighbors," combining individualism with a strong sense of community and a heavy sprinkling of idiosyncrasy. This is true whether we are speaking of the academics and intellectuals in the Boston area or the environmentalists who have settled in and transformed Vermont in the last two decades. Successive waves of settlers and immigrants to New England have absorbed much of this New England character.[27]

A special relationship has existed between New England and ethno-religious pluralism.[28] Originally this section was founded on the principle of territorial homogeneity, whereby different groups could occupy different territories and each particular political unit should be as religiously homogeneous as possible. This principle gave way to pluralism within a certain narrow Protestant band in the late eighteenth century. Then in the mid-nineteenth century, Catholic immigrants, particularly the Irish, came into the section. The strong antagonism that developed between the old-line Yankees and the newcomers gradually disappeared through the acculturation of the immigrants and the softening of the Yankees. Since

World War II, the pluralism of primordial groups, predominantly expressed through religious ties, has been the norm.

All of these trends have been played out in New England's educational system.[29] Committed to universal education from the first, schools in New England started as public or quasi-public institutions. Then in the nineteenth century, as a result of the Yankee-Irish struggle, the best schools were privatized. Today, in the public-private mix, the private schools stand at the top of the educational hierarchy. Once the preserve of the solid middle, at least in the cities, public education is now becoming the province of the underclass.

In many respects New England has been the section most independent of the federal government.[30] With the exception of the late nineteenth century, its political involvement has tended in the direction of pressing for major political reforms, whether abolitionist or environmentalist in nature. This section has benefited only modestly from federal aid, usually in the form of direct federal expenditures devoted to river and harbor improvements in the nineteenth century and federal contracts in the twentieth. In return, New England has provided Washington with much of its reformist and expert leadership.

Politically, New England is best characterized as progressive conservative—appearing very conservative in its traditions, yet among the leaders in progressive responses to new challenges. It is a section that has been divided in its partisan allegiance, originally between Federalists and Jeffersonians, later between Whigs and Democrats, and finally between Republicans and Democrats. It was the last bastion of the Federalist party. And from the Civil War era to the New Deal it was predominantly Republican. Now it is highly competitive, although Massachusetts is probably the most Democratic state in the Union, rivaled only by Minnesota.[31]

THE MIDDLE ATLANTIC STATES: AMERICA'S "MAIN STREET"

The Middle Atlantic states constitute the second section, which is distinctive, too, because of both its role as the "Main Street" of the United States and its immediate hinterland.[32] The dominant feature of this section is the big city, with its extensive urbanization and metropolitanization. Along the East Coast are densely developed suburban and exurban areas that have developed into a megalopolis, the first and greatest of all the city-belts. Less well known is the rurban hinterland along the edge of the mountains, which is rapidly developing as a secondary citybelt in its own right, bounded by mountain and forest recreation areas that serve the weekend leisure-time culture of the section.

The Middle Atlantic states, like those of New England, have been first on every frontier. They have also been best able to exploit the various frontiers in other sections as the corporate capitals of the country. As a result, this section has been the richest in the United States by most measures, most of the time.

Society in the Middle Atlantic states has tended to be fast-paced and highly competitive, certainly relative to the rest of the country. It has also been the most urban for the longest time, the most ethnic, and, for the past 150 years, the most "foreign." The Middle Atlantic states have fostered ethnic and religious pluralism from the first—either deliberately, as in Pennsylvania, or because other goals such as a free competitive market have been most important, as in New York. Anyone willing to participate in the game was more or less accepted as a player. This pluralism, though more egalitarian today than ever in the past, has always been the dominant feature of the section. The section's educational system has reflected this fact, inasmuch as private, parochial, and public education has shared in the provision of educational services for the different populations. There are as many varieties of educational institutions in this section as have existed in the United States overall.

As the "Main Street" of America, anchored at its southern end by Washington, D.C., the Middle Atlantic states have enjoyed a very cozy relationship with the federal government. Throughout much of American history, this section has dominated the political and administrative institutions of the federal government (except to the extent that the elected representatives of the rest of the country have been able to modify that domination). Its leaders have articulated the prevailing opinions that guide federal policies, and its people have benefited from federal activities in both more direct and more subtle ways, especially in matters such as monetary and industrial policy, even when more tangible forms of intergovernmental aid programs have favored other sections as a kind of compensation for their lesser influence in Washington.

This section has had a highly competitive party system throughout most of its history. Its state and local parties have been the most professionalized in the country and, in many cases, the most ideological as well. A combination of professionalized, even machine, politics—with relatively (for the United States) clear-cut ideological positions—has made for a very intense politics involving two kinds of payoffs: jobs, contracts, and other favors for the party faithful, on the one hand, and programmatic advantages for the leadership, on the other.[33]

THE NEAR WEST: THE NORTH'S FIRST FRONTIER

The Near West is the third section with a big-city culture.[34] As already suggested, to the extent that there is a Rustbelt in the United States, it is concentrated in the Near West—a curious amalgam of big and small industrial cities and open farmland, retaining many of the values of an older America except in the innermost core of the largest cities.

The location of the Near West has always made it the second section to shift to the next frontier stage. In the case of the land, urban, and metropolitan frontiers, it has been located in such a way as to benefit from them. This is less true with regard to the rurban frontier, however, since those who seek rurban living normally gravitate to physically attractive areas where there is an appropriate mix of interesting topography, pretty scenery, and good climate—all of which are notably lacking in most of the Near West. This fact, indeed, helps account for the economic difficulties in which the section currently finds itself.

The society of the states of the Near West retains much of what are known as traditional American virtues, which, in fact, it was able to introduce into its urban areas to no less a degree than in its rural ones. As a relatively egalitarian society, it absorbed settlers and immigrants from all parts of the world; and it did so with relatively little tension, in contrast to the problems encountered by New England and the Middle Atlantic states. The reason has to do with its ethnoreligious pluralism, primarily a pluralism of associations rather than of primordial groups. Every individual in this section is theoretically free to choose the group with which he or she wishes to associate. And groups are organized as formal associations, whether churches, political parties, or even ethnic communities. The only limitation is that the most important associations such as churches and political parties are expected to be permanent, even intergenerational. Hence this pluralism combines maximum flexibility with maximum stability.

Since Near Western pluralism is a pluralism of associations, it is assumed that people will utilize the instrumentalities of government to serve their common goals. Thus, the Near West was the first section in which education was almost fully vested in public institutions from kindergarten through university. Although private education has grown in recent years, public education is still the norm, and it is in this section that the best public universities are found.[35] Only California and the trans-Mississippi states immediately to the west can rival it in that respect.

The states of the Near West were the first to be carved out of the federal public domain.[36] Hence the federal government's presence was critically important in their founding years, with federal land grants providing the first sources of support for public, educational, and eleemosynary institutions. Subsequently, however, the federal government role diminished drastically, and in the twentieth century these states have probably benefited least from the federal connection. They have had the least influence in Washington; have gotten the least in the way of federal grants-in-aid because they fare the worst in terms of most of the formulas used; and, except for the section's defense industries during World War II and the Korean War, have performed least well in the competition for federal contracts. The pattern in this respect is quite distinctive.

Politically, this section has been greatly fragmented, with each state exhibiting its own pattern. The character of politics, the organization of the party system, and the patterns of partisanship vary so much throughout the section that no generalization can be made for the Near West as a whole. That in itself is a sectional characteristic.[37]

What can be said is that the Near West is a section that was particularly receptive to populist reforms. Its politics took form in the Jacksonian era and, whether predominantly Whig or Democrat, was strongly influenced by such principles of Jacksonian democracy as universal suffrage and professionalized politics. After the Civil War the Near West was much influenced by populism, although because it had already moved on to the urban-industrial frontier, the Populist Party did not do as well as the populist program. At the turn of the century, Progressivism was strong—but this was a progressivism in the Western style of seeking to improve the responsiveness of the political system, not to remove government from politics.[38] In the 1930s, the Near West was the site of the great and successful struggles of industrial workers to organize, as it had been for crafts workers a generation or two earlier. Characteristically these were all middle-class protest movements. Even the drive for unionization was spearheaded by people from essentially middle-class, rural backgrounds who had moved to the cities and had become factory workers.

Since the union organizing days of the 1930s, there has been no domestic middle-class protest movement. Instead, the period of the postwar generation was devoted to less dramatic forms of political and constitutional change in most of the states. Michigan and Wisconsin developed well-based Democratic parties capable of winning and holding office. Michigan and Illinois rewrote their constitutions. And Illinois, Indiana, and Ohio on various occasions elected blue-ribbon or reform tickets to state office to respond to the challenges of the metropolitan frontier.

THE UPPER SOUTH

Given the substantial homogeneity of the greater South as a whole, the differences among its three sections are relatively unpronounced. They were sharpest in the early days, when the Upper South relied on tobacco farming and was punctuated by areas settled by backwoods mountaineers. The Lower South was cotton country, punctuated by areas of rice cultivation, and the Western South emphasized cattle and a small-farm economy. The urban-industrial frontier appeared in pockets in all three sections, although it had its most dramatic impact in the Piedmont of the Upper South.[39]

In the Upper South, the metropolitan frontier had two dimensions: the rise of indigenous metropolitan areas, and the extension of the Northeastern megalopolis into northern Virginia. As a section, it is particularly suited to the rurban frontier and has attracted a great deal of urban settlement to its rural areas. Since World War II its economy has been increasingly tied in with the country's metropolitan and rurban frontiers.

Socially and culturally the Upper South was the greater South's principal region of small farmers, accompanied by a small plantation class and a mountain population famed for its backwoods character and way of life. With urbanization, the middle-class smallholders' society was transferred from the farms to the cities and suburbs.[40] This section exhibits little in the way of ethnic pluralism, although there are pockets of people not of British origin; however, in the framework of Southern Protestantism it does reveal a measure of religious pluralism. By and large, the Upper South has shared with the greater South the pluralism of caste, dividing whites and African-Americans to the detriment of the latter.

Like those in the rest of the South, the people of the Upper South have tended to leave education in private hands—indeed, in the hands of families rather than those of schools, public or private. Public education came late; and, designed only for the poorer strata who could not afford any kind of private schooling, it was far from universal. On the other hand, the states in this section established public universities early on, to educate the children of their elites.[41]

As in the rest of the South, the dominant feature in the relationship of the Upper South with the federal government was the race issue, in connection with slavery, the Civil War, Reconstruction, and Jim Crow segregation. With the passing of this issue as a sectional one, a whole new stage in that relationship is in the process of being opened.[42] Secondarily, the Upper South has benefited from federal aid over the years and, in Virginia, from the federal presence.[43]

Politically, the Upper South has wavered between elitism and the involvement of a relatively broad middle class. Like the rest of the South, the Upper South was for many years part of the solid South. Before that, it was primarily a Whig rather than a Democratic area; and even during the years of Democratic dominance there were pockets of equally dominant Republicanism in the mountain areas, a reflection of the perennial struggle between the mountaineers and the lowlanders. Also like the rest of the South, this section is by every measure a region of lower political participation. Nevertheless, with the end of segregation and the rise of neo-conservatism, the Upper South has developed a more competitive party politics.[44]

THE LOWER SOUTH

The Lower South, once an extraordinarily homogeneous section, is now undergoing great diversification because of the dramatic changes occurring in its economic base.[45] Today it embraces perhaps the sharpest contrasts of any section, from the booming rurban-cybernetic frontier of Florida and the Gulf Coast to the older rural interior. The older society of the Lower South was one of self-made elites and plantation culture, where slavery in its worst form was practiced. In time, most of the states of the Lower South fell within the Blackbelt, where the African-American population was in the majority, first as slaves and then as a segregated and repressed people. The culture and politics of race were central to the development of the section. The only pluralism to exist was a pluralism of caste.

Since World War II, the Lower South has added the Sunbelt dimension to its fringes, which have totally transformed the character of the section by bringing in millions of non-Southerners seeking a better climate. These newer arrivals, however, do not share the old mores and ways of the South and have built an entirely different culture and society. In this endeavor they were aided by the civil rights revolution and the general abandonment of old patterns of racial discrimination, although whatever residue of caste pluralism exists in the United States survives in the Lower South.[46]

As in the rest of the South, the states of the Lower South left education to families, maintaining few schools and even weaker public education systems. They did not even foster serious universities, since their elites were not at all education-minded. University became a kind of finishing school for young gentlemen and ladies, if that. In this context, too, the metropolitan and rurban frontiers have transformed matters. The new people coming in wanted good public schools and public universities, and used normal channels of political and governmental action to try to obtain them. These efforts, in turn, have stimulated some to seek better private facilities as well, on every level.

The relations of the Lower South with the federal government were much like those of the South as a whole, only more so—shaped and colored by the race issue in its various forms and for the most part intensely antagonistic. Like the other states in the Union, however, those in the Lower South learned over time how to mobilize federal aid in its various forms for local purposes, including direct federal assistance, grants-in-aid, contracts, and the siting of federal installations, all of which the Lower South states cultivated in abundance.

In politics, the Lower South was for a century the very heart of the solid South. Before the 1850s, there had been a substantial Whig vote in many of these states. But since the civil rights revolution, the section has become increasingly Republican in presidential elections and two-party competitive for state and other federal offices, all the while keeping its local vote Democratic.[47]

THE WESTERN SOUTH

Like the Near West, the Western South spans the fault line between spheres (in this case, the South and the West), leading to continuing dispute as to whether it is more Southern than Western. In that sense it is the South's West.[48] As such, it was the South's last frontier. In its eastern portions it followed the pattern of the Southeast and the Mississippi River, combining small farms, backwoods mountaineers, and a sprinkling of plantations, although the latter never developed west of the river as they did to the east. Its western portions developed the typical Western cattle culture; one could even say it was the classic version of same—the West of Texas Rangers and cattle drives.

In the later stages of its land frontier and during the urban industrial frontier of the rest of the country, the Western South became associated with legendary oil booms and wildcatting, two more aspects of the classic West. During the metropolitan frontier era, its cities grew by annexation to gigantic proportions, embracing vast pieces of the surrounding countryside in the process. More recently it has embraced the rurban frontier in several locations—along the Gulf Coasts of Texas and Louisiana, in the Ozarks of Missouri and Arkansas, and along the interstate highway that cuts across Oklahoma almost diagonally between St. Louis and Dallas–Ft. Worth.[49]

Despite this seemingly easy transition between frontier stages, the economy of this section has been of the boom-and-bust variety, again in the manner of the West. The section's culture and society have also been Western—indeed, legendarily so in its Texas and Oklahoma forms, given the emphasis in these states on physical prowess and the accumulation of great wealth. At the same time, the Western South has had a substantial share of hard-scrabble farmers, poor but respectable; and in its eastern reaches, African-Americans, first as slaves, then as sharecroppers.

Like the rest of the South, these states have not placed the same emphasis on public education as in the North and West; but as a section, the Western South has placed more emphasis than the others in its sphere. However neglected they might be, public schools were not an afterthought but part and parcel of the section's development. Public universities, devoted primarily to agriculture and the mechanic arts, also had their place.

The Western South is somewhat more ethnoreligiously pluralistic than the other two sections in the sphere, having attracted settlers directly from

Europe to some of its vast reaches. Some were Catholics; others were Protestants of many denominations. (The southern half of Louisiana was solidly Catholic from its founding as a French colony.) This religious pluralism was more or less submerged from view by the Southern pluralism of caste and has reemerged in the public eye only as the latter has declined.

As in the rest of the South, the predominant relationship between the Western South and the federal government has been antagonistic because of the race issue. Yet, as in the rest of the West, it has also been close and dependent. For historic reasons, the states of the Western South, with the exceptions of Arkansas and Missouri, were not public-land states in the traditional sense, so they did not have the experience of the Northwest of being tied to the federal government through the public domain. Nevertheless, they depended on federal troops to defend them against Native Americans; on federal assistance to construct their railways, waterways, and aviation facilities; on federal contracts to deliver their mail; and on federal installations to even out some of the effects of the boom-and-bust economy.

In politics, most of the Western South was born into the solid South and left it in our times in the same way as the other Southern sections. It has also been characterized by an active and continuous populism, which at one time combined the racism of Southern populism with the progressivism of the West. Although populism as a movement has disappeared, populist politics has not; in fact, it still dominates the Western South.[50]

THE NORTHWEST

The Northwest, embracing the plains and mountain states between the Mississippi and the Great Basin, contains what historically was the last of the Old West. The last frontier lasted longest in this section; six of its states celebrated their centennials in 1989 and 1990. The urban frontier had the least impact on the Northwest, and the metropolitan frontier manifested itself only on its eastern and western fringes. At present, the rurban frontier seems to be developing only along the eastern edge of the Rocky Mountains. Its economy remains heavily tied to the land, in terms of both agriculture and the extraction of natural resources, although there are pockets of advanced cybernetic technologies around Minneapolis–St. Paul and Denver. In typically Western fashion, it has a boom-and-bust economy, although the booms and busts are softened as one moves further east within the section.[51]

The culture and society of this section come closest to the American stereotype—egalitarian, open, friendly, small-town, rural, agrarian in spirit if not in actuality, with a felicitous combination of individualism and communitarianism, civic spirit, and neighborliness. These patterns carried over from the early days of the land frontier (which was far less violent in this section than in the Western South) through subsequent frontier stages.

Although this section may appear to the outsider to be very homogeneous, in fact it is highly pluralistic, both ethnically and religiously, in virtually all of its parts.[52] It was an area of first settlement for Europeans who came to America in the nineteenth century. Hence they were able to participate in the very founding of the states in which they settled—as was not the case in the sections of the greater Northeast or the greater South, where most immigrants direct from continental Europe came later and had to make do with integration through sufferance. Religiously, the region is divided among Protestants, Catholics, and the unchurched. Protestants are further divided into denominations with origins in the British Isles and Central and Northern Europe; indeed, every branch of Protestantism is well represented. Moreover, this is a section that still celebrates its ethnic and religious differences.

Like the states in the Near West, those in this section are highly committed to public education. By contrast to the Near West, however, the public educational system of the Northwest has not been weakened by the development of private education in recent years, and the public school and the public university remain the norm. If the public universities are not always of the first rank, the reason has more to do with small populations and a shortage of resources than with lack of will. At the least, one might say that education is this section's secular religion.

All of the states in this section are public-domain states; all that were in existence at the time of the Civil War not only sided with the North but were opposed to slavery and, along with the Near West, "responded to the colors" to provide the Union armies of the West. These states were born and bred in a close and continuing relationship with the federal government and generally have had a strong identification with federal policies as long as they were not policies blatantly favoring the special interests of the Northeast. Even then, with their belief in the efficacy of politics, the people of this section organized in a series of Populist and Progressive actions designed to bring federal policies more in line with their own interests, which they understood to be those of "the people."

Nevertheless, the Northwest has suffered from something of a colonial relationship with the federal government and the other institutions of the Northeastern "Main Street," embodied principally in higher transportation costs and, after the founding period, lower levels of federal aid. For many years, its natural resources were exploited by absentee owners or investors.[53] This section is not particularly attractive as a site for federal installations except in its mountain areas, and even there only limited kinds of installations can be sited. Its rivers and waterways also lend themselves only to limited kinds of federal improvements. In short, the Northwest has had to fight for formulas that serve its needs in federal grant programs.

Politically, most of these states became heavily Republican at the time of the Civil War. Only the mountain states became two-party competitive. After the war, the rise of populist and farmer-labor parties prevented anything like a true Republican monopoly in the state and local arenas. Then, subsequent to World War II, the states increasingly became two-party competitive, although most remained strongly Republican in presidential elections. Minnesota, where the Democratic-Farmer-Labor party is dominant, is strongly Democratic in presidential politics. The politics of this section in general is middle-class populist and has a strong reputation for being very "clean."[54]

THE FAR WEST

With its frontier characteristics and economy, the Far West falls squarely within the patterns of the greater West, with the added dimension of the special attractiveness and orientations of the Pacific coast. These are mountain and desert states, whether very hot or very cold. They are also states looked upon by Americans as the closest thing to paradise on earth, where people aspire to settle for their climate, scenery, and styles of life.[55]

The Far West acquired its stamp during the cattle and mining frontier— the rural-land frontier. It was minimally affected by the urban-industrial frontier, but it blossomed as a result of the metropolitan technological frontier. It became a mecca for millions of Americans who continued to move westward in their search for happiness. It was during this latter period that California became the leading state in the American Union and the section became the powerhouse that it is.

Rurban settlement, even citybelts, grew easily out of the patterns of the metropolitan frontier, whereas the region's lifestyle encouraged both the cybernetic and the settlement elements out of the latest frontier stage. From Seattle's Boeing to the San Francisco Bay area's Silicon Valley to New Mexico's nuclear testing centers, this section has become the springboard to new frontiers. Its economy has come to rest to no small extent on those functions.[56]

In a United States that has become increasingly casual and oriented toward leisure-time activities, the Far West plays an even more pronounced role. In a sense, its way of life has *defined* casual and leisure time; and because of the opportunities offered within it, its citizens are perhaps the most aggressive in taking advantage of casual leisure-time activities. The society of this section is also the most experimental in the United States with regard to lifestyles, always seeking new panaceas for human ills. In that sense its people are also the most restless Americans, changing jobs; places of residence; religious, political, and other affiliations; and even marriage partners at a pace far beyond the national average. If the Northwest is the epitome of American sobriety and stability, then the Far West is the epitome of American fluidity and experimentation. In this the mainland states are joined equally by Alaska and Hawaii. This is also the section with the fewest number of church members and the most fluid political parties.[57]

Pluralism in the Far West is a pluralism of individuals. Primordial groups, even permanent associations, are peripheral. If they exist at all, they are residues of a pluralism of caste in the Southwest, where Anglos and Hispanics have tried to lead separate lives for generations; but the pluralism of caste, too, is rejected these days. The pluralism of individuals, whereby every individual may choose his or her lifestyle and make whatever changes in it are desired at any time, is a product of the fluidity of society in this section.

Like the people in the rest of the West, those of the Far West are highly committed to education and principally to public education. For them, however, education is less a secular religion than a vehicle for helping individuals to find their way to paradise or, at the very least, to "right living." Hence their educational institutions are among the first to embrace fads, and there is a large, private continuing-education sector offering every imaginable kind of training for nirvana.

The relationship of the Far West with the federal government may best be described as dependent and ambivalent. Not only are all the states of the Far West public-land states, but the federal government still owns substantial percentages of all of them except Hawaii. Strong groups in each of the states are unhappy about this situation. Periodically the states demand that the land be turned over to them, as in the recent Sagebrush Rebellion.[58] Yet these federal public lands provide important props for the section's economy: for tourism and recreation, for stock-grazing, and for the maintenance of water resources.

Beyond that, federal installations and defense contracts have been extremely important in this section's economy. The federal military and naval presence in Hawaii have an effect equivalent to that of the public domain elsewhere in the section. Defense industries, weapons test sites, and the like are critically important in all of the Far Western states. These states have also done well with regard to federal contracts, grants, and entitlements. In short, the economic power of this section is in no small measure a result of the federal presence, which also serves to level out the boom-and-bust tendencies of its Western economy.

Politically, as the Far West has more or less always featured active competition between the two major parties, its states can be classified as two-party competitive. With the possible exception of Hawaii, it is also very populist and civic in its politics, with a citizenry active as political amateurs and readily mobilized to secure political change, whether through the two major parties, through third parties, or through constitutional and legislative initiatives and referenda (devices that have become common in this section). As in the Northwest, the politics of the Far West has a reputation for being "clean."[59]

SUMMARY

Chapter 6 completes our discussion of the American generational rhythm, the process whereby earlier sectional, class, and ethnic patterns were integrated and then reshaped in the twentieth century. In particular, this chapter has examined the impact of the third and early part of the fourth stages of the continuing frontier and the American response to external events in the world at large in the twentieth century. Much of this century has involved conflicts between old social values and new, within a political system that has had to both adapt to changed circumstances and absorb social changes while trying to remain as faithful as possible to its original form. In essence, the chapter discusses the massive changes in the moral and socioeconomic dimensions of the American Constitution and the ways in which these changes have been reflected in as well as balanced by the continuation of the almost-unchanged frame of government.

The century began with the demise of the Protestant consensus. It was replaced first by a tripartite religious pluralism involving whites only, then by an ethnoreligious pluralism embracing nonwhites as well. It began with a surge in class consciousness not heretofore experienced in the United States, which in turn was dissolved by post–World War II prosperity and the thrust toward egalitarianism that accompanied it. In short, the century began with the last stages of the land frontier coming to an end and the urban-industrial frontier in full bloom, moved on to the metropolitan-technological frontier, and, in its last generation, confronted the challenge of the rurban-cybernetic frontier.

This chapter completes the discussion of the columns in Table 2.1, having concluded with a survey of the expression of those patterns on a section-by-section basis.

NOTES

1. Melvyn Bulosky, *The United States in the Twentieth Century* (Englewood Cliffs, N.J.: Prentice-Hall, 1978); Walter Lafeber, Richard Polenberg, and Nancy Woloch, *The American Century: A History of the United States,* 3rd ed. (New York: Alfred A.

Knopf, 1986); Morris Janowitz, *The Last Half-Century: Societal Change and Politics in America* (Chicago: University of Chicago Press, 1978).

2. See Alfred B. Rollins, Jr., *Woodrow Wilson and the New America* (New York: Dell Publishing Co., 1965); Gene Smith, *When the Cheering Stopped: The Last Years of Woodrow Wilson* (New York: Morrow, 1964); and Ruth Cranston, *The Story of Woodrow Wilson* (New York: Simon and Schuster, 1945). See also the following books by Arthur S. Link: *Wilson the Diplomatist: A Look at His Major Foreign Policies* (Baltimore: Johns Hopkins Press, 1957), *Woodrow Wilson and the Progressive Era 1910–1917* (New York: Harper and Row, 1963); *Wilson: Confusion and Crises 1915–1916* (Princeton, N.J.: Princeton University Press, 1964), and *Wilson and the New Freedom* (Princeton, N.J.: Princeton University Press, 1956).

3. George Soule, *Prosperity Decade: From War to Depression 1917–1929* (New York: Harper and Row, 1968); Mark Sullivan, *Our Times,* 6 vols. (New York: Charles Scribner's Sons, 1930).

4. Kristi Anderson, *The Creation of a Democratic Majority 1928–1936* (Chicago: University of Chicago Press, 1979).

5. See the trilogy by Arthur Schlesinger, Jr., entitled *The Age of Roosevelt,* particularly vols. 1 and 2: *The Crisis of the Old Order 1919–1933* (Boston: Houghton Mifflin, 1957) and *The Coming of the New Deal* (Boston: Houghton Mifflin, 1959). See also Frank Friedel, *F. D.R. and the South* (Baton Rouge: Louisiana State University Press, 1965).

6. For an overview of these culminating events, see John R. Craf, *A Survey of the American Economy: 1940–1946* (New York: North River Press, 1947); and Richard B. Morris, *The Encyclopedia of American History* (New York: Harper and Row, 1965).

7. Seymour E. Harris, ed., *American Economic History* (New York: McGraw-Hill, 1961); Harold C. Halcrow, *American Agriculture: 1899–1939* (New York: National Bureau of Economic Research, 1942); William Greenleaf, ed., *American Economic Development Since 1860* (Columbia: University of South Carolina Press, 1968); Harry N. Scheiber et al., *United States Economic History: Selected Readings* (New York: Alfred A. Knopf, 1964); Howard R. Smith, *Economic History of the United States* (New York: Ronald Press, 1955); Harold Underwood Faulkner, *American Economic History,* 8th ed. (New York: Harper and Row, 1960).

8. Vaughn D. Bornet, *Labor Politics in a Democratic Republic: Moderation, Division, and Disruption in the Presidential Election of 1928* (Washington, D.C.: Spartan Books, 1964); D. M. Gordon, Richard Edwards, and Michael Reich, *Segmented Work, Divided Workers: The Historical Transformation of Labor in the United States* (Cambridge, England: Cambridge University Press, 1982); Marguerite Green, *The National Civic Federation and the American Labor Movement 1900–1925* (Washington, D.C.: Catholic University Press, 1956).

9. On the transformation of agriculture after 1920, see Harold C. Halcrow, *American Agriculture: 1899–1939* (New York: National Bureau of Economic Research, 1942); Grant McConnell, *The Decline of Agrarian Democracy* (Berkeley: University of California Press, 1953); and Theodore Saloutos and John D. Hicks, *Twentieth-Century Populism: Agricultural Discontent in the Middle West, 1900–1939* (Lincoln: University of Nebraska Press, 1951).

10. Thomas Sowell, *Ethnic America* (New York: Basic Books, 1981); Stephen Steinberg, *The Ethnic Myth: Race, Ethnicity and Class in America* (New York: Atheneum, 1981).

11. On Prohibition, see Joseph Gusfield, *Symbolic Crusade: Status Politics and the American Temperance Movement* (Urbana: University of Illinois Press, 1963); David E. Dyving, *Repealing National Prohibition* (Chicago: University of Chicago Press, 1979); Charles Merz, *The Dry Decade* (Seattle: University of Washington Press, 1969); James H. Timberlake, *Prohibition and the Progressive Movement, 1900–1920* (Cambridge, Mass.: Harvard University Press, 1963); and Jack H. Mendelson and Nancy K. Mello, *Alcohol: Use and Abuse in America* (Boston: Little, Brown, 1985).

12. Henry Steele Commager, *The Struggle for Racial Equality: A Documentary Record* (New York: Harper and Row, 1967); Sowell, *Ethnic America;* Steinberg, *The Ethnic Myth;* Paul Lewinson, *Race, Class and Party: A History of Negro Suffrage and White Politics in the South* (New York: Grosset and Dunlop, 1965).

13. Edward W. Washburn, *The Indian and the White Man* (Garden City, N.Y.: Doubleday, 1964); Francis Paul Prucha, *Great Father: The United States and the American Indians* (Lincoln: University of Nebraska Press, 1984); S. Lyman Tyler, *A History of Indian Policy* (Washington, D.C.: Bureau of Indian Affairs, 1973).

14. Morton Grodzins, *The American System* (Chicago: Rand McNally, 1966); William Anderson, *The Nation and the States: Rivals or Partners?* (Westport, Conn.: Greenwood Press, 1974).

15. Marvin E. Gettemen and David Mermelstein, *The Great Society Reader: The Failure of American Liberalism* (New York: Vintage Books, 1966).

16. G. Theodore Mitau, *The Decade of Decision: The Supreme Court and the Constitutional Revolution 1954–1964* (New York: Charles Scribner's Sons, 1967).

17. Archibald Cox, *The Warren Court: Constitutional Decision as an Instrument of Reform* (Cambridge, Mass.: Harvard University Press, 1968); Harold J. Spaeth, *The Warren Court: Cases and Commentary* (San Francisco: Chadler Publishing Co., 1966); Stanley I. Kutler, ed., *The Supreme Court and the Constitution: Readings in American Constitutional History*, 3rd ed. (New York: W. W. Norton, 1984).

18. Arthur Schlesinger, Jr., *The Bitter Heritage: Vietnam and American Democracy, 1941–1966* (New York: Fawcett Crest, 1967); Anthony A. D'Amato and Robert M. O'Neil, *The Judiciary and Vietnam* (New York: St. Martin's Press, 1972).

19. Theodore H. White, *Breach of Faith: The Fall of Richard Nixon* (New York: Dell Publishing Co., 1975).

20. Harold G. Vatter, *The U.S. Economy in the 1950s: An Economic History* (New York: W. W. Norton, 1963); George Steinlieb and James W. Hughes, eds., *Post-Industrial America: Metropolitan Decline and Inter-Regional Job Shifts* (New Brunswick, N.J.: Center for Urban Policy Research, Rutgers University, 1975); Daniel P. Moynihan, "How Has the United States Met Its Major Challenges Since 1945?" *Commentary* (November 1985): 25–107.

21. Howard L. Fromkin and John J. Sherwood, eds., *Intergroup Minority Relations: An Experimental Handbook* (La Jolla, Calif.: University Associates, 1976); Thomas Sowell, ed., *Essays and Data on American Ethnic Groups* (Washington, D.C.: Urban Institute, 1978); David R. Colburn and George E. Pozzetta, eds., *America and the New Ethnicity* (Cambridge, Mass.: Belknap Press of Harvard University Press, 1982); Richard Polenberg, *One Nation Divisible: Class, Race and Ethnicity in the United States Since 1983* (New York: Viking Press, 1980) .

22. See Edwin Gaustad, *Historical Atlas of Religion in America* (New York: Harper and Row, 1962); Will Herberg, *Protestant-Catholic-Jew: An Essay in American Religious*

Sociology (Garden City, N.Y.: Doubleday, 1955) and *Study of Religion's Impact on Politics, Economics, and Family Life* (Garden City, N.Y.: Doubleday, 1963).

23. For a discussion emphasizing class factors, see Richard F. Hamilton, *Class Politics in the United States* (New York: Wiley, 1972).

24. Robert S. Lynd and Helen Merrell Lynd, *Middletown: A Study in American Culture* (New York: Harcourt, Brace and World, 1929); W. Lloyd Warner, *American Life: Dream and Reality* (Chicago: University of Chicago Press, 1953); Reinhard Bendix and Seymour Martin Lipset, *Class, Status and Power* (Glencoe, Ill.: Free Press, 1953).

25. One problem in understanding the influence of sectionalism on politics concerns the proper identification of specific sectional issues from among many apparent ones. During the heyday of nineteenth-century Populism, Western and Southern Populists made common cause against what they believed to be Northeastern exploitation, despite the great cultures and even doctrinal differences separating them. When the movement failed, the temporary intersectional alliance came to an end for lack of binding common interests. Today certain students of American reform fail to distinguish between the two kinds of populism simply because they are aligned at one point in time. Richard Hofstader, one of the most distinguished students of American reform, succumbs to this kind of overgeneralization; see, for example, his *The Age of Reform* (New York: Alfred A. Knopf, 1955). See also Eric F. Goldman, *Rendezvous with Destiny* (New York: Alfred A. Knopf, 1952), for the history of the populist alliance and its dissolution.

26. On the economy and settlement patterns of New England, see Robert W. Eisenmenger, *The Dynamics of Growth in New England's Economy, 1870–1964* (Middletown, Conn.: Wesleyan University Press, 1967).

27. On New England society, see Perry Miller, *The New England Mind: From Colony to Province* (Boston: Beacon Press, 1957) and *The New England Mind: The Seventeenth Century* (Boston: Beacon Press, 1939). See also John Fiske, *The Beginnings of New England as a Puritan Theocracy and Its Relations to Civil and Religious Liberty* (Boston: Houghton Mifflin, 1889).

28. On pluralism in New England and other sections, see Daniel J. Elazar, *The American Constitutional Tradition* (Lincoln: University of Nebraska Press, 1988), ch. 2; George W. Pierson, "The Obstinate Concept of New England: A Study in Denudation," *New England Quarterly* (March 1955); Oscar Handlin and Howard Mumford Jones, "The Withering of New England, " *Atlantic Monthly* (April 1950); Merrill Jensen, ed., *Regionalism in America* (Madison: University of Wisconsin Press, 1965); and "Toward a United New England," containing remarks by James C. Cleveland made during the midyear meeting of the New England Council in 1973.

29. On education in New England and other sections, see Edwin E. Slosson, *The American Spirit in Education* (New York: Harper, 1956); James H. Risley, *How It Grew: A History of the Public Schools* (Denver: University of Denver Press, 1953); Thomas H. Eliot, *State Politics and the Public Schools* (New York: Alfred A. Knopf, 1964); and Harmon Zeigler and Karl F. Johnson, *The Politics of Education in the States* (Indianapolis: Bobbs-Merrill Co., 1972).

30. On relations with the federal government in New England and the other sections, see Daniel J. Elazar, *The American Partnership* (Chicago: University of Chicago Press, 1964); William Anderson, *The Nation and the States: Rivals or Partners?* (Minneapolis: University of Minnesota Press, 1955); Robert Goldwin, ed., *A Nation of States*

(Chicago: Rand McNally, 1962); Carol L. Jesenius and Larry C. Ledebur, *Where Have All the Firms Gone? An Analysis of the New England Economy* (Washington, D.C.: Economic Development Administration, Department of Commerce, Government Printing Office, 1977); Lynn E. Browne and John S. Hekman, "New England's Economy in the 1980s," *New England Economic Review* (January-February 1981); and *Regional Growth: Historical Perspective* (Washington, D.C.: U.S. Advisory Commission on Intergovernmental Relations, 1980).

31. On politics in New England, see Duane Lockard, *New England State Politics* (Princeton, N.J.: Princeton University Press, 1959); Betty Flanders Thomson, *The Changing Face of New England* (New York: Macmillan, 1958); and Joe McCarthy, *New England* (New York: Time-Life Library of America, 1967).

32. John T. Cunningham, *New Jersey: America's Main Road—Shaping of America: A Geographical Perspective on 500 Years of History.* Vol. 1, *Atlantic America 1492–1800* (New Haven, Conn.: Yale University Press, 1986).

33. On politics in the Middle Atlantic states, see Eric F. Goldman, "The Middle States' Regionalism and American Historiography: A Suggestion," in Eric F. Goldman, ed., *Historiography and Urbanization* (Baltimore: Johns Hopkins University Press, 1941).

34. See John H. Fenton, *Politics in the Border States* (New Orleans: Hauser, 1957).

35. On public education in the Near West, see Frank Levy, Arnold J. Meltoner, and Aaron Wildavsky, *Urban Outcomes, Schools, Streets, and Libraries* (Berkeley: University of California Press, 1974); Nicholas A. Masters, Robert H. Salisbury, and Thomas H. Eliot, *State Politics and the Public Schools* (New York: Alfred A. Knopf, 1964).

36. On the settlement of the Near West and the federal role in this process, see Daniel J. Elazar, *Cities of the Prairie* (New York: Basic Books, 1970), ch. 3; and Elazar, *The American Partnership* (Chicago: University of Chicago Press, 1962).

37. On the politics of the Near West, see Austin Ranney, *Illinois Politics* (New York: New York University Press, 1960); Emil F. Faith, *Government and History of the State of Illinois* (Chicago: Mentzner, Bush, and Company, 1956); and Leon D. Epstein, *Politics in Wisconsin* (Madison: University of Wisconsin Press, 1958).

38. On Western versus Eastern Progressivism, see Elazar, *Cities of the Prairie;* George Mowry, *California Progressives* (Chicago: Quadrangle, 1963); Russel B. Nye, *Midwestern Progressive Politics* (East Lansing: Michigan State College Press, 1951); Lewis L. Gould, *The Progressive Era* (Syracuse, N.Y: Syracuse University Press, 1974); and Daniel Aaron, *Men of Good Hope: A Story of American Progressives* (London: Oxford University Press, 1951).

39. On the economy of the South and its sections, see Thomas Dye, *Politics, Economics and the Public: Policy Outcomes in the American States* (Chicago: Rand McNally, 1966); K. Moreland, *The Millways of Kent* (Chapel Hill: University of North Carolina Press, 1958); George B. Tindall, *The Emergence of the New South 1913–1945* (Baton Rouge: Louisiana State University Press, 1967); Howard Odum, *Southern Regions of the United States* (Chapel Hill: University of North Carolina Press, 1967); and J. Carlyle Stitterson, ed., *Studies in Southern History* (Chapel Hill: University of North Carolina Press, 1957).

40. On the social characteristics of the South and its sections, see W. J. Cash, *The Mind of the South* (New York: Alfred A. Knopf, 1941); Raymond D. Gastil, *Cultural Regions of the United States* (Seattle: University of Washington Press, 1975).

41. On education in the South and its sections, see Odum, *Southern Regions of the United States;* Tindall, *The Emergence of the New South;* and Stitterson, *Studies in Southern History.*

42. On the South and the federal government, with respect to the racial issue, see Paul Lewinson, *Race, Class, and Party: A History of Negro Suffrage and White Politics in the South* (New York: Grosset and Dunlap, 1965).

43. On the South and federal aid, see the reports on federal aid of the U.S. Advisory Commission on Intergovernmental Relations (ACIR) for the years since 1962.

44. On politics in the Upper South, see V. O. Key, Jr., *Southern Politics* (New York: Alfred A. Knopf, 1949); J. Kenneth Morland, ed., *The Not So Solid South: Anthropological Studies in a Regional Subculture* (Athens: University of Georgia Press, 1971); A. K. McClure, *The South: Its Industrial, Financial and Political Condition* (Philadelphia: J. B. Lippincott Co., 1884); T. Harry Williams, *Romance and Realism in Southern Politics* (Baton Rouge: Louisiana State University Press, 1966); and Theodore Saloutos, *Farmer Movements in the South 1865–1933* (Lincoln: University of Nebraska Press, 1960).

45. See Neal R. Peirce, *The Border South States* (New York: Norton, 1975); Key, *Southern Politics;* Morland, *The Not So Solid South.*

46. Ibid.

47. Ibid.

48. Ibid.

49. Ibid.

50. Ibid.

51. On the Northeast, see Peirce, *The New England States* (New York: W. W. Norton, 1976); John Gunther, *Inside U.S.A.* (New York: Harper, 1947); and Henry G. Alsberg, ed., *The American Guide: A Source Book and Complete Travel Guide for the United States* (New York: Hastings House, 1949).

52. On ethnic and religious pluralism in the Northwest, see Gastil, *Cultural Regions of the United States.*

53. Neal R. Peirce, *The Great Plains States* (New York: W. W. Norton, 1972).

54. June D. Holmquist, ed., *They Chose Minnesota* (St. Paul: Minnesota Historical Society Press, 1981); Rhoda R. Gilman and June D. Holmquist, eds., "The Democratic Farmer Labor Party Schism of 1948," in *Selections from Minnesota History* (St. Paul: Minnesota Historical Society Press, 1965), pp. 298–308.

55. Gunther, *Inside U.S.A.;* Jensen, *Regionalism in America.*

56. Ibid.

57. Neal R. Peirce, *The Pacific States of America* (New York: W. W. Norton, 1972) and *The Mountain States of America* (New York: W. W. Norton, 1972).

58. Robert H. Nelson, "The Subsidized Sagebrush: Why Privatization Failed," *Regulation* 8, no. 4 (July-August 1984); Frank J. Pepper, "The Timely End of the Sagebrush Rebellion," *The Public Interest* 76 (Summer 1984): 61–73; *National Journal* (November 11, 1979): 1928.

59. See Peirce, *The Pacific States of America* and *The Mountain States of America.*

CHAPTER 7

The Peoples of the United States and Their Cultures

WHO ARE THE PEOPLE OF THE UNITED STATES?

The religious, ethnic, and racial groups that make up the people of the United States have become one people by choice. As early as 1782, the French-American observer Hector St. John Crevecoeur could view the result as constituting a "new American man."[1] The new nation came about as a consequence of what President Lyndon B. Johnson described as the people's "covenant with the land" and the civil society that has given it political form.[2]

This implicit covenant is, in most cases, based on the separate decisions of millions of individuals and families to leave their homelands and migrate to a new land where they hoped to build new lives (see Tables 7.1 and 7.2). The act of migration—"voting with one's feet," as it were—was the first step for all Americans, whether the first English settlers in the seventeenth century or the latest waves of Mexicans, Filipinos, Koreans, Cubans, and others. But in making the choice to become Americans (and ultimately every American has had to make this choice, even the Native Americans and African-Americans who had it forced upon them), they also have chosen to reserve certain basic rights to maintain other linkages—religious, ethnic, social, and cultural—as befits a covenantal arrangement among diverse peoples.

At one time there were no Americans. Although it is impossible to pinpoint the exact moment in the eighteenth century when the sense of being American became widespread in the English colonies, it is known that this sense developed out of the historical experiences of the colonists by the 1760s, before the revolution.[3] In other words, the sense of being Amer-

TABLE 7.1   Immigration: 1820–1989 (in thousands)

Period	Number	Rate[a]
1820–1989	55,458	3.4
1820–1830	152	1.2
1831–1840	599	3.9
1841–1850	1,713	8.4
1851–1860	2,596	9.3
1861–1870	2,315	6.4
1871–1880	2,812	6.2
1881–1890	5,247	9.2
1891–1900	3,688	5.3
1901–1910	6,795	10.4
1911–1920	5,736	5.7
1921–1930	4,107	3.5
1931–1940	526	.4
1941–1950	1,035	.7
1951–1960	2,515	1.5
1961–1970	3,322	1.7
1971–1980	4,493	2.1
1981–1989	5,802	2.7

[a]Annual rate per 1,000 U.S. people.

Source: U.S. Statistical Yearbook, 1990 (Washington, D.C.: Government Printing Office, 1990).

ican is at least implicitly a matter of conscious choice rather than something taken for granted.

RELIGION, ETHNICITY, AND CULTURE IN AMERICA

The people who make up the population of the United States come from as wide a range of religions and ethnic backgrounds as have ever congregated in one civil society. Herman Melville (1819–1891), whose classic novel *Moby Dick* captures the spirit—and problems—of America, summarizes the global meaning of America's human diversity: "Americans are not a narrow tribe of men. ... No: our blood is as the flood of the Amazon, made up of a thousand noble currents all pouring into one. We are not a nation so much as a world."[4]

However, not simply the *fact* of diversity is important in American politics but also the *character* of that diversity—in the nation as a whole as well as in its states and localities. To a greater or lesser degree, each group brings something to the overall American synthesis—each in its own way and in terms of its particular location in American civil society. When Paul Revere rode out to Lexington and Concord in April 1775, he rode through a homogeneous land of New England Yankee farmers. In 1975, on the occasion of the bicentennial of that ride, *Time* magazine published a map showing the ethnic (and commercial) diversity that would have greeted Paul Revere had he reenacted his ride two hundred years later (see Map 7.1).

The common factor uniting virtually all of the immigrants who came voluntarily to American shores (and stayed) was their desire to become Americans.[5] As a result, they eagerly embraced what they found to be the American way of life and, in the process, were able to invent a common culture that united them as Americans.

At the same time, most of those who came to the New World reserved the right to maintain some elements from their original heritage. Although American society required conformity in most matters involving overt behavior, almost from the first there has been an understanding that, as part of their right to maintain their own religious beliefs, Americans can use their religious communities to sustain their desire for maintaining their differences. Consequently, socioreligious communities have become the primary vehicles for the expression of subcommunal differences, including ethnic ones.

American peoplehood, then, is not the same as that of European nations in which national or communal ties are considered to be simply a matter of birth and descent and are preeminent over all other ties. Given the realities of American life, there is a sense in which the peoplehood of Americans exists on the basis of consent and is not expected to be exclusive or to replace all other ties.

In the traditional American view, the political ties that bind Americans are considered secondary to their religious ties. The idea that one's relationship to God supersedes human ties was brought to this country by the very first settlers, so many of whom came to seek religious freedom. We see this reflected in the American language. We speak of American Protestants, American Catholics, and American Jews.[6] The order of words is significant. The essence is the religious tie; *American* is its modifier. When we speak of ethnic groups, it is just the opposite. We speak of Irish-Americans, German-Americans, Italian-Americans, and all of those who once were referred to as "hyphenated Americans." The order of words indicates that we consider their ethnic origins to be limited modifiers of their principal identity as Americans.[7]

GENERATIONS AND ETHNORELIGIOUS INTERRELATIONSHIPS

The changes in the relationships among racial, ethnic, and religious groups (and their various combinations) coincide closely with the flow of generations and centuries. North America's first generation of settlement

TABLE 7.2   Immigrants by Country of Birth: 1961–1989 (in thousands)

Country	Total	
All countries		13,616.6
Europe		2,633.1
Czechoslovakia	41.7	
France	72.4	
Germany	328.6	
Greece	210.3	
Hungary	37.0	
Ireland	79.0	
Italy	366.4	
Netherlands	49.0	
Poland	193.8	
Portugal	219.8	
Romania	66.7	
Soviet Union	117.4	
Spain	74.4	
Sweden	32.0	
Switzerland	29.1	
United Kingdom	480.2	
Yugoslavia	104.7	
Asia		4,559.9
Afghanistan	25.8	
Cambodia	122.0	
China	641.0	
Hong Kong	126.7	
India	439.2	
Iran	184.4	
Iraq	47.6	
Israel	71.1	
Japan	123.9	
Jordan	71.8	
Korea	614.3	
Laos	157.9	
Lebanon	77.3	
Pakistan	87.7	
Philippines	893.2	
Syria	35.5	
Thailand	104.6	
Turkey	43.8	
Vietnam	536.9	

continues

TABLE 7.2 (cont.)

Country		Total
North America		5,163.5
Canada		503.9
Mexico		2,054.7
Caribbean		2,056.6
Barbados	46.0	
Cuba	682.2	
Dominican Republic	451.7	
Haiti	216.1	
Jamaica	401.8	
Trinidad & Tobago	119.2	
Central America		542.6
Costa Rica	42.2	
El Salvador	183.8	
Guatemala	96.6	
Honduras	70.2	
Nicaragua	55.6	
Panama	66.7	
South America		882.8
Argentina		87.5
Brazil		53.7
Chile		48.5
Colombia		248.1
Ecuador		130.7
Guyana		138.7
Peru		96.4
Venezuela		30.4
Africa		288.2
Egypt		70.0
Nigeria		36.8
South Africa		29.7
Australia		36.3
Other countries		55.7

Source: U.S. Statistical Abstract, 1990 (Washington, D.C.: Government Printing Office, 1990).

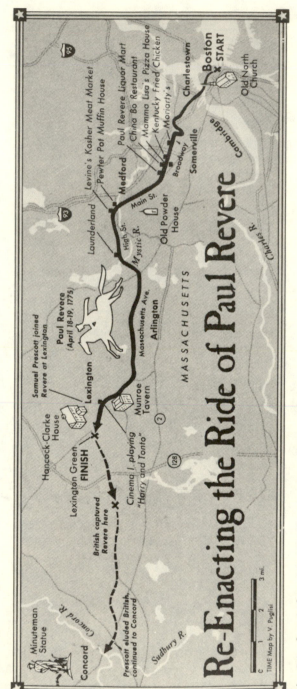

Map 7.1 *Source:* Copyright 1975 Time Inc. Reprinted by permission.

saw an attempt to allow religious pluralism on a strictly territorial basis—that is, by giving specific religious groups exclusive control over particular territories. For example, Massachusetts was for Puritans, Virginia for Anglicans, and Maryland for Catholics. At the same time, Africans were introduced as indentured servants, thereby creating a racial division in the country.

The colonies founded (or brought under English control) in the second and third generations, such as Pennsylvania and New York, recognized ethnic diversity and religious differentiation from the first. Beginning with the conquest of New Amsterdam by the English in 1660, which obliged them to recognize (at least *de facto*) the legitimacy of ethnic pluralism and, more particularly, with the founding of William Penn's noble experiment in Pennsylvania in 1682, there was a shift toward the idea that the polities being established on the new continent could rightfully be settled by people of different national origins who, while retaining their identities as English, Scottish, Welsh, Irish, Dutch, German, Swedish, and Jewish people, would share a common citizenship.[8] Heterodoxy spread during these decades, while the Africans were reduced to slavery. Thus, by the end of the first century of settlement, a modified religious pluralism was the norm, with locally favored churches and tolerated ones existing side by side. At the same time a racially based caste system was in the making, primarily in the South.

During the three generations of the second century, ethnic and sectarian pluralism increased dramatically, rendering most of the original territorial arrangements obsolete and resulting in the virtual elimination of established churches in the new nation. Slavery, after increasing gradually in the South, was given a new lease on life by technological change at the same time that it was being abolished in the North.

The first generation of the nineteenth century saw the unofficial establishment of a generalized Protestant republicanism, which was almost immediately challenged by the rise in non-Protestant immigration. The second generation was one of transition to a new post-Protestant pluralism, which remained an antagonistic one through the third generation, the years when non-Protestant, non-British migration reached its height.[9] Slavery boomed, was abolished at mid-century, and then was allowed to reappear near the end of the century in the form of a caste system reaffirmed through racial segregation.

Another revival of positive attitudes toward ethnic identity occurred during the post–Civil War period. By the very end of the nineteenth century, descendants of the non-English peoples of the British Isles (Scots, Welsh, and Scotch-Irish) and those of Northwestern Europe (particularly the Dutch and Germans), who were among the first settlers of the country, claimed credit for their share in the development of the United States.[10]

Their claims emerged in reaction to a generation or more of the public proclamation of what we might call "Anglo-Saxonism"—an ideological expression of the view that the genius of the "Anglo-Saxons" purportedly built the country single-handedly.

This effort on the part of the non-English "old-stock" groups to assert their rightful place as peoples in American history was at least partially aborted by the mass immigration from Southern and Eastern Europe, which united all old-stock Americans through a common interest in defending their own position and securing the Americanization of the newcomers. "Americanization" meant assimilation. Despite the suggestion in some quarters that cultural pluralism should be the goal of the new America, it was the "melting pot" ideology that prevailed. As Israel Zangwill put it in his popular play of 1908, *The Melting Pot:* "America is God's Crucible, the great Melting Pot where all the races of Europe are melting and reforming!"[11] However, this issue should not be construed entirely as one involving established groups forcing their worldview on new arrivals; the newcomers themselves, in the main, sought to be Americanized almost without reservation.

From the first, the twentieth century has been one of increasingly open pluralism—religious, ethnic, and racial—in American life. The barriers against full participation by women, later immigrant groups, and non-whites began to fall in the tenth generation, and the elimination of those barriers was the priority problem of the eleventh. Indeed, by the late 1960s, pluralism in morals and lifestyles began to shape up as the great issue of the coming generation.

It remained for one of the oldest groups of Americans to initiate the most recent revival of ethnic feeling. Since 1619, African-Americans had been passive witnesses to the ebb and flow of the tides of ethnicity, excluded by the tacit or active consensus of whites from participation as equals in American civil society. Their assertion of the right to equality as individuals in the 1950s led in the 1960s to a great discovery on their part: that they could become fully equal as Americans only if they had a sufficient sense of group identity, at least to the extent of a common African-American heritage. Their search for a usable past has taken a variety of forms, ranging from simple interest in African-American history to extreme separatist and anti-white outlooks. Taken as a whole, however, the African-American civil rights movement was the proximate cause of what has now become at least an intellectual movement of ethnic revival among Poles, Italians, Jews, Native Americans, and others.[12]

The blacks were not the first group to acquire a group identity based on a sense of common origin after coming to the United States. Most of those who came to the United States were from countries that had not yet forged their own sense of national identity. Hence the process of doing so took place simultaneously in the "old country" and among its immigrant groups in the New World. This is particularly true of Norwegians, Irish, Germans, and Italians.[13]

The African-Americans' assertion of ethnic unity came at a time when a host of factors had combined to support the movement triggered by that assertion: Among these were the Vietnam student rebellion crisis in American society, the growing alienation of the person-on-the-street from the country's leadership, and the search for identity on the part of many of the new and historically large generation of the postwar baby boom. It is important to note, however, that the movement itself fits into the overall cyclical pattern of emphasis on national homogeneity, followed by a period of emphasis on ethnic diversity that has persisted since the seventeenth century.

In the past, the emphasis on ethnicity by various groups has been a first step toward claiming equal status in America as a whole. At the same time, that emphasis led, temporarily, to intergroup conflict as the "outs" struggled against the "ins" to claim what they believed to be their rightful place (or their share of places) in the overall society. Although this conflict is itself well known, it has usually been treated as if it were *simply* a matter of "ins" and "outs," a matter of who got where first. In fact, the relationship between ethnic groups is conditioned not only by temporal and spatial factors but also by the degree of cultural affinity or dissimilarity that has served to bind or alienate particular peoples to or from one another. These patterns of intergroup affinity or dissimilarity have influenced the immediate character of interethnic conflict in the United States; they have also played a great role in determining the lines of assimilation over the long haul.

CULTURAL AND STRUCTURAL ASSIMILATION

We can see in the American experience thus far the difference between *cultural* and *structural* assimilation. Cultural assimilation, or acculturation, involves learning the values and public lifestyle of the new society. Structural assimilation involves the actual absorption of the group into that society, particularly on the level of intimate friendships, marriage patterns, and personal values. In the United States, acculturation has apparently proceeded at a far more rapid pace than has structural assimilation.

One consequence is that the very notion of who is "ethnic" needs reexamination. It is commonly assumed that "ethnics" are those still-not-fully-assimilated immigrants from non-"Anglo-Saxon" countries or their children. Ethnic identity is thus limited to first- and second- or, on occasion, third-generation Americans. So old-stock Americans are excluded from consideration as members of ethnic groups when, in fact, they are as sharply—if more subtly—divided ethnically as are newer arrivals.

Ethnicity seems to wax and wane and perhaps wax again. Many people see it as having faded out around the third or fourth generation. By then, the ties that maintained the descendants of the original group had become more religious, associational, or fraternal than communal. To an extent, these other ties were masks. The ethnicity still persists, ready to spring back into view in times of crisis. Acculturation, then, serves to mask the lag in structural assimilation.

What, then, is the impact of ethnicity in the United States today, and how does it manifest itself? Most determinations of *ethnic group* attachment are based on country-of-origin without taking other factors into account. Realistically speaking, however, country-of-origin is a convenient but often poor measure, since the countries themselves may be newer than the groups they purportedly identify. They may also contain groups with widely different national identities. In addition, *racial* groups such as African-Americans or Native Americans, *sociocultural* groups such as New England Yankees or Southern whites, *ethnoreligious* groups such as Jews, *socioreligious* groups such as Mormons, and *sociolinguistic* groups such as French-Canadians, all of which have become very real biocultural communities over generations of in-group marriage, must also be included in any full effort to delineate the "ethnic" groups of the United States.[14]

These five subsets are not mutually exclusive. Most ethnic groups are identified by several factors, even if one is primary. For example, the Ukrainians in the USSR, lacking political independence for centuries, have maintained themselves as a sociolinguistic group with a common church, elements of a common culture, and a common territory. Likewise, in coming to the United States many Ukrainians, particularly those who came after World War II, have sought to maintain their identity by establishing Saturday schools, supporting a national association, holding cultural events, and agitating on behalf of Ukrainian political prisoners in the Soviet Union.[15] The sense of having a common country of origin as well as a degree of sociocultural and linguistic unity has created a sense of common ethnicity among Italian-Americans that transcends even what were (and still are) sharp internal divisions in Italy. Similarly, one can speak of Hispanics as members of a sociolinguistic group with elements of a sociocultural subset (occupation and community structure) and elements of a socioreligious subset (their own variety of Roman Catholicism) as well. On the other hand, there are clear distinctions separating Hispanics from Puerto Ricans, Cubans, and Mexicans.

CONSCIOUS AND SUBCONSCIOUS ETHNICITY

Although ethnic self-consciousness is central to ethnic identity, it would be a mistake to overlook the persistence of group distinctiveness even where members of the group in question may not be conscious of their ethnic ties. Culture, in the anthropological sense, has a way of persisting at a subconscious level—as second nature—even when the overt sense of group consciousness has well-nigh disappeared. The New England Yankees are a case in point. In the twentieth century, the sense of a common New England heritage has substantially disappeared among the descendants of the migrants from that section. Nevertheless, the cultural patterns that their ancestors passed on to them are fully visible in their public and private behavior. This can be seen in the way that Presbyterians and Congregationalists (the two denominations that are pronouncedly Yankee in their membership) actively participate in public life because of their sense of civic obligation, as distinct from members of equally prestigious and "WASP" churches who are not of Yankee stock, such as many Episcopalians; or in the way they send their children back to New England for schooling while at the same time providing support significantly in excess of the national average for their local educational institutions; or in the moralistic approach they tend to take toward politics.

Similarly, the descendants of Southern whites are as distinguishable from other segments of the population in southern Illinois and southeastern Oregon as in Alabama or Texas. Descendants of the older migrations in the Middle States are distinctive in yet other ways. In fact, the myth of the existence of a homogeneous and monolithic WASP group is as much a figment of the white ethnics' imagination as was the view of African-Americans in years gone by that there existed a homogeneous, monolithic white community. All in all, as the data in Table 7.3 indicate, it is as much a mistake to ignore latent manifestations of ethnicity as to ignore more manifest ones.

The past few years have shown that ethnicity has a far greater staying power than many scholars had heretofore thought possible. Ethnicity becomes politically important for particular groups when (1) the group is very large and has great potential power; (2) the group is small but highly visible, or a well-organized minority; (3) a sophisticated group suddenly becomes conscious that it has become a minority and is surrounded by many other well-organized ethnic groups.

POLITICAL WILL AND GROUP CONSCIOUSNESS

Both manifest and latent forms of ethnicity are important factors in American politics, each in its own way. Latent cultural patterns, though harder to discern, are invariably present wherever there are human communities.

TABLE 7.3   Religio-Ethnicity and Political Participation, Family Income, and Education

Religio-Ethnic Group	Overall Political Participation[a]	Voting Participation[b]	Real Family Income, 1974	Average Years of Education
Irish Catholic	41.0[c]	30.7[c]	$13,451	12.8
Scandinavian Prot-estant	32.0	31.2	11,284	11.3
Jewish	19.0	22.9	14,577	13.9
Slavic Catholic	11.2	35.6	11,499	10.8
German Catholic	10.7	29.3	12,543	11.6
British Protestant	10.4	6.2	12,208	12.4
German Protestant	9.0	10.1	11,500	11.3
Polish Catholic	6.2	37.5	12,257	11.1
Italian Catholic	−14.3	17.6	12,473	11.1
Irish Protestant	−18.0	−6.3	10,714	10.9

[a]This column contains summary measures of scores on four participation scales: voting, campaigning, communal participation, and particularized contact.

[b]Scores in this column represent participation in the 1960 and 1964 presidential elections and the 1966 congressional election.

[c]Scores represent deviations from the mean in standardized units.

Sources: Columns 1 and 2, Andrew H. Greeley, Ethnicity in the United States (New York: Wiley, 1974), pp. 126–127; Columns 3 and 4, Andrew M. Greeley, "The Ethnic Miracle," The Public Interest, no. 45 (Fall 1976), pp. 26, 28.

Their influence is pervasive but subtle. Overt ethnic interests are not only more easily recognized but actively seek to influence political life. In a country like the United States, such manifest interests are more likely to be products of political will than the simple force of circumstances. That is to say, the very openness of American society, with its emphasis on individual liberty—from one's "native group" as well as in relation to government—enables most people to choose whether or not to maintain an ethnic identity. However, it is true that for some—African-Americans, for example—freedom of choice is circumscribed by the circumstances of birth (in their case, color) and that for others—Jews, for example—there are strong circumstantial incentives for preserving group consciousness. Still, no group in the United States takes form as a group unless there are enough people to will it.[16]

The Native Americans are a good example of a group that can choose to assimilate entirely or actively seek separatism almost to the point of political secession (a choice not accorded to other groups in American society).[17] Today in most parts of the country, Native American ancestry can be something of a "plus." Consequently, most Native Americans are able to assimilate, and many have done so. Oklahoma, once the stronghold of Native Americans, offers the best example of this process, with many of the state's "first families" boasting of their Native American ancestry but otherwise unidentified with the Native American life. Other Native

Americans have chosen to remain identified with their respective tribes and, through them, have become participants in American society while otherwise acquiring the ways of whites. Today they form the backbone of organized Native American life in the United States.

In the 1960s, Native American militants challenged all Indian efforts to assimilate within American society. They allied themselves with the surviving old-line traditionalists on the reservations and demanded restoration of national status to the tribes. Although they succeeded only partially in securing their demands, they did attract a certain sympathy, because the Native Americans, more than any other group, have a claim to separate sovereignty in American territory.[18]

The rise of the Native American movement is a good example of how people can will themselves a sense of group identity if they have something upon which to base that identity. The experience of African-Americans is a good example of how people *must* have some kind of group identity in order to strengthen their own individual identities. The African-American struggle for civil rights and opportunities as individuals was able to gain momentum when a critical mass of African-American people acquired a sense of group identity and began to act upon it. As that sense grew, the struggle passed more fully into African-American hands. As Stokely Carmichael and Charles V. Hamilton commented during the 1960s at the height of the African-American struggle:

> Black people must redefine themselves, and only *they* can do that. This means we will no longer call ourselves lazy, apathetic, dumb, good-timers, shiftless, etc. Those words are used by white America to define us. If we accept these adjectives, as some of us have in the past, then we see ourselves only in a negative way, precisely the way white America wants us to see ourselves. . . .
>
> Only when black people fully develop this sense of community, of themselves, can they begin to deal effectively with the problems of racism in this country.[19]

The American political system has had to respond, at least partially, to these new ethnic demands—in the case of the excluded groups, to provide favorable conditions for their full integration into society without losing their identity. Thus African-Americans have successfully demanded affirmative action programs; Hispanics, bilingual education; and various ethnoreligious and socioreligious groups, the right to be protected in their expression of religious differences in dress, Sabbath observance, and the like.[20]

Ethnic influences on American foreign policy are well known and well documented, whether with regard to the Jews and Israel, the Irish and the status of Ireland, or the various East European groups and Soviet domination of Eastern Europe. More recently, the Turks and the Greeks have entered the arena on behalf of their respective claims to Cyprus.[21]

If the still-active ethnic movements succeed in their goals, they may fundamentally transform American politics by creating a new right—that of group identity—to accompany the country's traditional emphasis on the rights of the individual. The right to other linkages could offer Americans a means to restore the sense of community that is so hard to find in this very large, highly mobile society. However, intergroup rivalries and conflicts could also create new tensions in American life.

ETHNIC GROUPS AND THE CONTINUING FRONTIER

The strength as well as the geography of ethnicity is directly related to the continuing American frontier. In ethnic terms, the rural-land frontier was characterized by the predominance of British and Northwestern European migrants, at least half of whom were identified with Reformed churches (principally Puritan, Presbyterian, and Dutch). The way of life generally associated with "old America" was formed by those groups through their frontier experiences.

It was the urban-industrial frontier that generated the great migration from Ireland and Germany, and, later, Southern and Eastern Europe, to bring the bulk of the families of today's "white ethnics" to American shores. They came to provide labor for the mines, mills, and factories that were the economic core of the urban frontier. Today many of their descendants are searching for a heritage lost in the process of Americanization.

The metropolitan-technological frontier, too, has stimulated new forms of ethnic interaction. Its first thrust was to encourage the great African-American migration from the rural South and the migration of Spanish-speaking groups from Latin America to Northern and Western cities. Most important, it created the conditions for both the civil rights revolution and the new ethnicity.

A look at Tables 7.1 and 7.2 reveals that immigrants still come to the United States every year to join the American people, whereas very few of those born in America emigrate. In the early stages of the rurban-cybernetic frontier, there was a shift in the direction of immigration. Changes in the immigration laws at the end of the metropolitan-frontier era, along with U.S. involvement in Asia, opened the door to large numbers of Asians on a competitive basis. (The earlier immigration of Chinese, Japanese, and Filipinos was essentially an importation of foreign labor.) Immigrants from almost every country in East Asia flocked to the United States and, in general, did well almost from the first. They were also well received as manifesting new incarnations of the American dream, embodying the willingness to work hard to get ahead. They won the respect and even the affection of old-stock Americans who saw in them the promise of revitalization of a nice country gone a little soft. Less noticed was the way in which these new populations transformed the United States into a truly universal melting pot, with connections not only to Europe and Africa but to Asia as well. As the United States moves into its third century, the American promise is being extended in yet another direction.

Meanwhile, those Americans of European and African stock, most of whose families have been in the United States for three, four, or many more generations, have pursued two contradictory trends. The metropolitan frontier and, even more so, the rurban frontier have hastened the process of assimilation and even amalgamation of peoples. As the younger generations move out of areas of ethnic concentration (even upper-class suburbs could be seen in that light until very recently) and go to college, they begin to meet and marry people from other ethnic, religious, and social backgrounds, extending and deepening the kinship connections among all Americans regardless of their ethnic background or religious identification. Propinquity, the major determinant of who marries whom, has ceased being parochial and become cosmopolitan for most Americans.

On the other hand, despite the loss of their unique kinship ties, many Americans have sought to overtly express their distinctive ethnic identities. Beyond that, even where they do not seek overt or visible distinctions, the patterns of behavior transmitted from their ethnic background persist in less visible ways. Nowhere is this more so than in the case of politics.

The "new ethnicity" of the last half of the eleventh generation was, as wiser heads understood at the time, not so much an assertion of cultural pluralism as the last step in the process of integration of the Southern and Eastern European ethnics and, to some extent, the African-Americans, Hispanics, and Asians into American society. In that respect, it paralleled the burst of ethnicity of the late nineteenth century, when the Northwest European groups underwent the same process. In other words, the demands of the new ethnics were not so much to be able to live culturally separate lives as to be recognized as having made their contribution to the common American culture and society.

The truth is, most of them had little that was distinctively ethnic to hang on to. A few foods, shared myths, and their own historical experiences in the United States did not add up to cultural differentiation in any significant way. Thus, once their contributions to American life had been recognized, they were content to continue the process of assimilation.

Indeed, it was at the beginning of the twelfth generation that the breakdown of previous barriers to intermarriage came to be felt in massive proportions. Intermarriage soared not only in connection with groups that had little to preserve other than heritage but also among groups such as the Jews, who traditionally had avoided intermarriage in order to maintain their own rich way of life.

By the end of the eleventh generation, overt ethnicity, as such, turned out to be far less important than anticipated by its apologists; but the less overt manifestations of ethnicity did not disappear. Quite to the contrary, they entered politics through political culture.

POLITICAL CULTURE:
A MAJOR FORCE FOR ETHNIC INTEGRATION

Political culture is one of the primary sources shaping politics. Political culture has been defined as the "particular pattern of orientations to political action" in which each political system is embedded.[22] A political culture is related to the general culture of a particular society but is by no means identical with it. As Gabriel Almond says: "Because political orientation involves cognition, intellection, and adaptation to external situations, as well as the standards and values of the general culture, it is a differentiated part of the culture and has a certain autonomy."[23] Like all culture, political culture is so rooted in the cumulative historical experience of particular groups that it has become second nature to those within its embrace.

General culture has a direct impact on politics from the outside, as it were. Political culture, that differentiated aspect of the overall culture which is itself a truly political phenomenon, has its direct impact from the inside.

The United States is a single land of great diversity inhabited by what is now a single people of great diversity. The singleness of the country as a whole is expressed through political, cultural, and geographic unity. Conversely, the country's diversity is expressed through its states, subcultures, and sections. In this section, we will focus on the political dimensions of that diversity-in-unity—on the country's overall political culture and its subculture.

Political culture is the summation of persistent patterns of underlying political attitudes and characteristic responses to political concerns that is manifest in a particular political order. Its existence is generally unperceived by those who are part of that order, and its origins date back to the very beginnings of the particular people who share it. Political culture is an intrinsically political phenomenon. As such, it makes its own demands on the political system. For example, the definition of what is "fair" in the political arena—a direct manifestation of political culture—is likely to be different from the definition of what is fair in family or business relationships. Moreover, different political cultures will define fairness in politics differently. Political culture also affects all other questions confronting the political system. For example, many factors go into shaping public expectations regarding government services, and political culture will be significant among them. Political systems, in turn, are in some measure the products of the political cultures they serve and must remain in harmony with their political cultures if they are to maintain themselves.

THE "GEOLOGY" OF SETTLEMENT AND THE CULTURAL STREAMS

The ethnic groups that came to America brought diverse patterns of culture to be integrated, modified, and unified by a new environment. In the process, they formed alignments with some ethnic groups and came into conflict with others. Whatever the level of individuality the various ethnic and religious groups wished to maintain, there were also points of convergence that united peoples of different backgrounds through shared common values. From these points of convergence have developed the major political subcultures in the United States, with their respective variations on American political culture as a whole.

Out of that process has come much of the present configuration of American politics. In order to identify and understand that configuration, we must explore the human "geology" of settlement across the country (which represents the primary structural impact of migration) as well as the differing manifestations of that geology in each locality. The ethnic mosaic in each community is reflected in the local geological pattern. The political impact, however, is considerably less fragmented. In some communities, especially those in the greater Northeast, politics seems to be heavily oriented toward balancing the "classic" national-origin ethnic groups (Irish, Italians, Jews, etc.) and conciliating their members; however, in most of the country there has been a convergence of such groups within the political arena into several principal clusters based upon affinities of political culture.

The geology of settlement is given shape by the "human deposits" of fifteen migrational streams that have flowed across the United States at various times and with varying intensities since the initial settlement of North America.[24] Each of these fifteen streams, taken in the aggregate, represents a population that, although composed of myriad individuals and many different ethnic groups, possesses certain unique cultural characteristics shared in some measure by the people within it, all of whom must somehow respond to the way of life it embodies. Through its deposits, determined in significant measure by generational and sectional factors as well as by the dictates of each successive frontier, each stream has contributed its special ingredients to the evolving social and political structure of the states and localities through which it has passed. More-over, since the pattern of deposits (and the effects they have on one an-other) differs from locality to locality, the very movement of the streams has created unique social combinations from place to place. This relation-ship contributes much to the explanation of similarities of political behav-ior in apparently diverse communities and of differences in political be-havior in apparently similar ones.

The terms *stream* and *current* are used here for purposes of generalizing about the overall patterns of migration and settlement in the United States. They are designed to convey a sense of the dynamic yet somewhat blurred nature of migrational patterns in this country and the directional character of the various migrations that have molded American settle-ment patterns. Streams are not ethnic groups. In fact, the concept of streams is deliberately used here as a means to overcome the limitations of conventional "ethnic group" concepts, which do not account for the link-ages that form between groups, particularly after they have acculturated.

The history of settlement and migration in this country reveals three basic ethnocultural strata, manifested in three sets of political-culture streams.

1. On the first level, there is a triad of primary political subcultures—the Southern, Middle, and New England states—that were developed within the overall American culture by the first waves of European set-tlers, primarily during the colonial period. The *Southern subculture* origi-nated in Virginia, the Carolinas, and Georgia, and was originally based on slavery, the plantation system, a radically individualist conception of so-cial obligation, and a gentry-dominated political order.[25] The *Middle States subculture* originated in New York, New Jersey, Pennsylvania, Maryland, and Delaware, and was based on commercial enterprise, ethnic and reli-gious pluralism, freehold agriculture, and a political order that, virtually from the first, was maintained as a marketplace and serviced by profes-sional politicians.[26] The *Yankee subculture* originated in New England and was based on Puritanism, with its emphasis on individual enterprise within the context of an organized and powerful community. This third subculture was dedicated to social order and individual redemption and to the fostering of a political order that encompassed a tension between an oligarchy deemed to be the guardian of communal values and the funda-mentally democratic town meeting.[27] All three subcultures became what were in effect "native" streams carried westward as the people within them migrated across the continent.

2. On the second level, there are the discrete ethnocultural streams (North Sea, English, Continental, Anglo-Canadian, and so on) brought into American civil society by subsequent migrants.[28] Most of these groups arrived from Europe, mainly during the nineteenth century, and

have had to be integrated into the three primary subcultures. They effectively formed themselves into nine "European" streams. The settlement and migration of these groups can be viewed as laid on top of, fitted to, and affected by the bedrock of the three broader subcultures.

3. On the third level, there are those non-European ethnocultural groups (African-American, Hispanic, Asian) that gained admission to the mainstream of American life only as late as the eleventh generation. They represent once-excluded non-European streams.

In conventional discussions, important divisions in accepted "ethnic" categories disappear within larger general categories that cut across those divisions. For example, all residents of Germany as unified by Bismarck in 1871 tend to be lumped together as Germans without distinction, ignoring fundamental differences between northern Protestants and southern Catholics, Prussians and Rhinelanders, Bavarians and Saxons, and so on. At the same time, deeper transethnic patterns of similarity of great significance rooted in common religious and cultural ties are equally ignored because they disappear within the framework of the various national divisions and loyalties that have captured the consciousness of the people involved. For example, the peoples living in the coastal areas around the North Sea have more in common with one another in terms of political culture than with their countrymen in the interior.[29] (See Table 7.4 for a breakdown of the characteristics of comparable subcultural streams.)

The "streams" are, of course, abstractions. Abstractions settle no place. Rather, settlement is made by the individual households—families and individuals—that, together, make up the several streams. Thus, in the final analysis, when we speak of migrational streams, we are speaking of the aggregation of small impacts of household after household. Families, in turn, tend to be bearers of traditional values and even certain behavior patterns—even in rapidly changing American society. Nor is this to be wondered at. The first years of human socialization are, as Freud so strongly suggested, the most critical in the development of personality, the establishment of behavior patterns, and the inculcation of values. These early years are normally spent within the family group.[30]

The tendency for families to act as bearers and transmitters of established values and patterns of social behavior is reinforced by the normal patterns of religious attachment in our society. Nuclear families not only tend to share membership in the same religious community, but their members often marry endogamously within their religious community. This orientation is particularly important in American society, where religious pluralism plays a vital role in preserving ethnic identity. The streams themselves tend to take visible shape primarily through the religious affiliations of their constituent households, reinforced by the tendency of friendly cliques to be religiously and ethnically homogeneous.

TABLE 7.4   Characteristics of Comparable Subcultural Streams

	Streams		
Indigenous	*European*	*Non-European*	*Modal Characteristics*
Northern	North Sea Anglo-Canadian Jewish[a]		Calvinistic Protestant (Congregational or Presbyterian), Communitarian, entrepreneurial, middle-class, Republican, fiercely loyal as a group to one party or fiercely independent
Middle	English Continental Irish		Catholic or Hierarchical Liturgical Protestant, individualist and pluralist, multiclass, entrepreneurial, with mixed party loyalties
Southern	Mediterranean Eastern European French Canadian	Hispanic African-American Asian	Single dominant religion or "color," individualist but kinship oriented, originally working class, overt ethnic identity, Democratic

[a]The Jewish stream deviates from these modal characteristics in several respects.

Such cliques, moreover, usually involve households occupying reasonably adjacent space.

The composition of the streams and the manner in which they flow have tended to strengthen this pattern of cultural transmission. By and large, people who intended to settle permanently in the West moved in family groups. These family groups, whether they originated in other parts of the United States or overseas, generally moved with other families from the same place of origin and with similar interests and attachments. Whether this movement took the form of formal colonization in which a group of families would actually form a colonization company to promote the settlement of a particular site, or whether it was simply a matter of friends attracting other friends in a less systematic manner, settlements usually developed along relatively homogeneous lines in their early stages. From then on it was often a matter of like following like.[31]

As settlements grew into cities and gained larger populations, their demographic composition became more diverse. Other groups arrived, representing other streams. Generally, they, too, settled in groups of families, sometimes displacing established groups in older neighborhoods and sometimes creating new neighborhoods of their own, adding new "deposits" to the evolving community. Even where the later arrivals have submerged the original streams, making them well-nigh invisible, the latter often continue to exist within the community, perpetuated through the complex of family ties, religious communalism, and friendship patterns. Meanwhile, their original influence on the patterns of community life and politics to some degree continues to shape the ways of the later arrivals.

In most cases the various streams that located in each city continue to be reinforced by new immigrants. Although the heyday of land settlement passed with the passing of the land frontier and the closing of unlimited immigration, migration within the United States continues undiminished, and the flow of the streams also continues, though perhaps at a somewhat diminished rate.[32] Southerners continue to flow into areas settled by Southerners and even expand into contiguous ones; Yankees follow old migration lines established by their forebears; and new immigrants from overseas often go where their families and friends who preceded them have already settled. Cuban immigrants since 1960, for example, have congregated in Miami, Florida; Hudson County, New Jersey; New York City; and Los Angeles, California. Recent Egyptian immigrants, many of whom are Coptic Christians, have also tended to concentrate in Brooklyn, Jersey City, and Los Angeles. In not a few cases, reciprocal relationships have developed between the original sources of each stream and their cultural hinterlands (as, for example, when the young are sent "back East" to college in the states of the family's original culture area), thus tending to reaffirm the social influences of the stream as well.

POLITICAL CULTURE AND AMERICAN POLITICS

Political-culture factors stand out as particularly influential in shaping the operations of the national, state, and local political systems in three ways: (1) by molding the perceptions of the political community (the citizens, the politicians, and the public officials) as to the nature and purposes of politics and its expectations of government and the political process; (2) by influencing the recruitment of specific kinds of people to become active in government and politics—as holders of elective offices, members of the bureaucracy, and active political workers; and (3) by subtly directing the actual way in which the art of government is practiced by citizens, politicians, and public officials in the light of their perceptions. In turn, the cultural components of individual and group behavior are manifested in civic behavior as dictated by conscience and internalized ethical standards, in the forms of law-abidingness (or laxity in such matters) adhered to by citizens and officials, and in the character of the positive actions of government.[33]

CONTRASTING CONCEPTIONS OF THE POLITICAL ORDER

The American political culture is rooted in two contrasting conceptions of the American political order, both of which can be traced back to the earliest settlement of the country. In the first, the political order is conceived as a marketplace in which the primary public relationships are products of bargaining among individuals and groups acting out of self-interest. In the second, the political order is conceived as a commonwealth—a state in which the whole people have an undivided interest—whereby the citizens cooperate in an effort to erect and maintain the best government in order to implement certain shared moral principles.

The commonwealth is animated by a vision of the proper political order yet to be attained but in the process of being built upon existing foundations—and it maintains its strength only by maintaining the vitality of that vision. The marketplace, by contrast, is animated by a desire to keep the peace through a balance of interests without any necessary commitments other than the preservation of the marketplace itself. Access to the political marketplace is open to all interests that in any way acknowledge its legitimacy and are willing to abide by its rules (at least most of the time). No independent criteria are used to judge the legitimacy of these interests as a condition of participation, so any individual or group that can make its presence felt acquires the functional equivalent of citizenship. In the commonwealth, on the other hand, citizenship, or the right to participate legitimately in the government process, is a matter of very serious concern, and *a priori* moral criteria can legitimately be applied to determine which individuals or groups have this right.

These two conceptions have exercised an influence on government and politics throughout American history, sometimes by conflicting and sometimes by complementing one another. They are so intertwined as to be practically inseparable in any particular case or situation. That is, marketplace notions contribute to, or shape, the vision of commonwealth, and commonwealth ideals are given a preferred position in the marketplace.

MARKETPLACE AND COMMONWEALTH: THE AMERICAN CULTURAL MATRIX

The two conceptions just noted are reflected in the matrix of value concepts that forms the larger cultural basis of American civilization. This matrix is portrayed in Figure 7.1. Its component value concepts together provide the framework within which the value orientations of the American people are shaped, whereas the differences in emphasis in the interrelationships among them reflect the various subcultures in the United States.

The four elements of the matrix are located between power and justice, the two poles of politics between which are encompassed the basic political concerns of all civil societies—namely, "who gets what, when, and

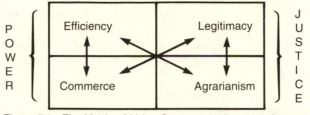

Figure 7.1   The Matrix of Value Concepts in American Culture.
Source: Daniel J. Elazar, *American Federalism: A View from the States*, 3d ed. (New York: Harper and Row Publishers, 1984), p. 113. Reprinted by permission of HarperCollins Publishers.

how" (power), on the one hand, and the development of the good society (justice), on the other. The major continuing task of every civil society is to shape an immediately practical relationship between the two poles in a manner that best fits its situation. Indeed, the character of any civil society is in large measure determined by the relationship between power and justice that shapes its political order. Accordingly, a particular civil society's conceptions of the uses of power and the nature of justice are important aspects of its political culture.

Efficiency may be defined operationally in this context as the achievement of the system's goals in a manner that involves the least wasteful or minimum expenditure of resources. Legitimacy refers to those aspects of a polity that are believed to be supported by the underlying values of its citizenry, particularly as embodied in its constitutional system. Both efficiency and legitimacy represent tendencies found in every civil society that are given meaning by each society's culture (general as well as political).

In the United States, efficiency is measured in predominantly commercial terms—as befits a civil society, which *The Federalist* correctly described as a commercial republic. Commerce, in turn, is a cardinal feature of American civilization that embodies the exchange of goods, services, and ideas. Indeed, one might readily argue that the federal republic was founded to advance and protect commerce and that it has adhered quite closely to that original purpose. Commerce is particularly valued because it is an efficient means of organizing, harnessing, and diffusing power in light of American values. Americans characteristically rely upon various kinds of marketplaces (e.g., the economic marketplace and the "marketplace of ideas") to protect and foster freedom as well as to foster property and enterprise. They have changed their conventional definition of what is efficient as the organization of their commercial enterprises has changed. So, in the eighteenth century, efficiency meant, first and foremost, the efficiency of competition among relative equals, thus reflecting the economic system of the time, which rested upon so many small enterprises. And in the twentieth century it has come to mean the hierarchical organization of enterprise, reflecting an economic system that rests upon complex bureaucratic corporations. In sum, both efficiency and commerce are primarily related to the concerns of power and its management.

Legitimacy, on the other hand, is given meaning in the United States by the peculiarly American complex of values and aspirations here termed agrarianism. The ideal of agrarianism envisions the United States as a commonwealth of self-governing freeholders, each with a tangible stake in the community (and, hence, in American society as a whole), raised to new heights of human decency through the general diffusion of knowledge, religion, and morality. This ideal stems from both the Puritan and Jeffersonian roots of American life; it has also undergone adaptation to the changing circumstances of American history. As the embodiment of the nation's social and political mystique, it is the major source and test of legitimacy in the United States. Both agrarianism and legitimacy relate to the problem of the attainment of justice and are expressions of the continuing effort to create a more just society in the United States.

Each of the four tendencies is pulled in the direction of power or justice and is also modified by every other tendency. In every form it has taken, American agrarianism has had a strong commercial aspect, beginning with the desire of many Americans to make a profit from the use of the land even while valuing closeness to it for moral reasons. Unlike feudal or peasant agrarianism, American agrarianism has represented the effort to create a moral commonwealth of religiously inspired freeholders actively engaged in commerce in its various manifestations. By the same token, the values of this agrarianism modify commercial efficiency at crucial points. Accordingly, the maximization of profits is not the only measure of efficiency in American life, even though the agrarian values themselves are sometimes tailored to meet the demands of efficiency.

The politically defined limits of commerce in America are set by the demands of agrarian legitimacy. Periodically, the commercial aspects of American society have run wild, only to be pulled back in line, sooner or later, on the grounds that they have been set free illegitimately. (For example, "trusts" are illegitimate even if they are efficient from a commercial point of view.) This common sense of legitimacy is defined in what are essentially agrarian terms. At such points, political action is forthcoming to reshape the commercial order so as to reintegrate it in accordance with the principles of agrarian legitimacy. At the same time, what is commonly deemed legitimate is itself shaped by the attachment to commerce as a key aspect of American civil society.

SUMMARY

In Chapter 7 we turn away from a consideration of geo-historical location to examine cultural location in the United States. The chapter begins by examining the similarities and diversities of the people of the United States. It follows the formation of the American people as the country developed from one of overwhelmingly British and North European background (nonwhites such as African slaves and Native Americans were excluded from the polity for their own reasons) to one characterized by a pluralism of European migrants in the nineteenth century and then, in our times, by a pluralism of peoples who originated from all continents, races, and religions.

The chapter also looks at contemporary religiosity and ethnicity as the basis for American pluralism and examines how shared constitutional-political ties have transformed diverse groups into a single American people. Then it examines the political manifestations of various kinds of group consciousness. This, in turn, brings the chapter to the issue of political culture as a major force for ethnic and religious integration; through the establishment of common rules of the game in which all can share, the people have been united beyond the diversities of ethnicity, religion, and the sequence of arrival on American shores.

NOTES

1. *The American Heritage History of the American People* (New York: American Heritage Publishing Company, 1971).

2. See Lyndon B. Johnson, Presidential Inaugural Address, 1964. Strictly speaking, of course, Native Americans and African-Americans (the latter having been brought to the new nation as slaves) are exceptions to this covenant. The forcible incorporation of both groups into American civil society has been termed America's original sin and has plagued the body politic from the first. It is clear by now, however, that even they remain by choice, as reflected in their struggle to gain equal rights within the system.

3. Richard Merritt explores and documents the rise of this sense of Americanism among the colonists in the decade before the Revolutionary War in *Symbols of American Community, 1735–1775* (New Haven, Conn.: Yale University Press, 1966).

4. Herman Melville, *Moby Dick* (New York: Holt, Rinehart and Winston, 1962).

5. Although most immigrants came to stay, a certain percentage found it desirable or necessary to return to the Old World. The rate of reemigration from the United States varied across ethnic groups and with economic conditions. For example, about one-third of all the immigrants who came to the United States between 1908 and 1924 did not remain here permanently. However, 94.8 percent of the East European Jews who came during that period chose to stay. See Irving Howe, *World of Our Fathers* (New York: Harcourt, 1976), p. 58.

6. For further discussion of religious groups in the United States, see Edwin Scott Gaustad, *A Religious History of America* (New York: Harper and Row, 1966); Sidney E. Ahlstrom, *A Religious History of the American People* (New Haven, Conn.: Yale University Press, 1972); Leo Rosten, ed., *Religions in America* (New York: Simon and Schuster, 1975); Parker J. Palmer, *The Company of Strangers: Christians and the Renewal of America's Public Life* (New York: Crossroad, 1981); Theodore Caplow et al., *All Faithful People: Change and Continuity in Middletown's Religion* (Minneapolis: University of Minnesota Press, 1983); Dean R. Hoge, *Converts, Dropouts, Returnees: A Study of Religious Change Among Catholics* (Washington, D.C.: United States Catholic Conference; New York: Pilgrim Press, 1981); and Dean R. Hoge and David A. Rich, ed., *Understanding Church Growth and Decline, 1950–1978* (New York: Pilgrim Press, 1979).

7. For several perspectives on ethnicity in the United States, see Andrew M. Greeley, *Ethnicity in the United States* (New York: Wiley, 1974); Colin Greer, *Divided Society: The Ethnic Experience in America* (New York: Basic Books, 1974); Paul Jacobs and Saulo Landau, with Eve Pell, *To Serve the Devil* (New York: Vintage, 1971); Nathan Glazer, *Beyond the Melting Pot* (Cambridge, Mass.: MIT Press, 1970); Stanley Lieberson, *Ethnic Patterns in American Cities* (New York: Free Press, 1963); Thomas Sowell, *Ethnic America* (New York: Basic Books, 1981); and Stephen Steinberg, *The Ethnic Myth: Ethnicity and Class in America* (New York: Atheneum, 1981).

8. The difference between the marketplace pluralism of New York and the morally grounded pluralism of Pennsylvania is discussed in Daniel J. Elazar's *The American Constitutional Tradition* (Lincoln: University of Nebraska Press, 1988), ch. 2.

9. For further discussion of immigration, see Oscar Handlin, *The Uprooted*, 2nd ed. (Boston: Little, Brown, 1973); Marcus Hanson, *The Atlantic Migration* (New York: Harvard University Press, 1961); and Maldwyn Allen Jones, *American Immigration* (Chicago: University of Chicago Press, 1960).

10. For an exemplary late-nineteenth-century ethnic apologia, see Albert B. Faust, *The German Element in the United States*, 2 vols. (Boston, 1909). See also E. Allen McCormick, ed., *Germans in America: Aspects of German-American Relations in the Nineteenth Century* (New York: Social Science Monographs, Brooklyn College Press, 1983); LaVern J. Rippley, *The German-Americans* (Boston: Twayne Publishers, 1976); and Frederick C. Luebke, *Germans in the New World* (Urbana: University of Illinois Press, 1990).

11. Zangwill was the first to use the term *melting pot*. Horace M. Kallen invented the term *cultural pluralism* and developed the conception in "Democracy Versus the Melting Pot," *The Nation*, no. 100, parts 1 and 2 (February 18 and February 25, 1915): 190–194 and 217–220. See also Horace M. Kallen, *Cultural Pluralism and the American Idea* (Philadelphia: University of Pennsylvania Press, 1956).

12. See, for example, Michael Novak, *The Rise of the Unmeltable Ethnic* (New York: Macmillan, 1972); and Richard Krickus, *Pursuing the American Dream: White Ethnics and the New Populism* (Garden City, N.Y.: Doubleday, 1976).

13. On the discovery of group identity by immigrants in the United States, see Marcus Hanson, *The Great Atlantic Migration* (New York: Harvard University Press, 1961); Oscar Handlin, *The Uprooted* (New York: Grosset and Dunlap, 1951); Stanley Lieberson, *A Piece of the Pie: Black and White Immigrants Since 1850* (Berkeley: Univer-

sity of California Press, 1980); and Rudolph Vecoli, ed., *Italian Immigrants in Rural and Small Town America* (Staten Island, N.Y.: The Association, 1987).

14. Ellsworth Huntington refers to such groups as "kiths" in *The Mainsprings of Civilization* (New York: Mentor, 1972). For further discussion of "kiths," see Gifford Geertz, *Interpretation of Cultures* (New York: Basic Books, 1973).

15. Leon Tolopko, *Working Ukrainians in the USA* (New York: Ukrainian American League, 1986); Paul R. Magocsi, ed., *The Ukrainian Experience in the United States: A Symposium* (Cambridge, Mass.: Harvard Ukrainian Research Institute, 1979); Myron B. Kuropas, *The Ukrainians in America* (Minneapolis: Lerner Publications, 1972); June D. Holmquist, ed., *They Chose Minnesota: A Survey of the State's Ethnic Groups* (St. Paul: Minnesota Historical Society Press, 1981).

16. See Raymond E. Wolfinger, "The Development and Persistence of Ethnic Voting," *American Political Science Review* 59 (December 1965): 896–908; Michael Parenti, "Ethnic Politics and the Persistence of Ethnic Identifications," *American Political Science Review* 61 (September 1967): 717–726; Harry A. Bailey and Ellis Katz, eds., *Ethnic Group Politics* (Columbus, Ohio: Charles E. Merrill, 1969); Mark R. Levy and Michael Kramer, *The Ethnic Factor: How America's Minorities Decide Elections* (New York: Simon and Schuster, 1972); Thomas Sowell, ed., *Essays and Data on American Ethnic Groups* (Washington, D.C.: Urban Institute, 1978); David R. Colburn and George E. Pozzetta, eds., *America and the New Ethnicity* (Cambridge, Mass.: The Belknap Press of Harvard University Press, 1982); and Richard Polenberg, *One Nation Divisible: Class, Race and Ethnicity in the United States Since 1938* (New York: Viking Press, 1980).

17. Constitutionally, the Native American tribes are, in the words of Chief Justice John Marshall, "domestic dependent nations," potentially similar in status to Puerto Rico. Hence they can assert extensive rights of self-government recognized in law. See S. Lyman Tyler, *A History of Indian Policy* (Washington, D.C.: Bureau of Indian Affairs, 1973); Francis Paul Prucha, *The Great Father: The United States Government and the American Indians* (Lincoln: University of Nebraska Press, 1984); and Russell L. Barsh and James Y. Henderson, *The Road: Indian Tribes and Political Liberty* (Berkeley: University of California Press, 1980).

18. See, for example, Vine Deloria, Jr., *Custer Died for Your Sins: An Indian Manifesto* (New York: Macmillan, 1969); Stan Steiner, *The New Indians* (New York: Dell, 1968); Hazel W. Hertzberg, *The Search for an American Indian Identity* (Syracuse, N.Y.: Syracuse University Press, 1971); and Thorstein Sellin, ed., "American Indians and American Life," *Annals of the American Academy of Political and Social Science* (May 1957): 1–220.

19. Stokely Carmichael and Charles V. Hamilton, *Black Power* (New York: Random House, 1967), pp. 37–39.

20. On the recognition of special allowances for different groups, see Levy and Kramer, *The Ethnic Factor*; and Polenberg, *One Nation Divisible*.

21. On ethnic groups and foreign policy, see George Kennan, "Foreign Policy and the Christian Conscience," *Atlantic Monthly* (May 1959): 63–97 and "Morality and Foreign Affairs," *Foreign Affairs* (Winter 1985-1986): 205–218. See also Dexter Perkins, *The American Approach to Foreign Policy* (New York: Atheneum, 1968); Perkins, *The Evolution of American Foreign Policy* (New York: Oxford University Press, 1966); Gabriel A. Almond, *The American People and Foreign Policy* (New York:

Harcourt Brace Jovanovich, 1950); Robert Osgood, *Alliances and American Foreign Policy* (Baltimore: Johns Hopkins University Press, 1968); and Marshall H. Segal et al., *Human Behavior in Global Perspective: An Introduction to Cross-Cultural Psychology* (New York: Pergamon Press, 1990).

22. See Gabriel Almond, "Comparative Political Systems," *Journal of Politics* 18 (August 1956): 396. See also Lucian W. Pye and Sidney Verba, eds., *Political Cultural and Political Development* (Princeton, N.J.: Princeton University Press, 1965); Donald J. Devine, *The Political Culture of the United States* (Boston: Little, Brown, 1972); Raymond D. Gastil, *Cultural Regions of the United States* (Seattle: University of Washington Press, 1975); Aaron Wildavsky, *Cultural Theory* (Boulder, Colo.: Westview Press, 1990); and Edward K. Hamilton, ed., *America's Global Interests: A New Agenda* (New York: W. W. Norton, 1989).

23. Almond, "Comparative Political Systems," p. 396.

24. See Daniel J. Elazar, *Cities of the Prairie* (New York: Basic Books, 1970), chs. 4–6, and *American Federalism, A View from the States,* 3rd ed. (New York: Harper and Row, 1984), ch. 5.

25. See Charles S. Sydnor, *American Revolutionaries in the Making: Political Practices in Washington's Virginia* (New York: Collier Books, 1962); William R. Taylor, *Cavalier and Yankee* (New York: Braziller, 1961); Richard R. Beeman, "Robert Manford and the Political Culture of Frontier Virginia, " *Journal of American Studies* 12, no. 3 (August 1978): 169-184; W. J. Cash, *The Mind of the South* (New York: Vintage Books, 1945); V. O. Key, Jr., *Southern Politics in State and Nation* (New York: Vintage Books, 1949).

26. André Moore, *Political Culture in Pennsylvania: An Empirical Analysis* (Philadelphia: Center for the Study of Federalism, 1970); David M. Ellis, "New York and Middle Atlantic Regionalism," *New York History* 25, no. 1 (January 1954): 13–32; Eric F. Goldman, "Middle States Regionalism and American Historiography: A Suggestion," in Eric F. Goldman, ed., *Historiography and Urbanization* (Baltimore: Johns Hopkins University Press, 1941); Digy Baltzell, *Puritan Boston and Quaker Philadelphia: Two Protestant Ethics and the Spirit of Class Authority and Leadership* (New York: Free Press, 1979); Sam Bass Warner, *The Private City: Philadelphia in Three Periods of Its Growth* (Philadelphia: University of Pennsylvania Press, 1941); and D. G. Thompson, *Gateway to a Nation: The Middle Atlantic States and Their Influence on the Development of a Nation* (Peterborough, N.H.: William Banham, 1956).

27. Merle Curti, *The Making of an American Community* (Stanford, Calif.: Stanford University Press, 1959); Perry Miller, *Errand into The Wilderness* (New York: Harper and Row, 1964); Baltzell, *Puritan Boston and Quaker Philadelphia;* Taylor, *Cavalier and Yankee.*

28. See, for example, Stephen Thernstrom, ed., *Harvard Encyclopedia of American Ethnic Groups* (Cambridge, Mass.: Harvard University Press, 1980).

29. Daniel J. Elazar, *Covenant Tradition in Politics,* Vol. 2 (forthcoming).

30. See Erik H. Erikson, *Childhood and Society* (New York: W. W. Norton, 1963); Richard E. Dawson and Kenneth Prewitt, *Political Socialization* (Boston: Little, Brown, 1969); Richard G. Niemi and Associates, *The Politics of the Future Citizens* (San Francisco: Jossey Bass, 1974); M. Kent Jennings and Richard G. Niemi, *The Political Character of Adolescence: The Influence of Families and Schools* (Princeton, N.J.: Princeton University Press, 1974); Dean Jares, *Socialization to Politics* (New York:

Praeger, 1973); Fred I. Greenstein, *Children and Politics* (New Haven, Conn: Yale University Press, 1965); and Frederick W. Bozett and Shirley M. H. Hanson, eds., *Fatherhood and Families in Cultural Context* (New York: Springer, 1991).

31. Daniel B. Creamer et al., *Migration and Economic Opportunity* (Philadelphia: University of Pennsylvania Press, 1935).

32. In the latter part of the nineteenth century, Congress imposed restrictions on the entry of Chinese persons, certain "undesirables," and contract laborers. The Immigration Act of 1924 established country-of-origin quotas that limited immigration, particularly from Asia as well as Southern and Eastern Europe. The Immigration Act of 1965 allowed a more equal distribution of immigration from countries outside the Western Hemisphere. And in 1976, Congress approved legislation designed to remedy some of the inequalities in the procedures involved in Eastern and Western Hemisphere immigration.

33. This section is adapted from Daniel J. Elazar, *American Federalism: A View from the States*, 3d ed. (New York: Harper and Row, 1984).

CHAPTER 8

The Political Subcultures of the United States

The national political culture of the United States is itself a synthesis of three major political subcultures. These subcultures jointly inhabit the country, existing side by side or sometimes overlapping one another. All three are of nationwide proportions, having spread, in the course of time, from coast to coast. Yet each subculture is strongly tied to specific sections of the country, reflecting the streams and currents of migration that have carried people of different origins and backgrounds across the continent in more or less orderly patterns.[1]

Given the central characteristics that define each of the subcultures and their centers of emphasis, the three political subcultures may be called individualistic, moralistic, and traditionalistic. Each reflects its own particular synthesis of the marketplace and the commonwealth.

It is important, however, not only to examine this description and the following ones very carefully but also to abandon the preconceptions associated with such idea-words as individualistic, moralistic, marketplace, and so on. Thus, for example, nineteenth-century individualistic conceptions of minimum intervention were oriented toward *laissez-faire*, with the role of government conceived to be that of a policeman with powers to act in certain limited fields. And in the twentieth century, the notion of what constitutes minimum intervention has been drastically expanded to include such things as government regulation of utilities, unemployment compensation, and massive subventions to maintain a stable and growing economy—all within the framework of the same political culture. The demands of manufacturers for high tariffs in 1865 and the demands of labor unions for worker's compensation in 1965 may well be based on the same theoretical justification that they are aids to the maintenance of a working marketplace. Culture is not static. It must be viewed dynamically and defined so as to include cultural change in its very nature.

THE INDIVIDUALISTIC POLITICAL CULTURE

The *individualistic political culture* emphasizes the conception of the democratic order as a marketplace. It is rooted in the view that government is instituted for strictly utilitarian reasons, to handle those functions demanded by the people it serves. According to this view, government need not have any direct concern with questions of the "good society" (except insofar as the government may be used to advance some common conception of the good society formulated outside the political arena, just as it serves other functions). Emphasizing the centrality of private concerns, the individualistic political culture places a premium on limiting community intervention—whether governmental or nongovernmental—into private activities, to the minimum degree necessary to keep the marketplace in proper working order. In general, government action is to be restricted to those areas, primarily in the economic realm, that encourage private initiative and widespread access to the marketplace.

The character of political participation in systems dominated by the individualistic political culture reflects the view that politics is just another means by which individuals may improve themselves socially and economically. In this sense politics is a "business," like any other that competes for talent and offers rewards to those who take it up as a career. Those individuals who choose political careers may rise by providing the governmental services demanded of them and, in return, may expect to be adequately compensated for their efforts.

Interpretation of officeholders' obligations under the individualistic political culture vary among political systems and even among individuals within a single political system. Where the standards are high, such people are expected to provide high-quality government services for the general public in the best possible manner in return for the status and economic rewards considered their due. Some who choose political careers clearly commit themselves to such norms; others believe that an officeholder's primary responsibility is to serve him- or herself and those who have supported him or her directly, favoring them at the expense of others. In some political systems, this view is accepted by the public as well as by politicians.

Political life within an individualistic political culture is based on a system of mutual obligations rooted in personal relationships. Whereas in a simple civil society those relationships can be direct ones, those with individualistic political cultures in the United States are usually too complex to maintain face-to-face ties. So the system of mutual obligation is harnessed through political parties, which serve as "business corporations" dedicated to providing the organization necessary to maintain that system. Party regularity is indispensable in the individualistic political culture because it is the means for coordinating individual enterprise in the political arena; it is also the one way of preventing individualism in politics from running wild.

In such a system, an individual can succeed politically, not by dealing with issues in some exceptional way or by accepting some concept of good government and then by striving to implement it, but by maintaining his or her place in the system of mutual obligations. A person can do this by operating according to the norms of his or her particular party, to the exclusion of other political considerations. Such a political culture encourages the maintenance of a party system that is competitive, but not overtly so, in the pursuit of office. Its politicians are interested in office as a means of controlling the distribution of the favors or rewards of government rather than as a means of exercising governmental power for programmatic ends; hence competition may prove less rewarding than accommodation in certain situations.

Since the individualistic political culture eschews ideological concerns in its "business-like" conception of politics, both politicians and citizens tend to look upon political activity as a specialized one—as essentially the province of professionals, of minimum and passing concern to laypersons, and with no place for amateurs to play an active role. Furthermore, there is a strong tendency among the public to believe that politics is a dirty—albeit necessary—business, better left to those who are willing to soil themselves by engaging in it. In practice, then, where the individualistic political culture is dominant, there is likely to be an easy attitude toward the limits of the professional's perquisites. Since a fair amount of corruption is expected in the normal course of things, there is relatively little popular excitement when any is found, unless it is of an extraordinary character. It is as if the public were willing to pay a surcharge for services rendered, rebelling only when the surcharge becomes too heavy. Of course, the judgments as to what is "normal" and what is "extraordinary" are themselves subjective and culturally conditioned.

Public officials, committed to "giving the public what it wants," are normally not willing to initiate new programs or open up new areas of government activity on their own initiative. They will do so when they perceive an overwhelming public demand for them to act, but only then. In a sense, their willingness to expand the functions of government is based on an extension of the *quid pro quo* "favors" system, which serves as the central core of their political relationships. New and better services are the reward they give the public for placing them in office. The value mix and legitimacy of change in the individualistic political culture are directly related to commercial concerns.

The individualistic political culture is ambivalent about the place of bureaucracy in the political order.[2] In one sense, the bureaucratic method of operation flies in the face of the favor system that is central to the individualistic political process. At the same time, the virtues of organizational efficiency appear substantial to those seeking to master the market. In the end, bureaucratic organization is introduced within the framework of the favor system; large segments of the bureaucracy may be insulated from it through the merit system, but the entire organization is pulled into the political environment at crucial points through political appointment at the upper echelons and, very frequently, also through the bending of the merit system to meet political demands.[3]

The individualistic political culture is a product of the Middle States stream, with its overriding commitment to commercialism and acceptance of ethnic, social, and religious pluralism. It has been reinforced by the English, Continental, East European, Mediterranean, and Irish streams, whose products either brought that political culture with them or adapted to it as their traditional cultures broke down. Most recently, substantial segments of the Southern and African-American streams are adapting to it for similar reasons, as they are transplanted from their original areas of settlement. The individualistic political culture is strong or dominant in those areas where the products of the streams manifesting its characteristics are strong or dominant.

THE MORALISTIC POLITICAL CULTURE

To the extent that American society is built on the principles of "commerce" (in the broadest sense) and that the marketplace provides the model for public relationships, all Americans share some of the attitudes that are of great importance in the individualistic political culture. At the same time, substantial segments of the American people operate politically within the framework of two political cultures—the moralistic and traditionalistic political cultures—whose theoretical structures and operational consequences depart significantly from the individualistic pattern at crucial points.

The *moralistic political culture* emphasizes the commonwealth conception as the basis for democratic government. Politics, to this political culture, is considered one of the great human activities: the search for the good society. True, it is a struggle for power, but it is also an effort to exercise power for the betterment of the commonwealth. Accordingly, in the moralistic political culture, both the general public and the politicians conceive of politics as a public activity centered on some notion of the public good and properly devoted to the advancement of the public interest. Good government, then, is measured by the degree to which it promotes the public good and in terms of the honesty, selflessness, and commitment to the public welfare of those who govern.

In the moralistic political culture, individualism is tempered by a general commitment to utilizing communal (preferably nongovernmental, but governmental if necessary) power to intervene in the sphere of "private" activities when it is considered necessary to do so for the public good or the well-being of the community. Accordingly, issues have an important place in the moralistic style of politics, functioning to set the tone for political concern. Government is considered a positive instrument with a responsibility to promote the general welfare, although definitions of what its positive role should be may vary considerably from era to era.

As in the case of the individualistic political culture, the change from nineteenth- to twentieth-century conceptions of what government's positive role should be has been great; for example, support for Prohibition has given way to support for wage and hour regulation. At the same time, care must be taken to distinguish between a predisposition toward communal activism and a desire for federal government activity. For example, many representatives of the moralistic political culture oppose federal aid for urban renewal without in any way opposing community responsibility for urban redevelopment. The distinction they make (implicitly, at least) is between what they consider legitimate community responsibility and what they believe to be central government encroachment; or between communitarianism, which they value, and "collectivism," which they abhor. Thus, on some public issues we find certain such representatives taking highly conservative positions despite their positive attitudes toward public activity generally. Such representatives may also prefer government intervention in the social realm—that is, censorship or screening of books and movies—over government intervention in the economy, holding that the former is necessary for the public good and the latter, harmful.

Since the moralistic political culture rests on the fundamental conception that politics exists primarily as a means for coming to grips with the issues and public concerns of civil society, it embraces the notion that politics is ideally a matter of concern for all citizens, not just those who are professionally committed to political careers. Indeed, this political culture considers it the duty of every citizen to participate in the political affairs of his or her commonwealth.

Accordingly, there is a general insistence within this political culture that government service is public service, which places moral obligations upon those who participate in government that are more demanding than the moral obligations of the marketplace. There is an equally general rejection of the notion that the field of politics is a legitimate realm for private economic enrichment. Of course, politicians may benefit economically because of their political careers, but they are not expected to *profit* from political activity; indeed, they are held suspect if they do.

Since the concept of serving the community is the core of the political relationship, politicians are expected to adhere to it even at the expense of individual loyalties and political friendships. Consequently, party regularity is not of prime importance. The political party is considered a useful political device, but it is not valued for its own sake. Regular party ties can be abandoned with relative impunity for third parties, special local parties, or nonpartisan systems if such changes are believed to be helpful in gaining larger political goals. People can even shift from party to party without sanctions if such change is justified by political belief.

In the moralistic political culture, rejection of firm party ties is not to be viewed as a rejection of politics as such. On the contrary, because politics is considered potentially good and healthy within the context of that culture, it is possible to have highly political nonpartisan systems. Certainly nonpartisanship is instituted not to eliminate politics but to improve it, by widening access to public office for those unwilling or unable to gain office through the regular party structure.[4]

In practice, where the moralistic political culture is dominant today, there is considerably more amateur participation in politics. There is also much less of what Americans consider to be corruption in government and less tolerance of those actions considered to be corrupt. Hence politics does not have the taint it so often bears in the individualistic environment.

By virtue of its fundamental outlook, the moralistic political culture creates a greater commitment to active government intervention in the economic and social life of the community. At the same time, the strong commitment to *communitarianism*[5] characteristic of that political culture tends to channel the interest in government intervention into highly localistic paths, such that a willingness to encourage local government intervention to set public standards does not necessarily reflect a concomitant willingness to allow outside governments equal opportunity to intervene. Not infrequently, public officials themselves will seek to initiate new government activities in an effort to come to grips with problems as yet unperceived by a majority of the citizenry. The moralistic political culture is not committed to either change or the status quo *per se* but, rather, will accept either depending upon the morally defined ends to be gained.

The major difficulty of this political culture in adjusting bureaucracy to the political order is tied to the potential conflict between communitarian principles and the necessity for large-scale organization to increase bureaucratic efficiency, a problem that could affect the attitudes of moralistic culture states toward federal activity of certain kinds. Otherwise, the notion of a politically neutral administrative system creates no problem within the moralistic value system and even offers many advantages. Where merit systems are instituted, they are rigidly maintained.

The moralistic political culture is a product of Puritan New England and the Yankee stream derived from it. It has been strongly reinforced by the North Sea and Jewish streams, who shared the same political culture when they came to the United States. Finally, it is strong or dominant in those areas where Yankees, Scots, Dutch, Scandinavians, Swiss, and Jews are strong or dominant.

THE TRADITIONALISTIC POLITICAL CULTURE

The *traditionalistic political culture* is rooted in an ambivalent attitude toward the marketplace coupled with a paternalistic and elitist conception of the commonwealth. It reflects an older, precommercial attitude that accepts a substantially hierarchical society as part of the ordered nature of things, authorizing and expecting those at the top of the social structure to take a special and dominant role in government. Like its moralistic counterpart, the traditionalistic political culture accepts government as an actor with a positive role in the community, but in a very limited sphere—mainly that of securing the continued maintenance of the existing social order. To do so, it functions to confine real political power to a relatively small and self-perpetuating group drawn from an established elite who often inherit their "right" to govern through family ties or social position. Accordingly, social and family ties are paramount in a traditionalistic political culture; in fact, their importance is greater than that of personal ties in the individualistic political culture, where, after all is said and done, a person's first responsibility is to him- or herself. At the same time, those who do not have a definite role to play in politics are not expected to be even minimally active as citizens. In many cases, they are not even expected to vote. In return, they are guaranteed that, outside of the limited sphere of politics, family rights (usually labeled "individual rights") are paramount, not to be taken lightly or ignored. As in the individualistic political culture, those active in politics are expected to benefit personally from their activity, though not necessarily through direct pecuniary gain.

Political parties are of minimal importance in a traditionalistic political culture, inasmuch as they encourage a degree of openness and competition that goes against the fundamental grain of an elite-oriented political order. Their major utility is to recruit people to fill the formal offices of government not desired by the established power-holders. Political competition in a traditionalistic political culture is usually conducted through factional alignments, as an extension of the personalistic politics that is characteristic of the system; hence political systems within the culture tend to have a loose one-party orientation if they have political parties at all.

Practically speaking, a traditionalistic political culture is found only in a society that retains some of the organic characteristics of the pre-industrial social order. "Good government" in the political culture involves the maintenance and encouragement of traditional patterns and, if necessary, their adjustment to changing conditions with the least possible upset. Where the traditionalistic political culture is dominant in the United States today, political leaders play conservative and custodial rather than initiatory roles unless pressed strongly from the outside.

Whereas the individualistic and moralistic political cultures may encourage the development of bureaucratic systems of organization on the grounds of "rationality" and "efficiency" in government (depending on their particular situations), traditionalistic political cultures tend to be instinctively anti-bureaucratic. The reason is that bureaucracy by its very nature interferes with the fine web of informal interpersonal relationships that lie at the root of the political system and have been developed by following traditional patterns over the years. Where bureaucracy is introduced, it is generally confined to ministerial functions under the aegis of the established power-holders.

The traditionalistic political culture is a product of the plantation agrarianism of the Southern stream. It was supplemented by the African-American stream, whose "products" were originally absorbed into the Southern way of life as slaves. Secondary reinforcement has come from the Hispanic stream. The traditionalistic political culture is strong only where it has become the dominant political culture in those areas settled almost exclusively by the streams that manifest its characteristics. When those streams have moved into environments where other political cultures have been dominant, the traditionalistic political culture has tended to break down. In fact, as the possibilities for maintaining more than semblances of traditionalistic life have continued to decline in the United States, traditionalistic political culture has also diminished, undergoing subtle but serious changes—generally in the direction of the individualistic political culture, except where strong secondary tendencies toward the moralistic political culture have been present. (The characteristics of the three political cultures are summarized in Table 8.1.)

Returning to the matrix of value concepts undergirding the overall American culture, we see that the political subculture variations manifest themselves in two ways: (1) in the differences in shades of meaning attached to each of the four tendencies—for example, the differences between the communitarian agrarianism of the moralistic New England town, the individualistic agrarianism of the Middle States, and the plantation agrarianism of the traditional South; and (2) in the degree of emphasis placed on each of the four tendencies—for example, the greater emphasis on commerce and commercial efficiency in the individualistic Middle

States, the particular conception of aristocratic (read oligarchic agrarian) legitimacy based on caste in the traditionalistic South, and the special kind of populist agrarian efficiency of the moralistic Northwest.

More generally, we see that the individualistic political culture draws most heavily from the value orientations of commerce, the moralistic political culture from those of agrarianism, and the traditionalistic culture from those of legitimacy (as its representatives understand the concept). Each of these different emphases weights the matrix as a whole in a different direction, even while those in the matrix are preserving all its elements intact—thereby reflecting *subcultural* rather than cultural differences. Hence we are reminded that, although the differences among the three subcultures are measurably real, they are not as extreme as they would be if they were reflections of different *cultures* (see Exhibit 8.1).

THE "GEOLOGY" OF POLITICAL CULTURE

The individualistic, moralistic, and tradionalist political subcultures arose out of very real sociocultural differences found among the peoples who came to America over the years—differences that date back to the very beginnings of settlement in this country and even back to the Old World. Because the various ethnic and religious groups that came to these shores tended to congregate in their own settlements, and because they continued to settle together as they or their descendants moved westward, the political patterns they bore with them are today distributed geographically. Indeed, it is the geographic distribution of political cultures as modified by local conditions that has laid the foundations for American sectionalism. Sectional concentrations of distinctive cultural groups have helped create the social interests that tie contiguous states to one another even in the face of rather marked differences in the standard measures of similarity.

In order to portray the overall pattern of political culture, we must draw upon the full understanding of location presented in this book: Not only spacial but also temporal and cultural location have to be considered. Geography, too, must be taken into account. There is also a kind of human or cultural "geology" that adds another dimension to the problem. In the course of time, the different streams of migration have passed over the American landscape in response to the various frontiers of national development. Those streams, which in themselves are relatively clear-cut, have left residues of population in various places—residues that, in a sense, have become the equivalent of geological strata. As these populations settled in the same location, sometimes side by side, sometimes overlapping, and frequently on top of one another, they created hardened cultural mix-

TABLE 8.1   Characteristics of the Three Political Cultures

Concepts	Individualistic	Moralistic	Traditionalistic
	Government		
How viewed	As a *marketplace* (means to respond efficiently to demands)	As a *commonwealth* (means to achieve the good community through positive action)	As a means of maintaining the *existing order*
Appropriate spheres of activity	Largely economic (encourages private initiative and access to the marketplace) Economic development favored	Any area that will enhance the community although nongovernmental action preferred Social as well as economic regulation considered legitimate	Those that maintain traditional patterns
New programs	Will not initiate unless demanded by public opinion	Will initiate without public pressure if believed to be in public interest	Will initiate if program serves the interest of the governing elite
	Bureaucracy		
How viewed	Ambivalently (undesirable because it limits favors and patronage, but good because it enhances efficiency)	Positively (brings desirable political neutrality)	Negatively (depersonalizes government)
Kind of merit system favored	Loosely implemented	Strong	None (should be controlled by political elite)

continues

tures that must be sorted out for analytical purposes, city by city and county by county, from the Atlantic to the Pacific.

Quite clearly, the various sequences of migration in each locale have determined the particular layering of its cultural geology. Yet even as the strata were being deposited over generations and centuries, externally generated events, such as depressions, wars, and internal cultural conflicts, caused upheavals that altered the relative positions of the various groups in the community. Beyond that, the passage of time and the impact of new events have eroded some cultural patterns, intensified others, and modified still others, to make each local situation even more complex. The simple mapping of such patterns has yet to be done for more than a handful of states and communities; and although the gross data that can be

TABLE 8.1 (cont.)

Concepts	Individualistic	Moralistic	Traditionalistic
Politics			
Patterns of Belief			
How viewed	Dirty (left to those who soil themselves engaging in it)	Healthy (every citizen's responsibility)	A privilege (only those with legitimate claim to office should participate)
Patterns of Participation			
Who should participate	Professionals	Everyone	The appropriate elite
Role of parties	Act as business organizations (dole out favors and responsibility)	Vehicles to attain goals believed to be in the public interest (third parties popular)	Vehicle of recruitment of people to offices not desired by established power holders
Party cohesiveness	Strong	Subordinate to principles and issues	Highly personal (based on family and social ties)
Patterns of Competition			
How viewed	Between parties; not over issues	Over issues	Between elite-dominated factions within a dominant party
Orientation	Toward winning office for tangible rewards	Toward winning office for greater opportunity to implement policies and programs	Dependent on political values of the elite

Source: Daniel J. Elazar, *American Federalism: A View from the States,* 3d ed. (New York: Harper and Row Publishers, 1984), pp. 120–121. Reprinted by permission of HarperCollins Publishers.

used to outline the grand patterns as a whole are available in various forms, they have been only partially correlated. However, by utilizing the available data, we can sketch with reasonable clarity the nationwide geography of political culture.

THE DISTRIBUTION AND IMPACT OF POLITICAL SUBCULTURES

Both Map 1.3 and Map 8.1 show how migrational patterns have led to the concentration of specific political subcultures in particular states and localities. The basic patterns of political culture were set during the period of the rural-land frontier by three great streams of American migration

EXHIBIT 8.1   Political Cultural Differences and Watergate

The *New York Times* of April 26, 1973, under the headline "The Voter and Watergate Case," ran the article from which the following paragragraphs were excerpted.

"Using the Easter recess to gauge the impact of the Watergate scandal, members of Congress from around the country report a sense of frustration and impotence on the part of increasingly concerned voters at home.

"Reports from Congressmen in both parties in 20 states this week indicate that the issue has begun to define itself in the minds of voters more as a moral than a political problem. ...

"Typical of the responses are the following:

"'The Republicans here are unhappy,' says Representative Henry P. Smith, 3d, of upstate New York. 'Most of them because it was such a stupid thing and, as I said in a television interview, "I hate to belong to a stupid party."'"

"Representative Frank Thompson, Jr., Democrat of New Jersey, reports little reaction from his constituents but has concluded that 'most people believe the House of Representatives can't do anything about the situation.'" ...

"A Republican state Senator in Minnesota is urging party members to withhold contributions to the national party until they can be assured that 'it will be spent in a manner consistent with the highest political ethics.'"

This *New York Times* account is very revealing. The general disgust with Watergate is a reflection of the country's common political culture. Unlike some other peoples, Americans are not willing to accept law-breaking by the ranking authorities as the expected way of doing government business. Of course, people of different subcultural backgrounds are indignant for different reasons. The individualistic New Yorkers hate to belong to a "stupid party"; the moralistic Minnesotans are disturbed that the highest political ethics were violated; and, as for the Southerners (though none were interviewed in this article), their traditionalistic political culture initially put them in the position of expressing confidence in their leaders *because* they were leaders.

that began on the East Coast and moved westward after the colonial period. Each stream moved from east to west along more or less fixed paths, following lines of least resistance that generally led them due west from the immediately previous area of settlement.

Greater New England

Across the northern part of the United States, thrusting westward and slightly southwestward, is an area settled initially by the Puritans of New England and their Yankee descendants. From the first, they established a moralistic political culture.

After five generations of pioneering in New England, where they established several versions of their commonwealth in the New England states, the Puritans had developed a set of deeply rooted cultural patterns. Then, moving westward into New York State, the Yankees began their great cross-country migration. Across New York, northern Pennsylvania, and the upper third of Ohio, the Yankee current moved into the states of the upper Great Lakes and Mississippi Valley. There they established a greater New England in Michigan, Wisconsin, Minnesota, and Iowa, and attempted to do the same by settling in northern Illinois.

Beginning in the mid-nineteenth century, the Yankees were joined by Scandinavians and other Northern Europeans who, stemming from a related tradition (particularly in its religious orientation), reinforced the basic patterns of Yankee political culture, sealing them into the political systems of those states. Pressing westward, the Yankees settled Oregon, then Washington, and were the first "Anglos" to settle California. As Mormons, they settled Utah; then, as abolitionists, they settled Kansas. They became the leaders of the permanent settlements in Colorado and Montana, and even moved into northern Arizona. In each of these states, they were joined or followed by the same Scandinavian–Northern European group; and in each they established the moralistic political culture to the extent of their influence. Within these states and the smaller ones colonized from them, the moralistic political culture flourishes even today.[6]

The Middle States

Groups of quite different ethnic and religious backgrounds, primarily from England and the interior Germanic states, settled the middle parts of the nation, beginning with the Middle Atlantic states of New York, New Jersey, Pennsylvania, Delaware, and Maryland. Together the majority of these highly diverse groups established the basic patterns of American pluralism. They were united by one common bond in particular—the search for individual opportunity in the New World. Unlike the Puritans who sought communal as well as individualistic goals in their migrations, the pursuit of private ends predominated among the settlers of the Middle States.

Though efforts were made to establish morally purposeful communities, particularly in Pennsylvania, the very purpose of those communities was to develop pluralistic societies dedicated to the individual freedom to pursue private goals, to the point of making religion a private matter (an unheard-of step at the time). The political culture of the Middle States reflected this distinctive emphasis on private pursuits from the first. By the end of the colonial period, a whole system of politics designed to accommodate itself to such a culture had been developed with distinctive state-by-state variations, modified by moralistic traits only in Pennsylvania and by traditionalistic ones in Maryland and Delaware.

Map 8.1   The Regional Distribution of Political Cultures Within the States. *Source:* Daniel J. Elazar, *American Federalism: A View from the States,* 3d ed. (New York: Harper and Row Publishers, 1984), pp. 124–125. Reprinted by permission of HarperCollins Publishers.

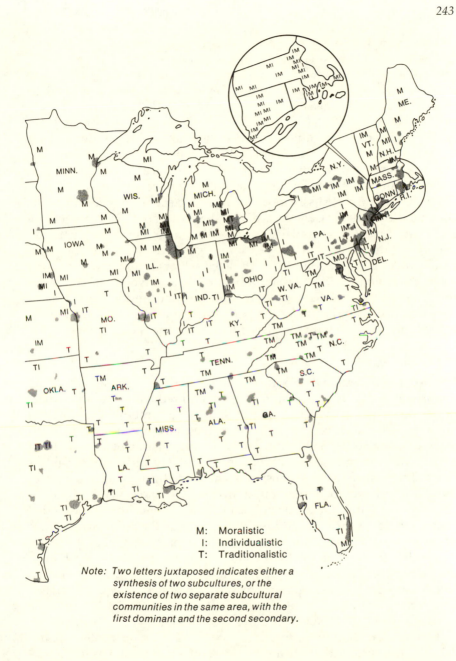

M: Moralistic
I: Individualistic
T: Traditionalistic

Note: Two letters juxtaposed indicates either a
synthesis of two subcultures, or the
existence of two separate subcultural
communities in the same area, with the
first dominant and the second secondary.

These groups also moved westward across Pennsylvania into the central parts of Ohio, Indiana, and Illinois, and then on into Missouri. There, reinforced by immigrants from Western Europe and the lower Germanic states who shared the same attitudes, they developed extensions of their pluralistic patterns. Since these states, too, were settled by representatives of the other two political cultures, giving no single culture clear predominance, pluralism became the only viable alternative. So the individualistic political culture became dominant at the state level in the course of time, whereas the moralistic and traditionalistic political cultures retained pockets of influence in the northern and southern sections of each state.

After crossing the Mississippi, this middle current jumped across the continent to northern California during the 1849 gold rush (an activity highly attractive to individualistic types). Its groups subsequently helped to populate the territory in between. The areas of Nebraska and South Dakota bordering the Missouri River attracted settlers from Illinois and Missouri; the Union Pacific railroad populated central Nebraska and Wyoming; and Nevada was settled by migrants from the California gold fields. Today there is a band of states (or sections of states) across the belt of the country in which the individualistic political culture is dominant.[7]

The South

The people who settled the Southern tier of states were seeking individual opportunity in ways similar to those of their brethren to the immediate north. But whereas the latter sought their opportunities in commercial pursuits, either in business or in a commercially oriented agriculture, those who settled the South sought opportunity in a plantation-centered agricultural system based on slavery and essentially anti-commercial attitudes. This system, as an extension of the landed-gentry agrarianism of the Old World, provided a natural environment for the development of an American-style traditionalistic political culture in which the new landed gentry progressively assumed ever-greater roles in the political process at the expense of the small landholders, while a major segment of the population, the slaves, were totally excluded from any political role. Elitism within this culture reached its apogee in Virginia and South Carolina. In North Carolina and Georgia, meanwhile, a measure of equalitarianism was introduced by the arrival of significant numbers of migrants from the moralistic and individualistic cultures, respectively.

This peculiarly Southern agrarian system and its traditionalistic political culture was carried westward by the southern current. Virginia's people dominated in the settlement of Kentucky; North Carolina's influence was heavy in Tennessee; and settlers from all four states covered the southern parts of Ohio and Illinois as well as most of Indiana and Missouri. Georgians, with a mixture of other settlers, moved westward into

Alabama and Mississippi. Louisiana presented a unique situation in that it contained a concentration of non-Anglo-Saxons rare in the South, but its French settlers shared the same political culture as the other Southerners, regardless of their other cultural differences. Ultimately, the Southern political culture spread through Texas, where it was diluted on that state's western fringes by individualistic-type European immigrants, and Oklahoma; into southern Kansas, where it clashed directly with the Yankee political culture; then across New Mexico and into Arizona, eventually overlapping the Yankee current in southern and central California.[8]

The character and degree of complexity of the geology of specific local settlements in the United States determine whether a particular state or civil community comes closer to resembling one of the three political-culture models or combines elements of more than one within its boundaries. Most states, except those on the peripheries of the country, are situated geo-historically such that representatives of all three political subcultures have contributed to their settlement and development in significant numbers. Settlements and bands of settlements dominated by all three can be found in those states in varying conditions of cultural development and change. Accordingly, their present statewide political cultures were amalgams created out of varying degrees of conflict generated by the initial meeting of the representatives of the three and by the struggle between them for the dominant position of influence within the emerging state political systems.

The general outcome of that original struggle has long since been determined. It created a relationship between political culture and political system in each of the states that continues to set the limits for political behavior within them. At the same time, within the framework of the statewide political subculture, a conflict between products of the original political cultures (substantially modified and disguised though it may be) continues to be waged. Indeed, the very conflict itself has become institutionalized as one of the "moving parts" of the state political system.

The only major departures from the east-west pattern of cultural diffusion during the settlement of the land frontier came when the emigrants encountered the country's great mountain systems. The mountains diffused the cultural patterns because they were barriers to easy east-west movement. Thus, in the East, the Appalachian chain deflected the moralistic Scotch-Irish emigrants southward from Pennsylvania, where they were isolated in the Southern mountains. There they developed traditionalistic patterns of culture over a moralistic base and created special cultural pockets dominated by a synthesis of the traditionalistic and moralistic cultures, especially in the Piedmont areas of Virginia, the Carolinas, Georgia, and even Alabama.

In the West, the Rocky Mountains blocked the neat westward flow of the cultural currents and diverted people from all three political cultures into their valleys, from north to south, in search of fortunes in mining and specialized agricultural pursuits. There the more individualistic types from all three subcultures diffused from Montana to Arizona, creating cultural pockets in all the mountain states of the West that in some cases— Wyoming, for example—altered the normal regional patterns of political culture.

The development of the urban-industrial frontier coincided with the arrival of other immigrant groups that concentrated in the burgeoning cities of the industrializing states. These groups, primarily from Ireland, Italy, Eastern Europe, and the Balkans, also moved from east to west but settled in urban pockets, thereby adding new cultural strata to communities scattered throughout the country. Most of these settlers, though bound at first by traditional ties, soon adopted more individualistic attitudes and goals, which brought them into the individualistic political culture. Since most of them settled in cities, their cultural impact was less universal in scope but more concentrated in force. In some states (such as Massachusetts) they disrupted established cultural patterns to create new ones; in others (such as New York) they simply reinforced the existing individualistic-dominated pluralism; and in still others (such as Illinois) they tipped the balance between competing cultural groups.

The communal deposits left by these subcultural streams have, of course, given rise to a diversity of state and local characteristics and lifestyles in the United States.[9] The impact of political culture on local community life is partially reflected in Table 8.2, which shows the relationship between political culture and the overall "quality of life" of 83 medium-sized SMSAs (each encompassing from 200,000 to 500,000 people) at the end of the 1970s. These quality-of-life ratings include 123 indicators of each city's political, social, health, educational, economic, and environmental characteristics. As the table indicates, and as we would expect given the nature of the three political subcultures, cities having a dominant moralistic political culture tend to have "outstanding" (A) and "excellent" (B) quality-of-life ratings; individualistic cities tend to have middle (B, C, and D) ratings; and traditionalistic cities tend to have "adequate" (D) and "substandard" (E) ratings.[10] Although these ratings should be read with some caution, because what is "outstanding" or "substandard" is itself subject to cultural definition, they do suggest that moralistic cities, for example, tend to have the highest levels of public expenditure for health, education, and welfare; more equal distributions of public goods and services; and higher levels of education, health care, and political participation. Moreover, all of these criteria conform to the "commonwealth" conception of the polity.

TABLE 8.2   Political Culture and Quality of Urban Life
for Medium-Sized SMSAs (percentages)

Quality of Life	Political Culture								
	M	*MI*	*MT*	*IM*	*I*	*IT*	*TM*	*TI*	*T*
Outstanding	71	36	–	15	6	–	–	–	–
Excellent	29	28	100	62	–	–	12	10	–
Middle	–	36	–	15	56	50	38	30	–
Adequate	–	–	–	8	38	50	25	40	17
Substandard	–	–	–	–	–	–	25	20	83
N =	7	14	1	13	16	2	8	10	12

I: Individualistic; M: moralistic; T: Traditionalistic. The juxtaposition of two letters indicates either a synthesis of two subcultures or the existence of two separate subcultural communities in the same area, with the first dominant and the second secondary.

Source: Center for the Study of Federalism Workshop in Political Culture; table prepared by John Kincaid (1980).

ETHNICITY, POLITICAL CULTURE, AND CONTEMPORARY MIGRATION PATTERNS

Migration as a social phenomenon continues to be of the utmost importance in American life. When the number of immigrants drops internal migration once again comes to the fore as a means of reshaping local social and political patterns. Internal migration today has two aspects. On the one hand, there is the continuing cross-country flow of people seeking better opportunities of one sort or another. On the other hand, the predominant cross-country flow is still westward. From the end of World War II until the late 1960s, the northern flow from the greater South was a close second. Since then, it has been replaced by a northern flow southward. At the same time, intrametropolitan migration has become an even more important phenomenon.[11]

With the advent of the metropolitan frontier after World War II, Americans abandoned sedentary patterns that had become widespread between 1910 and 1945 and began to move again. About one-fifth of the American people change their residence every year. These migrations from farm to city to suburb and from section to section no longer follow a simple east to west pattern.

The first kind of migration—from farm to city, from town to metropolis, or from city to suburb—usually takes place within the same section of the country, if not the same state. It barely alters the local patterns of political culture, even though it may lead to substantial internal changes in the political culture itself. Iowans moving off their farms to Des Moines or Philadelphians moving from the central city to the suburban counties may simply reinforce existing patterns of culture.[12]

The second kind of migration may lead to the alteration of the cultural geology of particular areas. Southerners moving to Detroit have brought a traditionalistic culture into a moralistic environment, whereas Northerners moving southward have altered the states of the Lower and Western South in important ways. In some cases this movement cannot be identified as group migration, but in others the continuity of older modes of cultural diffusion and change is marked.

California is a case in point.[13] Its cultural patterns remain in flux because of the continuous intensity of migration into the state (the highest in the nation since 1910), even though fairly well-defined cultural lines had been established within it by the turn of the century. In a reversal of the national pattern, southern California became the center of the moralistic culture because the Yankees and their midwestern descendants predominated there. Northern California, on the other hand, attracted the Middle State migrants and became the locus of the individualistic culture, whereas central California attracted many Southerners who brought to the region strong traces of the traditionalistic culture. The sharp cultural division between north and south (the central area was still too weak to be of importance) had already helped intensify the well-known conflict between the two sections of the state that came strongly to the fore during the Progressive era.

Until recently, at least, the great migrations of the twentieth century have generally reinforced the original patterns of culture in California. Midwesterners from moralistic culture states continued to seek the Los Angeles area, and individualistic culture types, particularly from the East, flocked to the San Francisco Bay area. Each group has generally blended in well with the original political culture of its area of choice.

During the Great Depression, "Okies" and "Arkies"—migrants from the Western South—settled in great numbers in central California. After World War II, the increased migration of Southerners into all parts of the state, with greatest intensity in the southern part and progressively less intensity moving northward, added a strong strain of the traditionalistic culture (or the particular individualistic manifestation that occurs when its people leave their traditionalistic environment) in areas where that strain was previously weak or nonexistent. What happened in those cases was the development of a conflict between the two cultures as a consequence of the contrast between them. By and large, the radical right of southern California consists of former Southerners in revolt against what were, to them, unacceptable patterns of political and social life created by the dominant non-Southerners.

Two other significant migrational streams became stronger in California after World War II. The Latino migration from Mexico—at first principally illegal, but then publicly recognized—grew to mass proportions to the extent that, by the 1980s, it was projected that Spanish would become the most widely spoken language in the state sometime in the early twenty-first century. Southern California, in particular, acquired a major Hispanic presence.[14]

Beginning in the 1970s, immigration from Asia assumed major proportions. First triggered by the collapse of the American military effort in Southeast Asia, it also featured many Koreans, Filipinos, and others who simply came in search of opportunity, as generations of immigrants from all over the world had done before them. Although the Asians settled throughout the state, they continued to concentrate in northern California.[15] The Hispanics settled in areas already strongly influenced by the traditionalistic political culture as modified, whereas the Asians joined those reflecting the individualistic political culture. Hence these groups, too, tended to reinforce previous patterns rather than bringing major cultural changes with them.

Thus, although the major impact of the three native streams came in the early days of settlement, the streams themselves persist. Since World War I, the Southern stream, transformed into one segment of the overall rural-to-urban migratory movement, has sent fingers northward again, establishing significant colonies of Southerners, particularly unskilled Southern mountain folk in the North, even where none existed before. These groups did not become politically articulate in their new homes until the beginning of the twelfth generation, with the rise of the religious fundamentalists in politics; but their presence and somewhat "alien" ways had presented the civil communities with substantial minority-group problems even earlier.

To a lesser extent, the migration from the farms to the cities has also represented a continuation of the nineteenth-century streams. The original cultural patterns of those streams were best preserved in the rural areas where families, friendship cliques, and religious ties were most stable, having encountered less pressure to change. Thus many of the descendants of the original Yankee, Middle States, and Southern settlers, moving into the cities two, three, or more generations later, have brought with them infusions of a more faithfully preserved form of the original native cultures.

Although continued migration has helped maintain the fluid nature of cultural patterns, the values of the various political cultures have undergone internal change. Moral demands have generally stiffened within the American political culture as a whole. For example, what is today considered to be conflict of interest was considered perfectly proper even by the moralistic political culture in the days of Daniel Webster. Though an authentic Yankee, Webster, without any qualms, could take an annual retainer from a leading Boston bank while serving in the U. S. Senate. At the same time, the moralistic subculture has kept at least a step ahead of the others in its demands for political morality. On another level, when the general culture was so oriented as to demand public standards of social and sexual morality, governments within the orbit of the moralistic political culture tended to enforce the law as fully as possible. Once the general cultural styles changed, the same governments could zealously support the canons of the permissive society on the grounds of individual freedom of choice as a paramount good.

Politicians who developed within the individualistic political culture are suffering most from the new standards of political morality. These new standards have opened up opportunities for everyone—from the FBI to rival politicians in their own bailiwicks—to investigate or entrap them and then drive them out of office for practices that were formerly considered standard behavior in their circles. At the same time, the recent decline in the role of political party organizations has introduced some elements previously associated with the traditionalistic subculture into individualistic culture areas; one such element is the organization of politics around individuals who are able to appeal to the voters and who thereby attract followings among the politicians. In another context, the individualistic political culture, originally the home of the rugged individualist, has taken on something of a collectivist tinge in the twentieth century. Many of those within it have come to believe that big government offers opportunities for individuals that are unobtainable in any other way. Thus its representatives are often found at the forefront of the drive for greater government intervention in the economy.

Meanwhile, the traditionalistic political culture has tended to adopt individualistic elements as its traditional social bases have eroded. With its older elites no longer in positions of power because of economic and social changes, many of its traditionalistic attitudes were transformed into bigotries designed to maintain the old racial caste system, or became unchallenged efforts, by individuals seeking personal profit from the changes, to maintain the political status quo. On the other side of the coin, traditionalistic modes of operation have been adapted by the economic leadership in major Southern cities to create organized business-dominated oligarchies committed to civic progress as a means of economic betterment. The Dallas Citizens' Council is one of the best known of these organizations; others can be found in most major Southern cities.

A certain amount of assimilation from one culture to another is based on changes in individual interests and attitudes. Under certain circumstances, cultural values change because of changing social status. There is some evidence to suggest that, as some people move upward into the middle- to upper-middle-class range, they may adopt, at least for external purposes, some of the values of the moralistic political culture (which has always been a middle-class phenomenon), particularly if those values are the more acceptable ones in their communities. In true frontier fashion, such change often occurs in conjunction with a change of residence, such as migration to the suburbs. This phenomenon was reflected during the 1950s and 1960s in the rise of new-style Republican parties in the suburbs that gained a measure of power by opposing, on moralistic grounds, the old-style machine politics of the Democrats and the GOP old guard, both of which symbolized the individualistic political culture in its least attractive form.

The most visible ethnic manifestations in the United States are found among those people who are products of the later set of European streams. Generally speaking, there are substantial communities of first- and second-generation Americans drawn from those streams that can still be identified without much difficulty. The flow of the European streams radically diminished in intensity with the close of mass immigration after World War I but reintensified briefly after World War II. The trickle that persists today continues to follow the same patterns as the earlier streams: Like attracts like to each locality. Since the revision of immigration laws in the 1960s, there has been an increase in immigration. Approximately 7.5 million immigrants from Europe have entered the United States since 1945, of whom a substantial percentage settled among or near their brethren who had preceded them generations earlier.

In many states and localities where ethnic groups representing different cultural streams have come to rest within the same political system, early conflicts between the groups have given way to cultural synthesis as their descendants have found some common ground of communication. For example, in Massachusetts, where the conflict of political cultures between the moralistic Yankees and the individualistic Irish was extraordinarily intense, the present generation has witnessed a kind of rapprochement in which many of the descendants of the Yankees have adopted the political techniques of the Irish, while many of the descendants of the Irish have adopted the sense of political goals and purposes of the Yankees. The Kennedys illustrate this point. John F. Kennedy was at one and the same time a quintessential Yankee and the leader of an "Irish mafia." Former Senator and Secretary of State Edmund Muskie of Maine, of Polish descent, is another such example. Only by becoming the galvanized Yankee that he is could he have been the first Democrat to break the grip of the Republican party on that state in the 1900s. More recently, Michael Dukakis, of Greek descent, became governor of Massachusetts and the 1988 Democratic candidate for the presidency by doing the same. The Yankees and the Irish, such formidable antagonists in generations past, could begin to meet on common ground because they shared many common values from their respective general cultures, not the least of which was a common "puritanism."

POLITICAL CULTURE: SOME CAVEATS

By now the reader has no doubt formed his or her own value judgments as to the relative worth of the three political subcultures. For this reason a particular warning against *hasty* judgments must be added here. Each of the three political subcultures contributes something important to the configuration of the American political system, and each possesses certain characteristics that are inherently dangerous to the survival of that system.

The moralistic political culture, for example, is the primary source of the continuing American quest for the good society, yet there is a noticeable tendency toward inflexibility and narrow-mindedness among some of its representatives. The individualistic political culture is the most tolerant of out-and-out political corruption, yet it has also provided the framework for the integration of diverse groups into the mainstream of American life. When representatives of the moralistic political culture, in their striving for a better social order, try to limit individual freedom, they usually come up against representatives of the individualistic political culture, to whom individual freedom is the cornerstone of their pluralistic order, though not for any noble reasons. Conversely, of course, the moralistic political culture acts as a restraint against the tendencies of the individualistic political culture to tolerate anything as long as it is in the marketplace.

The traditionalistic political culture contributes to the search for continuity in a society whose major characteristic is change; yet in the name of continuity, its representatives have denied African-Americans (as well as Native Americans and Latinos) their civil rights. When it is in proper working order, the traditionalistic culture has produced a unique group of first-rate national leaders from among its elites; but without a first-rate elite to draw upon, traditionalistic political-culture systems degenerate into oligarchies of the lowest level. Comparisons like these should induce caution in any evaluation of a subject that, by its very nature, evokes value judgments.

It is equally important to use caution in identifying individuals and groups as belonging to one cultural type or another on the basis of their public political behavior at a given moment in time. Immediate political responses to the issues of the day may reveal the political culture of the respondents, but not necessarily. Often, in fact, people will make what appear to be the same choices for different reasons—especially in public affairs, where the choices available at any give time are usually quite limited. Deeper analysis of what is behind those responses is usually needed. In other words, the names of the political cultures are not substitutes for the terms *conservative* and *liberal*, and should not be taken as such.

THE IMPLICATIONS OF AMERICAN DIVERSITY

As a new society the United States consists of an extraordinary diversity of religious, ethnic, and cultural groups, many of whose original members made more or less conscious decisions to settle in America. However, although a common citizenship, language, and culture unites these groups, considerable differences remain; indeed, they remain because they are tolerated and at various times even encouraged by the society as a whole, and because the groups themselves often insist on retaining subcommunal identities of varying degrees. It is important to note that ethnicity rests not only on country-of-origin but also on racial, sociocultural, socioreligious, and sociolinguistic bases. Ethnic groups have maintained their distinctiveness for various reasons, whether religious, communal, political, associational, and/or fraternal. Ethnicity becomes politically important when (1) a group is large and has potential power; (2) a group is small but highly visible or well organized; or (3) a group is conscious of being a minority and of being surrounded by other well-organized ethnic groups.

The migration of these groups to and within the United States is responsible for settlement of the country. Continuing internal migration has contributed to social mobility and to a national identity by eroding static provincialism. At the same time, the fifteen migrational streams that have flowed across the United States have created a mosaic of cultural patterns consisting of three basic ethnocultural strata: (1) the primary political subcultures of the Southern, Middle, and New England states; (2) the discrete European ethnocultural groups such as the Irish; and (3) the non-European ethnocultural groups such as the Chinese. The bases for the coexistence of these groups have shifted over the course of American history from territorial pluralism during the colonial period, to an attempt to impose Protestant republicanism during the nineteenth century, and then to an increasing emphasis on open religious, ethnic, and racial pluralism during the twentieth century.

Political culture has been defined as the summation of persistent patterns of underlying political attitudes and characteristic responses to political concerns within a particular political order. Thus political culture is a kind of "second nature" that is generally unperceived by those who are part of that order. Its origins date back to the beginnings of the people who share it. Political culture influences people's perceptions and expectations about the proper roles of politics and government, the recruitment of specific kinds of people into political life, and the actual practice of government and politics.

As earlier noted, American political culture encompasses two contrasting views of politics: (1) the political order as a marketplace, characterized by bargaining among essentially self-interested individuals and groups; and (2) the political order as a commonwealth, in which people have an undivided public interest in building the best government on the basis of shared moral principles. Also as noted, the national political culture is made up of three major subcultures. The individualistic political culture, a product of the Middle States stream, emphasizes the conception of the democratic order as a marketplace. The moralistic political culture, a product of Puritan New England and its Yankee stream, emphasizes the conception of the democratic order as a commonwealth. Finally, the traditionalistic political culture, a product of the plantation agrarianism of the Southern stream, exhibits an ambivalent attitude toward the marketplace and a paternalistic and elitist conception of the commonwealth.

The movement of the center of population westward since 1790 closely reflects the shifting limits of the three great spheres and their relationship to the three political subcultures. The line of movement, indicated in Map 8.2, follows almost precisely that of the division between the greater Northeast and the greater South, whereas the center point marks the general beginning of the greater West as that sphere has taken shape over time. Since the West was initially a product of the land frontier, its boundaries shifted substantially as long as pioneering on that frontier continued in a meaningful way. In the twentieth century, these shifts have slowed considerably and the eastern limits of the greater West have hardened. Roughly speaking, the individualistic political culture proceeds westward along the northern edge of the center of the population line, reaching approximately 150 miles north of that line. It then begins to shade off into the area of moralistic political culture. South of the line, it begins to shade off into the traditionalistic culture area almost immediately. And west of the center of population, the spread of the three cultures is generally more diffused.

SUMMARY

This chapter continues our discussion of the role of political culture, examining the three great political subcultures of the United States and how they draw their strength from fifteen cultural streams. These streams provided the means for integrating people of diverse ethnic and religious backgrounds who have shared similar conceptions of the role of government in politics. The chapter first examines the moralistic, individualistic, and traditionalistic political cultures and their relationship to the market-

Map 8.2   Center of Population: 1790–1990. "Center of population" is that point at which an imaginary flat, weightless, and rigid map of the United States would balance if weights of identical value were placed on it so that each weight represented the location of one person on the date of the census. *Source: Statistical Abstract of the United States, 1992* (Washington, D.C.: U.S. Department of Commerce, 1992).

place and commonwealth elements in American political culture as a whole. It then examines the geology of political culture established through past and present migrational patterns.

NOTES

1. For a fuller description of these political cultures, see Daniel J. Elazar, *Cities of the Prairie* (New York: Basic Books, 1970); Daniel J. Elazar et al., *Cities of the Prairie Revisited* (Lincoln: University of Nebraska Press, 1956); Daniel J. Elazar and Joseph Zikmund II, *The Ecology of American Political Culture: Readings* (New York: Thomas Y. Crowell, 1975); and John Kincaid, ed., *Political Culture, Public Policy and the American States* (Philadelphia: Institute for the Study of Human Issues, 1982).

2. The "good" meaning of *bureaucracy:* Administration of a government chiefly through bureaus staffed with nonelective officials, selected on the basis of merit. The "bad" meaning: Any administration in which the need to follow complex procedures impedes effective action.

3. Political leaders in such an environment often argue that merit systems are impersonal, rigid, and ultimately inefficient. As Thomas Whelan, former mayor of Jersey City (1963–1971), once remarked: "You have to have the power to hire and fire. Civil Service examinations may measure intelligence but they don't measure courage, drive or curiosity. You wind up with a guy with nine heads who can't even get the men out of the garage." In 1972, Whelan and several other leaders of this highly

individualistic city were convicted of various charges of conspiracy and accepting kickbacks on public contracts.

4. In this context, it should be noted that regular party systems are sometimes abandoned in local communities dominated by the individualistic political culture so that nonpartisan electoral systems can be instituted in an effort to make local governments more "business-like" and to take local administration "out of politics." Such anti-political efforts are generally products of business-dominated reform movements and reflect the view that politics is necessarily "dirty" and illegitimate.

5. On communitarianism, see Robert N. Bellah et al., *Habits of the Heart: Individualism and Commitment in American Life* (New York: Harper and Row, 1985); and Daniel J. Elazar, *The American Constitutional Tradition* (Lincoln: University of Nebraska Press, 1988).

6. See Stewart H. Holbrook, *The Yankee Exodus* (Seattle: University of Washington Press, 1968); James R. Gibson, ed., *European Settlement and Development in North America* (Toronto: University of Toronto Press, 1978); and Louis K. Matthews, *Expansion of New England* (New York: Russell and Pursell, 1936).

7. See Eric F. Goldman, "Middle States Regionalism and American Historiography: A Suggestion," in Eric F. Goldman, ed., *Historiography and Urbanization* (Baltimore: Johns Hopkins University Press, 1941).

8. See W. J. Cash, *The Mind of the South* (New York: Alfred A. Knopf, 1960).

9. Raymond Gastil describes this phenomenon as the "cultural matrix" of a particular area. See his *Cultural Regions of the United States* (Seattle: University of Washington Press, 1975).

10. These results are based on research by John Kincaid as presented in "Political Cultures and the Quality of Life," *Publius* 10, no. 2 (Spring 1980). The quality-of-life ratings are taken from Ben-Chieh Liu, *Quality of Life Indicators in U.S. Metropolitan Areas, 1970: A Comprehensive Assessment* (Washington, D.C.: U.S. Environmental Protection Agency, 1975). Similar results were obtained for large and small SMSAs.

11. See Richard Bensel, *Sectionalism and American Political Development* (Madison: University of Wisconsin Press, 1984); Everett C. Ladd, Jr., with Charles D. Halley, *The Transformation of the American Party System: Political Coalitions from the New Deal to the 1970s* (New York: W. W. Norton, 1975); Everett C. Ladd, Jr., *American Political Parties: Social Change and Political Response* (New York: W. W. Norton, 1970); Jeff Fishel, ed., *Parties and Elections in the Anti-Party Age* (Bloomington: Indiana University Press, 1978); and Seymour Martin Lipset, ed., *Party Coalitions in the 1980s* (San Francisco: Institute of Contemporary Studies, 1981).

12. See, for example, Elazar, *Cities of the Prairie Revisited*, ch. 3.

13. On postwar California, see Gladwin Hall, *Dancing Bear: An Inside Look at California Politics* (Cleveland: World Publishing Company, 1968); and Michael P. Ragin, *Political Change in California: Critical Elections and Social Movements, 1890–1996* (Westport, Conn.: Greenwood, 1970).

14. On the Hispanic migration, see John J. Burma, *Mexican Americans in the United States* (Cambridge, Mass.: Schenkman Publishing Co., 1970); Lyle Saunders, "The Social History of Spanish-Speaking People in Southwestern United States 1846," First Congress of Historians from Mexico and the United States, *Memoria* (1950); Carey McWilliams, *North from Mexico: The Spanish-Speaking People of the United States* (Philadelphia: J. B. Lippincott, 1949); Kingsley Davis and Clarence Senior, "Immi-

gration from the Western Hemisphere," *American Academy of Political and Social Science: Annals*, no. 262 (March 1949); Norman S. Goldner, *The Mexican in the Northern Urban Area: A Comparison of Two Generations* (San Francisco: R and E Research Associates, 1974); and T. Allen Caine, *Social Life in a Mexican-American Community* (San Francisco: R and E Research Associates, 1974).

15. See June D. Holmquist, ed., *They Chose Minnesota* (St. Paul: Minnesota Historical Society Press, 1981); and Oscar Handlin, *Immigration as a Factor in American History* (Englewood Cliffs, N.J.: Prentice-Hall, 1959).

CHAPTER 9

Territorial Democracy and the Metropolitan Frontier

No, my friend, the way to have good and safe government is not to trust it all to one, but to divide it among the many, distributing to everyone exactly the functions he is competent to do. Let the national government be entrusted with the defense of the nation and its foreign and federal relations; the State governments with the civil rights, laws, police, and administrations of what concerns the counties, and each ward direct the interests within itself. It is by dividing and subdividing these republics from the great national one down through all its subordinations, until it ends in the administration of every man's farm by himself, by placing under everyone what his own eye may super-intend, that all will be done for the best. What has destroyed liberty and the rights of man in every government which has ever existed under the sun? The generalizing and concentrating all cares and powers into one body, no matter whether of the autocrats of Russia or France, or of the aristocrats of a Venetian senate. And I do believe that if the Almighty has not decreed that man shall never be free (and it is a blasphemy to believe it), that the secret will be found to be in the making himself the depository of the powers respecting himself, so far as he is competent to them, and delegating only what is beyond his competence by a synthetical process to higher and higher orders of functionaries, so as to trust fewer and fewer powers in proportion as the trustees become more and more oligarchical. The elementary republics of the ward, the county republics, the State republics, and the republic of the Union, would form a gradation of authorities, standing each on the basis of law, holding every one its delegated share of powers, and constituting truly a system of fundamental balances and checks for the government.

—Thomas Jefferson to Joseph C. Cabell, February 2, 1816

In the previous chapters we saw how the peoples who came to America forged themselves into a single, if highly diverse, nation, spreading that diversity unevenly across the continent to give it a certain geographic basis. We also looked briefly at the way in which the nation's diversity has acquired local expression through cultural streams and their political subcultural differences that stop considerably short of separate nationhood. (Even the South, the most distinctive of American sections, set off as it is by a set of distinct historical experiences, is not a separate nation.) Nevertheless, it is on the basis of territorial democracy that we can see how the political culture is manifested through political structure.

Territorial democracy is closely linked with the principle of federalism in American life. Beyond that, it is the American expression of what popular writer Robert Ardrey has labeled the "territorial imperative."[1] As noted at the very beginning of this book, living things, including humans, seem to have a need to stake out a territory of their own in which they feel secure to pursue their own interests and development. In this sense, too, the American system seems to have been designed to harmonize with human nature.

Territorial democracy as expressed through federalism is the American way to attempt to accommodate these human needs. Federalism also accommodates the need for a proper institutional framework for democratic self-government. In both respects, federalism is the integrating principle of the American polity. The patterns of religion, ethnicity, sectionalism, and political culture, as well as territoriality, find their expressions through the American federal system, which has also come to play a critical role in the generational rhythm of American politics. In this chapter we will explore how the federal system functions in this role.

A SYSTEM OF SYSTEMS

The realities of the American federal system only begin with the relations between the national government and the states. The states themselves are in many respects congeries of local communities, cities, schools and special districts and, in some cases, townships or boroughs. In 1987, when they were last counted, there were 83,186 such local governments within the fifty states and the District of Columbia, as follows:

3,042   *counties* (called "parishes" in Louisiana and "boroughs" in Alaska) in every state but Connecticut and Rhode Island.

19,200 *municipalities* (cities, boroughs, and incorporated towns) in all 50 states.

16,691 *townships* (called "towns" in the six New England states, New York, and Wisconsin; "plantations" in some cases in Maine;

and "locations" in parts of New Hampshire) in 21 northern states.

14,721 *school districts* in 46 states (all except Hawaii, Maryland, North Carolina, and Virginia, where all public schools are managed by general government bodies).

29,885 *special districts* in every state but Alaska. (Most special districts were created for the purposes of natural resource management, fire protection, water supply, and other public utilities.)[2]

Most Americans live within the jurisdiction of many local governments simultaneously. One student of American federalism identified the following constellation of jurisdictions to which citizens in the particularly well-endowed suburb of Park Forest south of Chicago paid taxes:

The United States of America
The State of Illinois
Cook (or Will) County
Cook County Forest Preserve District
Suburban Tuberculosis Sanitary District
Rich (or Bloom) Township
Bloom Township Sanitary District
School District 216 (or 213)
Rich Township High School District
Elementary School District 163
South Cook County Mosquito Abatement District[3]

All of these local governments, whether general-purpose municipalities like the city of Chicago or very specialized districts like the South Cook County Mosquito Abatement District, are endowed with legal authority to act; they also possess substantial powers to translate that authority into reality to achieve the purposes for which they were established, whether broad or limited. Somehow all of these governments have to fit together in a system that will serve the differing needs of the American people in their various capacities—as citizens of a single nation and fifty separate states, as residents of a single nation and fifty separate states, as residents of specific (and often complex) local communities, and as individuals with family and group ties. These different capacities reflect varying and at times contradictory loyalties and interests. Nevertheless, they are all parts of a system of systems built around the original and basic political bargain that links the federal government and the states.

TERRITORIAL DEMOCRACY

Common to all these governments is a territorial base. That is, their jurisdiction extends over a particular piece of territory with definite boundaries. Modern governments in general tend to organize themselves territorially so as to serve equally all people residing within them. In other epochs, governmental jurisdictions were designed to encompass particular estates, ethnic communities, socioeconomic groups (guilds), or castes. The modern nation-state developed as part of an effort to do away with such forms.

In this respect, the United States itself is the epitome of modernism, having never organized its population under any other system. In fact, the American situation is just the reverse of the premodern experience. Americans have frequently utilized territorial divisions to make possible the autonomy of particular groups rather than giving those groups autonomy within shared territories, precisely because of the principle that equality of political attachment should prevail within every territorial jurisdiction.

The system of territorial democracy was further reinforced by the agrarian foundations of American society. The country was initially settled by people who earned their livelihood from the land, mostly as farmers living on territorially bounded economic units. It was natural for them to base their new governments on larger territorial units—each, in effect, an aggregation of the smaller units within its compass.

Not only the governmental units themselves but also the systems of representation within them were territorially based. Representatives were elected from districts, either following the political boundaries of constituent units or drawn specially for the particular purpose at hand. As political parties emerged, they developed parallel bases for their organizations.

The traditions of federalism, combined with those of an agrarian society, have shaped political organizations in the United States within a territorial mold. Hence American politics is organized around units of territory rather than around economic or ethnic groups, social classes, and the like. All such groups gain formal representation in the councils of government according to their location in particular places and through their ability to capture political control of territorial units. Alexis de Tocqueville described the situation in the following manner in his classic *Democracy in America:*

> In New England, townships were completely and definitely constituted as early as 1650. The independence of the township was the nucleus round which the local interests, passions, rights, and duties collected and clung. It gave scope to the activity of a real political life, thoroughly democratic and republican.[4]

The phrase *territorial democracy* was coined by the American journalist and political analyst Orestes Brownson in the 1850s. He wrote that "the United States of America form a republic in which territorial democracy prevails. ..." Brownson contrasted territorial democracy with *Jacobin democracy*, the infatuation with an abstract, infallible People, and the concentration of "popular" power in an absolute, centralized government. In doing this contrast, Brownson used the terms almost as a synonym for federalism. In theory, the two are not quite the same; but in the American system, where federal democracy is expressed mainly through territorial divisions, they come very close to coinciding.[5]

More recently, Russell Kirk revived the concept in somewhat different form.[6] Contemporary experts on the political party system emphasize the degree to which both *access* and *representation*[7] in the American political system are interwoven with the country's territorial divisions (see Figure 9.1). The struggle over reapportionment in the eleventh generation was a dramatic case in point. Since territorial districts form the basis for political life, the character of those districts is necessarily of central importance. The drive for legislative reapportionment after World War II culminated in a series of landmark decisions by the U.S. Supreme Court, starting in 1962 with the case of *Baker* v. *Carr*.[8] This decision was based on the view that a system of state legislative and congressional districts (which in most states had gone unchanged for decades or, if changed, had been redrawn in the absence of population parity) was inherently undemocratic because it denied citizens equal access.[9]

The argument against basing apportionment strictly on equal population—or one-person, one-vote—also has roots in a conception of territorial democracy which holds that pluralism is protected by the use of territorial divisions to protect specific groups, interests, or ways of life. This argument maintains that there are polities, groups, or interests that deserve or require representation regardless of whether they meet the minimum population requirements (e.g., farmers who need protection in an urban society, African-Americans who need representatives of their own among a white majority, people from small cities in a metropolitan environment) and that the apportionment system must take them into account.

THE TWO FACES OF TERRITORIAL DEMOCRACY

Territorial democracy in America has two faces.[10] Characterizing the first are specific groups that frequently choose to settle in specific territories in order to create and maintain communities and to gain the requisite political power to secure their common goals. This territorial distribution of power has served to mitigate the effects of great national diversity by

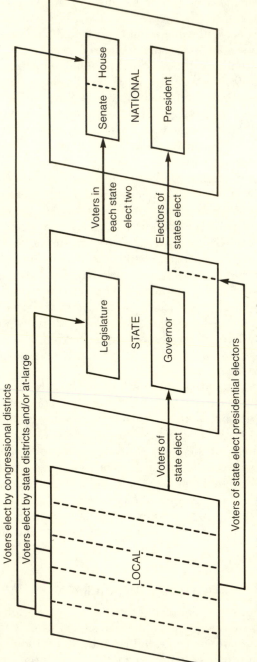

Figure 9.1   The Territorial Basis of Representative Democracy in the United States

allowing subnational territorial communities to interpret national demands in such a way as to reflect their own local values as well.

The second and more frequently visible face of territorial democracy emphasizes the openness of American communities. In the United States, most localities are open to virtually anyone who chooses to settle within them, thereby enabling different groups to gain political power or access to power simply by virtue of their location. In many respects this is the most neutral kind of representation. As soon as one interest declines in importance and a new one rises, it can gain representation because the people who make up that interest are located in some particular political subdivision and can vote there.

The first face of territorial democracy was introduced by the Pilgrims and Puritans, extended by various groups of settlers of the West, and then revived in our own times by some of the advocates of "black power," among others. This form of territorial democracy has enabled diverse groups to maintain their own respective integrities and particular ways of life while at the same time sharing in the larger American society.

In the days of the rural-land frontier, it was assumed that people with like backgrounds, views, or interests would settle together within the same political jurisdiction. If there were only a few of them, they would settle a particular town or township; if there were more, a county; and if there were enough, a whole state. This pattern was most pronounced during the colonial period, when Massachusetts was founded by and for the Puritans, Maryland by and for the Catholics, New Amsterdam by and for the Dutch, and so on. In the nineteenth century, the settlement of Utah by the Mormons was a pronounced reflection of this pattern, but so, too, were the settlements of Alabama and Mississippi by people from the lower Southeast and of the Dakotas by Scandinavians.

In New England, efforts were made to enforce uniformity within political jurisdictions. Baptists were not welcome in Congregationalist Massachusetts and were forcibly evicted. However, the Puritan fathers did not particularly object to their settlement of a new territory to the south, Rhode Island, where they could follow their "heretical" ways. Meanwhile, Connecticut was founded by Puritans whose doctrines differed from those of the Massachusetts "establishment."

This pattern of statewide conformity and interstate differentiation soon proved untenable. There were just too many people coming to the New World with too many different ideas. On the local plane, however, there were nearly unlimited opportunities—if not for complete homogeneity, then at least for the association of two or three compatible groups within a particular locality. This latter pattern was spread across the continent in the nineteenth century. Given the limited population density of agrarian settlement, it was possible to have "Protestant" or "Catholic" towns and counties nearly everywhere; and in many parts of the country, the division was even finer, whith whole counties predominantly Baptist or Lutheran, not to mention the many settlements overwhelmingly populated by single ethnic groups (e.g., the German cities, towns, and counties that covered the Mississippi Valley).[11]

Where religious or ethnic homogeneity was lacking, there was often at least a homogeneity of interest, as in the case of the cow towns and mining camps of the West or the coal and mill towns of the Northeast and South. The formal structure of government in each of these territorial political communities was essentially the same, varying only according to the sectional patterns that emerged from the three "mother" political cultures as they moved westward. But within that formal structure, each community provided its own content, utilizing the opportunities of federalism to maintain local values and interests while functioning as an integral part of the larger society.

The coming of the urban-industrial frontier made the maintenance of this face of territorial democracy more difficult. The densely populated cities that emerged in the nineteenth century did not easily permit the separation of peoples that was necessary for its maintenance. Still, in the smallest cities a great deal of homogeneity could be obtained, whereas in the largest ones, different groups managed to settle neighborhoods within which they could preserve their own ways. The political organization of the great cities reflected their desire to do so. The division of the city into wards and the development of the political machine (which was almost invariably ward-based) provided a vehicle for maintaining subcommunities within the city. Ward leaders negotiating with one another within the framework of the city's formal and informal political structure could win for their constituents practical control over everything from police to schools.

Thus, during the heyday of the urban-industrial frontier, American cities offered opportunities for the maintenance of territorial democracy. However, neighborhood autonomy led to a conflict of political cultures and became suspect as a result. Reformers seeking to restore "good government" attacked the system that allowed the survival of neighborhood control. As they succeeded in weakening or destroying the city political machines, the possibilities for this face of territorial democracy diminished. In this respect, the thrust upward and outward into the larger American society of the various ethnic groups provided additional support for the reformers' efforts.

Manifestations of the first face of territorial democracy can be found in everything from liquor laws to racial discrimination. Take the former. Some local communities and one state (Mississippi) prohibit the sale of liquor within their boundaries; others restrict the sale to state or municipal liquor stores; others allow sales by the bottle but not by the drink. Nor do the laws tell the whole story. In most states, enforcement of liquor laws is informally left to local authorities who handle it according to local mores and expectations. Thus the legal prohibition in Mississippi is virtually unenforced in most localities. In Iowa, Davenport and all of Scott County are allowed greater discretion in selling liquor because the population there is generally recognized to be more tolerant in such matters than that of the rest of the state. In some communities with strong ethnic traditions of regular drinking, though in moderation, even under-aged youths are informally allowed to imbibe.

In general, *local option*,[12] whether formal or informal, prevails in such matters, as it does in the matter of Sunday sales limitations, gambling, and many other issues involving cultural standards and personal morality. Under the Constitution, the states retain the power to regulate in these areas, subject only to federal constitutional limits involving civil rights. In practice, the states tend to delegate these regulatory powers to their local subdivisions. Here sectional and political factors play a role. Southern states tend to enact very specific legislation in this area and then allow their localities to enforce it or not. Western states tend to keep both state and local legislation in these matters to a minimum, so as to allow a maximum of private choice, formally as well as informally. And Northern states inherited a great deal of restrictive legislation from their early days and now enforce it in a mixed manner, to the extent that U.S. Supreme Court decisions have not undercut enforcement of blue laws.

The "noble experiment," with nationwide prohibition of the sale or consumption of liquor between 1920 and 1933 as dictated by the Eighteenth Amendment of the Constitution, was a clear violation of the idea of territorial democracy. The total failure of this prohibition has since generally served as an object lesson for Americans about the limits of government intervention into private morality. It should also serve as an object lesson regarding the limited possibility of developing a single national standard in such matters. Prohibition was an example of the unnecessary application of a single moral standard by law, in part occasioned by the desire of an older, rural America to secure a symbolic victory over the newer, urban America with its lower level of social control.

Half a century later, Americans again tried setting uniform national standards in morals, albeit in reverse. Until 1957, regulation or prohibition of pornographic material was left to local authorities who set policy according to the standards then prevailing in their localities. So, for example, "hit" plays in New York could be banned in Boston. Then the U.S. Supreme Court ruled that "contemporary community standards" were to be defined in terms of the *national* community.[13]

This decision was expanded over the following fifteen years to cover most of the communications media, particularly publishing and films, but ultimately led to a double set of problems. On the one hand, the Court itself had to become a *de facto* national censorship board as it was called upon to review case after case in which publishers and film-makers attempted to eliminate restrictions nationwide—and it was overwhelmed by the burden. On the other hand, as the tastes of the most "with-it" sectors of American society began to be imposed on the rest of the country, there was a popular outcry of growing proportions. Finally, in 1973, the Court found it necessary to restore the rights of the states and communities to apply their own standards, within certain broad limits,[14] thus demonstrating in another way the utility of territorial democracy as a means of providing for the expression of widely divergent viewpoints in a large and diverse country with a minimum of conflict.

If territorial democracy has offered opportunities for the maintenance of necessary and proper diversity, it has also enabled some segments of the population to discriminate against other segments, particularly in the South. In this respect, it is like every other human institution, capable of being used for good or ill. For the better part of the past two centuries, whites used their dominant position in the Southern states to oppress African-Americans first through slavery and then through racial segregation. Moreover, except during the Civil War and Reconstruction, the majority in the North avoided interference in this oppression on the grounds of "states rights," one aspect of territorial democracy. The freedom of action of the territorial polities in this sphere was progressively limited beginning in the 1920s on constitutional grounds and eliminated as an option by the Supreme Court's school desegregation ruling in 1954 and subsequent civil rights decisions.[15]

In this case, as in the others, the principle of checks and balances allows for intervention when one constitutional principle is used to violate another. Yet the original principle is not destroyed, only redirected. Although maximum federal pressure was brought to bear on the states and localities that maintained racial segregation through a combination of legal and other means, the ultimate responsibility for desegregation was necessarily left to the territorial polities in line with constitutional requirements. The federal Supreme Court could hold that Alabama was acting unconstitutionally when it maintained segregated schools; the Congress of the United States could enact legislation cutting off federal aid to segregated schools; the president could even send troops to protect the civil rights of African-American students. But under the Constitution, there was no way for the federal government to open its own schools in Alabama or forbid the state to maintain its school system.

Thus, in the end, change had to be effected through intergovernmental cooperation, albeit antagonistic cooperation in this case. This may or may not have meant that desegregation took longer to be achieved than under some other approach (there is no way to be certain that desegregation by federal order coupled with the exercise of force would not have provoked even greater resistance on the part of Southern whites and thereby prolonged the struggle for equality). The ultimate achievement of this change took place in such a manner that a consensus was developed, with most Southern whites ultimately persuaded of the justice of the change, even if they did not like it personally, and hence more willing to support it.

A key element in the desegregation struggle was the opening of the ballot box to African-Americans in the Southern states, just as the anti-slavery struggle a century earlier had to culminate in the institution of constitutional guarantees for African-American enfranchisement in the country as a whole. The importance of the right to vote in local, state, and national elections is directly connected to territorial democracy.

Access to the country's political mechanisms, a crucial concern for those seeking to gain their place in the sun, has always involved location in territorial units of government. Recent gains by African-Americans in the protection of their constitutional rights on the federal plane, for example, are being translated into political realities because of the concentration of African-Americans in certain territories where they can gain important local representation and also make their numbers count for more than their 12 percent of the nation's total population. Indeed, by obtaining the ballot in the Southern states where they form majorities in some counties, they have been able to gain significant representation in local offices and a voice in state politics.

That potential is illustrated by the political career of Alabama's late governor, George Wallace. Wallace rose to power in the 1950s on a typical Southern populist platform, combining attacks on privilege with low-key racism. Seeing the opportunity to strengthen his power base by opposing the federal government over the issue of racial desegregation, he took up the cudgels for "the Southern way of life" and demonstrably stood in the doorway of the University of Alabama to prevent African-Americans from enrolling.

His success with his constituency led him to take his racist campaign nationwide. Twice he tried to run for the presidency of the United States. At his high-water mark he received 14 percent of the vote nationwide. (The results of this election offer a very good illustration of the location of the traditionalistic political subculture in the United States.) Then he was shot in an assassination attempt, returned to Alabama, and, semi-paralyzed, successfully ran again for governor.

By this time the tide had turned on racial matters, African-Americans had begun to vote, and Wallace needed their support. In his new incarnation he became the African-Americans' best friend, gave them jobs in his administration, and returned to the University of Alabama to bestow his blessing on the university's first African-American homecoming queen, receiving in return the blessing of leading civil rights activist Charles Evers. In one sense, this was political cynicism refined to a high art. In another, it was a reflection of the impact of the democratic process whereby politicians were being led to adjust to changing realities as expressed through territorial democracy.

In the Northern and Western states, the sheer increase in their numbers has transformed the African-Americans into a potent bloc, particularly in the major cities where they now constitute from one-fourth to more than one-half of the total population. Until the 1960s, African-American city council members were hard to find; but by the 1980s, African-Americans had been elected mayors in most of these cities, including all the biggest ones.[16]

The neutrality of territory has reinforced the second face of territorial democracy such that it remains the fundamental basis for political representation even in today's highly urbanized America. Thus the federal protection of Southern African-Americans' right to vote has meant that they have gained a certain potential political power automatically (like all other groups), because the permanent boundaries of the states and the well-nigh permanent boundaries of their major subdivisions serve not only as major mechanisms for access to positions of influence but also as strong bulwarks for the diffusion of power. As permanent boundaries, they offer continued opportunities for diverse interests to exercise power without fear of retribution from "higher authority"; but, inasmuch as they possess the neutrality of "artificial boundaries," they also prevent the confinement of power to select interests. Since every interest, new or old, is located willy-nilly in some formally defined political territory, each can potentially make its voice heard simply by making use of the country's political mechanisms.

The state of Florida, for example, once a typical representative of traditional Southern interests, now speaks for the pioneers of the space frontier and the new world of leisure. Another example is Detroit, Michigan, a locus of power for Yankee commercial and craft interests in the nineteenth century. Along with its economic transformation into an automobile center, it was politically transformed into a stronghold for "ethnic" and African-American autoworkers without having to alter significantly its basic political structure or institutions. African-Americans, some of whom felt the need to riot in 1968 to make themselves heard, first elected one of their own (Coleman Young) as mayor of Detroit in 1973, within the same boundaries and under the same ground rules.

Even in the colonial period, the face of territorial neutrality developed side by side with the face of territorial communalism. The Middle States, in particular, emphasized pluralistic settlement in their territories. Ultimately, all the states followed their lead to a greater or lesser degree. In the end, with a few exceptions, most political units have some characteristics of both faces, functioning as neutral arenas to the extent that they are open to all who seek to settle within them and, at the same time, as communities to the extent that those who do settle within them seek to use their political structure to maintain their own values or way of life.

The U.S. Supreme Court has ruled that states and localities cannot formally prohibit American citizens from settling in their midst, although they can regulate some of the conditions under which the settlement takes place.[17] At the same time, on the most immediately local plane, informal methods have been devised to keep communities more or less homogeneous, ranging from outright violence against "undesirables" to more subtle devices such as control of home sales and rentals or simple exclusion of those who "do not fit" from the local and social networks. Most of these devices have been challenged in the courts and ruled unconstitutional or legally unenforceable.[18] Many have been outlawed by state and federal legislation.

Rural America still retains much of the first face of territorial democracy. It is most evident among such truly separatist groups as the Amish, but it is equally strong in communities that consider themselves full participants in American life while still preserving their own variant of American mores. At the same time, it is under pressure as a result of the new-style settlement movement.

The opening of the metropolitan-technological frontier brought with it renewed opportunities to strengthen both faces of territorial democracy. On the one hand, the new mobility led to a breakdown of many territorially based local communities. Out-migration from rural areas and older urban neighborhoods depleted old, established ones, while the migrants themselves, in resettling themselves, often upset other communities. On the other hand, the settlement of the suburban frontier, with its opportunities for the development of many politically separate suburbs within a metropolitan area, created new opportunities for the development of territorial polities consisting of peoples with similar backgrounds and values. In some cases, specific ethnic or religious groups settled together in suburbs; in others, political or economic homogeneity was the source of local unity. Indeed, suburbia has been attacked in some quarters for fostering communities in which one group or another isolates itself to maintain its own particular patterns of life, whatever they might be.[19]

The attacks on suburban self-segregation reflect a significant aspect of the ideology of the metropolitan-technological frontier—namely, that traditional group distinctions that lead to segregation, even self-segregation, are anti-democratic and should be broken down. This ideology emerged out of the struggle to eliminate the divisions in American life between the older, white Protestant "establishment" and the newer ethnic groups and previously excluded racial groups. It is oriented toward the use of territorial democracy in the most neutral manner. Despite their acceptance of the ideology, many if not most Americans still retain a pragmatic desire to protect real interests by means of their territorial polities, using a variety of means such as police and zoning powers to preserve local control. Those who do not have the opportunity to control their own polities—inner-city African-Americans, for example—seek equivalent opportunities through demands for community control.[20]

THE STATES AS THE KEYSTONES IN THE GOVERNMENTAL ARCH

A useful definition was provided by Chief Justice Salman P. Chase in 1869:

> [The word *state*] describes sometimes a people or community of individuals united more or less closely in political relations, inhabiting temporarily or permanently the same country; often it denotes only the country or territorial region, inhabited by such a community; not infrequently it is applied to the government under which people live; ... In the Constitution the term *state* most frequently expresses the combined idea ... of people, territory, and government. [21]

The fifty American states, located between the powerful federal government and the burgeoning local governments in a metropolitanized nation, are the keystones of the American governmental arch. This was the case when the Constitution was adopted in 1789, and it remains so despite the great changes that have taken place in the intervening years.

This assertion, if it had been made at the end of the eleventh generation of American history or even early in the twelfth, though as true then as it is now, would have been greeted with disbelief. Today, as a result of the failures of the federal government at the end of the eleventh generation, the Reagan revolution at the beginning of the twelfth, and the natural rhythm of the generations (which emphasizes the resurgence of state and local powers in the periods of generational consolidation and generational buildup), a situation has been created in which the states have once again become the leading innovators and sources of energy in American government. Nevertheless, if this assertion were based upon an analysis

of the present position of the states in light of formal *constitutional* interpretations alone, there would be great difficulty in substantiating it. In
fact, the states maintain their central role because of their *structural* and *political* position in the overall framework of the nation's political system, a
position that is supported by the Constitution but transcends its formal
bounds.

By *structural* position I mean the very existence of the states, with their
own political institutions, tax bases, and congeries of interests that make
them players in the American game of government. By *political* I mean the
power of the states and their representatives operating through the political process to make their demands felt and to satisfy their needs.

Unlike the more or less visible constitutional status of the states, their
structural and political position is generally of low visibility, not only to
the public at large but often even to those people involved in the day-to-
day operations of American government.

When we speak of a state doing this or that or taking one position or
another and of states responding to federal actions in different ways, we,
like Chief Justice Chase, are using a convenient way of speaking about the
actions of those people and the interests within each state's civil society
that dominate its political system. This is not to say that the dominant
forces leading a state represent all or even a majority of the citizens of their
state every time they act in its name. Cross-pressures of varying degrees
exist within each state on every issue. On most issues that attract
nationwide attention, the cross-pressures extend across state lines. Therefore, contesting groups within the state's civil society may momentarily
find that they have more in common with their counterparts in other
states than with their immediate compatriots.

Nevertheless, there is a wide range of issues in which the dominant interests in any state can act as if they had a statewide consensus behind
them. These include certain substantive issues in which the welfare or interests of the majority of a state's citizenry are clearly involved (such as
state economic development); certain fundamental procedural issues that
are important because they concern the maintenance of the state itself
(such as the right of the state to determine the terms of employment in its
government); and at least a few issues that, although they do not necessarily reflect a "state" interest as such, do reflect the opinions of a solid majority of the state's citizens (such as the anti-government bias widespread
among citizens of the sparsely populated states of the mountain-and-
plains West or the racial bias of the white majority that once was so powerful in the Southern states).

Proper use of the systemic aspects of a state's civil society enhances the
possibility that the people and interests dominating a state's political system will speak in the name of that state. There are many ways in which

each state, as a reasonably autonomous civil society, can capitalize on its potential for internal unity in the face of outside pressure. States can take appropriate legislative and executive action. Local officials can enforce regulations and ordinances that, taken at face value, may seem irrelevant to the issue at hand but can be applied discreetly in a relevant way. Private exercise of property and personal rights backed by state and local law-enforcement agencies can be used as a countervailing power.

Nor is this ability to mobilize the state's citizens and institutions simply a matter of negativism, of opposition to national goals or norms. Minnesota, for instance, protects itself against organized crime by a combination of the same instruments: state legislation against the "betting" sports (horse and dog racing), a vigilant and uncorruptible judicial system, cooperation among local law enforcement officers to expel "undesirable elements" when they enter the state, and an attitude among the citizenry that provides both tacit and active support for the state's activities. In a more subtle way, Oregon mobilizes its resources as a state to maintain its "pristine" character by encouraging environmental protection and discouraging economic development that might bring an influx of new settlers in the pattern of California and Washington, its two principal neighbors. Even a highly diverse state like New York is capable of this kind of mobilization when its standing as the nation's economic and cultural center comes into question.

Take a different kind of case involving defense against "outside encroachment." State law-enforcement agencies are often able to reshape certain Supreme Court rulings on criminal procedures if they can foster agreement among the courts, the prosecutors, the police, and the bar in the states and in the state's communities regarding the means by which the individual's basic rights are to be protected under the state's scheme and the degree of discretion that law-enforcement agencies are to be allowed.[22]

A state's formal constitutional position, taken alone, would hardly be an adequate line of defense in cases where the state has a paramount interest in preserving local patterns or customs, just as (to take a far different example) the states in general have no constitutional guarantee that their citizens will receive a specific share of federal defense expenditures. Even the states' role as the bases of the nation's party system would not provide sufficient defense against concentrated national pressure, though it helps considerably. The states' first line of defense (or, in the case of the defense contracts, offense) lies in their ability to function as civil societies, to mobilize many facets of their internal and external powers through their own political systems to resist "encroachments" (or to gain benefits) from the outside.

In the militant states of the South, the state police, the local school boards, the senators in Washington, the governor, the local fire inspectors, and the network of Citizens Councils all joined together to fight desegregation after 1954. Their collective effort was such that federal authorities, including the courts, implicitly recognized that these states were functioning as civil societies, stamping as equally unconstitutional both direct state action and private actions sanctioned by the states and thereby reinforcing racial segregation. In all of the states, relevant groups of similar diversity—the state's economic development agency, state and local chambers of commerce, the governor and the mayors, and the state's representatives in Congress—join to secure defense contracts, federal installations, or public works.

More recently this kind of effort has been mobilized for purposes of economic development, especially in the way of exports to foreign countries and foreign investment. This foreign economic activity may well be the new frontier of the states as civil societies. States not only serve their own interests but also play a role of critical national importance, recognized by the federal government as one that only they can perform well.[23]

The states are also becoming more visible as civil societies in matters of lifestyle, where moral questions are involved. Though less differentiated than they used to be regarding issues related to gambling and liquor consumption, they are more differentiated in such matters as abortion rights, control of obscenity and pornography, sexual preference, and other concerns of the new-style politics.[24] It is their ability to join together and to fight their common battle on a number of fronts that has given certain states such a large measure of success in these various endeavors.

THE STATES AS POLITICAL SYSTEMS

The means by which the states and localities organize themselves as political systems to exercise power within the national political system are vitally important to the functioning of American government.

The term *state*, as used in the United States, can be said to refer to those people, interests, and institutions that at any given time are bound together within a territory organized constitutionally as an equal constituent unit of the federal system and are capable of speaking for the political system of the state in question. No state speaks for any specific ethnic, racial, or religious group or interest *per se*, since it is the people of the state who maintain their state's separate identity apart from their common American identity. People do identify with their states, often very strongly. Texans, Virginians, and Californians are assumed to have a highly developed sense of their respective state's identities. Southerners tend to maintain a sense of themselves as citizens of their state. Coloradans and Minnesotans have equally avid, if less well-known state attachments. But in no case, not even among Hawaiians or Alaskans, does state identity stand apart from the sense of being American; rather, one's state attachments are generally considered to be a function of one's being an American. If nothing else, the migratory habits of Americans tend to discourage any contrary development.

Consequently, it is very difficult to determine which people, interests, and institutions speak for a particular state at any given time. Certainly, no particular group or institution can claim to be the custodian of a state "ism" or culture. Although the likelihood is that the governor and the legislature will be a state's prime spokespersons, that is not always the case. Courts, political leaders, heads of government departments, important interest groups—even public opinion, broadly defined—may speak for the state in particular instances. It is under these conditions that each state's existence as a civil society—a complex social institution organized for civil, or political, purposes—becomes clear.

The political system of each state can be said to include the following components:

1. the state government in its several branches and parts (including its local parts);
2. those agencies of the federal and local governments that, although not formally attached to the state government, function primarily to serve the state and its citizens (e.g., the U.S. District Court for the state);
3. the public nongovernmental institutions organized on a statewide basis that serve the state's civil society (e.g., the state's Red Cross);
4. the state's political parties; and
5. the various interests regularly concerned with and involved in the state's political life for reasons of their own (e.g., the state's trade and labor council).

All of these components have some place in the state's constitution, both in the immediate sense of the document that sets forth its frame of government and in the larger sense of the documents, traditions, and rules of the game that define the state's particular orientation as a civil society.

In each state the various institutions, organizations, groups, individuals, and values involved in these components form the basis for the network that is the state's political system, which in turn allows its civil society to function in pursuit of its civic and political goals, even as the state is an integral part of the nation. But not every state functions as a unit to the same degree. Some choose not to do so by design and, occasionally, by default. Obviously, the more successful a state is in formulating common goals shared by the greater part of its citizenry, forging a network of institutions that embraces all the variegated elements within its boundaries, and utilizing its own government to set its pace as a state, the more important it will be to its citizens and the better able it will be to promote those goals.

THE STATES AS CIVIL SOCIETIES

The subtle and sometimes-not-so-subtle differences among the states are worth noting and considering as part of any discussion of American politics. Every state has its own distinctiveness—in terms of the composition of its people, its political goals and processes, and the way in which its people respond to those goals and processes. Yet those differences are not like the differences among the six republics (states) that once made up Yugoslavia, each of which represents a different nationality. Nor do they even approach the differences that set Quebec apart from the rest of Canada.

Every state has its own character as a civil society because it has its own laws, institutions, and history (or, better, geo-historical location). Some enjoy the advantage of being easily perceived as distinctive by their citizens and others. Some are not easily seen in a distinctive light, but, on closer examination, their distinctiveness becomes visible. What every state does have is a history of its own, which continues to shape future events; its own legal system, which sets the framework for much of its economic and political activity; and its own conception of justice, upon which it builds its social and economic policies as a state. As a civil society every state has its own means of organizing power, developed over time and, in part, encapsulated in its system of laws. Each also has its own conception of justice, manifested through its policies and their manner of execution.

What, then, is the substance of state differences? We can identify several ways in which particular states are unique. These include (1) substantial cultural distinctiveness, (2) substantial and self-conscious public attachment, (3) a widely shared sense of a common historical experience of substantial worth or distinctiveness, (4) substantial state distinctiveness in policy matters, and (5) substantial geographic isolation and/or distinctiveness. These five categories frequently reinforce one another.

Some examples are in order. Perhaps the most distinctive state is Utah. Its overwhelmingly Mormon population is more internally homogeneous than that of any other state and, at the same time, very different. Because Utah is the Mormon "homeland," its citizens are self-consciously identified with it as a state and with its history as the center of Mormonism. Because of the special role of the Mormon church, Utah maintains very distinctive governmental policies, both internally and externally. Finally, Utah is geographically one of the most isolated and self-contained of the states; the Mormons chose to settle where they did for precisely that reason.[25]

California is another highly distinctive state, but in the mainstream (if not the avante-garde) of American life. The "California way of life" is a well-recognized American subculture. Californians identify strongly with it and with their state as its home. The state pursues distinctive policies, especially in the realm of social relations, that flow from this way of life and support it. California's history has acquired an especially romantic flavor in the minds of its people, who follow it avidly, while its geographic character and position give it a measure of separation from the rest of the country.[26]

Minnesota is as distinctive as California, but in a lower-key way. It gains room for its distinctiveness from its geographic position away from the country's mainstream. Its government has consistently pursued distinctive policies, especially in the areas of education, social welfare, and human rights. The state has a special ethnic heritage that is well known, yet the political culture of its population is as homogeneous as that of Utah because of the cultural convergence of the streams that settled it. Moreover, Minnesotans are highly conscious of their distinctiveness and of the virtues of their state, especially after they travel outside its boundaries. The weakest link in this chain is that, although Minnesotans have been conscious of their history from the first (note that the state's oldest institution is the Minnesota Historical Society), they do not have a real sense of how distinctive that history is.[27]

On the other end of the scale, New Jersey is usually pictured as an artificial and even accidental creation with no real identity of its own.[28] That image is not entirely false, but it disregards the very real coherence within the Garden State forged out if its historical experiences. From its first settlement in the seventeenth century until the end of the eleventh generation, New Jersey was a satellite of New York City and Philadelphia, with its northern half pulled toward the former and its southern half toward the latter. It was so much a "colony" of its neighbors that it depended upon them for its mass media, having no major newspaper, radio, or television station within its boundaries. Yet as a result of its historical experiences, the state acquired a personality of its own. Its people share a common pattern of settlement in small cities and towns; they are heavily suburbanite in their orientation; and they join together to oppose substantial state taxation, preferring to maintain a relatively low level of public services instead. At the same time, they rely upon their state government for far more than do the two cities in New York and Pennsylvania that function as their states' centers of gravity.

The twelfth generation has marked the turning point for New Jersey. Today the state is coming into its own as the very center of action on America's "main street." The headquarters of major corporations moved from New York City across the Hudson. New Jersey acquired some major sports teams (some of which are still identified as New York teams even though they play in the Garden State). A political leadership visible for its progressiveness and quality has emerged and attracted national attention. And New Jersey finally acquired television service of its own. By the middle of the 1980s the rurban-cybernetic frontier epitomized New Jersey's pattern of settlement, and suddenly the state found itself the heartland of the new frontier. Its people began to develop a new sense of identity, purpose, and state pride.[29]

Similarly, Ohio has a certain anonymity as a state, fostered by its location well within the mainstreams of American life. Contrast Ohio's stance in defining the state's role with that of Minnesota. In Ohio, it has been assumed that the basic task of state government is to create a proper climate for business to prosper, on the assumption that such prosperity will lead to prosperity in the state as a whole, leaving to its many different cities and counties the task of defining what constitutes the good life for their residents. Thus Ohio has consistently pursued a tax policy that favors business investment and has widely advertised that fact. Or, in a slightly different context, Ohio began to provide substantial support for higher education when it became clear that good universities were an integral part of the "package" needed to attract growth industries.[30] In the Gopher State (Minnesota), it has long been assumed that state government exists to equalize opportunity and benefits even at the expense of what is often termed "a good business climate." It has levied taxes accordingly, with a steeply progressive income tax at the core of its revenue-raising system. Moreover, the state has always supported higher education handsomely because its people believe in the social and moral efficacy of education.

In sum, every state has its own particular identity, matched by the realities of its distinctiveness. In many cases, that identity is widely perceived. What does "Texas" evoke as an image? Virginia? Indiana? Hawaii? Vermont? In these cases the image is clear; but even where it is not, a moment's reflection does bring something special to mind. And behind that "something special" there is a reality forged by history, geography, and culture and embodied in particular patterns of political organization focusing on a particular conception of justice.

THE FEDERAL SYSTEM AND THE POLITICAL SETTING

Each of the fifty states responds to the intergovernmental system described in the foregoing chapters in its own way. Understanding their responses requires an appreciation of (1) the way in which the states' functioning as political systems influences the operations of the general government; and (2) the way in which the states—still functioning as political systems—adapt national programs to their own needs and interests. For such an appreciation, it is first necessary to understand the fundamental social and political factors that serve to shape the states and the political setting in which they operate.

The three overarching factors of *political culture*, *sectionalism*, and the continuing *frontier* appear to be especially important in shaping the individual states' political structures, electoral behavior, and modes of organization for political action. All three of these factors represent dynamic processes that generally act upon the states and the federal system, and interact with one another in ever-changing ways. The three factors embrace and shape the primary social, economic, and psychological thrusts that influence American politics. Indeed, it is suggested here that other factors, often presented as basic to the shaping of political systems, and ranging from the class system to urbanization, can best be understood in light of these three factors and are accordingly secondary in their influence.

Political culture is particularly important as the historical source of differences in habits, perspectives, and attitudes that influence political life in the various states. Sectionalism is particularly important as a major source of geographically rooted variations that influence state-by-state differences in responses to nationwide political, economic, and social developments. The frontier is particularly important as the generator of the forces of change. These forces influence patterns of settlement and human economic, social, and political organization throughout the federal system; they stimulate governmental action in new fields on all planes and thus compel the continual readjustment of the federal balance.

FEDERALISM AND POLITICAL CULTURE

One observation coming out of the various studies of state-federal relations is that the states themselves (or their local subdivisions) largely shape the impact of federally aided activities within their boundaries. Take the case of the impact of federal aid on the administration of state government. In those states where the executive branch is organized along hierarchical lines and the governor is usually strong, federal aid has tended to strengthen executive powers by giving the governor more and better tools to wield. In those states where power is widely diffused among the separate executive departments, federal aid has tended to add to the diffusion by giving the individual departments new sources of funds outside of the normal channels of state control. These can be used to obtain more money and power from the legislature. Finally, in those states where earmarked funds reflect legislature or lobby domination over programs, earmarked federal funds tend to follow the same pattern. Despite many protestations to the contrary, only in rare situations have federal grant programs served to alter state administrative patterns in ways that did not coincide with already established state policies, although such grants have often sharpened certain tendencies in state administration.

During the past generation, in state after state, constitutions were revised, gubernatorial tenure and powers were strengthened, legislative sessions were lengthened, legislators' salaries were increased, and state tax systems were overhauled. Although indirect federal influence (in the sense of U.S. Supreme Court decisions or the threat of federal encroachment on their prerogatives) should not be ignored, these changes were self-generated and were not the result of any direct influence by federal authorities or programs.

In the case of federal merit-system requirements, states dominated by political attitudes conducive to notions of professionalization and to the isolation of certain forms of government activity from the pressures of partisan politics have had little problem adjusting their programs to meet federal standards. They had either adopted similar standards earlier or were quite in sympathy with the standards when proposed. Minnesota, for example, has tighter merit-system requirements than those applicable to its federally aided programs under the Hatch Act. By contrast, states dominated by a political outlook having little sympathy for nonpartisanship in government administration (e.g., Kentucky, Pennsylvania, and West Virginia) have had a more difficult time adjusting to federal requirements of this sort, and have often worked to find ways to circumvent them, even while conforming superficially. States with a similar lack of interest in civil service reform but with an environment shaped by advanced industrial and commercial organization are generally open to the organizational aspects of the federal requirements, if only because their dominant economic organizations already reflect the modern organizational approach. So, even if the dominant political interests in states like Massachusetts, Pennsylvania, or Illinois object to the *political* aspects of Hatch Act requirements, they are in reasonable harmony with the act's *organizational* demands.

A parallel situation exists in regard to the substance of the federal programs. Every state has certain dominant traditions about what constitutes proper government action, and every state is generally predisposed toward the federal programs it can accept as consistent with those traditions. Many states have pioneered programs that fit into their traditions before the initiation of similar ones on the federal plane or on a nationwide basis through federal aid. This factor, too, tends to lessen the impact of federal action on the political systems of those states and also lessens any negative state reaction to federal entrance into particular fields.

Wisconsin's pioneering efforts in social welfare before the New Deal are well known. They became the models for many of the new federal-aid programs that were often drawn so as to minimize the dislocation to that state's established programs. The majority of Minnesota's congressional delegation is continually at the forefront in supporting new federal-aid education, welfare, and internal improvement programs because, as a state, Minnesota is predisposed toward positive government action and finds such programs useful in supporting its own goals. In matters of national defense, the Southern states have a long tradition of supporting state militia and National Guard units, such that over the years they have taken greater advantage of federal subventions for the maintenance of military reserve units than have most of their sister states.

States like California accept federal aid and its requirements for mental health programs as a reinforcement of programs they have developed themselves. By contrast, professional mental health workers in states like New Jersey rely upon the same federal grants to keep their programs free of internally generated political pressures, arguing with the patronage-inclined legislatures that federal regulations demand maintenance of professional standards. Their colleagues in states like Pennsylvania use federal-aid requirements to force the hands of their legislatures to expand state activities in new directions. And reformers interested in mental health in states like Mississippi are interested in federal aid to inaugurate new programs. Many of these and other differences in state responses within the federal system appear to be stimulated by differences in political culture among the states.

THE POLITICAL CULTURES OF THE STATES

The amalgam of the political subcultures in the several states is varied because representatives of each are found within every state to varying degrees. In fact, unique aggregations of cultural patterns are clearly discernible in every state. These cultural patterns give each state its particular character and help determine the tone of its fundamental relationship, as a state, to the nation. Map 9.1 presents the particular pattern of political culture in each state; Table 9.1 presents the configuration of states on a nationwide scale. In general, the states of the greater South are dominated by the traditionalistic political culture; the states stretching across the middle section of the United States in a southwesterly direction are dominated by the individualistic political culture; and the states of the far North, Northwest, and Pacific Coast are dominated by the moralistic political culture.

Seventeen states are predominantly or overwhelmingly influenced by the moralistic political culture, sixteen by the traditionalistic political cul-

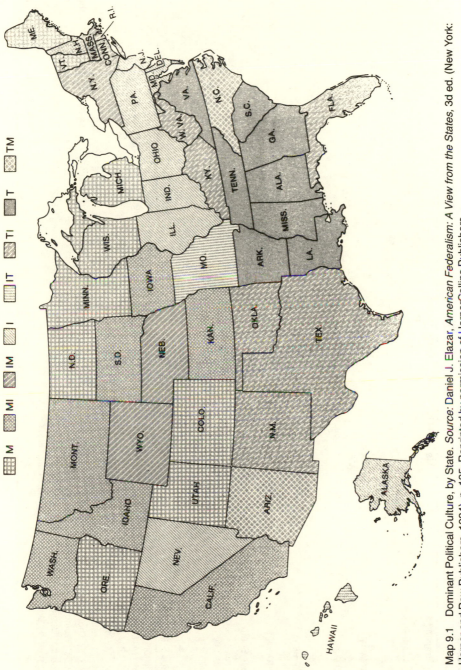

Map 9.1 Dominant Political Culture, by State. *Source: Daniel J. Elazar, American Federalism: A View from the States,* 3d ed. (New York: Harper and Row Publishers, 1984), p. 135. Reprinted by permission of HarperCollins Publishers.

TABLE 9.1 State Political Cultures: The National Configuration

Section	M	MI	IM	I	IT	TI	T	TM
New England	Vt.	Me. N.H.	Conn. Mass. R.I. N.Y.					
Middle Atlantic				Penna. N.J. Del. Md.				
Near West	Mich. Wis.		Ohio[a] Ill.[a]	Ind.				
Northwest	Minn.	Iowa Kan. N.D. Colo. Mont. S.D. Wyo. Neb.						
Far West	Utah Ore.	Calif. Wash. Idaho		Nev.				
Southwest					Mo.	Tex. Okla. N.M.		Ariz.
Upper South						W. Va. Ky. Fla.	Va. Tenn.	N.C.
Lower South						Ala. Ga. Ark. La.	S.C. Miss.	
Pacific				Alas.	Haw.			

[a]Illinois and Ohio have strong traces of M in their northern counties and T in their southern counties.

KEY: M: Moralistic dominant.
MI: Moralistic dominant, strong Individualistic strain.
IM: Individualistic dominant, strong Moralistic strain.
I: Individualistic dominant.
IT: Individualistic dominant, strong Traditionalistic strain.
TI: Traditionalistic dominant, strong Individualistic strain.
T: Traditionalistic dominant.
TM: Traditionalistic dominant, strong Moralistic strain.

NOTE: The eight columns in the table should be viewed as segments on a forced continuum that actually has elements of circularity. The specific placing of the individual states should be viewed cautiously, considering the limits of the data.

Source: Daniel J. Elazar, American Federalism: A View from the States, 3d ed. (New York: Harper and Row, Publishers, 1984), p. 136. Reprinted by permission of HarperCollins Publishers.

ture, and seventeen by the individualistic political culture. This division is paralleled by the relative populations of the three groupings of states, as shown in Table 9.2. The states dominated by the individualistic political culture used to be fewer in number, but with a far greater share of the nation's population. Now they have reached parity in number and declined to parity in population. Thus, although the aggregate population of all three groupings is growing in absolute numbers, their relative share of the nation's population has shifted considerably. Moreover, because several of the traditionalistic states are undergoing subtle changes in the direction of the individualistic political culture, the role of the traditionalistic subculture nationally is further diminished. In terms of population, the relative strength of the moralistic states is increasing. The figures do not tell, however, whether the population increase in those states is reinforcing the established political subculture or injecting new elements foreign to it. Neither can the figures reveal to what extent the moralistic political subculture is gaining strength in the individualistic states as a result of social and cultural change.

What we do see is an overall shift of American national political culture in a moralistic direction. This shift is evidenced by the new standards of public and private rectitude demanded of politicians. Although the shift is the product of many trends, it suggests that the changes in state-by-state population aggregations reflect real change in the nation as a whole.

THE WIDESPREAD APPLICATION OF
FEDERAL PRINCIPLES

The basic federal division of powers is supplemented by widespread acceptance of the idea that federal principles should apply to relations between all governments in the United States. Hence local governments—formally the creatures of their states—have been effectively endowed with a seat at the bargaining table hardly inferior to that of the states, despite the nominally unitary state-local relationship. Formal structures have a certain legal force that contributes to the shaping of the state and local roles in the American system. They have certainly contributed to reliance upon grants-in-aid and similar efforts to stimulate state activity in fields deemed by the national legislature to demand national effort in place of direct federal action in those fields.

At the same time, the constitutionally unitary character of the states proclaimed by the courts (often in the face of clear expressions of the public will to the contrary) sets certain very definite legal limits to local powers. This latter view, although it can be challenged, has been adopted by the U.S. Supreme Court, which has reaffirmed it in a series of decisions beginning with the reapportionment case in 1962. The Court has made it a

TABLE 9.2   Populations of the Cultural Groupings, by State, 1940–1990

Political	Number	Total Populations (in millions)					
Culture	of States	1940	1950	1960	1970	1980	1990
M/MI	17	30.9	38.1	47.8	51.4	63.7	72.2
I/IM/IT	17	51.8	66.6	77.4	87.3	71.9	91.2
T/TM/TI	16	39.9	45.2	52.9	58.4	70.5	81.6

Source: *U.S. Statistical Abstract 1991* (Washington, D.C.: Government Printing Office, 1991).

point to refer to the unitary character of the states as distinct from the federal character of the Union in justifying its rulings. The people of most states have succeeded in modifying this doctrine by introducing home-rule provisions into the state constitution or adopting them by statute to maintain the principle of local autonomy. Advocates of home-rule argue that, when cities (and counties, in some cases) are granted the right to determine their own governmental structures and full power over all local activities except those of the states' concern, local government is substantially enhanced and improved. Since 1875, thirty-three states have provided for home rule on a constitutional or statutory basis, and more than two-thirds of cities with populations greater than 250,000 have adopted home-rule charters.[31] Moreover, in some states, particularly (but not exclusively) those of New England, strong traditions hold the states to be federations of towns or counties on much the same basis that the United States is a federation of states.

Beyond that, philosophical traditions, historical processes, and political realities have substantially modified the practical application of both principles of constitutional law. Today there is no question that, rightfully or not, there are few practical limits on the scope of federal activities as the result of the expansion of that government's delegated and implied powers. On the other hand, at no time in American history has local government more vociferously demanded that the localities also partake of the autonomy that comes with federal arrangements.

In the actual business of everyday problem-solving, political leaders and the public rarely stop to consider constitutional nuances. Rather, they respond according to their sense of the immediate need and overall "fitness" of things from the perspective of an outlook that has become second nature. Hence in the course of the normal give and take of policymaking and program implementation, the spokespersons for the localities assert their "federal autonomy"—their right to be considered as autonomous as any other plane of government in the federal system.

At times, the federal system even takes on elements of a caricature of itself in reverse, with the public and Congress treating the federal-state relationship as a unitary one and the state-local relationship as federal in character. Big-city mayors, for example, have insisted that the federal government force the states to recognize their cities' "independence." The fact that there were a number of big cities larger than some of the smaller states also contributed to this *de facto* extension of federal principles. For a while, in the 1960s and 1970s, the big cities succeeded in gaining this recognition. However, as they actually declined in population size so, too, did their influence. The Reagan administration proclaimed this shift as a matter of federal policy, emphasizing federal-state relations to the exclusion of direct federal-local relations. By the same token, as the population of the country grew, the predominance of the larger cities diminished. The states, capitalizing on the decline of federal aid and the increasing financial problems of those cities, reasserted their role, albeit with new activism and greater assistance for the big cities. This sequence of events is almost a natural one in a political system so heavily influenced by federal principles.

In the final analysis, the institutions, politics, and policies of a state and its localities are so closely intertwined that no real separation between them is possible. Even when the biggest cities deal directly with Washington, they usually do so with their states' active or tacit consent, operating as arms of their states to the same extent as do state administrative agencies when dealing with their federal counterparts. On the other hand, home rule has not significantly altered the state-local relationship. The reason for this lies in the fact that virtually all local activities are of state concern or have been so defined by the state legislatures. The Colorado constitution, for example, grants the right to adopt home-rule charters to every city with at least 2,000 residents. Once a city does so, it gains full power over all local activities, subject to state intervention only in matters of statewide concern. While on paper this appears to be an extreme grant of local autonomy, in fact the Colorado state legislature has ruled that wherever state laws or funds are involved, the home-rule provision is superseded. Those actions cover virtually every subject except the adoption of the charter itself. Home rule has proved useful in giving the cities and counties in home-rule states greater power over the structure of their governments; but in this highly integrated society, it has done little else to advance their autonomy.

THE CIVIL COMMUNITY:
THE VEHICLE FOR LOCAL ACTION
IN THE FEDERAL SYSTEM

The diffusion of powers and functions among many local governments is the most characteristic feature of local governmental structures.[32] In most cases it is even difficult to determine which is the principal government in the local constellation—the city or the county, the borough or the township. Only the largest cities and some of the larger counties (those with populations of more than half a million) have governmental structures sufficiently comprehensive to resemble those of the states. But they account for no more than one-fifth of the country's urban population. For the majority of localities, and the vast majority of Americans, the network of governmental, quasi-governmental, and public bodies that give each locality a political form is less neat and therefore harder to discover. In them, political form is determined by the organized sum of the political institutions that function in a given locality to provide the bundle of governmental services and activities that, in turn, can be manipulated locally to serve local needs in light of the local value system.

Under this definition, a locality becomes a community insofar as it is organized for political or civil purposes. A civil community of this kind is, in effect, a smaller and more limited counterpart of the two civil societies in which every American lives. The civil community is designed to meet the immediate civic needs of people living in close proximity rather than the more comprehensive purposes served by civil societies. Among its politically significant components are:

1. the formal local governments serving the locality (e.g., city, township, school districts, special districts, county);
2. the local agencies of the state and federal governments, to the extent that they have become adjuncts of the local community functioning primarily to serve it (e.g., the state employment office, the local post office);
3. the public nongovernmental bodies that function in governmental or quasi-governmental capacities locally (e.g., the community welfare council, the chamber of commerce);
4. the political parties, factions, or groupings that organize political competition locally;
5. the interest groups operating within the local political arena; and
6. the body of written constitutional material and unwritten tradition that serves as a framework within which sanctioned political action must take place and as a check against unsanctioned political behavior.

Every locality with its own comprehensive political system is a civil community. Such a system provides a wide variety of governmental services for those who live under it, ranging from the maintenance of law and order to the provision of recreation and welfare services. The extent and character of the latter depend, in great measure, on local demands. The civil community also functions to manipulate activities not of local concern alone, such as the Selective Service and public educational systems, so as to ensure their conformity with local values.

Not every locality is equally successful in making the transition from a congeries of political institutions to a civil community, because not every one is able to create the necessary network of relationships among the institutions involved. What is clear is that a civil community is far more capable of asserting its claims within the federal system in terms of both policymaking and administration than any single local government acting alone, including the occasional city government that possesses and exercises broad powers under its state's constitution.

American civil communities have existed in a variety of forms, ranging from the traditional New England town or rural Southern county of yesteryear to the metropolitan center of today. The New England town and the Southern county were easily envisioned as civil communities because, in a simpler age, the community and its political boundaries were identical. Today, however, the complexities of government are reflected in the complexities of governmental structure, at least at the local level. Although city, town, or county lines may indeed delimit the civil community adequately in many cases, the limits of specific civil communities may be less easily discovered within formal political boundaries. In metropolitan America, city boundaries do not necessarily encompass the entire population of the civil community, and city governments only partially encompass the institutions of the local political system. At the same time, counties are often too large or politically complex to be coterminous with the civil community, either because urban-rural divisions within them are sharp or because they contain too many different forms of urban life.

Most Americans today live in metropolitan areas that are, in effect, congeries of civil communities in various stages of internal organization and development and with varying levels of intercommunity contact. But it must be recognized that most metropolitan areas themselves are not civil communities, regardless of how integrated they are economically. That is why suggestions to consolidate metropolitan areas under a single government have not been adopted. In the final analysis, local sentiment, political interest, and lines of civic communication are far more important determinants than commuter flows or bank clearings.

Even though there is no such legal entity as the civil community, Americans—particularly those involved in local affairs—act as if it were a very real entity indeed. Hence the civil community is an *operational* reality, because it represents a characteristically American adaptation of the principle of local community. America's very fluid, highly mobile, and socially pluralistic society is not oriented toward the development of the kind of rooted, homogeneous, "organic" community of our European ancestors.

Properly developed, even such limited communities can exert a great deal of influence over the political matters that affect them and their residents.

As suggested by the etymology of the words themselves, the key to *community* is to be found in the ongoing existence of a particular sphere of *communication* among relevant communicants—that is, communication in its original sense of sharing as well as in the sense of transaction. Obviously, the key to civil community is the existence of a particular sphere of political communication. It is not at all amiss to see the problem of creating and maintaining civil communities as a problem of communication, especially in the sense of sharing a particular kind of political life. Since the existence of a civil community is more a matter of the interrelationships between its public and private, governmental and nongovernmental, and political and civic parts than simply a question of political boundaries, the primary measure of that existence is the ambit of a particular kind of political communication; on the other hand, the primary measure of its effectiveness rests on the level and pattern of political communication between and among its parts. That is where the question of scale takes on added significance.

Some political jurisdictions, even if they are legally cities, are simply too large to foster the requisite kind of sharing among their components necessary for the existence of a civil community. This is true even if their leaders are able to manipulate the organized media of communications so as to give the illusion of community. The proof of that pudding is invariably demonstrated when the city, confronted by internal and external pressures, cannot produce anything like a common front. By the same token, some political jurisdictions are simply too small to contain a complete local communications network. If properly located, they become, in effect, neighborhoods within some larger civil community. If not, they remain suspended with no civil community.

One of the primary tasks of any civil community today is to function as an active power in the complex network of federal-state-local relations that is responsible for delivering most governmental services and benefits to its residents. In many respects, the test of a civil community lies in its ability to acquire state and federal aids, adapt them to local needs, and combine them with locally provided services into a comprehensive governmental "package" responsible to the needs and interests of the local citizenry.[33]

TERRITORIAL DEMOCRACY
ON THE METROPOLITAN FRONTIER

The mosaic of American governments and the patterns of territorial democracy that it reflects and sustains were originally products of the rural frontier. Although those patterns were tested, in some cases severely, by urbanization (the urban-industrial frontier), the mosaic survived in basic form to be reinvigorated by metropolitanization. Thus the 1980 census showed some apparently contradictory trends that can be understood only in light of the principles of federalism as Americans understand them. On the one hand, 73.5 percent of all Americans lived in what the Census Bureau defines as urban places (essentially, places of 2,500 inhabitants or more), and 76.6 percent lived in Standard Metropolitan Statistical Areas. At the same time, only 31 percent of the population lived in central cities of 50,000 or more people, while 37 percent lived in the suburbs and 32 percent in open country or small towns. Even with the increased number of very large metropolitan areas (in 1985, there were thirty-seven with more than 1 million people within each SMSA, containing some 45 percent of all Americans), the overwhelming majority of the people in these areas live in small cities. Refer back to Table 3.1 and it becomes apparent how much metropolitan America is still a land of relatively small local jurisdictions. In an age of great complexity, and despite the efforts of many who have sought, in the name of reform and modernization, to change the organization of American local government and the distribution of powers within the federal system as a whole, the mosaic and its animating principles have survived.

Territorial entities such as states, counties, cities, boroughs, townships, school districts, special districts, congressional districts, wards, and precincts form the basis of American political life. Territorial democracy is such that people gain formal political representation through their location in particular places and their ability to capture political control of those places. In fact, territorial democracy is a neutral kind of representational system in the sense that specific groups such as the Mormons may choose to settle in a particular place in order to gain sufficient political strength to secure their own goals; or specific groups such as African-Americans, who have been discriminated against or have migrated into already-established places, may develop sufficient political clout to compete with or even displace the old "establishment."

In the scheme of American territorial democracy, the states are the keystones. It is important to note that the position of the states rests not only on constitutional guarantees but also on their ability to function as civil societies by orchestrating the components of their political systems for successful action. These components include the formal state government, the agencies of the federal and local governments within the state, the public's nongovernmental institutions serving the state, the state's political party organs, the various interests involved in state politics, and the state's "constitution." In a similar manner, the political power of localities rests not so much on legal provisions for local autonomy or home rule as on the ability of localities to function as civil communities with the capacity to gain seats at the state and federal bargaining tables.

SUMMARY

Chapter 9 focuses on territorial democracy as a key aspect of the American political system, manifested primarily but not exclusively through federalism and changed significantly by the impact of the metropolitan frontier. The chapter begins by explaining the meaning of territorial democracy, in the context of the United States as a system of systems. It then describes the two faces of territorial democracy and the extent to which territorial democracy has been influenced by the continuing frontier. The chapter places special emphasis on the states as civil societies with comprehensive political systems of their own—as the keystones of the governmental arch. It also examines the federal system in its political setting, focusing especially on the question of how institutions in all territories are affected by the political cultures in which they are embedded.

NOTES

1. Robert Ardrey, *The Territorial Imperative* (New York: Atheneum, 1967).

2. U.S. Bureau of the Census, *U.S. Census of Governments, 1988* (Washington, D.C.: U.S. Government Printing Office, 1988).

3. Morton Godzins, *The American System,* edited by Daniel J. Elazar (Chicago: Rand McNally, 1966), pp. 3–4.

4. Alexis de Tocqueville, *Democracy in America,* Vol. I (New York: Schocken Books, 1961), p. 42.

5. Orestes Brownson, *The American Republic,* facsimile edition (Clifton, N.J.: A. M. Kelley, 1972).

6. Russell Kirk, "The Prospects for Territorial Democracy in America" (1963), in Robert Goldwin, ed., *A Nation of States* (Chicago: Rand McNally College Publishing Company, 1974).

7. *Access:* The ability to contact official decisionmakers to present a case in such a way that it will receive serious considerations. *Representation:* The ability to participate in the selection of official decisionmakers so that they will have reason to seek to represent the selectors' interests.

8. *Baker* v. *Carr,* 369 U. S. 186 (1962).

9. On the reapportionment debate and struggle, see U. S. Advisory Commission on Intergovernmental Relations, *A Framework for Studying the Controversy Concerning the Federal Courts and Federalism* (Washington, D.C.: U.S. Advisory Commission on Intergovernmental Relations, 1986); and Daniel J. Elazar, *American Federalism: A View from the States,* 3rd ed. (New York: Harper and Row, 1986), and *The American Constitutional Tradition* (Lincoln: University of Nebraska Press, 1988).

10. This section draws heavily on Elazar, *American Federalism: A View from the States,* 3rd ed.

11. For a graphic illustration of this phenomenon, see the large map of the distribution of religions in Edwin Gaustad's *Historical Atlas of Religions in the United States* (New York: Harper, 1962). See also *The Economist World Atlas and Almanac* (New York: Economist Books, Prentice-Hall Press, 1989).

12. *Local option:* The right of a local community under state law to choose its own policy and enact appropriate regulations to enforce it, usually on matters relating to the health, safety, and morals of the population.

13. *Roth* v. *United States,* 354 U.S. 476 (1957).

14. *Miller* v. *California,* 413 U.S. 15 (1973).

15. *Brown* v. *Board of Education,* 347 U.S. 483 (1954); *Cooper* v. *Aaron,* 358 U.S. 1 (1958); *Swann* v. *Charlotte-Mecklenburg Board of Education,* 402 U.S. 1 (1971).

16. Marcus D. Pohlman, *Black Politics in Conservative America* (White Plains, N.Y.: Longman, 1990); Michael Preston et al., *The New Black Politics* (White Plains, N.Y.: Longman, 1982); Hanes Walton, Jr., *Invisible Politics: Black Political Behavior* (Albany: State University of New York Press, 1985); James A. Barnes, "Into the Mainstream," *National Journal* (February 3, 1990), pp. 262–266.

17. *Edwards* v. *California,* 314 U.S. 160 (1963).

18. For an example of a Supreme Court case on housing discrimination, see *Jones* v. *Alfred H. Mayer Co.,* 392 U.S. 409 (1968).

19. One particular area of recent contention concerns the right of lower-income people and nonwhites to move into suburban communities. See, for example, Anthony Downs, *Opening Up the Suburbs* (New Haven, Conn.: Yale University Press, 1973); Michael N. Danielson, *The Politics of Exclusion* (New York: Columbia University Press, 1976); John J. Harrigan, *Political Change in the Metropolis,* 3rd ed. (Boston: Little, Brown, 1985); and Daniel J. Elazar, *Building Cities in America* (Lanham, Md.: Hamilton Press, 1987).

20. On African-American demands for "community control," see Milton Kotler, *Neighborhood Government: The Local Foundations of Political Life* (Lanham, Md.: University Press of America, 1969); Stokely Carmichael and Charles V. Hamilton, *Black Power: The Politics of Liberation in America* (New York: Random House, 1967); August Maier, ed., *The Transformation of Activism* (New Brunswick, N.J.: Transaction Books, 1973); and Marguerite Ross Barnett and James A. Hefner, eds., *Public Policy for the Black Community: Strategies and Perspective* (New York: Alfred Publishing Company, 1967).

21. Chief Justice Salmon P. Chase, quoted in *Texas* v. *White,* 7 Wallace 700 (1869).

22. See Theodore L. Becker and Malcolm H. Feeley, eds., *The Impact of Supreme Court Decisions* (New York: Oxford University Press, 1973); and Stephen L. Wasby, *The Impact of the United States Supreme Court* (Homewood, Ill.: Dorsey, 1970). See also Stanley I. Kutler, ed., *The Supreme Court and the Constitution: Readings in American Constitutional History,* 3rd ed. (New York: W. W. Norton, 1984).

23. On the states' foreign economic activities, see John Kincaid, "American Governors in International Affairs," *Publius* 14, no. 4 (Fall 1984): 95; and John Kline, "The International Economic Interests of U.S. States," *Publius* 14, no. 4 (Fall 1984): 81.

24. On the states in the context of lifestyle issues, see Robert N. Bellah, *Habits of the Heart* (New York: Harper and Row, 1985); and John Kincaid, "Political Cultures and Quality of Life," *Publius* 10, no. 2 (Spring 1980): 1–16.

25. See Wallace Turner, *The Mormon Establishment* (Boston: Houghton Mifflin, 1966); and Frank H. Jones, "Utah: The Different State," in Frank H. Jones, ed., *Politics in the American West* (Salt Lake City: University of Utah Press, 1969).

26. See Carey McWilliams, *California, the Great Expectation* (New York: Current Books, 1949); Todd LaPorte and C. J. Adams, "Alternative Patterns of Postindustria: The California Experience," in Leon N. Lindberg, ed., *Politics of Industrial Society* (New York: McKay, 1976).

27. June D. Holmquist, ed., *They Chose Minnesota*; Theodore G. Blegen, *Minnesota: A History* (Minneapolis: University of Minnesota Press, 1964); Clifford E. Clark, ed., *Minnesota in a Century of Change: The State and Its People Since 1900* (Minneapolis: Minnesota Historical Society, 1989).

28. In the first issue of the *New Jersey Monthly* (November 1976), the publisher noted that the magazine would try to break down "The Myth of New Jersey," which "holds that [the state] is not really a place. True, it is a state in which 7.5 million people have chosen to live. True, it has a governor and a legislature and its own laws and roads and cities and shopping centers. But it isn't *really* a place. It has no identity of its own; it is merely a large suburb of New York and Philadelphia; it is smelly and dirty; it is run by the Mafia; it is corrupt; it is crowded; and worst of all, nobody who lives in New Jersey really *cares* about New Jersey" (p. 5).

29. See John T. Cunningham, *New Jersey: America's Main Road* (Garden City, N.Y.: Doubleday, 1966); and Alan Rosenthal and John Blydenburgh, eds., *Politics in New Jersey* (New Brunswick, N.J.: Rutgers, 1975). See also Barbara Salmore and Stephen Salmore, *Politics and Government in New Jersey* (Lincoln: University of Nebraska Press, 1993).

30. On Ohio, see John H. Fenton, *Midwest Politics* (New York: Holt, Rinehart and Winston, 1966); Dick Perry, *Ohio: A Personal Portrait of the 17th State* (Garden City, N.Y.: Doubleday, 1969); and Robert McLaughlin, *The Heartland* (New York: Time-Life Library of America, 1967).

31. See Stephanie Cole, ed., *Partnership Within the States* (Urbana: University of Illinois, Institute of Government and Public Affairs; and Philadelphia: Temple University, Center for the Study of Federalism, 1976). See also Joseph Zimmerman, ed., *Government of the Metropolis* (New York: Holt, Rinehart and Winston, 1968).

32. This section can be supplemented by reference to the following books by Daniel J. Elazar: *Cities of the Prairie* (New York: Basic Books, 1970), ch. 9, p. 45; *Cities of the Prairie Revisited* (Lincoln: University of Nebraska Press, 1986), pp. 38–45; *Building Cities in America* (Lanham, Md.: Center for the Study of Federalism and University Press of America, 1987); and *The Politics of Belleville* (Philadelphia: Temple University Press, 1971).

33. See Daniel J. Elazar, "Local Government in Intergovernmental Perspective," in Elazar, ed., *The Politics of American Federalism* (Lexington, Mass.: C. C. Heath, 1969); and Paul Finkelman and Stephen E. Gottlieb, eds., *Toward a Usable Past: Liberty Under State Constitutions* (Athens, Ga.: University of Georgia Press, 1991).

CHAPTER 10

A New Generation and
a New Frontier

BEGINNING THE TWELFTH GENERATION

In 1977, the United States moved into the first phase of the twelfth generation (see Figure 10.1). The founding events of that generation were the
American withdrawal from Vietnam, the shifting of public respect and expectations away from the federal government in the aftermath of the perceived excesses and failures of the Great Society, and the development of a
new anti-government, anti-Washington attitude in the country.[1] With the
end of the Vietnam venture, the American people rejected the role of the
United States as the world's policeman and a period of neo-isolationism
began.[2]

By 1979, the culminating events of the generational founding included
the Carter administration's semi-intended assistance to the Sandinistas in
overthrowing the Somoza regime in Nicaragua and the installation of a
Cuban-style Communist dictatorship in that country (the abandonment of
our dictators for theirs, who were crueler, demonstrated Carter's inability
to defend the West or even the United States) and the fall of the shah in
Iran, again, after the Carter administration ceased its support for him, followed by the rise of a fundamentalist Islamic regime there, which
heralded what was to become a principal international problem in the
new generation—namely, a highly militant and aggressive Islam that was
not afraid to strike at Western targets.

Carter's failures in foreign policy led to the election of Ronald Reagan
in 1980, returning the Republicans to the White House. It may very well
be that the 1980 elections (when Reagan won a relatively narrow victory)
and the 1984 elections (when he smashed the opposition) were the critical
elections of the twelfth generation. As in the case of the Civil War generation, the results confirmed the deadlock between the two parties, perhaps
in transition to a new majority rather than in affirmation of an old major-

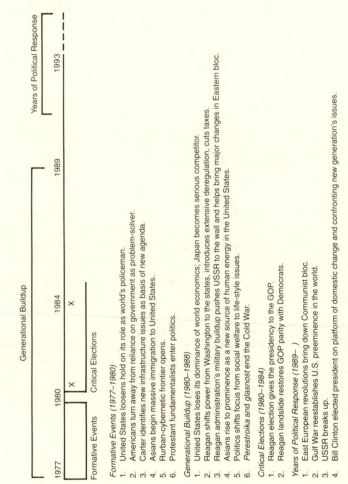

Generational Buildup

Years of Political Response

1977   1980   1984   1989   1993

Formative Events   Critical Elections

Formative Events (1977–1980)

1. United States loosens hold on its role as world's policeman.
2. Americans turn away from reliance on government as problem-solver.
3. Carter identifies new infrastructure issues as basis of new agenda.
4. Asians begin massive immigration to United States.
5. Rurban-cybernetic frontier opens.
6. Protestant fundamentalists enter politics.

Generational Buildup (1980–1988)

1. United States loses its dominance of world economics; Japan becomes serious competitor.
2. Reagan shifts power from Washington to the states, introduces extensive deregulation, cuts taxes.
3. Reagan administration's military buildup pushes USSR to the wall and helps bring major changes in Eastern bloc.
4. Asians rise to prominence as a new source of human energy in the United States.
5. Politics shifts focus from social welfare to life-style issues.
6. *Perestroika* and *glasnost* end the Cold War.

Critical Elections (1980–1984)

1. Reagan election gives the presidency to the GOP.
2. Reagan landslide restores GOP parity with Democrats.

Years of Political Response (1989–)

1. East European revolutions bring down Communist bloc.
2. Gulf War reestablishes U.S. preeminence in the world.
3. USSR breaks up.
4. Bill Clinton elected president on platform of domestic change and confronting new generation's issues.

Figure 10.1   Patterns and Trends in the Twelfth Generation

ity. In any case, Reagan, as a new president, assumed that he had a broad mandate for change and proceeded to inaugurate the "Reagan revolution," which consisted of (1) an effort to restore dual federalism and transfer responsibility back to the states, in particular; (2) deregulation of the economy and increased support for private enterprise; (3) transformation of the nation's tax structure to encourage investment (i.e., reinvestment in the rich); and (4) more aggressive foreign policy, emphasizing the American acceptance of the challenge to fight Soviet Communism, which Reagan described as "the evil empire." Although Reagan's self-confidence began to restore America's self-confidence, his economic policies led to a substantial erosion of America's position in the world economy and an end to its sole dominance.

By the end of the decade, the United States had to share economic dominance with the rapidly strengthening European Community (which was increasingly being driven by Germany in the economic sphere) and a surging Japan. Meanwhile, in the mid-1980s, Mikhail Gorbachev took over the reins of the Soviet government, whose rigidity under the previous regimes had brought the USSR to the brink of economic disaster. Gorbachev introduced *glasnost* and *perestroika* in an effort to liberalize the Soviet Union without abandoning Communism or Communist party control. Within a short time the Soviet Union had withdrawn from Afghanistan, in which it had intervened in the last year of the Carter administration, leading to a successful Afghani resistance encouraged by the Reagan administration and to the abandonment of most of the Soviet Union's foreign adventures.

In November 1988, Republican George Bush, Reagan's vice-president, was elected president in his own right. Popular satisfaction with the Reagan years gave the Republicans another four years in the White House. Within a year of Bush's taking office, the peoples of Eastern Europe revolted against Communist domination, both by indigenous Communists and by the Soviet Union. In a remarkably short time and with remarkably little violence, they succeeded in replacing the Communist regimes of their countries with democratic ones and in ending COMECON (the Communist economic community parallel to the EC that basically served to harness the East European economies for Soviet purposes) as well as the Warsaw Pact (the Communist agreement parallel to NATO). The Soviet Union began to withdraw its troops from its former satellites and Germany was reunified within the EC and NATO. But the climax of the generation came when the Cold War ended in a decisive and dramatic Western victory. The Soviet Union was in disarray and suffering from internal dislocation and revolt. Gorbachev had succeeded in liberalizing the country but was unable to contain or control the results. In 1991, President Bush was able to put together a worldwide coalition against

Iraq, led by dictator Saddam Hussein who had attempted to seize Kuwait. A breathtaking military victory by the American-led coalition completed the restoration of American self-confidence. The United States emerged once again as the dominant world power.

Bush came out of the Gulf War with the highest popularity ratings of any president since public opinion polling began, and pundits firmly stated that his reelection was ensured. A year and a half later he was decisively defeated by Arkansas Governor Bill Clinton, the Democratic candidate who exploited Bush's domestic policy weaknesses in a time of severe economic downturn to secure victory. Clinton promised a program of domestic change based on economic revival, policy shifts on several lifestyle issues, and health insurance coverage for all. His inauguration in January 1993 was accompanied by a call for a period of federal government activity similar to those in response to previous periods of generational climax. It was being said that George Bush was the last president of the World War II generation whereas Bill Clinton was the first of his, that of the postwar baby boomers. Clinton presented himself as such in the most obvious and forthright manner.

Perhaps Carter's greatest insight during his presidency was his recognition that the government issues of the new generation would again be infrastructure issues, now having to do with energy and communications—this in contrast to the previous two generations, when the principal issues on the domestic governmental agenda were social ones. Carter was premature in pressing these infrastructure issues; but his concerns, which were not picked up between 1977 and 1981, will undoubtedly resurface as the major domestic issues of this generation in the 1990s.[3]

Major Political Patterns and Events

Domestically, the states continued to take the initiative in responding to the domestic problems of the United States and even those related to the resettlement of refugees from Southeast Asia and the development of foreign trade relations—areas that previously would have been considered the exclusive or near-exclusive province of the federal government. These years witnessed an explosion of ecological concern. The old conservationism, which emphasized the wise use of natural resources and the preservation of natural beauty, was replaced by a new notion of an integrated biosphere in which all life contained within it was deemed holy. The new ecological activists struck hard at any human activity that to them seemed to lower the quality of life.[4] Indeed, the phrase *quality of life* became the standard around which to rally in the new generation.

The new ecology was strengthened by the end of the metropolitan frontier. In the hiatus between that frontier and the new rurban-cybernetic frontier, arguments that the world (or at least the West) had reached "the limits of growth" became fashionable, squaring well with the quality-of-life arguments of the new ecologists. As the world entered the generation that marked five hundred years since the opening of Europe's great frontier by Portuguese, Spanish, and other explorers, the very language of human activity, which referred to taming wilderness, conquering frontiers, and exploiting natural resources, was challenged as immoral.

This was a period, too, for the legitimation of the lifestyle revolution that had begun a decade earlier. This legitimation took several forms. In particular, older issues of government intervention to preserve moral standards—as in the areas of liquor, gambling, pornography, and obscenity—underwent changes, both subtle and direct. For example, restrictions on drinking ceased to be a matter of religious concern and became more a matter of concern for health. Gambling, which was no longer confronted by public religious objections and did not evoke any in the dimension of health, was legalized in various forms by many states. Obscenity and pornography continued to be regulated, but on the basis of "contemporary community standards," which were far more permissive than in the past. The primary restrictions concerned the protection of minors or responded to the feminist attack on pornography as a manifestation of the degradation of women.[5]

Freedom of sexual preference and choice expanded, whether in regard to marriage or cohabitation, hetero- or homosexuality, or prostitution. Again, the major limitations were those derived from health considerations (compounded in the 1980s by the spread of AIDS) and feminist concerns for the dignity of women. Sexual freedom became accepted.[6]

The new generation also featured a shift away from the intensive concern for personal involvement in public service that had characterized the previous generation, especially its last half. The new direction was far more egoistic in nature, emphasizing personal financial success, health, and appearance. Private concerns replaced public ones, either foreshadowing or paralleling a general shift toward the view that government was part of the problem rather than a source of solutions.[7]

The election of Ronald Reagan to the presidency in 1980 inaugurated the period of generational buildup. For the first time since the 1920s, Protestant fundamentalists entered politics in a big way.[8] The more than 40 million born-again Christians in the United States became a major political force and were particularly important in the election of Reagan to the presidency.

Reagan and his administration embodied the thrust toward reducing the size and role of government, privatization, decentralization (with far more emphasis on the states in cases where government was deemed to have to act), deregulation, and a general freeing of the economy from whatever dimensions of government control existed. Up to a point, the

Reagan administration succeeded in shifting the course of American civil society.[9] The forward thrust of government, particularly the federal government, was halted. The states continued to assume more important roles and, during the Reagan years, became the cutting edge of governmental innovation in the United States. There was substantial deregulation, and, perhaps most important, the Reagan administration (whether deliberately or not) encouraged such huge federal deficits through the combination of tax cuts and supply-side economics that no new federal initiatives could be forthcoming. The resources for such initiatives simply did not exist.

Yet government was not significantly reduced in scope. Intergovernmental cooperation continued to be the norm. Even the Reagan administration had to acknowledge that government had a role to play in responding to ecological crises.

In world affairs, Reagan was able to pull the United States out of its neo-isolationist posture. Attacking the Soviet Union as the "evil empire," he initiated a major defense buildup that, although limited by Americans' reluctance after Vietnam to become too involved overseas, did present a major challenge to the Soviets. Their effort to respond to that buildup seems to have forced them into even more difficult economic straits than before. In the meantime, the United States adopted a more aggressive posture in world affairs, which was manifested in the invasion of Grenada, pressure on Libya, support for the Contras against the Sandinista government in Nicaragua, support for the Afghanis who were resisting the Soviet occupation of Afghanistan, and intervention in Lebanon and the Persian Gulf.

Much of this activity amounted to image rather than reality, and the immediate results were distinctly mixed. But by the end of the 1980s, Reagan's policy had paid off. Mikhail Gorbachev became the Soviet leader and proclaimed *perestroika* and *glasnost,* confessing the bankruptcy of the Soviet economy, withdrawing Soviet forces from Afghanistan, and beginning a slow withdrawal of Soviet involvement outside of its borders and a major liberalization within the country. In the USSR these events led to the awakening of forces seeking democracy. Upheavals in the Soviet Union's East European satellites followed in 1989, ending Communist party dominance in all of them and putting them on the road to multiparty democracy and neutralization in the confrontation between the two superpowers. When the Berlin Wall came down in November 1989, many people proclaimed that the Cold War had ended. The USSR itself disappeared three years later by the common consent of its member republics. Certainly, as the period of generational buildup came to an end and the 1990s began, it was clear that an agenda had come before the United States that was very different from that of the eleventh generation.[10]

Government and the Economy

In the 1980s, the United States lost its economic hegemony in the world.[11] It became a debtor nation. The Japanese surpassed it as a world economic power in a number of critical areas, from automobiles to banking to hi-tech products. The dollar was repeatedly and significantly devaluated, partly as a reflection of new realities and partly in an effort to make American exports more competitive in the world market. On the horizon, the European Community also threatened to surpass the United States as an economic power, especially in light of its decision to further economic and political integration in 1992.

Back home, the Reagan administration shifted the federal government's role in the economy to one of self-limitation and deregulation. Although Reagan's efforts to reduce the size of the federal government had only limited success, he was quite successful in his deregulation campaign. The court-ordered breakup of AT&T, which was accepted by the telephone industry and turned to its advantage, ended the monopoly in the telecommunications field; soon, competitive telephone and other telecommunications services had developed. Indeed, the new competition among the airlines, transport, and telecommunications industries, along with technological transformations in the latter, was characteristic of the rurban-cybernetic frontier. On the other hand, despite the Reagan administration's desire to create a situation in which government would be reduced at all levels, state regulation of the economy grew slightly after 1977.

Principal Ethnoreligious Manifestations

The shift toward comprehensive pluralism that constituted the major feature of the eleventh generation continued into the twelfth.[12] The civil rights revolution had come to an end in the final years of the eleventh generation. The major problems of poverty-stricken urban African-Americans remained unsolved and may have intensified as the breakdown of the ghetto social order continued under the impact of the new drug culture and the increasing number of out-of-wedlock births to younger and younger mothers. The African-American middle class also grew, and the participation of African-Americans in politics became increasingly important. African-American mayors were elected in most American cities, especially the biggest ones, culminating in the election of David Dinkins as mayor of New York City in 1989. The same year witnessed the election of the first African-American governor in any American state since Reconstruction. Significantly, that state was Virginia, one of the centers of massive resistance to racial desegregation a generation earlier. All told, thousands of African-Americans were elected to political office around the country. Nevertheless, by the end of the period of generational buildup, African-Americans were again feeling left behind.[13]

This feeling was exacerbated by the great success of the massive new Asian migration to the United States.[14] That migration, which began in the 1970s, became visible in the early years of the twelfth generation as Asians seemed to become a new version of the traditional American "get-up-and-go." Asian entrepreneurs made their appearance from street corners to hi-tech industries, and Asian students became the most notable achievers in the universities. An examination of the pattern of Asians' settlement in the United States revealed their attraction to the new rurban-cybernetic frontier. Aside from their natural concentration on the West Coast near their ports of entry, Asian concentrations were found primarily in the college towns around the country, gateways to the new frontier. These new concentrations of Vietnamese, Koreans, Chinese, Cambodians, Laotians, Japanese, and Filipinos were on their way to becoming important in the United States' effort to remain competitive on the world scene and in its connection to the Asian-Pacific world whose importance was growing rapidly.

The Ibero-Indian migration from Latin America also continued in growing numbers. The Hispanic population, though less achievement-oriented as a group than the Asians, were noted for their faithfulness to their language and culture. Hence the Spanish language became an increasingly important force, especially in the American Southwest. Although the push toward bilingualism that featured heavily in the last part of the eleventh generation dropped out of the headlines, bilingual societies were in fact developing in the Southwestern states and Florida. A Spanish-speaking majority in California has been predicted to occur sometime during the first third of the twenty-first century—during the thirteenth generation. Meanwhile, Miami became one of the most important Latino cities in the world and the new commercial center of Latin America. In certain respects it became a Latin American intellectual and political center as well.[15]

The Hispanic population also spread nationwide. Its principal growth was to be found west of the Mississippi, in the Deep South, and along the American East Coast, but Latinos were moving inland as well. Moreover, various Latino groups developed their own achievers, who entered politics and gave the Latino population substantial representation in government for the first time—at the local, state, and federal levels.

The other big political news was the entrance of Protestant fundamentalists into the mainstream of American politics. After the failure of the Protestant fundamentalist crusade of the World War I period, evangelical Protestants had retreated into pietism, dropping out of politics, even local politics, and concentrating on the pursuit of individual salvation. Then, in the late 1970s, led by a group of celebrity television evangelists, they came back in full force. Acting in response to what they perceived as a degeneration of the United States into secular humanism and hedonism, they were instrumental in helping Ronald Reagan win the presidency and for a few years became a powerful force in every political arena. Ultimately, as had happened in the past, their leaders were shown to be mere humans with the usual human foibles, and the fundamentalist political movement collapsed in the wake of a series of financial and sexual scandals involving those figures. Although the fundamentalists remained an important force in the United States, by the end of the 1980s they had ceased to be a major political power.

While the ranks of the fundamentalists were growing, the mainstream Protestant churches were losing ground in response to the adoption by their leaders of religiously and politically liberal stances far in advance of their constituents.[16] In the churches, as in other voluntary organizations, people voted with their feet when they discovered that what was happening was not to their liking. Some shifted to more traditional or fundamentalist churches, whereas others who were likely to share the same liberal views as the church leadership ceased to have religious interests in the "me" generation and drifted away from religious ties altogether.

At the same time, the Catholic Church, now that its position in American life was secure, began to increase its activity in political and social issues, becoming more willing to enunciate Catholic political and social doctrines and positions on the issues of the day. In the meantime, the shift from welfare to lifestyle issues brought about major clashes between Catholics, on the one side, and liberal Protestants and Jews, on the other, over such issues as abortion and homosexuality. Ironically, the Catholic hierarchy turned to call for more government intervention in the economy and greater regulation of capitalism at a time when the rest of the country had shifted toward freer markets.[17]

Ethnicity *per se* continued to wane as a political force among Americans of European background, just as some had predicted would happen. Intermarriage among groups accelerated as mobility increased and as greater numbers of Americans went to college, where they met people of backgrounds different from their own. Issues of ethnicity gave way to nonethnic issues of lifestyle, which in turn led to the greater involvement of religion in politics. Although liberal commentators were defining this phenomenon as if it were new and inappropriate, in fact it was merely part of the continuing generational rhythm of American political life.

Finally, the women's movement gave rise to a new politics of gender in which women not only pressed for greater control over their own personal lives and for consciousness-raising vis-à-vis men in the economic and social spheres, but also sought to enter politics in numbers

more proportionate to their share in the population. Although these un-
dertakings proved difficult to achieve, notable advances were made in
the 1960s. Indeed, women became a factor to be reckoned with in American politics.

One response to these changes was the effort made by a coalition of racial, ethnic, and sexual minorities to develop a new educational agenda—
to turn the American people toward "multiculturalism," a redefinition of
American peoplehood that goes beyond pluralism (which was described
earlier in this book) to a new relativism. No longer was a major question
one of showing how Jews or African-Americans or women participated in
the great events of American history alongside George Washington, Abraham Lincoln, and Franklin Delano Roosevelt. Rather, what had now taken
hold was an approach to the American experience maintaining that whatever the "politically correct" minorities were doing at those critical mo-
ments was as important as what was being recorded in mainstream American history, and that their cultural contributions were as important as
those constituting mainstream American culture. Thus, they must be
given at least equal time in American educational and communications
circles, if not more—as a kind of affirmative action to rewrite American
history and recast the American experience in multicultural terms. In
other words, rather than asking to be let into the mainstream, the advocates of multiculturalism were rejecting that mainstream and seeking a
multistreamed approach. In the early 1990s, multiculturalism became
"politically correct" (a term developed to define and justify the actions of
the American left). Where it will take the American people remains to be
seen.

Toward a New Majority

Politically speaking, the new programs of each generation have invariably
been preceded by critical elections through which the reconstituted electorate—which changes from generation to generation as new people
reach voting age and old ones die—determines the basic pattern of party
voting for the new era, either by reaffirming the majority party's hold on
the public by granting the majority party an extended mandate or by elevating the minority party to majority status. These critical elections, which
attain their highest visibility in presidential contests, allow voters, blocs,
and interests to realign themselves according to the new problems that
face them.

Three times in American history the critical elections have elevated the
party of the minority to majority status. In the series of elections beginning in 1796 and culminating in 1800, the Jeffersonian Democratic-Republicans replaced the Federalists. In the 1856 and 1860 series, the Republi-

cans replaced the Democrats, who had become the heirs of the Jeffersonians. And in 1928–1932, the Democrats in turn replaced the Republicans.
Between each shift, the critical elections served to reinforce the majority
party, which was successful in adapting itself to new times and new conditions. Thus, in 1824–1828, the Jacksonian Democrats picked up the reins
from their Jeffersonian predecessors; in 1892–1896, the Republicans were
able to reconstitute their party coalition to maintain their majority position and even strengthen it; and in 1956–1960, the Democrats were able to
do the same thing. The old coalition put together by FDR and the New
Deal, which underwent severe strains in the late 1940s and early 1950s,
was reconstituted and reshaped by Adlai Stevenson and John F. Kennedy
to give the Democrats an even stronger majority than before, thus making
possible the programs of the 1960s.

With this record in mind, we can expect another major shift toward a
new majority party in the twelfth generation. In fact, the period from 1968
to the present seems very much like the period a century ago during
which the Republicans had become the favored party to win the presidency while the Democrats retained control of Congress—in other words,
a period of transition prior to the next set of critical elections that is likely
to shift party control to the Republicans if the past is any guide. In five of
the seven presidential elections beginning in 1968, Republicans have won.
The only Democratic victories came in the aftermath of the Watergate
scandal and the Vietnam debacle and the deep economic crisis of the late
1980s.

On the other hand, except for a brief period at the beginning of the
Reagan administration, the Democrats have continued to control both
houses of Congress. For a while it seemed as if the election of Ronald
Reagan would be in the nature of a critical election, but he was unable to
break the Democratic hold in Washington or even the Democratic majority in the states. The elections of 1980 and 1984 may have been critical
ones; but if so, they reaffirmed the stalemate between the two parties.
The Republican Party has slowly been gaining power in the states and localities, but the Democrats still maintain their overall control in the state
houses.

In increasing numbers across the country, Republican governors have
been making positive records, thereby strengthening themselves and their
party both for the immediate future and in the long term. Meanwhile, vigorous young chief executives have been open to positive programs with
political appeal and are seeking to participate actively in their formulation. In doing so, they are preparing the way for yet another round of critical elections in the progression of generations.

SOME IMPLICATIONS OF THE
GENERATIONAL THESIS

The temporal pattern that nature has imposed upon human events not only endows the progression of such events with a certain kind of meaning but also brings historical (i.e., civilized) man face to face with his biological origins to link history and biology in a common framework. That framework is bound together by the social and political patterns, events, and actions that have harnessed biological man to particular civil societies, thereby ordering his life in accordance with patterns larger than his own discrete allotment of days.

Here we have focused on the political manifestations of the pattern; however, as we have noted their connections with other aspects, we have substituted hints that, for other purposes, there are generational patterns organized in different ways. What does seem clear is that, whether immediately or ultimately, all the patterns interlock inasmuch as they are patterns that involve facets in the lives of the same people. This relationship may be analogous to the musical one between a simple base tone and the harmonics built upon it. If so, the theory also provides us with a link between the historical and physical sciences.

Although the possibilities for a predictive political science are still problematic, an understanding of the generational pattern set forth here is clearly essential as a basis for serious prediction—of when things will happen, if not of what will happen. The sources of the "what" lie elsewhere. It should be sufficient for the moment if we learn to use this thesis to properly point to the "when."

THE IMPACT OF SPACE, TIME, AND CULTURE
ON AMERICAN POLITICS: A FINAL WORD

In this book we have explored the ways in which space, time, and culture come together to help shape the American political mosaic—facets that must be treated as an inseparable triad, creating the environment in which humans function. The book has suggested that space and time are linked together through the continuing American frontier and the generational rhythm of American politics. It has also emphasized the degree to which the modern age is one in which the great frontier has been opened up, unleashing a frontier process extending from the frontier initiated by the European explorers and colonists of the New World through the American rural-land frontier that brought about the settlement of the North American continent and the founding of the United States of America.

We have seen how the rural-land frontier, in turn, gave rise to the urban-industrial frontier, whose advance across the United States transformed American patterns of settlement and civil society; and how it, in turn, gave rise to the metropolitan-technological frontier, which reshaped the United States in a similar way after World War II. We have noted how, after nearly a decade of lamenting the end of American expansion and headlining "the limits of growth," the United States actually entered into a new frontier stage generated by the metropolitan-technological frontier—this time as a rurban-cybernetic frontier, which is now once again transforming American settlement patterns and civil society. The continuing frontier, more than anything else, embodies the linkage of space and time in the shaping of human affairs.

The continuing American frontier has played itself out politically through the generational rhythm of American politics, the more or less regular organization of political time through which the civil society responds to new environmental challenges every thirty years or so. The process is one of identifying those challenges, testing responses to them, mobilizing politically to make the necessary additional responses, and then integrating these responses into the overall fabric of American civilization. It is through this generational rhythm that changes occur in civil society, but in such a way that an appropriate continuity is also maintained.

The existence of the frontier and the regularity of the generational rhythm reflect the fact that the United States is a new society, founded "from scratch" by migrants coming to its territory, initially from Europe and Africa but more recently from all parts of the world. Indeed, the United States is one of the greatest ethnic melting pots and religious mosaics that the world has ever known. Ethnically, the United States has been brewed from predominantly British and northwest European stock, supplemented by a population drawn from throughout Europe, with strong infusions of African-Americans, Ibero-Indians from Latin America, and, more recently, Asians, particularly from East and Southeast Asia. The country has changed, then, from one in which the population was divided between "two cities"—an "upper city" of those of British and northwest European stock and a "lower city" of Irish and southern and eastern European background, plus an "excluded" population of African-Americans, Ibero-Indians, Native Americans, and Asians—to one in which a major effort has been made using official and unofficial organs of power to achieve a basic equality for all.

A parallel transformation has taken place with regard to religious affiliation and association, but with a somewhat different result. From its earliest beginnings, the United States was a haven for those seeking freedom of religion. Indeed, from the first, a multiplicity of sects flourished on American shores, leading to the unique American constitutional doctrine and practice of the separation of church and state.

Initially, American religious pluralism was confined to Protestantism. The sects found expression through the first face of territorial democracy, with each religious community establishing itself as a monopoly or near-monopoly in a particular political jurisdiction—whether local or state. In the colonial period, these territorial divisions had an official character, whereby different churches were established in different political units.

Following the complete separation of church and state between the Revolutionary War and the end of the sixth generation, this pattern of territorial democracy persisted informally and voluntarily throughout the nineteenth century and the first half of the twentieth; then it was weakened by urbanization, which brought together people of many different faiths living cheek by jowl in the big cities. This form of territorial democracy was denied any governmental support by U.S. Supreme Court decisions of the 1950s and 1960s.

In the meantime, the nineteenth century brought with it a major influx of Catholics, Lutherans, and Jews, thus further extending American religious pluralism. Since the Catholics and, to some extent, the Lutherans were divided by country of origin, for them ethnicity became a major internal point of division. Jews took the lead in pressing for more pluralism; from their midst came both the melting pot idea and that of cultural pluralism. Twentieth-century changes in religious temper brought a further division among Protestants between liberal mainstream and evangelical fundamentalist churches.

Eastern religions outside the Judeo-Christian tradition became visible in the latter part of the twentieth century, in part through the entry of Asian religious ideas attractive to Americans of European background who had detached themselves from their original faiths even before the massive late-twentieth-century immigration of Asians. The eleventh generation brought the first signs of the presence of Buddhism; and the twelfth, the first visible signs of Islam.

As was not the case with the ethnic melting pot, religious differences in America maintained themselves to create a mosaic of religious communities in the United States that were considered legitimately able to pursue their search for the transcendent as long as they remained tolerant of the others in their pursuit. Despite these differences in outcome, links between ethnic background and religious association remain as important in American life as they always have been. Manifestations of these links have been channeled through the fifteen ethnoreligious streams that have migrated across America. These streams have shaped the American landscape, helped define the sectional differences that have emerged in the United States, and prepared the way for a national integration that transcends ethnic and religious differences.

The fullest expression of that national integration on a pluralistic basis is to be found through American political culture and its subcultures. Political culture has been a great integrative force in American life, linking ethnic and religious groups of similar political orientation early on by enabling them to identify common norms and goals around which they could coalesce even while their general cultures remained different from one another, and offering them a way to become part of an overall American political culture. That overall political culture, with its synthesis of marketplace and commonwealth orientations, somehow found room for all kinds of Americans, allowing them to preserve those differences deemed worth preserving. Shaped by the migrations associated with the successive frontier stages, the patterns of American political subcultures have acquired a sectional character, thus further strengthening sectionalism as a political force in American society.

Just as the first phase of territorial democracy helped establish the initial patterns of ethnic and religious pluralism in the United States, the second phase helped bring about the political integration of these different groups, offering them equal opportunities to find expression through the American federal system. In that respect, territorial democracy was itself critically important as a fair and neutral means of organizing political life in a democratic republic. Its fairness was further enhanced by its association with federalism: Not only was civil society organized on a territorial basis, but the critical territorial units were self-governing, with their powers of self-government anchored in the Constitution.

Federalism involves the combination of self-rule and shared rule: The various groups could achieve self-government through the territorial polities in which they found themselves; but they could also share in the government of all through the federal system. Through federalism, intergovernmental cooperation became the norm; at the same time, changes could be effected through critical elections and "New Deals" that encouraged the governments of the United States to respond to changing conditions and new frontiers.

SUMMARY

Chapter 10 begins by examining the first third of the twelfth generation, which is marked by the opening of the fourth stage of the continuing frontier and by major political and economic transformations on the world scene that, in themselves, were generally unexpected. Returning to Table 2.1, we find that this twelfth generation is considered on a column-by-column basis, accounting for various political, economic, and cultural transformations incuding the movement toward the formation of a new political majority. The chapter ends by reviewing the implications of the generational thesis and ties the whole together through a reconsideration of location and space, time and culture, of the contemporary United States and the American people.

NOTES

1. On changing American views of government, see *Changing Public Attitudes on Government and Taxes: 1989* (Washington, D.C.: U.S. Advisory Commission on Intergovernmental Relations, 1990); and Peter Dignan and Alvin Rabushka, *The United States in the 1980s* (Redding, Mass.: Addison-Wesley, 1980).

2. On the neo-isolationism of these years, see Richard M. Abrams and Lawrence W. Levine, *The Shaping of Twentieth-Century America: Interpretive Articles* (Boston: Little, Brown, 1965).

3. On Carter's attempts to address the new infrastructure issues, see Daniel J. Elazar, *Building Cities in America* (Lanham, Md.: Hamilton, 1980), pp. 59–62.

4. On the new ecology and the quality-of-life concept, see Stephen Toulmin, *The Return to Cosmology: Postmodern Science and the Theology of Nature* (Berkeley and Los Angeles: University of California Press, 1982); and John Kincaid, "Political Culture and the Quality of Urban Life," *Publius* 10, no. 2 (Spring 1980): 89–110.

5. On the lifestyle revolution, see Robert N. Bellah, *Habits of the Heart* (New York: Harper and Row, 1985).

6. On the sexual revolution, see John D'Emilio, *Intimate Matters: A History of Sexuality in America* (New York: Harper and Row, 1988).

7. On the new egoism and privatism, see James Oliver Robertson, *American Myth, American Reality* (New York: Hill and Wang, 1980); and Bellah, *Habits of the Heart*.

8. On the political activism of Protestant fundamentalists, see Daniel J. Elazar, "Religious Factors, Political Culture, and Political Geography in the United States," paper presented at the International Political Science Association, Washington, D.C., August 1988.

9. On the Reagan revolution, see Garry Wills, *Reagan's America* (New York: Penguin, 1988); Richard P. Nathan, *Reagan and the States* (Princeton, N.J.: Princeton University Press, 1987); David Stockman, *The Triumph of Politics: How the Reagan Revolution Failed* (New York: Harper and Row, 1986); Richard Williamson, *Reagan's Federalism: His Efforts to Decentralize Government* (Lanham, Md.: Center for the Study of Federalism and University Press of America, 1990); Donald T. Regan, *For the Record: From Wall Street to Washington* (New York: St. Martin's Press, 1989); and Kevin Phillips, *The Politics of Rich and Poor: Wealth in the American Electorate in the Reagan Aftermath* (New York: Random House, 1990).

10. On Reagan's foreign and defense policy and the changing world situation, see Joseph Richard Goldman, ed., *American Society in a Changing World* (Lanham, Md.: Center for the Study of Federalism and University Press of America, 1987); Strobe Talbott, *The Russians and Reagan* (New York: Vintage Books, 1984); and Edward K. Hamilton, ed., *America's Global Interests: A New Agenda* (New York: W. W. Norton, 1989).

11. On the changed economic position of the United States, see Daniel P. Moynihan, "How Has the United States Met Its Major Challenges Since 1945?" *Commentary* (November 1985): 25–107; Terry Boswell and Albert Bergensen, eds., *America's Changing Role in the World System* (New York: Praeger, 1987); and Larry May, ed., *Recasting America: Culture and Politics in the Age of the Cold War* (Chicago: University of Chicago Press, 1989).

12. On the further advance of pluralism, see William A. Gamson, *The Strategy of Social Protest* (Homewood, Ill. : Dorsey Press, 1975); Antony Black, *State, Community and Human Desire* (Hertfordshire, England: Harvester Wheatsheaf, 1988); and Stanislaw Ehrlich and Graham Wootton, eds., *Three Faces of Pluralism* (Brookfield, Vt.: Ashgate Publishing Company, 1980).

13. William H. Chafe and Harvard Sitkoff, eds., *A History of Our Time: Readings on Postwar America* (New York and Oxford: Oxford University Press, 1983), pp. 117–147.

14. Nathan Glazer, ed., *Clamor at the Gates: The New American Immigration* (San Francisco: Institute for Contemporary Studies, 1985). See especially Chapter 8 by Ivan Light, "Immigrant Entrepreneurs in America: Koreans in Los Angeles," pp. 161–181, and Chapter 9 by Peter I. Rose, "Asian Americans: From Pariahs to Paragons," pp. 181–213.

15. See Neal R. Peirce, "Florida: The Man-Made State," in *The Megastates of America* (New York: W. W. Norton, 1972), pp. 450–495. See also Rodolfo O. de la Garza, "Mexican Americans, Mexican Immigrants, and Immigration Reform," in Nathan Glazer, ed., *Clamor at the Gates: The New American Immigration* (San Francisco: Institute for Contemporary Studies, 1985), ch.5, pp. 93–109.

16. For further information on church reform, see Ronald C. White, Jr., and C. Howard Hopkins, *The Social Gospel: Religion and Reform in Changing America* (Philadelphia: Temple University Press, 1976).

17. George Gallup, Jr., and David Poling, *The Search for America's Faith* (Nashville: Abingdon Press, 1980); White and Hopkins, *The Social Gospel*.

About the Book
and Author

The American Mosaic presents Daniel J. Elazar's theory of American political be-havior in a concise, accessible manner ideal for all students of political science. Drawn together here for the first time are the outlines of several major themes and concepts essential to Elazar's understanding of the way the U.S. political system works: American pluralism, historical change, federalism, urbanization and the metropolitan shift, and the forces of political culture.

Elazar examines the question of location in American politics from a spatial, temporal, and cultural point of view. He looks at our frontier society as a continu-ing challenge to political flexibility and shows its relationship to territorial democ-racy. He then puts these factors together with generational rhythms in our history and the contemporary amalgam of ethnic, racial, and religious groups to compose the mosaic of American politics that distinguishes—and sometimes confounds—our federal system.

Maps, tables, figures, timelines, and special-interest vignettes add to the picture that *The American Mosaic* creates. This text is ideal as a supplement in introductory American government courses as well as in courses on federalism, state and local government, and political culture.

Daniel J. Elazar is director of the Center for the Study of Federalism at Temple University, president of the Jerusalem Center for Public Affairs, and Senator N. M. Paterson Professor of Intergovernmental Relations at Bar-Ilan University.

Index

Abolitionism, 137, 147, 149, 152, 241
Abortion, 275, 303
Acculturation. *See* Assimilation
Adams, John Quincy, 143
Adams, Samuel, 127
Administrative Procedures Act, 169
Affirmative action, 211, 304
Afghanistan, 297, 300
AFL. *See* American Federation of Labor
Africa/Africans, 51, 59, 74, 205
African-Americans, 21(map), 91–92, 94,
    96, 108, 109, 114, 126, 139, 157, 160,
    171–172, 175, 177, 179, 185, 186,
    187, 206, 207, 208, 209, 210 211,
    213, 217, 223(n2), 232, 236, 252,
    269–270, 270–271, 272, 291, 301–
    302, 307
  political office-holders, 301
  See also Black power; Slavery
Aggression, 3
Agrarianism, 155, 222, 236, 237, 244, 262.
    See also Agriculture
Agriculture, 15, 16, 78, 84, 94, 114, 121,
    139, 159, 167, 184, 216, 246
  agribusiness, 78, 91, 142
  implements industry, 150
  See also Agrarianism; Farmers
Aid programs, 181, 182, 185, 186, 188,
    233, 268, 280–281, 282, 290
Alabama, 245, 265, 268
  University of Alabama, 269, 270
Alaska, 22, 24, 56
Albany Plan of Union, 123
Almond, Gabriel A., 9, 214

Amateurs, political, 234
American Association for the
    Advancement of Science, 149
American Federation of Labor (AFL), 159
American Medical Association, 149
Andros, Edmund, 115
Anglicanism, 115, 118, 122, 205
Anglo-Saxons, 84, 147, 206
Anthropology, 3, 165
Anti-Semitism, 160
Apaches, 154
Appalachian barrier, 123
Apportionment, 263, 285
Ardrey, Robert, 260
Armed services, 172
Art, 43
Articles of Confederation, 125
Asians, 25, 139, 160, 172, 178, 179,
    202(table), 212, 217, 249, 298, 302,
    307
Assimilation, 206, 207–208, 210–211,
    212, 213, 216, 250
AT&T, 301
Atlanta, 140
Attitudes, 3, 9, 79, 94, 246, 250
Australia, 74
Austria, 23
Authority, 11
Automobiles, 17, 88, 90–93, 92(table), 167

Bacon's Rebellion, 109
Baker v. Carr, 263
Balance of power, 129
Balkans, 246

Baltimore, 121
Banks, 125, 129, 143, 147, 149, 152, 153, 159, 167, 170
Baptists, 113, 130, 265, 266
    Southern Baptists, 139
Bauer, Raymond A., 43
Behavior, 1, 3, 6, 9, 11, 12, 14, 154, 201, 217, 252, 288
    civic, 219
    differences/similarities in political, 216, 245
    learned, 4
Beliefs, 3, 8, 9, 201
Benton Harbor, Michigan, 96
Bering Strait, 24
Berkeley, William, 109
Bible, 7, 41–42, 69
Bilingualism, 211, 302
Billington, Ray Allen, 73
Biology, 2, 3, 4–5, 10, 11, 45, 47, 48–49, 306. *See also* Generations
Black Hawk War, 35
Black power, 178, 265
Bonds of association, 83
Booms, 155, 188, 191
Boosterism, 81, 84
Born-again Christians, 299
Boston, 121, 138, 154
Boundaries, 3
Braddock, Edward, 123
Brownson, Orestes, 263
Bryan, William Jennings, 155
Buddhism, 308
Buffon, Comte Georges de, 46
Bureaucracies, 231–232, 234, 236, 255(n2)
Burnham, Walter Dean, 44
Bush, George, 68, 297–298

Calhoun, John C., 143
California, 23, 24, 150, 160, 183, 190, 244, 245, 275, 278, 302
    southern vs. northern, 248–249
Calvinism, 7, 8, 118
Canada, 121, 137, 143
    French-Canadians, 208
Canals, 147, 148

Capitalism, 58, 143, 146, 148, 152, 153, 155, 158, 159, 176, 303
    financial, 170
Carmichael, Stokely, 211
Carter, Jimmy, 67, 95, 176, 298
    administration, 295
Caste system, 59, 60, 185, 186, 205, 250
Catholicism, 83, 84, 108, 109, 114, 149, 159, 177, 180, 188, 189, 205, 208, 217, 303, 308
    anti-Catholics, 154, 160
Censorship, 233, 268
Censuses, 81, 291. *See also* United States, Census Bureau
Centuries, 49–55, 52–54(table), 58–59, 75, 201, 205–207
    eighteenth, 119–131, 199, 221
    historical vs. chronological, 49–50
    nineteenth, 137, 139, 140, 142, 143, 205, 213, 216, 229, 233, 249, 253, 265–266
    seventeenth, 50, 51, 104–119, 131
    three-generation, 42, 43, 69
    twentieth, 165–192, 206, 222, 229, 233, 250, 253, 254, 308
Challenges/responses, 51, 52–54(table), 55, 57, 59, 60–61, 63, 74, 75, 79, 94, 99(n9), 103, 125, 131, 152, 154. *See also* Generations, generational buildup/responses
Champaign-Urbana, Illinois, 95
Change, 7, 8, 10, 16–19, 36, 49, 75, 80, 84, 90, 94–95, 126, 159, 170, 177, 186, 192, 205, 229, 231, 249, 250–251, 269, 280, 285, 297, 298, 299
    institutionalization of, 16
Charles II (English king), 113
Charleston, 121
Chase, Salman P., 272
Checks and balances, 259, 268
Chicago, 33, 35, 82
Chicago Rivers and Harbors Congress of 1847, 150
Children, 66, 92
China, 176
Chinese/Chinese-Americans, 154, 160, 172, 227(n32), 253, 302

Choice, 199, 200, 201, 210, 223(n2), 250, 252

Christianity, 7, 25. *See also* Catholicism; Protestants; Religion

Cities, 17–18, 28, 56, 81, 83, 91, 93, 100(n14), 139, 179, 185, 218, 219, 246, 266, 270, 301
  annexations, 87, 89, 187
  and civil communities, 289, 290
  growth of, 82, 85, 87, 88, 119, 166
  and home rule, 286, 287
  sizes of, 85, 138, 286, 287, 288, 291
  two cities, upper/lower, 159, 177, 178, 307
  See also Metropolitan areas; Urban areas

Citizenship, 113, 126, 154, 205, 220

Civil communities, 287–290, 292

Civil rights, 157, 160, 172, 175, 178, 186, 252, 267, 268
  civil rights movement, 94, 166, 206, 211

Civil service, 83, 281

Civil society, 4–7, 16, 18, 74, 77–78, 103, 199, 221, 222, 230, 273, 274, 275, 276, 288, 291, 307, 309. *See also* Civil communities

Civil War, 27(map), 50, 59, 66, 152, 161, 173, 175, 185, 190, 268, 295

Class issues, 79, 83, 96–97, 122, 192. *See also* Conflict, class conflict; Middle class

Clay, Henry, 146

Climate, 23

Clinton, Bill, 67, 68, 298

CMSAs. *See* Metropolitan areas, consolidated metropolitan statistical areas

Coalitions, 44, 64, 65, 68, 127, 146, 150, 152, 169, 171, 173, 297, 304, 305

Cold War, 57, 173, 175, 297, 300

Collectivism, 233

Colonialism, 160

Colonization companies, 218

Colorado, 18, 275–276, 287

Columbus, Christopher, 74

Commerce, 114, 126, 159, 216, 221, 222, 231, 232, 236, 237, 244

Commonwealths, 220–222, 229, 232, 235, 246, 254, 309

Communication(s), 4, 6, 11, 290, 298, 304

Communism, 8, 55, 57, 295, 297, 300

Communitarianism, 233, 234, 236

Competition, 3, 231, 235, 301

Computers, 95

Comte, Auguste, 42

Confederation, 112, 114, 125, 180. *See also* Federalism

Conflict, 3, 12, 97, 112, 118–119, 139, 146, 159, 207, 238, 245, 248, 266
  class conflict, 83, 179–180
  ethnic, 83, 215, 251
  intersectional, 137, 142, 171
  labor-business, 170–171, 177, 179
  urban-rural, 173
  of values, 165, 192

Conformity, 201, 265

Congregationalists, 209, 265

Connecticut, 105, 108, 113, 265

Conservatism, 44, 71(n24), 97, 139, 181, 185, 233, 253

Constitutions, 46, 61, 115, 221, 288
  amendments, 152, 158, 267
  constitutional conventions, 125, 126
  home-rule provisions in, 286, 287
  intracolonial constitutional activity, 112–113
  of states, 276, 281, 286, 287, 291
  U. S. Constitution, 71(n27), 126, 127, 143, 157, 158, 268, 272, 273, 274, 309
  See also United States, Supreme Court

Continental Congresses, 123, 125

Contracts, 143, 181, 182, 184, 185, 191, 274, 275

Cooperation, 3, 6

Corporations, 58, 83, 112, 148, 153, 157, 158–159, 170, 222, 278
  ownership/management, 177

Corruption, 83, 231, 234, 252

Cotton, 139, 184
  cotton gin, 59, 126, 130

Counties, 260, 286, 288, 289

Cournot, Antoine Augustin, 42

Courts. *See* Judiciary

Crawford, William, 143
Crevecoeur, Hector St. John, 199
Crime, 14, 166, 175, 274
Crises, 8, 170, 208, 300, 305
    energy, 2, 57, 67, 92, 176
    of 1960s, 50, 207
    religious, 118
    See also Depressions
Cubans, 208, 219
Culpepper's Rebellion, 109
Culture, 1, 200–201, 214, 221, 247
    American cultural matrix, 220–222
    American stereotype, 188
    biological basis of, 4–5
    change/continuity, 7, 8, 10, 229, 248,
        285
    and civil society, 4–7
    as concealed, 4
    cultural affinities/differences, 7, 201,
        207, 215, 216, 237, 251, 265, 271,
        278
    cultural convergence. *See* Political
        culture, and converging ethnic groups
    definitions, 3, 6
    east-west diffusion, 245, 246, 247, 248
    as integrating factor, 6. *See also*
        Political culture, and cultural
        synthesis
    mainstream, 304
    rural, 165, 185
    and sections, 180, 181, 182, 185, 186,
        187, 188
    vs. society, 6
    subcultures, 5, 6, 7, 141, 142,
        218(table), 278. *See also* Political
        subcultures
    themes, 9–15
    transmission of, 217–218
    urban, 121, 165, 182
    See also Assimilation; Multiculturalism;
        Political culture
Currency, 152
Custer, George Armstrong, 154
Customs, 19, 274
Cybernetics. *See* Frontiers, rurban-
    cybernetic; Technology, cybernetic
Cycles. *See* Political cycles

Cyprus, 212

Dakotas, 265
Dallas, 140, 250
Dartmouth College Case, 143
Darwinism, 165
    Social Darwinism, 158, 160
Decentralization, 299
Decisionmaking, 79, 170, 176, 292(n7)
Declaration of Independence, 125, 127
Deficits, 300
Definitions, 6
Deism, 130
Delaware, 112, 118
Demands, 5, 10, 57, 58, 104, 142, 153,
        155, 159, 173, 211, 214, 231, 249,
        265, 272, 273, 286, 288
Democracy, 79, 94, 140, 148, 230, 300
    Jacksonian, 137, 141, 184
    Jacobin, 263
    territorial, 97, 108, 130, 259–292,
        264(fig.), 308
Democracy in America (Tocqueville), 262
Democratic-Farmer-Labor Party, 190
Democratic Party, 63–64, 68, 139, 152,
        155, 171, 173, 175, 181, 184, 187,
        305
Democratic-Republicans, 68, 127, 129,
        146, 304
Demographics, 84
Denver, 188
Depressions, 83, 147, 155, 238. *See also*
        Great Depression
Deregulation. *See* Regulations/
        deregulation
Desegregation. *See* Segregation/
        desegregation
Detroit, 270–271
De Voto, Bernard, 147
Differences, 7, 43, 137, 179, 201, 211,
        237, 277, 308. *See also* Culture,
        cultural affinities/differences;
        Diversity; Pluralism; United States,
        diversity in
Dilthey, Wilhelm, 42
Dinkins, David, 301
Direct-dialing, 95, 96

Discontent, 44

Discrimination, 160, 186, 268, 271

Dissenters, 108

Districts, 261, 263, 264(fig.), 291

Diversity, 59, 205, 207, 268. *See also*
Differences; Pluralism; *under* United
States

Dred Scott case, 150, 154

Drerup, Engelbert, 43

Dukakis, Michael, 251

Dutch people, 108, 112, 114, 205, 212,
235, 265

EC. *See* European Community

Ecology. *See* Environment

Economic issues, 11, 15, 17, 28, 51, 52–
54(table), 55, 57, 58, 68, 83, 91, 97,
139, 184, 186, 187, 190, 191, 222,
233, 297, 298
economic growth, 76, 78, 114, 273, 274,
275
foreign economic activity, 275
government–economy relationship, 105,
108, 114, 118, 122, 125–126, 129,
141, 143, 146, 148–149, 153, 158–
159, 170–171, 176–177, 229, 250,
299, 301, 303. *See also* Aid programs;
Grants; Regulations/deregulation
internationalization, 177
supply-side economics, 300
See also Trade

Edison, Thomas, 82

Education, 143, 147, 154, 160, 167, 209,
210(table), 211, 219, 246, 278, 279,
282, 303, 304
continuing-education, 191
public education, 83, 181, 182, 183,
185, 186, 187, 189, 191. *See also*
School districts

Efficiency, 221–222, 232, 234, 236, 237

Egyptians, 219

Eisenhower, Dwight D., 64, 173

Eisenstadt, S. N., 43

Elections, 44, 158, 269
critical, 45, 51, 52–54(table), 63–66, 68,
123, 127, 146, 155, 157, 169, 173,
295, 304–305

presidential, 44, 65, 68, 94, 97, 123,
146, 152, 155, 173, 190, 295
See also Voting

Electoral college, 146

Elites, 186, 235, 244, 250, 252

Elizabeth I (English queen), 49]

Energy, 15, 16, 67, 298. *See also under*
Crises

Entrepreneurs, 82, 141, 153, 158, 170, 302

Environment, 16, 57, 79, 274, 298, 300

Episcopalians, 209

Equality, 12, 50, 77, 78, 84, 92, 93, 94,
99(n9), 103, 126, 206, 244, 262

Equilibrium, 11, 44

Era of good feeling, 143, 146

Establishment, 139, 169, 172, 272, 291

Ethnicity, 51, 83, 94, 96, 139, 215, 247–
252, 278, 303, 307
conscious/subconscious, 209
and continuing frontier, 212–214
ethnic identity/attachments, 207–212,
213, 217, 253
ethnocultural strata, 253
See also Ethnoreligious issues; Racial
issues

Ethnoreligious issues, 52–54(table), 59–
60, 108, 112, 114, 118–119, 122, 126,
129–130, 149, 154, 159–160, 171–
172, 177–179, 180–181, 182, 183,
200–201, 205–207, 210(table), 271,
301–304, 308, 309. *See also* Ethnicity;
Pluralism, ethnoreligious/religious;
Religion

Europe, 55, 79, 143, 201, 206, 211, 212,
216–217, 241, 244, 246, 251, 253,
297, 300, 301

European Community (EC), 297, 301

Evers, Charles, 270

Experimentation, 190–191

Fairness, 214

Families, 11, 66, 92, 217–218, 219, 235

Farmers, 153, 155, 171, 179, 185, 187,
200, 262. *See also* Agrarianism;
Agriculture

Favors system, 231, 232

Federal government, 180. *See also* Aid
  programs; Federalism; Grants; New
  Deal; Sectionalism, federal
  government–section relations
Federalism, 7, 50, 51, 58–59, 67, 112, 119,
  123, 127, 134(n22), 147, 170, 176,
  260–261, 262, 263, 266, 279–282,
  285–287, 291, 297, 309
Federalist, The, 20, 221
Federalist Party, 127, 143, 181, 304
Federal reserve system, 142, 167, 170
Feminism, 299. *See also* Women, women's
  movement
Ferrari, Giuseppe, 42
Fertile crescent, 25
Fitzgerald, F. Scott, 165
Florida, 121, 140, 270, 302
Ford, Gerald, 51, 176
Foreign affairs/foreign policy, 129, 175,
  176, 211, 295, 300
Fort Ross, 24–25
Foundings, 18–19, 48, 103, 104, 105, 122,
  127, 131, 295
France/French people, 23–24, 25, 26, 33,
  50, 118, 119, 208, 245. *See also*
  French and Indian Wars
Franklin, Benjamin, 121, 123
Freedom, 14, 76, 78, 80, 83, 94, 241, 250,
  252
  of religion, 201, 307
  See also Liberty
Freeways, 93. *See also* Roads/highways
French and Indian Wars, 115, 118, 123
French Revolution, 50
Freudianism, 165, 217
Friendship, 207, 219
Frontiers, 20, 36, 49, 73–98, 192, 299
  access to, 76, 78, 93
  casualties of, 79
  continuing, 58, 75–76, 80, 95, 103,
    212–214, 280, 306, 307
  criteria for, 76–77, 78, 82
  feedback from, 77
  frontier lines, 89, 155
  and generational rhythms, 74–75
  land frontier. *See* Frontiers, rural-land

  metropolitan, 84–95, 97, 140, 141, 170,
    172, 173, 176, 180, 185, 186, 187,
    188, 190, 212, 213, 247, 271, 272,
    290–292, 298, 307
  periods, 52–54(table), 55–57, 97–98
  psychological orientation concerning,
    77, 78, 80, 84, 94
  rural-land, 77–81, 82, 97, 122, 140, 141,
    142, 155, 158, 179, 187, 189, 190,
    212, 239, 245, 254, 265, 290–291,
    306
  rurban-cybernetic, 95–97, 98, 183, 185,
    186, 187, 188, 190, 212, 213, 279,
    298, 301, 307
  space, 270, 302
  specialized, 78, 93
  urban-industrial, 81–84, 89, 94, 97, 137,
    138, 139, 140, 150, 152, 153, 157,
    158, 171, 177, 180, 184, 187, 188,
    190, 212, 246, 266, 291, 306–307
Full Employment Act of 1946, 169
Fundamentalists. *See under* Protestants
Furs, 24, 123, 148

Gallatin, Albert, 129, 143
Gambling, 275, 299
Gender issues, 166, 303
Generations
  baby boom, 207, 298
  classification of, 42
  differences among, 43
  eighth, 150–154, 151(fig.)
  and electorates, 66, 68
  eleventh, 166, 172–179, 174(fig.), 213,
    214, 217, 263, 272, 301, 308
  and ethnoreligious issues, 201, 205–207
  fifth, 122–126, 124(fig.)
  first, 104–108, 106–107(fig.)
  fourth, 119–122, 120(fig.)
  generational buildup/responses, 62(fig.),
    66, 67, 104, 105, 108, 112, 113, 115,
    121, 122–123, 127, 146, 150, 154,
    155, 157, 167, 169, 173, 175, 272,
    299, 300. *See also* Challenges/
    responses
  generational rhythms, 15, 36, 41–69,
    52–54(table), 103, 131, 260, 306, 307.

See also Frontiers, and generational rhythms
implications concerning, 306
intergenerational contacts, 49
ninth, 155–160, 156(fig.), 170
second, 108–114, 110–111(fig.)
seventh, 143–149, 144–145(fig.)
sixth, 127–130, 128(fig.), 147
span of, 41, 45, 46, 47. *See also*
  Centuries, three-generation
stages, 60, 61, 62(fig.), 66
studies of, 42–43
tenth, 166, 167–172, 168(fig.), 206
third, 115–119, 116–117(fig.)
three-generation periods, 50
twelfth, 213, 249, 272, 278, 295–305,
  296(fig.), 308
Geography. *See* Location, geo-historical;
  United States, political geography of
Georgia, 119, 121, 140, 244–245
Germany/Germans, 51, 115, 121, 122,
  126, 149, 154, 205, 212, 217, 244,
  266, 297
Ghost towns, 17, 79, 91
Global village, 97, 98
Glorious Revolution, 115
Goals, 7, 35, 76, 93, 143, 149, 221, 241,
  246, 263, 276–277, 282, 291, 309
Gold, 150, 244
Good society, 230, 233, 252
Gorbachev, Mikhail, 297, 300
Gorges, Sir Ferdinand, 113
Gottman, Jean, 95
Governments, local, 260–261, 285–290,
  291. *See also* Local option/control
Government's role, 229, 230, 233, 234,
  253. *See also* Economic issues,
  government–economy relationship;
  Laissez-faire issues; Regulations
Governors, 301, 305
Granger laws, 153
Grants, 157, 159, 183, 186, 190, 191, 285.
  See also Aid programs; Land grants
Great Awakening, 122
Great Britain/British people, 22, 23, 50,
  108, 112, 118, 119, 121, 122, 123,
  126, 205, 212

Civil War, 105, 109, 113
  Restoration, 109, 113
  See also North America, British
    colonies in
Great Depression, 80, 85, 89, 166, 167,
  169, 171, 179, 248
Great Lakes, 161(n5)
Great Society, 67, 175, 295
Greece, 170, 212, 251
  ancient Greeks, 5, 25
Gusfield, Joseph, 43

Half-way Covenant, 113
Hall, Edward, 4, 11
Hamilton, Charles V., 211
Hartford Convention, 129
Hatch Act, 281
Hawaii, 22, 178, 191, 192
Health issues, 246, 299
Hedonism, 166, 303
Henry, Patrick, 127
Heresy, 113
Highways. *See* Roads/highways
Hispanics, 139, 141, 154, 191, 208, 211,
  213, 217, 236, 302. *See also* Ibero-
  Indians; Latinos
History, 142, 278, 304, 306
  historical revisionism, 99(n9), 304
  periods in United States, 45
  strata of, 16, 18
  study of, 18–19, 42
  See Location, geo-historical; Time
Hofstader, Richard, 195(n25)
Home rule, 286, 287
Homosexuality, 303
Houston, 140
Huguenots, 115, 118
Humanism, 130, 303
Human nature, 260
Human rights, 278. *See also* Civil rights
Hussein, Saddam, 298

Ibero-Indians, 302, 307. *See also*
  Hispanics
Ideals, 140, 172, 222
Ideology, 5, 11, 14, 15, 139, 149, 172, 182,
  231, 272

Illinois, 28, 33–35, 34(map), 153, 184,
    246, 281
Immigrants, 17, 51, 59, 82, 87, 94, 115,
    122, 130, 139, 149, 152, 154, 159,
    169, 171, 180, 189, 201, 206, 212–
    213, 216–217, 219, 227(n32), 247,
    249, 302
    numbers of, 200(table), 202–203(table),
    251
    reemigration from United States,
    223(n5)
    See also Migrations
Immigration Acts of 1924/1965, 227(n32)
Improvement Acts of 1841, 147
Income, 138, 210(table)
Indiana, 23, 184
Indiana Territory, 33
Indian Restoration Act of 1934, 172
Indians. *See* Native Americans
Indian Wars, 109, 114, 119, 143, 155. *See
    also* French and Indian Wars
Individualism, 50, 166, 180, 188, 191,
    233. *See also* Political subcultures,
    individualistic
Industry, 138, 140, 146, 150, 152, 166,
    170, 179, 246
    industrialization, 66, 84, 89, 91, 94, 139,
    143
    industrial revolution, 56, 148, 150, 158
    See also Frontiers, urban-industrial
Infrastructure, 173, 298. *See also* Internal
    improvements
Innovation, 176, 272, 300
    legislative, 61, 63, 66, 67, 152, 175
Interests, 210, 218, 220, 250, 263, 265,
    266, 270, 273, 276, 288, 290, 292(n7)
Intergovernmental relations, 52–54(table),
    300. *See also* Federalism
Internal improvements, 147, 148, 153,
    282. *See also* Infrastructure
Interventions, 230, 233, 250, 268, 287. *See
    also* Government's role
Investment, 275, 297
Iowa, 267
Iran, 295
Iraq, 298

Ireland/Irish, 122, 149, 154, 180, 207, 211,
    212, 246, 251, 253. *See also* Scotch-
    Irish settlers
Islam, 295, 308
Isolationism, 166, 167, 295
Israel, 25
Italians, 206, 207, 208, 246

Jackson, Andrew, 66, 146–147, 149, 173.
    See also Democracy, Jacksonian
Jamestown colony, 49
Japan/Japanese, 55, 160, 297, 301
Jefferson, Thomas, 46–47, 66, 69, 127,
    130, 146
    Jeffersonians, 181, 305
Jersey City, 255(n3)
Jews/Judaism, 5, 8, 25, 83, 84, 94, 114,
    159, 177, 206, 208, 210, 211, 214,
    223(n5), 235, 303, 308
Jobs, 91, 182. *See also* Occupations
Johnson, Lyndon B., 67, 68, 175, 199
Judiciary, 127, 172, 274
Jurisdictions, 261, 262, 265, 290, 291
Justice, 7, 15, 16, 220–221, 222, 277, 279

Kallen, Horace M., 224(n11)
Kansas, 245
Kennedy, John F., 64, 68, 173, 175, 251,
    305
Kentucky, 281
Key, V. O., Jr., 44, 63, 65
King George's War, 121
King Philip's War (1676), 114
King William's War (1689–1697), 115,
    118
Kirk, Russell, 263
Kluckhohn, Clyde, 4, 9, 10
Korean War, 173
Ku Klux Klan, 171

Labor issues, 179. *See also* Conflict,
    business-labor; Jobs; Labor unions;
    Occupations; Unemployment
Labor unions, 83, 149, 153, 159, 170–171,
    177, 184, 229
Laissez-faire issues, 158, 170, 176, 229
Land Grant College Act (1862), 153

Land grants, 129, 149, 152, 153, 157, 167, 183
Land use, 76, 81, 89–90
Language, 5–6, 7, 9, 201, 208, 211, 249, 302
Latinos, 160, 177, 178, 179, 212, 248–249, 252, 302. *See also* Hispanics
Law enforcement, 274. *See also* Police
Laws, 19, 266–267. *See also* Legislation
Leaders, 47, 61, 105, 127, 130, 166, 169, 176, 181, 182, 236, 250, 252, 255(n3), 279, 303
Legislation, 147, 148, 157, 158, 169, 172, 178, 192, 227(n32), 251, 267, 268, 274. *See also* Innovation, legislative; Laws
Legislative Reorganization Act, 169
Legitimacy, 221, 222, 237
Leisure, 181, 190, 270
Lewis and Clark expedition, 33
Liberalism, 44, 71(n24), 97, 253, 303, 308
Liberty, 12, 46, 99(n9), 103, 121, 171, 210, 259. *See also* Freedom
Lifestyles, 60, 97, 140, 190, 191, 206, 207, 246, 275, 298, 299, 303
Limerick, Patricia Nelson, 99(n9)
Lincoln, Abraham, 13, 22, 66, 150
administration, 152
Linton, Ralph, 4, 6
Liquor, 266–267, 275, 300
Literacy, 7
Little Big Horn, Battle of, 153
Local government. *See* Governments, local
Local option/control, 267, 272, 293(n12)
Location, 237, 262
cultural, 13, 165, 223
dimensions of, 1, 2, 14, 35–36
geo-historical, 13, 14, 15, 16–17, 137, 165, 166, 277
spatial/temporal, 13, 14. *See also* Location, geo-historical
See also Territorialism
Lorenz, Ottokar, 42
Los Angeles, 219, 248
Louisiana, 187, 245
Louisiana Purchase, 23

Loyalists, 125–126
Lumber, 140
Lutherans, 266, 308
Lynchings, 171

McCarthyism, 173
McCulloch v. Maryland, 143
McDonald, Thomas H., 91
McKinley, William, 155, 173
McMurtry, Larry, 99(n9)
Maine, 113, 251
Manhattan Island, 105
Mannheim, Karl, 43
Manufacturing, 138, 159. *See also* Industry
Marketplaces, 216, 220–222, 229, 230, 252, 254, 309
Marriage, 207, 208, 213–214, 217, 303
Marshall, John, 143
Marshall Plan, 170
Maryland, 108, 109, 115, 205, 265
Mason, George, 127
Massachusetts, 104, 105, 108, 113, 180, 181, 205, 246, 251, 265, 281
Meaning(s), 5, 6
Media, 94, 268, 278. *See also* Television
Melting Pot, The (Zangwill), 206
Melting pot idea, 206, 308. *See also* Assimilation
Melville, Herman, 200
Mental health programs, 282
Mentre, Francois, 43
Mercantilism, 58, 114, 118, 122, 146, 148, 153
Merit system, 232, 234, 255(n3), 281
Methodism, 130
Metropolitan areas, 28, 56–57, 61, 81, 138, 139, 140, 181, 247, 289
consolidated metropolitan statistical areas (CMSAs), 100(n14)
Metropolitan Statistical Areas (MSAs), 96, 100(n14), 101(n24)
Standard Metropolitan Statistical Areas (SMSAs), 85, 90, 100(n14), 101(n24), 246, 247(table), 291
See also Frontiers, metropolitan
Mexican War, 22, 150, 154

Mexico/Mexicans, 22, 24, 150, 208
Miami, 140, 219, 302
Michigan, 91, 184
Michigan, Lake, 33
Middle class, 166, 179, 181, 184, 185,
    190, 250–251, 301
Migrations, 17, 29(map), 73, 76, 81, 89,
    93, 115, 122, 159, 171, 199, 302, 309
  contemporary patterns, 247–252
  kinds of internal, 247–248
  migrational streams, 215–219, 229, 232,
    237, 238–239, 249, 251, 253
  rural-urban, 247, 249
  Yankee currents, 240–241, 245, 249
  See also Immigrants
Mill, John Stuart, 42
Milwaukee, 154
Mining/minerals, 15, 17, 18, 150, 155, 246
Minneapolis, 14, 154, 188
Minnesota, 181, 190, 274, 276, 278, 279,
    281, 282
Mississippi, 265, 266, 267, 282
Mississippi River, 22, 33
Missouri, 187
Missouri Compromise, 146
Missouri River, 22, 33
Mobility, 23, 73–74, 80, 247, 276, 303.
    See also Social mobility
Moby Dick (Melville), 200
Monopolies, 58, 105, 114, 129, 148, 301
Monroe, James, 143, 146
Monroe Doctrine, 143
Montreal, 24
Moral issues, 14, 60, 99(n9), 165, 175,
    206, 209, 220, 222, 249–250, 251,
    254, 267, 275, 285, 299. *See also*
    Political subcultures, moralistic
Mormonism, 8, 80, 208, 241, 265, 278,
    291
Mortality tables, 46
Mountains, 23, 245
MSAs. *See* Metropolitan areas,
    Metropolitan Statistical Areas
Multiculturalism, 50, 60, 304. *See also*
    Pluralism
Municipalities, 260
Music, 166

Muskie, Edmund, 251

Napoleon Bonaparte, 50, 129
Napoleonic wars, 129
National character, 19
National Guard, 282
Nationalism, 51
Native Americans, 8, 21(map), 33, 79,
    98(n6), 108, 114, 118, 126, 130, 141,
    149, 153, 154, 160, 172, 177, 178,
    179, 188, 206, 208, 210–211, 223(n2),
    252, 307
  militants, 211
  See also French and Indian Wars; Indian
    Wars
Natural resources, 16, 157, 159, 298, 299
Nature, idea of, 5
Navigation Acts, 109
Neighborhoods, 266, 271, 290
Netherlands, 51. *See also* Dutch people
Neumann, Sigmund, 43
New Amsterdam, 112, 205, 265
New Conservatism, 139
New Deal, 44, 66, 67, 68, 96, 169, 171,
    172, 173, 175, 305
New deals, 63, 66–68, 152, 309. *See also*
    New Deal
New England, 22, 26, 95, 105, 112, 115,
    121, 129, 130, 147, 180–181, 200,
    208, 209, 236, 253, 262, 265, 286,
    289
  Greater New England, 240–241
  United Colonies of, 113
  Yankee subculture, 216, 235, 241
  See also United States, North/Northeast
New Federalism, 176
New Freedom programs, 167
New Hampshire, 105, 108, 113
New Haven, Connecticut, 113
New Jersey, 112, 118, 219, 278–279, 282,
    294(n28)
New Jersey Monthly, 294(n28)
New Netherlands, 105, 109, 112. *See also*
    New York (colony)
Newspapers, 95
New York (city), 22, 26, 82, 87, 112, 121,
    138, 219, 278

New York (colony), 104, 105, 108, 114,
    118, 205
New York (state), 130, 182, 246, 274
New York Times, 240
New Zealand, 74
Nicaragua, 295, 300
Nixon, Richard M., 64, 67
    administration, 176
Nonconformists, 108, 114
Nongovernmental institutions, 276, 288,
    291
Norms, 7, 10, 12, 130, 230, 231, 309
North America
    British colonies in, 24, 25–26, 51, 59,
        104, 109
    settlement of, 16, 19, 20, 23–24, 28, 48,
        51, 73, 74, 77
    size of, 22
North Carolina, 109, 115, 244, 245
North Sea area, 217, 235
Northwest Ordinance, 125
Norwegians, 207
Nuclear issues, 2, 15

Obligation, 216, 230, 231, 233
Occupations, 77, 84, 94
Ohio, 184, 279
Ohio River, 22, 33
Oil, 92, 187
Oklahoma, 160, 187, 210
OMB. *See* United States, Office of
    Management and Budget
Opinions, 19. *See also* Public opinion
Opportunity, 76, 77, 80–81, 82, 83, 92, 94,
    241, 250, 279
Oregon, 274
Ortega y Gasset, José, 42

Paine, Thomas, 130
Panic of 1837, 147
Park Forest, Illinois, 261
Paths to the Present (Schlesinger), 71(n24)
Patronage, 65, 282
Patroon system, 105
Patterns/events/trends, 7, 9, 28, 45, 48, 51,
    57, 66, 68, 69, 279, 282, 306, 309
    behavior patterns, 217

    and individual generations, 104–105,
        106–107(fig.), 109, 112–114, 110–
        111(fig.), 115–118, 116–117(fig.),
        119, 120(fig.), 121, 122–125,
        124(fig.), 127, 128(fig.), 129, 143–
        147, 144–145(fig.), 150–153,
        151(fig.), 155–158, 156(fig.), 167–
        170, 168(fig.), 172–176, 174(fig.),
        296(fig.), 298–300
    latent cultural patterns, 209–210
    local vs. continental patterns, 104
    migrational/settlement patterns, 216,
        238–239
Penn, William, 205
Pennsylvania, 118, 130, 182, 205, 241,
    281, 282
Perception, 5
Persian Gulf, 298, 300
Personality, 6
Peterson, Julius, 43
Peyre, Henri, 43
Philadelphia, 83, 87, 121, 278
Philosophy, 25
Piedmont area, 121, 185, 245
Pinder, Wilhelm, 43
Pittsburgh, 13
Plessy v. Ferguson, 160
Plunkitt, George Washington, 83
Pluralism, 50, 108, 130, 223, 241, 244,
    252, 263, 271, 301
    of caste, 186, 191
    ethnoreligious/religious, 59, 112, 118,
        180–181, 182, 185, 187–188, 189,
        192, 205, 206, 216, 217, 232, 253,
        308–309
    in morals/lifestyle, 60
    territorial, 149, 154, 253
    See also Diversity; Multiculturalism
Plymouth colony, 105
Police, 92, 272, 275
Polish people, 206, 251
Political access/representation, 263,
    292(n7)
Political appointments, 232
Political bosses, 83
Political careers, 230
Political correctness, 304

Political culture, 3, 4, 7, 78, 140, 141,
    214–215, 221, 252–253, 309
    and converging ethnic groups, 215, 278
    and cultural synthesis, 12, 309
    definitions, 9, 214, 253
    and federalism, 280–282
    "geology" of, 237–239
    grass-roots action, 80
    of Illinois, 34(map)
    institutions, 142
    and political systems/structure, 219, 260
    political terms, 5–6
    regional distribution, 242–243(map)
    of states, 282, 283(map), 284(table),
        285
    study of, 9, 10–12, 14
    subcultures. *See* Political subcultures
    themes, 9–15
Political cycles, 43–45, 50, 71(n24)
Political deadlock, 68
Political life/death, 10, 48
Political order, conceptions of, 219–220
Political participation, 210(table), 219,
    220, 230, 233, 234, 246
Political parties, 44, 63, 83, 97, 127, 139,
    150, 182, 191–192, 230, 234, 235,
    250, 256(n4), 263
    minority/majority status, 68, 127, 169,
        304–305
    nonpartisanship, 281
    realignment in, 65–66
Political power, 47–48, 63, 67, 125, 129,
    209, 220–221, 222, 232, 235, 250,
    263, 270, 277, 280, 291–292
Political subcultures, 214, 215, 216, 229–
    255, 238–239(table), 247(table),
    283(map), 284(table), 309
    distribution/impact of, 239–246
    individualistic, 216, 229, 230–232, 235,
        236, 240, 241, 244, 246, 248, 249,
        250, 251, 252, 254, 282, 285
    moralistic, 229, 232–235, 237, 240–241,
        244, 246, 248, 250–251, 252, 254,
        282, 285
    populations, 286(table)
    and sectionalism, 237

traditionalistic, 229, 235–237, 240, 244,
        246, 248, 249, 250, 252, 254, 269,
        282, 285
    See also Political culture
Pomper, Gerald, 44
Population(s), 30–32(maps), 85, 138, 285,
    286(table)
    center of population, 255 (map)
    growth, 82, 119, 141, 287
    See also under Rural areas; Suburbs;
        United States; Urban areas
Populism, 137, 141, 155, 160, 175, 184,
    188, 189, 190, 192, 195(n25), 237
Populist Party, 155, 184
Pornography, 14, 267, 275, 299
Powell, G. Bingham, 9
Power, 138. *See also* Political power
Prediction, 306
Prejudice, 160
Presbyterians, 209, 212
Presidency, 127, 141, 146
    age requirement for, 71(n27)
    See also Elections, presidential
Price controls, 114, 129, 148
Primary message systems, 11
Private enterprise, 148, 153. *See also*
    Capitalism
Privatization, 299
Privilege, 80, 146
Professionalism, 149, 231, 281
Progress, 80
Progressives/progressivism, 166, 175, 181,
    184, 188, 189, 248
Prohibition period, 165–166, 171, 233,
    267
Prosperity, 166, 179, 192, 279
Prostitution, 14
Protestant Reformation, 8
Protestants, 59, 60, 83, 84, 96, 108, 114,
    122, 149, 154, 159–160, 165, 171,
    180, 185, 188, 189, 205, 217, 253,
    272
    fundamentalists, 299, 302–303, 308
    See also individual sects
Public good(s), 232–233, 246
Public image, 10
Public opinion, 63, 65, 273, 276, 298

Public schools, 83. *See also* Education,
    public education; School districts
Puerto Ricans, 208
Puritanism, 8, 26, 58, 105, 109, 112, 113,
    115, 118, 122, 205, 212, 216, 235,
    240–241, 252, 265

Quakers, 113, 126
Quality of life, 246, 247(table), 298, 299
Quebec, 24
Queen Anne's War, 50, 115, 118
Quotas, 227(n32)

Racial issues, 51, 59, 83, 130, 142, 205,
    273
  racism, 160, 172, 269
  riots, 171
  See also Caste system; Ethnicity;
    Segregation/desegregation
Radcliffe-Brown, A. R., 6, 7
Radicalism, 57
Railroads, 83, 147, 148, 150, 152, 153,
    154, 155, 244
Rainfall, 139
Reagan, Ronald, 51, 295, 303, 305
  administration, 57, 67–68, 139, 272,
    287, 297, 299–300, 301
Reapportionment. *See* Apportionment
Reconstruction, 173, 175, 185, 268
Recreation, 18, 191, 288
Reforms, 67, 147, 152, 157, 167, 169, 175,
    181, 184, 195(n25), 256(n4), 281
  reformers, 2, 159, 266, 282
Refugees, 298
Regional development, 142. *See also*
    Sectionalism
Regulations/deregulation, 58, 148, 153,
    155, 157, 170, 176, 177, 229, 233,
    282, 297, 299, 300, 301
Relativism, 165, 304
Religion, 7, 8, 12, 51, 115, 165, 191, 211,
    212, 222, 241, 249, 299, 307–308
  church-state relations, 126, 129–130,
    307, 308
  Eastern, 308
  religious vs. political ties, 201
  revivalism, 149

secular, 8, 189
  See also Catholicism; Ethnoreligious
    issues; Protestants
Report on Internal Improvements
    (Gallatin), 129, 143
Repression, 155
Republican Party, 63–64, 68, 139, 150,
    152, 155, 159, 173, 175, 181, 185,
    187, 190, 251, 304–305
Revere, Paul, 200, 204(map)
Revolutionary War, 22, 50, 125–126
Rhode Island, 105, 108, 265
Richmond, 121
Rights, 126, 160, 177, 199, 212, 223(n2),
    235, 259, 269, 274. *See also* Civil
    rights
Rintala, Marvin, 43
Risks, 76, 78, 83, 93
Rivers, 22, 23, 33, 153, 181, 189
Roads/highways, 88, 91, 92, 93, 147, 148,
    172
  freeways, 93
Robber barons, 82
Roman empire, 8
Roosevelt, Franklin Delano, 45, 66, 67,
    68, 80, 169, 305
Roosevelt, Theodore, 66, 157
Rostow, W. W., 83
Rules, 4, 6, 127
Rural areas, 55–56, 91, 165, 267, 271
  amenities of, 85, 87
  growth, 81, 140
  open-country density, 138
  populations, 85, 96, 138
  See also Frontiers, rural-land; Rurban
    development
Rurban development, 28, 57, 140, 180,
    181. *See also* Frontiers, rurban-
    cybernetic; Suburbs
Russia/Russians, 23, 24, 25, 26
Rustbelt, 138, 182–183

Sagebrush Rebellion, 191
San Francisco, 82, 248
Scandinavians, 8, 154, 235, 241, 265
Schlesinger, Arthur M., 43–44, 71(n24)
School districts, 261, 291

Science, 25, 89, 90, 93, 149, 165, 306
Scotch-Irish settlers, 118, 119, 121, 205, 245
Scots, 114, 115, 121, 126, 205, 235. *See also* Scotch-Irish settlers
Sectionalism, 26, 36, 96, 97, 137–161, 177, 179, 195(n25), 237, 280
  dimensions of identity, 180–192
  federal government–section relations, 180, 183, 188, 189, 191
  spheres as basis of, 138–141, 161(n5)
  See also Conflict, intersectional
Segregation/desegregation, 60, 94, 139, 157, 160, 172, 175, 177, 185, 205, 268, 269, 272, 275, 301
Self-conception, 11
Self-interest, 254
Self-reliance, 80
Sellers, Charles, 44
Separation of church and state. *See* Religion, church-state relations
Service(s), 230, 231, 233, 246, 278, 288
Seward, William, 24
Sexuality, 166, 275, 299, 303
Sherman Anti-trust Act, 157
Siberia, 24, 74
Silent Language, The (Hall), 4
Sioux-Cheyenne alliance, 154
Slavery, 28, 33, 50, 59, 109, 115, 126, 130, 137, 140, 146, 147, 149, 150, 154, 185, 186, 205, 216, 236, 244
  ex-slaves, 153, 160
Smith, Adam, 148
SMSAs. *See* Metropolitan areas, Standard Metropolitan Statistical Areas
Social control, 267
Social development, 75, 80, 82
Social mobility, 94, 141, 167, 253
Social welfare, 67, 147, 278, 282, 288
Society, definition of, 6
South Carolina, 147, 244, 245
South Vietnam, 176
Soviet Union, 55, 68, 208, 297, 300
Space, 1, 2, 3, 4, 306, 307
Spain/Spaniards, 23, 24, 25, 119
  Spanish language, 249, 302

Spanish-American War (1898), 157
Speech, protected, 14
Stability, 44, 125, 129, 152, 169, 176, 183
Stamp Act of 1765, 123
Standard of living, 179
States (in U.S.), 28, 141–142, 148, 157, 167, 172, 173, 175, 176, 178, 267, 272–287, 291, 298, 300
  as civil societies, 277–279
  definitions, 272, 275
  distinctiveness of, 277–279
  identification with, 275–276, 279, 294(n28)
  and local governments, 285–287
  political cultures of, 282, 283(map), 284(table), 285
  and political systems, 245, 275–277, 279–280, 291
  spokespersons for, 276
  states rights, 146, 147, 268
  See also Federalism; Governors
Stevenson, Adlai, 305
Streams. *See* Migrations, migrational streams
Strikes, 155, 176
Students, 166, 302
Stuyvesant, Peter, 105, 112
Style, 9, 10, 14
Subcultures. *See* Political subcultures; *under* Culture
Subsidies, 146, 148, 149, 159
Suburbs, 17, 56, 87, 88–89, 91, 97, 139, 170, 178, 179, 185, 213, 247, 251, 271–272, 278
  populations, 88, 291
  See also Rurban development
Suffrage, 146, 149, 184
Sugar and Currency Act of 1767, 123
Sunbelt, 28, 57, 93, 96, 97, 186
Swedes, 114
Switzerland, 23, 235
Symbols, 6, 9, 10

Talent, 84
Tariffs, 129, 147, 148, 152, 153, 159, 167, 170, 229

Taxation, 123, 261, 278, 279, 281, 297, 300
  income tax, 157, 158, 167
Tea Act of 1773, 123
Technology, 17, 56, 59, 76, 83, 88, 90, 141, 170, 177
  cybernetic, 17, 55, 56–57, 188. *See also* Frontiers, rurban-cybernetic
  obsolescence of, 84
  telecommunication, 18, 96, 97, 98, 301
  See also Frontiers, metropolitan
Telegraph, 150
Telephones, 95, 96, 301
Television, 57, 166
Tenements, 82, 87
Territoriality, 2–3, 4–5, 11, 260
  territorial neutrality, 270, 271
  See also Democracy, territorial
Texas, 23, 91, 140, 187, 245, 275
Time, 1, 2, 3, 4, 74, 306, 307
  temporal rhythms, 45–47
  time zones, 23, 138
  See also Centuries; Generations; Location, geo-historical
Time magazine, 201
Tobacco, 114, 139, 184
Tocqueville, Alexis de, 18–19, 22, 103, 262
  ...sm, 191
  ...nships, 260–261, 262, 291
  ...de, 108, 118, 121, 122, 125, 129, 170, 275, 298
Traditions, 3, 286, 288. *See also* Political subcultures, traditionalistic
Trends. *See* Patterns/events/trends
Truman, Harry, 172
Turkey, 170, 212
Turner, Frederick Jackson, 75–76, 79, 98(n9), 158

Ukrainians, 208
Unemployment, 93, 229
Unitarians, 130
United States
  Atlantic coast, 23, 25
  Census Bureau, 85, 96, 100(n14), 141, 155, 291. *See also* Censuses

colonial/post-colonial periods, 61, 265
Congress, 45, 64, 67, 71(n27), 127, 130, 152, 157, 158, 169, 173, 268, 305
Constitution. *See* Constitutions, U.S. Constitution
diversity in, 15, 23, 200, 201, 214, 263
ease of movement in, 23. *See also* Mobility
expansion westward, 26, 28, 35, 73, 75, 119, 123, 127, 137, 142, 143, 147, 148, 154, 216, 254. *See also* Frontiers
generations in, 15, 49. *See also* Generations
geo-historical location of, 13. *See also* Location, geo-historical
historical periods in, 45
historical study of, 18–19
maps, 21, 27, 29–32, 242–243, 255, 283
Middle states, 126, 181–182, 216, 232, 236–237, 241, 244, 248, 249, 253, 271, 282
as new society, 75, 307
North/Northeast, 138–139, 142, 148, 149, 150, 171, 172, 175, 205, 215, 248, 254, 267, 270, 282. *See also* New England
Northwest, 188–192, 237, 282
Office of Management and Budget (OMB), 96, 100(n14), 101(n24)
openness in, 265
political geography of, 20–28, 142
sections of, 26, 28, 29(map), 35, 137, 141–142, 229, 308. *See also* Sectionalism
self-confidence of, 297, 298
size of, 22–23
Southern, 96, 109, 118, 121, 126, 130, 138, 139–140, 142, 147, 149, 152, 160, 175, 184–188, 191, 205, 209, 216, 232, 236, 237, 244–245, 248, 249, 253, 254, 267, 268, 269, 273, 275, 282, 289
Supreme Court, 66, 143, 149, 150, 152, 153, 157, 158, 171, 175, 178, 263, 267–268, 271, 281, 285–286, 308
temporal rhythms in, 45–47

Western, 96, 138, 140–141, 142, 149,
    150, 171, 172, 182–184, 190–192,
    254, 267, 270, 273
world role, 55, 61, 67, 169–170, 295,
    300. *See also* Foreign affairs/foreign
    policy; Isolationism
Universities, 95, 185, 186, 187, 189, 279
Urban areas, 28, 29(map), 56, 165, 249,
    267
    growth, 81, 85
    number of, 85
    populations, 85, 86(table), 270, 287,
        288, 291
    urbanization, 81, 84, 89, 139, 173, 181,
        308
    urban renewal, 93, 172, 233
    urban sprawl, 89–90
    See also Cities; Frontiers, urban-
        industrial; Metropolitan areas
Utah, 277. *See also* Mormonism
Utrecht, Treaty of, 50, 118, 119

Values, 3, 9, 12, 154, 166, 178, 183, 192,
    207, 217, 221, 237, 249, 250–251,
    265, 266, 288
    value concepts, 6, 7, 220, 221(fig.), 236
Vermont, 112
Vietnam War, 64, 67, 175–176, 295, 305
Violence, 79, 83
Virginia, 104, 108, 109, 114, 115,
    134(n22), 185, 205, 244, 245, 275,
    301
Von Ranke, Leopold, 42
Voting, 44, 48, 60, 66, 68, 146, 269. *See
    also* Elections; Suffrage

Wages, 82, 233
Wallace, George, 269–270

Wards, 266, 291
War of 1812, 50, 103, 129, 143, 143
War of Independence. *See* Revolutionary
    War
War on poverty, 94
Warsaw Pact, 297
Washington, D.C., 138, 182
Washington, George, 82, 121, 127
WASP groups, 209
Watergate scandal, 67, 176, 305
Water issues, 142, 191
Way, idea of, 5
Wealth, 83, 91, 182
Webster, Daniel, 249
Welfare. *See* Social welfare
Welsh people, 115, 205
Western civilization, 25, 74
West Virginia, 23, 281
Whelan, Thomas, 255(n3)
Whigs, 146, 150, 181, 184, 185, 186
White Plains, New York, 95
Wilson, Woodrow, 50
    administration, 167, 171
Wisconsin, 184, 282
Women, 206, 299
    women's movement, 303–304
World War I, 50, 167
World War II, 15, 88, 166, 169, 171, 1
Wyoming, 23

Yamasee War, 119
Yankees. *See* New England; Migrations,
    Yankee currents
Young, Coleman, 271
Young people, 48, 104, 267

Zangwill, Israel, 206
Zeitlin, Maurice, 43
Zenger case, 121